Praise for *The Arc of Truth: The Think*

"Dr. King was a prophet who came to save our country, and Baldwin captures his spirit and his voice, ringing loud and clear, to arouse, inspire, and unite us. He brings Dr. King to our present era, speaking truth to us in the here and now, as we face rising white nationalism and cope with ongoing systemic racism and government mendacity. This book is extraordinary!"

—Susannah Heschel, Dartmouth College, and author of
The Aryan Jesus: Christian Theologians and the Bible in Nazi Germany

"Dr. King's prophetic wisdom speaks in this much-needed volume, especially in an age when truth is the victim of cultural biases and toxic political distortions. Baldwin not only highlights King's understanding of and commitment to 'the blazing light of truth' but brings to the surface the deep well of King's thought concerning the essence of beauty, goodness, love, and the rule of justice. A *tour de force* on the thinking of Dr. King!"

—Forrest E. Harris Sr., president, American Baptist College,
and author of *Ministry for Social Crisis:*
Theology and Praxis in the Black Church Tradition

"Baldwin has discovered in Dr. King's books, sermons, speeches, and conversations an enduring and clearly articulated trope regarding truth, not as a supplement but as the central thesis of his life. *The Arc of Truth* is more timely now than at any other period in modern history because politicians, preachers, and conservative talk-show hosts have elevated lying to a new art form. The depth and scope of Baldwin's understanding of King are simply unmatched, and this text uniquely fills a long-standing void in King scholarship. A must-read about a modern Black prophet who is as eloquent and substantive as Amos, Jeremiah, and Micah!"

—James H. Harris, Virginia Union School of Theology,
and author of *Black Suffering: Silent Pain, Hidden Hope*

"At a moment when truth is under assault in our public life, Lewis V. Baldwin—one of our foremost experts on Martin Luther King Jr.—shows us why King should be our lodestar. *The Arc of Truth* eloquently lays bare the depth and complexity of King's devotion to this ideal."

—Sophia Rosenfeld, University of Pennsylvania,
and author of *Democracy and Truth: A Short History*

THE ARC OF TRUTH

THE ARC OF TRUTH

The Thinking of
Martin Luther King Jr.

Lewis V. Baldwin

Foreword by Beverly J. Lanzetta

Fortress Press
Minneapolis

THE ARC OF TRUTH
The Thinking of Martin Luther King Jr.

All Scripture quotations, unless otherwise indicated,
are from the King James Version.

Scripture quotations marked (NRSV) are from New Revised Standard Version Bible, copyright © 1989 National Council of the Churches of Christ in the United States of America. Used by permission. All rights reserved worldwide.

Cover image: Martin Luther King
(Photo by Steve Schapiro/Corbis via Getty Images), 525580540
Cover design: Kristin Miller

Print ISBN: 978-1-5064-8476-1
eBook ISBN: 978-1-5064-8477-8

When I despair, I remember that all through history the ways of truth and love have always won.

—Mohandas K. Gandhi, *An Autobiography:*
The Story of My Experiments with Truth (1927)

Freedom is still the bonus we receive for knowing the truth.

—Martin Luther King Jr., *Where Do We Go from Here:*
Chaos or Community? (1967)

For the most important women in my life:

Wife
Jacqueline Loretta Laws

Mother-in-Law
Thelma Laws Bartholomew

Sisters
Mary, Edna, Dorothy, Carolyn, Yolanda,

and
those who first spoke to me about the arc of truth:

Mother
Flora Bell Baldwin

Paternal Grandmother
Fannie Bell Baldwin

Maternal Grandmother
Mary E. Holt

Aunt
Hattie Lyons

Extended Family Members
Amy Lynom
Mamie McDole

Contents

Foreword

In a time of global distress, racial injustice, and personal reckoning, Lewis V. Baldwin's identification of Martin Luther King Jr. as a modern prophet and a sign from God is more prescient and timelier than ever. Among the vast number of scholarly studies about Dr. King, Baldwin's brilliant, masterful book *The Arc of Truth* is unique in establishing King as a prophetic genius who carved a path of truth in the soul of America, a path that is working itself out now, even in the midst of all that labors to distort, deny, and destroy the quest for peace to which King devoted his life.

In earlier works, Professor Baldwin revolutionized King scholarship by shifting attention to the biblical influences, prayer life, contemplative yearning, and soul healing that were at the heart of King's commitment to ending racial injustice. *The Arc of Truth* builds on these studies, offering a detailed, historical account of King's intense spirituality and documenting as never before how the pursuit of truth was the foundational force that directed his personal life, civil rights campaigns, and theological focus.

With scholarly wisdom and extensive research, Baldwin presents Dr. King as a prophetic and contemplative thinker who gave his life to truth as a guiding principle and the most noble human and ethical ideal. From an early age, King was concerned with truth itself—its descriptions, usages, and meanings. "Convinced that untruth enslaves the mind and spirit of whomever it victimizes," Baldwin writes, "and that truth frees the mind and spirit of the enslaved, King challenged humans everywhere to think in more creative and even unorthodox ways" about truth-telling.[1] By following the dictates of truth in every circumstance and instance, King held, the means and ends toward which life aspires would be realized.

King's passion for truth stemmed from experiences as a child and later into adulthood of the terrible wounds a Jim Crow society inflicted on the bodies and souls of Black Americans. King's rare pathos was born of a mystical participation in suffering, for the human condition, for the pain we inflict on one another, and for the soul lament that is stifled and suppressed by our refusal to *feel* and *act* to rectify injustice. He understood that the path to dignity and equality, while having radical social implications, required a new integration of contemplation and action that was fundamentally interior and deeply spiritual in nature. And this is where Baldwin has done the rest of us a great service. He has painstakingly traced King's emphasis on the inner life, on the relationship of the integrity of the soul and the dignity of the body with the sacred commitment of equal rights for all.

It was through King's personal pain and solidarity with oppressed people that "a new dimension of prophecy was introduced through the civil rights movement: the prophecy of body and action."[2] King combined the prophetic rhetoric rooted in the Black church tradition with the Gandhian tactic of the peaceable body, which responds to violence with nonviolence. In this new dimension of prophecy, radical in its vision and depth, the value of the body and the presence of the divine in the body become for King a central locus of transformative power. His attention to the sanctity of the body, especially as a sacred vessel of nonviolence, is an exemplification of King's pathos for the cross of incarnation, for the wounds inflicted on the collective body, elevating his civil rights mission beyond the social and political into the realm of the timeless and universal.

The foundation was King's understanding that authentic transformation requires sacrifice and a "vocation of agony." Like prophets of every age, King identified with the feelings of God, which came about through his reflection of and participation in the divine pathos. He also realized that the command to live for truth was extended to the entire society, that it was not merely personal but a collective striving toward living out the divine will—to transform America morally, socially, politically, economically, and spiritually. On this point, no other book has achieved such an extensive analysis of the spiritual roots of Dr. King's alignment with God's command to love expansively and altruistically and yet not retreat from confronting the powerful forces of darkness and oppression that stalked the American experiment and fractured its ability to live up to its founding principles.

Baldwin begins his work by tracing King's quest for truth from his youth to his years in academia up to his experiences as a pastor and civil rights leader. It was during this process of intellectual and theological development that King, after a short period of agnosticism, centered his life on God, on what the Judeo-Christian heritage and his own profound experiences revealed about the nature of universal truth. From the beginning, King sought to combine biblical revelation, intellectual inquiry, and the facts of science. At the same time that he believed in absolute truth—Divine Truth—as the necessary claim on human life and action, he disavowed any rigid fundamentalism. Truth was ever evolving, a principle of infinite scope and variety that exerted a claim of authenticity on the life of every person.

Equally impressive was Dr. King's reverence for and openness to the world's great religions. King valued religious diversity and abhorred religious bigotry or intolerance, finding genuine meaning in other paths of truth, including Mohandas K. Gandhi's campaign of nonviolence, and in his kinship with Rabbi Abraham Joshua Heschel and the Vietnamese Buddhist monk Thich Nhat Hanh.

King envisioned that multifaith dialogue and cooperation among Hindu, Buddhist, Christian, Jewish, and Muslim leaders could work together to eliminate structures of oppression and exclusion.

The struggle for the inherent rights and dignity of Black Americans and an alleviation of the violent and pervasive subjugation of Black communities that fueled King's spiritual mission took on a larger global and spiritual context. He not only embraced concrete plans to transform the rights and livelihood of Black Americans but also forged a spiritual path for humanity, a path of global consequence that addressed the effects of racism, militarism, poverty, and economic injustice on the souls of individuals and nations. It became for King nothing less than a reckoning with and realization of the divine presence in history. It was for him a prophetic injunction to make actual, to embody and incarnate, the eternal truths of justice, compassion, love, and the dignity of all persons.

King was a transhistorical prophet of truth who became the voice of the world's soul, who called humanity to seek the higher self, and who dared to speak for the divine dignity of the disenfranchised and the sacred gift of life. He not only was in pursuit of social justice but also sought spiritual transformation and the coming into being of a new social order that would dispel the ancient, endemic, and worldwide fear and hate that fuels racism of all kinds. King was combatting the sectarianism, tribalism, and fundamentalism that mock truth, that distinguish the saved from the sinners, the chosen from the discarded, the financially elite from the poor. He was tackling the oppression and subordination of the human spirit—the spirit of God—in persons and institutions in the Black community, the nation, and around the world. He was pursuing an eternal but never before achieved global reckoning of nonviolence to protect and enshrine the inherent God-given gift of self-determination granted each person to be free from enslavement of the soul. For this reason and others, King opposed whatever wounded or destroyed the integrity of peoples and nations—decrying the tragedy of the Vietnam War, rampant militarism, and the cruelty of racism, poverty, homelessness, and economic injustice.

King was the architect of a literal path of global reconciliation, community, and spiritual love as radical as any in history. He saw that the remedy—the "promised land" of liberation—for the (ancient and modern) worldwide subjugation of people by one group over another could be realized in the context of a spiritual movement of moral and ethical forces striving for justice. King held that God was at work in history and that the true goal of human life was the formation of the "beloved community." This was not a convenient catchphrase but a profound mystical aspiration—that the highest order of human existence was to choose altruistic love, forging an alternative community of nonviolence in which "we must affirm that every human life is a reflex of divinity, and every act of injustice mars and defaces the image of God in man."[3]

King was profoundly aware that the movement was divinely inspired, holy—that it had an impact on the inner life of the person, on his or her strength to love and to heal the wounds of the soul scarred by the immorality of racism and the scandal of poverty.

The Arc of Truth culminates with an extended treatment of the problems involved in reconciling King's pursuit of truth in his own era with how he is remembered in our post-truth age. It explores the methods used to distort, misappropriate, or domesticate the more radical King, the creative and prophetic thinker who turned his moral outrage on the conscience of America. This final chapter also outlines how the practice of objective truth-telling yields insights about how to rescue and reclaim truth in an era of dubious ethical and moral norms. Baldwin's analysis is especially significant in reminding us of King's call for revolutionary change, which "has become, strangely enough, the target of so much untruth in this twenty-first-century age of conspiracy theories, deliberate deception, disinformation campaigns, and fake news." He declares that "we have done this to King in order to protect ourselves from his essential radicalism and from the radical demands with which his legacy still confronts us."[4]

In these challenging times, nothing is more important than to place the location of our struggle in the noble quest for truth—to call to mind the ancient injunction to be better, holier, and ever new. *The Arc of Truth* is this voice of prophecy and a clarion call to devote our lives to something important and eternal, to feel the passion within us, and to walk on the sacred path of truth, affirming and enacting humanity's higher potential—to truly create a just society and make actual the divinely sanctioned dignity of each body and soul. As Dr. King says,

> But when God speaks, who can but prophesy? The word of God is upon me like *fire* shut up in my bones, and when God's word gets upon me, I've got to say it, I've got to tell it all over everywhere.[5]

Beverly Lanzetta
July 2021

Preface

I have been reading, teaching, and writing about Martin Luther King Jr. for four decades and have often wondered why so little attention has been devoted to what he thought and said about truth over the course of his lifetime. This pattern of neglect in King studies is indeed inexcusable and perplexing, especially since King—a clergyman steeped in the southern Black Baptist Church tradition—said and wrote as much and perhaps more about truth and untruth than any other prominent figure in the twentieth-century Western world. The need for a major work on this topic became increasingly evident as I read through the collections of King's unpublished sermons, speeches, interviews, and letters and as I reread his books, articles, and the seven volumes of his published papers, edited by Clayborne Carson and others. Thus, I decided to write *The Arc of Truth: The Thinking of Martin Luther King Jr.* I simply felt that the time had come for this book to be written and that I, having lectured and published extensively on King, could bring an informed and insightful perspective to the subject matter. This feeling was reinforced by the countless conversations I have had over the years with colleagues and friends whose expertise lie in the fields of theology, philosophy, and ethics. While they did not read any portion of this work, it benefited from the intellectual excitement they provided.

Other considerations proved equally pressing as I outlined the chapters of *The Arc of Truth*. I thought this book might be especially appealing at a time when the lines between truth and untruth in our culture are becoming increasingly blurred and distorted, aided by the silence, blessings, and even active participation of many of the nation's most influential political and religious leaders. Terms like "alternative facts," "crisis of truth," "deliberate deception," "fake news," "half-truths," "conspiracy theories," "disinformation campaigns," and "war on truth" pepper our political and public discourse, and many cultural and social critics refer variously to "the credibility crisis," "the post-truth age," "the post-truth era," "the new age of lies," "the post-fact society," and "the post-truth world." All too many Americans have become desensitized to lies, distortions, misinformation, and misleading statements. Truth and truth-telling are in danger of becoming essentially meaningless and irrelevant on so many levels. We cannot allow the assault on objective truth to become firmly established as the new societal norm. Otherwise, we will become unable to sustain any semblance of moral and spiritual health and will ultimately find ourselves living in a valueless society and world. As this book shows, Martin Luther King Jr. has something to offer us at the levels of ideas and praxis as we face this critical dilemma.

The Arc of Truth is also designed to contribute yet another layer to the burgeoning field of King studies, particularly in terms of how King sought to translate ideas into practical action and reality. Although King viewed and spoke of truth as the goal of the philosophical-theological life and the socioethical quest, his search for and reflections on truth were not merely about ideas. Perhaps more importantly, he also organized truth into a strategy and method to fight social evil and injustice, a point not sufficiently explored in the extant works on King's ethics, philosophy, and theology. In more specific terms, the ways of truth for him became inseparable from the ways of the cross, the ways of love, the ways of nonviolence, and the ways of civil disobedience. When King spoke of the arc of the moral universe bending toward justice, he also had in mind the long arc of truth, for love and justice were for him dimensions and/or expressions of the activity of truth. In this sense, King bore a striking similarity to Mohandas K. Gandhi, one of his most important intellectual and spiritual sources.

I should also say that writing this book gave me a new perspective on and appreciation for the meaning and power of truth. I now have a better understanding of truth not simply as spoken words but as ways of living and acting in the world. I am now more convinced than ever before that *truth spoken* accrues special power and meaning when it is also *lived truth* and *truth applied* in the context of human life and struggles. Figures like King and Gandhi are endlessly fascinating, not simply because of what they believed and achieved in the context of the human condition and struggle, but because they epitomized that vital nexus between *spoken*, *lived*, and *applied truth*.

This book is not and should not be the last word on King's understanding of truth and on how he appropriated and applied truth to the struggle for human dignity, equal opportunity, justice, and peace. Hopefully, ethicists, philosophers, and theologians—especially those with a deep interest in King—will become more intentional about exploring the topic from their own perspectives. Undoubtedly, they can significantly build on my own treatment of the subject.

Lewis V. Baldwin
July 2020

Acknowledgments

Writing a book is always a cooperative endeavor. Although I alone am responsible for the conception and execution of this work, it benefited immensely from the many invigorating and substantive conversations I have had with friends and fellow academics over time. A special thanks to the late Professor Rufus Burrow Jr., a first-rate Martin Luther King Jr. scholar, who always provided both a listening ear and rich and fruitful advice whenever I approached him about my own book proposals. Burrow probably knew more about King's theology and ethics than any other King scholar writing today, and his work on King as a personalist and as an ethical prophet significantly enhanced and enriched this volume. Sadly, Burrow passed away while this book was still in press.

Much the same can be said of Professor Walter Earl Fluker, a former seminary classmate of mine and a highly respected King scholar as well. Fluker has written extensively and lectured widely on ethical leadership, including King among his major case studies. Fluker's conception of ethical leadership and the categories he uses to explain it proved quite useful in the very last chapter of this book, which highlights the relevance of King and his legacy for understanding and developing ethical leadership.

Professor DeWayne R. Stallworth, who teaches ethics and religious studies at American Baptist College, challenged me to think in new and more creative ways about King as a writer and man of ideas. We met in person and spoke via telephone on numerous occasions. Though he did not read my manuscript, he often questioned me about it, closely followed its development, and never hesitated to dialogue with me about King's understanding of and commitment to truth.

Special appreciation is also due to Dr. Beverly J. Lanzetta, the world-renowned theologian and spiritual teacher, who graciously agreed to write the foreword for this book. Lanzetta has published extensively on global spirituality, interfaith dialogue, and the new monasticism, and I have benefited immensely from the raw wisdom and the sheer brilliance she brings to her treatment of both the centrality of truth to the spiritual life and the human encounter with the realm of the sacred. Lanzetta's rich and powerful insights into Mohandas K. Gandhi's experiments with and understanding of truth proved quite helpful as I assessed Gandhi's impact on King's approach to the ways and/or arc of truth. She also provided much-needed critical feedback that significantly improved the very last chapter in this volume.

I owe a special debt to Dr. Monique Moultrie, an associate professor of African American studies and religious studies at Georgia State University, who assisted me in locating and getting access to issues of the *Atlanta Daily World*, the first Black-owned daily newspaper in the United States. Launched in the city of Atlanta, Georgia, in 1928, this newspaper is an important source for exploring the culture that shaped and nurtured Martin Luther King Jr.

This book would have been impossible without the great work of Dr. Clayborne Carson, the senior editor of the Martin Luther King, Jr. Papers Project, and his outstanding staff at Stanford University. Having collected, compiled, and published seven extant volumes of King documents through the University of California

Press, they—by making this material accessible—are largely responsible for this book coming to fruition. Carson and his staff must be highly commended for making the King Papers Project the richest resource for advancing King studies. Carson also deserves special praise for his own personal treatments of King's educational journey through Morehouse College, Crozer Theological Seminary, and Boston University, which are, in my opinion, the best resources we have on the subject. What he provides in essays and in the introductions to volumes one and two of the King Papers proved more helpful to me than what I found in other sources that explore King's Morehouse, Crozer, and Boston years.

The telephone conversations I had with the late Wyatt Tee Walker, Dorothy Cotton, and C. T. Vivian, all of whom worked closely with King, were immensely important as I conceptualized and sketched an outline for this book. I also exchanged letters with Walker and Cotton and was informed, enriched, encouraged, and inspired by what they shared. I shall always remember the amazing kindness and spirit of generosity they extended to me.

Many thanks to Cynthia P. Lewis and Elaine Hall, who worked for years in the library and archives at the King Center in Atlanta, for their assistance in locating and photocopying documents that still figure prominently in my research and publications on King. I will always be indebted to them for their unfailing aid, encouragement, and inspiration.

This book is dedicated to the Black women who have been most important to me over the course of my life. My wife, Jacqueline, richly deserves a special note for standing with and by me for more than forty years. I have often turned to her for advice and insight when writing about Martin Luther King Jr., and she has always been a dedicated and effective proofreader. She deserves a great deal of credit for every book I have written on King. Thelma Laws-Bartholomew, her mother and my mother-in-law, has also been kind, generous, and supportive over the years.

I am blessed to have five wonderful sisters—Mary, Edna, Dorothy, Carolyn, and Yolanda—who have never ceased to inspire and support me with their prayers and words of encouragement. I am also dedicating this book to them. They are all persons of deep faith, and they have said in so many ways that God is using me and my scholarship as part of a larger plan to keep Dr. King's dream and legacy alive. For this assessment, I am profoundly humbled.

I reserve a special measure of gratitude and appreciation for other women who impacted my life in decisive ways, all of whom are no longer with us. They include Flora Bell Baldwin (mother), Fannie Bell Baldwin (paternal grandmother), Mary E. Holt (maternal grandmother), Hattie Lyons (aunt), Amy Lynom (extended family), and Mamie McDole (extended family). While I was growing up in the rural Alabama Black Belt during the darkest days of segregation, these strong and God-fearing women taught me by word and deed the power of truth over untruth. They never bowed to Jim Crow, because they knew that it was rooted in structured and institutionalized evil and falsehood. They nurtured and shaped my life in profound and indelible ways and started me on a path that led to the academy and ultimately to this and numerous other books on Martin Luther King Jr. These women were among the first truth-tellers and truth-sharers I came to know. This book is also dedicated to their memory.

Finally, thanks to the God of the universe, who is the author and source of all truth.

Introduction

Martin Luther King Jr. said as much and perhaps more about truth than any other prominent figure in the 1950s and '60s. This should not be surprising, since he was at once a Christian minister, the spiritual leader of a movement, and a world figure. King was not only vastly influential as an advocate for and defender of truth; he also did more than anyone in his time to organize truth into a movement for the liberation, uplift, and empowerment of humanity. His efforts ultimately resulted in the loss of his life.

King believed that it was possible to proclaim and to live truth without lapsing into dogmatic fundamentalism or antirationalism, and he tried to help others discover this as well. Despite being labeled a "notorious liar," an "extremist," a "law breaker," and a "troublemaker" by racist and hate-filled detractors and opponents,[1] King found a special place in that noble tradition in which major platforms are used to advance truth in both theory and practice. In other words, King's name and image belong alongside those of Mohandas K. Gandhi, Abraham J. Heschel, Dorothy Day, Oscar

Romero, Mother Teresa, Thomas Merton, Thich Nhat Hanh, and others who constitute that pantheon of great thinkers and activists. They all believed, taught, and demonstrated by example that truth derives from a revolution in the heart, mind, and soul before it can be translated into institutions and structures that guarantee freedom, justice, human dignity, equality of opportunity, and peace.

The Arc of Truth: The Thinking of Martin Luther King Jr. is quite unlike any other book that has been written and published on King up to this point. It holds that King's life and thought must be understood largely in terms of an enduring search for and commitment to truth.[2] The roots of this kind of engagement with truth gradually took form during King's early childhood, when he displayed an amazingly inquisitive mind regarding life and the world around him, and it became quite evident toward the end of his Morehouse College years (1944–48), when the youngster "felt the urge to enter the ministry" and, more specifically, "to serve God and humanity."[3] In any case, King never separated this call to Christian service from what he described, in Gandhian terms, as "an experiment with truth."[4]

This book consists of six chapters. Chapter 1 traces important developments in King's lifelong search for truth. The significance of his upbringing in a family and church culture in which truth was considered a vital part of the spiritual quest and in which truth-telling was cherished as a supreme value is highlighted.[5] Attention is also given to King's childhood struggles with the biblical fundamentalism of southern Black Baptist Protestantism—particularly its lack of openness to critical inquiry as a path to truth—and how this drove him, while still in his teens, to "accept the liberal interpretation with relative ease."[6] King's willingness to "fall in line with the liberal tradition" as a more promising route to truth is attributed, first and foremost, to his education at Morehouse College.[7] His studies in biblical criticism, theology, philosophy, and ethics at Pennsylvania's Crozer Theological Seminary, Boston University, and other institutions in the Northeast are considered pivotal, especially since he also found in these institutions a liberalism that encouraged not only a "devotion to the search for truth" but also an "insistence on an open and analytical mind" and a receptivity to "the best lights of reason."[8] This chapter concludes with reflections on how King's search for truth progressed beyond his seminary and graduate school years through his involvements as a pastor, civil rights leader, and world figure. Generally, the emphasis is on a spiritual, intellectual, and practical quest that was serious, intense, and enduring.

Chapter 2 explores the answers and insights King provided as he struggled with age-old, perennial, and seemingly unanswerable questions concerning the meanings and categories of truth. While continuously influenced by a Black church and family-centered culture in which the fidelity to truth was real and unquestioned, King, as this chapter shows, approached these questions with the mind of a theologian, philosopher, and ethicist, knowing that truth is not reducible to a single definition, type, or category.[9] Considerable attention is devoted to King's thoughts on the correspondence of truth with fact and reality; on the "different though converging truths" of religion and science;[10] on relative versus absolute truth; on dialectical truth; on certain basic, immutable, and objective truths in the universe; and on the ways in which attitudes toward "final," "ultimate," and "finished truth" discourage an openness to "new truth,"[11] all of which are central to the question of definition and/or meaning. Of particular concern is King's stress on truths derived from the lessons of experience and history, biblical truths, theological truths, anthropological truths, philosophical truths, ethical truths, "truth in the natural law," and faith and reason as defining motifs in the advancement of truth.[12] This chapter also takes into account King's perspectives on the irreconcilability of truth and untruth, on the persevering quality of truth, and on the ultimate triumph of truth over untruth. Several conclusions can be drawn from the content provided: First, that truth, in King's thinking, mattered and has always figured prominently in the realm of human values. Second, that King addressed the meaning of truth in both definitional and descriptive terms. Third, that King never abandoned the Hegelian idea that "truth is the whole."[13] And finally, that King's approach to questions about the meanings and categories of truth had what might be called a distinctly "Kingian" quality,[14] especially since he brought to it both his deep commitment to truth as a preacher, pastor, and social activist and his inquiring and open mind as a theologian, philosopher, and ethicist.

King's rousing and persistent challenge to Americans to face the ugly truth about themselves, their history, and their heritage is covered in chapter 3, the content of which is framed on the basis of his sense of the dialectical or paradoxical nature of persons and society.[15] The chapter opens with significant references to King's childhood struggles in a society steeped in contradictions—a society claiming to be free while sanctioning human oppression and organized, institutionalized white supremacy. The discussion then turns to King's lifelong challenge to a nation that claimed certain truths about humanity and freedom "to be self-evident" in its founding and most sacred documents—the Constitution and the Declaration of Independence—while simultaneously holding hundreds of thousands of Africans in an inhumane and oppressive system of bondage.[16] As this chapter reveals, this coexistence of American democratic claims and the brutal oppression of Blacks and other people of color became clearer in King's thinking during his experiences and studies at Morehouse College,[17] Crozer Theological Seminary, Boston University, and other academic institutions in the Northeast[18] and as he increasingly applied W. E. B. Du Bois's "double consciousness" thesis, Georg Hegel's analysis of the dialectical process, and Reinhold Niebuhr's insights into the behavior of individuals and groups to the human situation in the United States.[19] King's use of the metaphors of "the ambivalent nation," "the American dilemma," and "the schizophrenic personality" are underscored in this chapter, for they reveal not only his significance as a dialectical thinker[20] but also his emotional, intellectual, and spiritual struggle with a nation that proudly proclaimed certain profound truths "on paper" while failing to honor those truths in its daily practices.[21] King emerges here as a sharp and synthetic critic of the nation's chronic ambivalence around the questions of race, poverty and economic injustice, and war and human destruction.[22] The chapter closes with references to King's dialectical perspective on America's founding documents of freedom; to his views on the relationship between the Declaration of Independence, the Constitution, and the Emancipation Proclamation; and to his oft-repeated pronouncements on the need for all Americans to genuinely recommit themselves to the fulfillment of the Jeffersonian idea of "self-evident truths" as a necessary step in the direction of a more perfect union.

Chapter 4 builds on the content shared in the previous chapter by focusing from a slightly different angle on King's messaging strategy as it related to truth and truth-telling. It treats King as an ethical prophet who felt called and inspired by God to speak truth to power and evil in high places.[23] King's upbringing in a family and church tradition that affirmed, through word and deed, the critical need to witness to truth in any form and at all cost—a tradition that owed much to the Black experience and a certain reading of the ancient Hebrew prophets, the life of Jesus, and the Apostolic Church—is explored in some detail.[24] King's emergence as a church pastor and civil rights leader in Montgomery, Alabama, in the mid-1950s is seriously considered, for it was at that point that he was compelled to ask himself the question that essentially defined his role as an ethical prophet—namely, *when* and *how* to speak truth to power that is fundamentally evil and untruthful. The kitchen vision King experienced as a leader in the city's bus boycott, during which he heard "an inner voice" saying "stand up for truth, and God will be at your side forever,"[25] is treated in this chapter in terms of how it impacted King's sense of his own prophetic leadership and the role of the prophet in general. King's constructive critique of powerful forces such as the mass media, white supremacist organizations, political advocacy groups, government officials, the judicial system, and the Christian churches in terms of their failure to pursue truth as a regulating or guiding principle is discussed in some measure. It is noted from this point that King increasingly called "witnessing to truth," at the risk of life and limb, "a sacrifice" or "a vocation of agony" for the prophet, likening it to cross-bearing—to acts of sacrificial love and redemptive suffering.[26] Some assessment of how King himself addressed and dealt with the challenges and even the danger of "the cross," of standing up for truth vis-à-vis untruth even until death, is offered. The chapter ends with a discussion of King's challenge to the people of God regarding the need to reclaim "the prophetic way"[27] as an avenue to much-needed church renewal and a revitalized spiritual life.

King's understanding and description of the civil rights movement as part of what he called "the new advancing" or "unfolding truth"[28] is examined in greater detail in chapter 5. It opens with a discussion of the white South's reaffirmation of certain aspects of its mythical past during the 1950s and '60s and with King's tireless efforts to refute the enduring myth that the South and North were "two different Americas" when it came to matters of race. The attention then shifts to King's insistence on viewing the movement in historical context, and especially his tendency to regard it as yet another example of "truth marching on."[29] Of special significance are the ways in which he and his associates made truth the basis and, indeed, the guiding principle, of a creative, concerted, and protracted thrust to "redeem" and "save the soul" of the South and the nation as a whole—to entirely transform America morally, socially, politically, economically, and otherwise—thus bringing into being "a new South" and "a new America,"[30] or the beloved community in both regional and national terms. The content provided affirms the Black psychologist Kenneth B. Clark's contention that nonviolent direct action was for King "not just a strategy" but "a truth"—an "assertion of the philosophical position that one cannot differentiate means from ends."[31] The leadership role King assigned to different segments of the American population in the struggle for the beloved community ideal—or a completely integrated society and world devoid of racial oppression, economic exploitation, and wars of aggression—is acknowledged. Of particular significance was the messianic role he ascribed to "the non-myth" or "new Negro" as "a creative minority" in this human struggle.[32] The final part of this chapter invites readers to imagine along with King "a new world"—a globalized beloved community in which humans take seriously and choose to live in accordance with higher human and ethical values, and especially the demands and dictates of truth.[33]

Chapter 6 is the concluding chapter of this book. It explores how the figure and significance of King are remembered, viewed, and appropriated in America in what some cultural and social critics variously call "the post-truth age," "the new age of lies," "the post-truth era," "the post-fact society," or "the post-truth world." The twenty-first-century reality of "alternative facts," "the crisis of truth," "deliberate deception," "fake news," "fictionalized propaganda," "half-truths," "conspiracy theories," "disinformation campaigns," and "the war on truth"[34]—a reality in which the lines between truth and untruth are too often unclear and indistinct—is taken seriously, particularly in light of its impact on how King is understood, on how his legacy is evaluated and appropriated, and on how certain elements within the ranks of the political and religious right assess their own obligation in terms of advancing the unfinished agenda of his sacred crusade. The presidency of Donald J. Trump and Trumpism, which escalated "the war on truth" to new and unprecedented levels, is discussed as a formidable challenge to both the Kingian model of ethical leadership and the King legacy as a whole. The essential point is that Trump and Trumpism epitomize what it means to live and function in a post-truth culture—a culture that fails to demand an unwavering devotion to those moral and/or ethical values and norms that King considered vastly important for those who assume the mantle of leadership in the quest for a more just, humane, and inclusive society and world. Finally, an assessment of the relevance and implications of King's ideas and activities for a society and culture in which a relentless assault on truth has become the new normal, even with the blessing of all too many political and religious leaders, is provided. The conclusion is that because King always advocated, cherished, and practiced objective truth-telling and the coherence of words and deeds as a part of a larger culture of basic moral and ethical standards, he provides some of the answers about how to rescue and reclaim truth in this social media world.

The significance of *The Arc of Truth: The Thinking of Martin Luther King Jr.* rests on essentially three levels. First, it contributes to the sustained conversation concerning the role of ideas in King's life. Second, it shows that King's significance for humanity cannot be limited to his contributions as a preacher, pastor, civil rights leader, and world figure—that he was and remains equally impactful as a theologian, philosopher, and ethicist. Finally, this book reveals that there is a certain timelessness about so much of what King believed, said, and practiced with regard to truth and truth-telling. Thus, he is still meaningful for the twenty-first-century American society and world.

1

Paths to Truth

The Enduring Search

The seeker after truth should be humbler than the dust. The world crushes the dust under its feet, but the seeker after truth should so humble himself that even the dust could crush him. Only then, and not till then, will he have a glimpse of truth.

—Mohandas K. Gandhi, *An Autobiography: The Story of My Experiments with Truth* (1993)

One does not need to be a profound scholar to be open-minded, nor a keen academician to engage in an assiduous pursuit for truth.

—Martin Luther King Jr., *Strength to Love* (1963)

Martin Luther King Jr.'s life may be viewed as a continuing pursuit of truth in a world consistently threatened by the evil, oppressive, and intransigent forces of untruth. In fact, King believed it

9

was impossible to be a Christian, and indeed an authentically moral and rational person, without engaging in an enduring process of tenacious truth-seeking. Although the precise forms of his own efforts to discover truth did not take shape until his college years, the search itself was evident from his early childhood, when he first raised questions about race relations and the established order of the world around him.[1] The search for truth, which entailed both an unfolding intellectual journey and a commitment to a way of life,[2] remained King's chief concern until the end of his days.

This chapter highlights critical stages in King's lifelong search for truth, a search that was inescapable for him in view of the Black experience in particular and the human condition in general. The discussion begins with some attention to the beginnings of this search in the context of a family and church life in which truth was viewed largely through the lens of history, culture, and a narrow and rigid biblical fundamentalism.[3] The focus then turns to King's training at Morehouse College, Crozer Theological Seminary, Boston University, and other academic institutions and how this freed him from his "dogmatic slumber" while opening him to a "liberal tradition" that encouraged the pursuit of truth through the channels of "objective appraisal" and critical-analytical thinking.[4] Special attention is devoted here to King's studies in biblical criticism, theology, philosophy, and ethics. The chapter ends with a focus on how King's pursuit of truth progressed beyond his college, seminary, and graduate school studies through his years as a pastor, civil rights leader, and world figure. The emphasis is on the ways in which the spiritual, intellectual, and practical dimensions of life came together in King's consciousness as he engaged in a search for truth.

Family, Faith, and a Reverence for Truth

David Cortright rightly includes Martin Luther King Jr. among the most influential "truth seekers" of the twentieth century.[5] King's pursuit of truth began in early childhood in the Jim Crow South—more particularly Atlanta, Georgia, where he was born and raised—and it came naturally as he increasingly developed a sense of what it meant to be Black in white America. "While I was still too young for school," he recalled, "I had already learned something about discrimination."[6] Perhaps the initial moment of truth for King came at age six, when he lost two white male playmates due to the white supremacist views of their parents. Being the questioning type and "somewhat precocious mentally," King asked his mother, Alberta Williams King, for an explanation: "My mother took me on her lap and began by telling me about slavery and how it had ended with the Civil War. She tried to explain the divided system of the South—the segregated schools, restaurants, theaters, housing; the white and colored signs on drinking fountains, waiting rooms, lavatories—as a social condition rather than a natural order. Then she said the words that almost every Negro hears before he can yet understand the injustice that makes them necessary: 'You are as good as anyone.'"[7] Young King came to see that his mother was "explaining the facts of life," and especially "the facts of segregation,"[8] to him—"facts" that lined up with truth as generations of his family had come to know it. As a result, he increasingly became a truth-seeker, living, struggling, and thinking in the shadow of untruth.

The lesson from Alberta King gave her son perhaps his earliest sense of truth and untruth as polar opposites. Lessons from King's father, Martin Luther King Sr., reinforced this sense of the irreconcilability of truth and untruth. The younger King variously described his father, affectionately called Daddy King, as a man of "fearless honesty," of "real integrity," and of "genuine Christian character"—one "deeply committed to moral and ethical principles": "He is conscientious in all of his undertakings. Even the person who disagrees with his frankness has to admit that his motives and actions are sincere. He never hesitates to tell the truth and speak his mind, however cutting it may be. This quality of frankness has often caused people to actually fear him. I have had young and old alike say to me, 'I'm scared to death of your dad.' Indeed, he is stern at many points."[9]

King witnessed not only Daddy King's willingness to speak truth but also his determination to act on truth. In the 1920s, before King was born, his father refused to ride the segregated buses in Atlanta and led in the struggle to eliminate Jim Crow elevators and to equalize the salaries of Black and white teachers. While in elementary school, King watched his father scold a white policeman for calling him "a boy" and storm out of a shoe store after a white clerk insisted that he sit in the colored section before being served. Truth was the motivating force driving these acts of resistance. Young King came to understand that Daddy King's struggle against white supremacy was about ensuring the triumph of truth over untruth. The example set by King Sr. and the facts of history as shared by Alberta King figured into King Jr.'s promise, expressed in early childhood, that he would one day take his own stand against injustice.[10]

The faith King Sr. and Alberta King evinced affirmed truth as a supreme value. In the eyes of King and his siblings, Willie Christine and Alfred Daniel, their parents were paragons of rectitude, instilling in their children the values of truth and truth-telling. Indeed, King Sr. and Alberta's roles as disciplinarians included an emphasis on truth-telling as essential to the Christian faith, and in the King home, there was always a strong push against untruthfulness. Daddy King constantly conveyed, in words and actions, that the challenge to be truthful or untruthful confronts every person who assumes the mantle of moral leadership, and he and Alberta taught their children that they had to actually become the truth that they so passionately sought in life. King and his siblings were exposed to these same teachings at Atlanta's Ebenezer Baptist Church, a congregation pastored by Daddy King, and at Yonge Street Elementary School, David T. Howard Elementary and Junior High School, Atlanta University Laboratory High School, and Booker T. Washington High School—all Black institutions at which they studied in Atlanta over time. The nobility of King Sr. and Alberta King's lives was always paramount in King's thinking whenever he stressed the need for parents to exemplify "an example of true Christian living."[11]

King always agreed with his parents' view that religion should be "concerned about values,"[12] including truth, truth-seeking, and truth-telling, and he shared their reverence for truth as an avenue to understanding God, life, and reality. He had no problem with the belief in Jesus Christ as "the way, the truth, and the life."[13] King also accepted the idea that the search for truth is in large measure a spiritual quest and that faith and worship are essentially about an encounter with truth in an absolute form, which is God.[14] But King reached a point during his childhood when he seriously questioned the viability of biblical fundamentalism, to which his parents adhered uncritically, as a path to truth. The Kings' family and church culture had long embraced the essential truths of old-line fundamentalism, passed down from the early twentieth century— especially doctrines such as the authority and inerrancy of the Bible, the virgin birth, the deity and resurrection of Christ, his substitutionary atonement, and the second coming—but King's skepticism surfaced at Ebenezer Baptist Church before he reached his teens:

> The lessons which I was taught in Sunday School were quite in the fundamentalist line. None of my teachers ever doubted the infallibility of the Scriptures. Most of them were unlettered and had never heard of biblical criticism. Naturally, I accepted the teachings as they were being given to me. I never felt any need to doubt them—at least at that time I didn't. I guess I accepted biblical studies uncritically until I was about twelve years old. But this uncritical attitude could not last long, for it was contrary to the very nature of my being. I had always been the questioning and precocious type. At the age of thirteen, I shocked my Sunday School class by denying the bodily resurrection of Jesus. Doubts began to spring forth unrelentingly.[15]

While still a teenager, King began to question the validity of other biblical fundamentals, such as the virgin birth and a literal conception of hell and eternal damnation.[16] Because he had become something of a dialectical thinker before completing his studies at Atlanta's Booker T. Washington High School in 1944, he faced no real difficulty in holding on to certain widely accepted biblical truths while either questioning or categorically rejecting others. King rejected biblical inerrancy and/or infallibility but never surrendered his belief in the Bible as an authoritative source of truth.[17] Moreover, he never denied that biblical fundamentalism, despite its tendencies toward narrow-mindedness and doctrinal rigidity, conveyed certain truths concerning the power inherent in the supernatural realm, the importance of matters of personal ethics, and the need for a vibrant and contagious spirituality, all of which he considered essential to the complete life.

King was able to deal with his parents' biblical fundamentalism because they were open to profound truths about the transformative potential of prophetic faith and the social gospel. This was not typical of the fundamentalism of white churches, especially in the South. King had long heard Daddy King and many other pastors in the Black church preach on the ancient Hebrew prophets and on the social implications and demands of the faith, and he shared their convictions concerning the necessity for an enduring prophetic critique of power and evil in high places and about putting the biblical principles of love and justice to the service of redeeming and transforming humanity and society. The point is that King and his father agreed on certain essential truths about faith even as they differed over the significance of biblical fundamentalism in the quest for truth. The emerging disagreements between the two over certain biblical and theological truths were real and at times led to unpleasant exchanges between them, but these were never such that they caused a rift in the family. Daddy King remained quite secure in his biblical fundamentalism and theological conservatism, and he never interfered with his son's intellectual journey into the exciting fields of biblical criticism and theological liberalism. Invitations for King to preach at Ebenezer Baptist Church never ceased, and his standing as a copastor of the congregation during certain time frames, with Daddy King and his brother, A. D., was never really in jeopardy.

King's family and church culture provided exactly what he needed to begin a lifelong search for truth. The very atmosphere this culture generated affirmed that truth itself is the means by which to arrive at truth and that it takes humility and an insatiable will to devote life to truth-seeking. There were always questions there about God, faith, life, humanity, the world, justice, and the meaning of ultimate reality, which have long inspired truth-seekers. Also, the challenges and struggles resulting from white supremacist ideas, policies, and practices were ever-present, highlighting certain dilemmas in the quest for truth. Equally important is the fact that in his family and church culture, King learned that pursuing truth is about committing life to a core of higher human and timeless values and norms. Small wonder that he came to see early on that truth-seeking is not only possible and necessary but inevitable and audacious.

Truth-Seeking within the Walls of Academia

The intellectual roots of Martin Luther King Jr.'s search for truth grew in the fecund soil of Morehouse College, a Baptist-affiliated, all-Black and male institution in Atlanta, Georgia.[18] King enrolled at Morehouse in the fall of 1944. His time there was not only "very exciting" but intellectually challenging. "At the age of fifteen I entered college," he wrote later, "and more and more I could see a gap between what I had learned in Sunday School and what I was learning in college." King went on to report that "this conflict continued until I studied a course in Bible in which I came to see that behind the legends and myths of the Book were many profound truths which one could not escape."[19] King never lost his reverence for Scripture, especially after studying the Bible with Morehouse's religion professor George D. Kelsey,[20] but he completely surrendered the desire to be associated with the fundamentalist label. "My college training, especially the first two years, brought many doubts in my mind," King declared. "It was at this period that the shackles of fundamentalism were removed from my body."[21] This disavowal of fundamentalism had lasting implications for King's quest for truth.

King eagerly embraced liberalism at Morehouse because it provided what he had not found in fundamentalism and, more particularly, Southern Black Baptist Protestantism—namely, a religion in line with modern thinking regarding biblical revelation and scientific facts.[22] King also valued liberalism's "appreciation for objective appraisal and critical analysis," its respect for "the power of human reason," and its commitment to truth-seeking.[23] Although King's studies at Morehouse were supervised to some extent by his parents, with whom he continued to differ biblically and theologically,[24] he never lacked the freedom to take courses that required explorations into the farthest reaches of truth. Indeed, King increasingly came to see that the only education worth having is one that advances freedom, including the freedom to think and pursue truth.

King said as much and more in essays he wrote on "The Purpose of Education" for the *Maroon Tiger*, the campus newspaper, during his junior year at Morehouse. He clearly had the pursuit of objective truth in mind when he noted that education "should discipline the mind for sustained and persistent speculation" and that it should also "integrate human life around central, focusing ideals." King went on to make the point in more specific terms: "Education should equip us with the power to think effectively and objectively. To think is one of the hardest things in the world, and to think objectively is still harder. Yet this is the job of education. Education should cause us to rise beyond the horizon of legions of half-truth, prejudices, and propaganda. Education should enable us to 'weigh and consider,' to discern the truth from the false, the relevant from the irrelevant, and the real from the unreal."[25]

Interestingly, in one of these essays, King acknowledged the human tendency "to let our mental life become invaded by legions of half-truths," which means that education has not "fulfilled its purpose." Education at its best "helps us" not only "know truth," he wrote, but "love truth" and "sacrifice for it."[26] King repeatedly said this throughout his life.[27] At some points, he equated "the call for intelligence" with "a call for open-mindedness, sound judgment, and love for truth." The call for intelligence "is a call for men to rise above the stagnation of close-mindedness and the paralysis of gullibility," he declared, to "engage in" a "devotion to truth" and "an assiduous pursuit for truth."[28] Although King was perceived to be "not brilliant" and "an academic 'underachiever'" at Morehouse,[29] he had "a good mind" and "good integrity" and was never unclear, even at that time, about how the quest for truth frees and empowers the truth-seeker. He already had a sense of how both truth and untruth impact not only human freedom but the larger moral and spiritual life.[30] "He who lives with untruth lives in spiritual slavery," King would write years later. "Freedom is still the bonus we receive for knowing the truth."[31]

Steeped in the history, culture, and values of the Black South, Morehouse was exactly where King needed to be to explore—in intellectual terms—deep questions around the inextricable relationship between truth and freedom. The race issue became the point of departure in this venture, as King himself noted: "There was a free atmosphere at Morehouse, and it was there I had my first frank discussion on race. The professors were not caught up in the clutches of state funds and could teach what they wanted with academic freedom. They encouraged us in a positive quest for a solution to racial ills. I realized that nobody there was afraid. Important people came in to discuss the race problem rationally with us."[32] Exploring the reality of the Black experience was a vital part of Morehouse's commitment to truth, and King became more mindful there of the centrality of truth-seeking and truth-telling to his people's efforts to survive and ultimately triumph over the forces of white supremacy.[33] In other words, the Morehouse experience reinforced and significantly enhanced much of what King had learned from his earliest childhood from his parents, Ebenezer Baptist Church, and the segregated public schools of Atlanta.

This range of influences proved equally significant as King turned to a more serious, formal study of the Hebrew prophets and Jesus of Nazareth, whom he found to be primary harbingers of truth. King had grown up hearing his father preach on these towering figures, but he developed a much greater understanding of them as ancient sources of truth in courses he had with Professor Kelsey, whose "critical approach to biblical studies" distinguished him from Daddy King's "scriptural literalism."[34] Kelsey, who was director of the Morehouse School of Religion in the late 1940s, not only taught classes but also sponsored institutes for Black Baptist ministers at various times that focused on the prophets and Jesus, some of which were more than likely attended by King.[35] King came to see that the prophets and Jesus had a fierce loyalty to truth and a contempt for untruth, and by the time he graduated from Morehouse in 1948, he believed that they had indeed been inspired by God and that the traditions passed down from these declarers of the absolute and eternal word of God constituted a major inspiration for the religious and cultural commitment of the Jewish people to justice.[36] As King moved through Morehouse, and later seminary and graduate school, he repeatedly read the prophetic writings in the Hebrew Bible and Jesus's teachings in the New Testament. Ultimately, he came to an understanding of scriptural revelation that was heavily informed by biblical criticism.[37] With his own intellectual growth as a biblicist in mind, King insisted that "liberalism's contribution to the philological-historical criticism of biblical literature has been of immeasurable value and should be defended with religious and scientific passion."[38]

King became familiar with other ancient sources of truth while studying with philosophy professor Samuel W. Williams during his senior year at Morehouse. King had "extensive training in philosophy," beginning with the classical Greek philosophers who, as he most certainly realized, struggled with profound and eternal issues such as reality and truth.[39] Of particular significance for King was Socrates, who—as was the case with Jesus—never wrote anything but became known through his disciples, Plato and Xenophon. King read parts of the Platonic dialogues in Williams's Introduction to Philosophy courses, and he most certainly learned about Socrates's willingness to "create tension in the mind" and to ultimately face death because of "his unswerving commitment to truth and his philosophical inquiries."[40] King would have also grasped that what Plato shared about Socrates was essential for understanding Plato himself, for Plato said much about truth as an ultimate value, equating it with beauty and the highest good.[41] In any case, King's introduction to the Platonic dialogues at Morehouse prepared the ground for his more intense study of Plato at Crozer Theological Seminary and later in a course at Harvard

University under Professor Raphael Demos.[42] Plato would become one of King's favorite philosophers, in part because of what he contributed to King's understanding of the various kinds of love and truth, but also because Plato engaged on some level the full range of philosophical and theological concerns.[43] King would say years later, after rising to national and international prominence, that Plato's *Republic* was the "one book," aside from "the Bible," that he would want in hand if he was "marooned on the proverbial desert island." "I feel that it brings together more of the insights of history than any other book," King declared. He added, "There is not a creative idea extant that is not discussed, in some way, in this work. Whatever realm of theology or philosophy is one's interest—and I am deeply interested in both—somewhere along the way, in this book you will find the matter explored."[44]

During those two semesters in Professor Williams's Introduction to Philosophy courses, King almost certainly had some exposure to a number of other ancient Greek philosophers—such as Aristotle, Euripides, and Aristophanes—but they seem not to have had the same impact on him and his truth-seeking as Plato. King was also introduced to the German philosopher Georg Friedrich Wilhelm Hegel,[45] who would have as much or perhaps more influence on him than Plato when it came to his search for truth. Although King's most intensive study of Western philosophy occurred later, during his PhD work at Boston University, the quality of his work in this vast field in both seminary and graduate school owed much to the foundation that had been laid in Professor Williams's philosophy courses at Morehouse. King left Morehouse fully mindful of the centrality of the pursuit of truth to the philosophical life. Largely because of Williams's influence, the young man was described during his very last semester at Morehouse, by a college staff person who recommended him highly for studies at Crozer Seminary, as a "clear thinker" and a "persistent searcher after the truth."[46]

King's evolving pursuit of truth was sparked in some measure by his introduction to liberal theology and ethics at Morehouse. This liberalizing process started as King was exposed, through the lectures and sermons of the college president Benjamin E. Mays and its religion professor George Kelsey, to the ideas of the Social Gospel—a movement primarily among liberal Protestants who applied the biblical principles of love and justice to the amelioration of the social order.[47] The same might be said of King's introduction to personalism, or personal idealism, which stressed the idea of the personal God of love and reason and the sacredness of persons. King had been exposed to certain ingredients of the Social Gospel and of personalism through the preaching and activism of his father, William Holmes Borders, Lucius M. Tobin, and other Black ministers in the Atlanta area, but the Morehouse experience brought more of an intellectual framework to King's understanding of these liberal streams of thought, thus blazing a path for his more serious academic studies at Crozer and Boston.[48] The liberalizing process at Morehouse helps explain why King, by the time he enrolled at Crozer Seminary, had no problem invoking philosophy, religiosity, and theology when framing his thoughts on truth.

It is conceivable that King arrived at certain truths about the moral universe and fundamental moral laws while sitting at the feet of Mays, Kelsey, and Williams at Morehouse. During King's time there, Mays affirmed in his writings that the universe is essentially moral and ethical and that moral and ethical laws govern the universe and the regulation of human life in ways similar to scientific and physical laws.[49] In a speech on moral laws delivered in Sales Chapel at Morehouse in 1948, Mays "declared to his listeners that the laws governing human conduct and behavior are just as objective and universal as those of chemistry, physics, mathematics, and other sciences."[50] "Moral laws" were occasionally highlighted in different ways as a theme for lectures at Morehouse in the mid- to late 1940s when King was studying there, and students as well as faculty were usually present.[51] Kelsey, with a PhD from Yale University, taught Christian ethics at Morehouse and actually published an essay on "The Nature of the Christian Ethic,"[52] and careful scholar that he was, it is difficult to imagine him not being knowledgeable about the objective moral order and the system of moral laws. The same is true of Williams, who studied philosophy at the University of Chicago and was apparently open to morally and scientifically based conceptions of truth.[53]

Although King studied the lives and works of several important thinkers at Morehouse—in philosophy, ethics, science, Bible, theology, sociology, and other fields of study—it appears that no one impressed him more than Henry David Thoreau, who was himself a great seeker of truth. King was introduced to Thoreau in one of Williams's philosophy classes. A naturalist, social critic, and transcendentalist, Thoreau wrote "On the Duty of Civil Disobedience" (1849), an essay in which he urged the citizens of Massachusetts to refuse to pay taxes in support of a system that sanctioned the evils of slavery, the slaughter of the American Indians, and the nation's imperialistic ventures in the war with Mexico. King was immediately fascinated with not only Thoreau's concept of noncooperation with evil but also his views on the supremacy of the moral law, the sacred rights of the individual conscience, the willingness to sacrifice and to suffer penalties in defense of a just cause, and the value of a creative minority in transforming an unjust system.[54] King's "first intellectual contact with the theory of nonviolent resistance" came with his reading of Thoreau's essay, and he was convinced that Thoreau had identified certain objective truths about the nature of the moral law and the responsibility of free, moral, just, and rational persons. Of course, King was equally mindful that Thoreau, inspired by his transcendentalism, had also sought a sense of life, reality, and truth through nature. Be that as it may, King read and reread Thoreau's "On the Duty of Civil Disobedience,"[55] and this, along with his reading of parts of the New Testament, prepared the ground for his interest in and reading of Gandhi once he enrolled in seminary and graduate school.

Because King was a sociology major at Morehouse, he tended to be as concerned about facts as he was about truth. At the same time, he understood that facts and truth are distinguishable on some levels and indistinguishable on others. King had ten courses with sociologist Walter R. Chivers, "an outspoken critic of segregation" who also became his adviser, and through Chivers he developed "an appreciation for social science methodology," which would be quite useful to him in "the civil and human rights movements." This methodology "stresses the importance of collecting facts" for the purpose of knowing "the actual state of affairs regarding specific social ills."[56] Probably at the urging of Chivers, King also took jobs during the summer—at places like Cullman Brothers' Tobacco Plantation in Simsbury, Connecticut; the Atlanta Railway Express Company; and Atlanta's Southern Spring Bed Mattress Company—and these experiences undoubtedly helped put a face on and bring more clarity to the data and facts he explored on a theoretical level in his sociology classes.[57] Thus, King was in a better position to understand the difference between truth and facts as theoretical processes and truth and facts as lived experiences.

Influenced by his father and by "academically trained" and "socially committed" ministers like Benjamin Mays, George Kelsey, and Samuel Williams, King answered the call to ministry during his junior year at Morehouse, at age eighteen.[58] Undoubtedly, the young-ster began to think of the search for truth in new and perhaps more challenging ways, or in ways more consistent with the requirements and demands of the profession. King most likely had the ministry in mind when he asserted, "As a young man with most of my life ahead of me, I decided early to give my life to something eternal and abso-lute. Not to these little gods that are here today and gone tomorrow, but to God who is the same yesterday, today, and forever."[59] There is no reason to doubt that the "eternal and absolute" in King's mind had much to do with truth-seeking on the highest levels. This was essential given the inescapable "inner urge" he felt "to serve God and humanity," a feeling that undoubtedly weighed heavily on his consciousness when he was ordained in February 1948, four months before graduating from Morehouse. By that time, King had strayed far from the biblical fundamentalism that had long empowered so many of his people, as evidenced by the fact that he reportedly denied the virgin birth when questioned by Daddy King, Benjamin Mays, Samuel Williams, and other ministers on his ordination com-mittee.[60] Liberalism would continue to be the driving force in both King's ministry and theological education, even after he found in neoorthodoxy a sobering and moderating influence.[61]

King enrolled at Crozer Theological Seminary in Chester, Pennsylvania, in the fall of 1948, at age nineteen, and began the next phase in his intellectual pilgrimage toward truth. Like Morehouse, Crozer was a Baptist institution, but it was distinguished by the sheer depth of its identification with the liberal theological tradition.[62] Thus, King was in the type of academic environment he needed to build significantly on much of what he had learned in college, especially in the areas of Bible, theology, philosophy, and ethics. His classwork during that first year reflected the spirit of a young man eager and even determined to engage modernistic trends in thought and in culture generally. During the fall semester of 1949, King—in the Christian Theology for Today course taught by George W. Davis, Crozer's professor of Christian theology— wrote a paper in which he was highly "scornful of fundamentalism" and essentially "uncritical of liberalism." In that paper, entitled "The Sources of Fundamentalism and Liberalism Considered Historically and Psychologically," King highlighted the narrowmindedness encouraged by fundamentalists, noting that when it comes to matters of human nature, they tend to ignore science and other important sources while finding all of their answers in the Bible. "They argue that if the Bible is true—that is, so divinely inspired as to be free from error," King wrote, "then all other truths follow inevitably, because they are based upon what the Bible says in language clear and unmistakable." King saw a healthy contrast in liberalism, which was far more accommodative of scientific discoveries and other sources of truth. He went on to write, "The liberal does not see the Bible as the only source of truth, but he finds truth in numerous other realms of life. He would insist that truth is not a one-act drama that appeared once and for all on the Biblical stage, but it is a drama of many acts continually appearing as the curtains of history continue to open. He sees the light of God shining through history as the blossom shines through the bud; God is working through history."[63] As far as King was concerned, liberalism was the kind of "progressive movement" humans everywhere needed in the mid-twentieth century, for it had come "into being in an attempt to adjust religion to all new truth."[64]

Not surprisingly, King brought this decisively liberal perspective to his work on the ancient Hebrew prophets and Jesus of Nazareth, whom he studied in much greater depth under Crozer's Hebrew Bible professor James Bennett Pritchard and its New Testament professor Morton Scott Enslin. Pritchard retained "vivid memories" of King in his classes and of King's "interest in the Hebrew Prophets."[65] In King's thinking, Isaiah, Amos, Micah, Jeremiah, and the other prophets spoke truth in the form of revelations from God. In a paper on "The Significant Contributions of Jeremiah to Religious Thought," written for Pritchard's course on the Old Testament, King—in his very first semester at Crozer—variously referred to Jeremiah as "a striving prophet" and "the weeping prophet," noting particularly his declarations against "false religion" and "his devotion to truth and civic duty." Jeremiah understood, King suggested, that truth, not ritual, can be perceived as an end within itself, and King went on to focus on Jeremiah's "contributions to the body of religious truth," chief among which were "his New Covenant," his denunciation of "artificial worship," and his conception of personal religion as "a relationship between Jehovah and the individual soul."[66] With its first-rate scholars in Bible, Crozer could not have been a more congenial atmosphere for King to advance his perspective on the prophets as proclaimers of truth. Due largely to the impact of the Crozer experience, the Hebrew prophets were always uppermost in King's mind when he thought in terms of divine revelation, of absolute or eternal truth, or of God as truth.

The same applies in the case of Jesus of Nazareth. King became increasingly convinced that Jesus stood squarely in the tradition of the Hebrew prophets—that Jesus so submitted his will to the divine will that God revealed God's word and plan to humanity through Jesus. Crozer's liberalism nurtured this position. In fact, King embraced "the liberal Jesus school of thought," which portrayed Jesus as "the prophet of a new righteousness"—as one who taught that "the Kingdom of God, conceived as an ideal social order," could come to earth through the Christianization of society based on love and justice.[67] Although King rejected Professor Enslin's emphasis on "the eschatological elements of Jesus' thought," he nonetheless appreciated Enslin's liberal approach to New Testament studies, which affirmed biblical criticism and reason as vital and necessary tools in the quest for truth. This is clear from what King reported about Enslin's course on the "History and Literature of the New Testament," which he also had during that first semester at Crozer. But interestingly enough, when it came to the relevance of the Hebrew prophets and Jesus for the Social Gospel, King parted with Enslin and sided with George W. Davis, from whom he took a number of courses in systematic and historical theology, the philosophy and psychology of religion, and comparative religions.[68]

During the fall term of his second year at Crozer, in Davis's Christian Theology for Today course, King read Walter Rauschenbusch's *Christianity and the Social Crisis* (1907). Rauschenbusch, the leader of the Social Gospel movement, devoted the first three chapters of this work to the Hebrew prophets, Jesus, and the early church, and King found here not only "a theological basis" but also an intellectual structure and conceptual framework for expressing "the social concern" he developed earlier at Ebenezer Baptist Church and Morehouse College.[69] Although Rauschenbusch "came perilously close to identifying the Kingdom of God with a particular social and economic system" and bowed to "the nineteenth century 'cult of inevitable progress'" and its "superficial optimism" concerning human nature—shortcomings that bothered King tremendously—King nonetheless believed that Rauschenbusch was right in "insisting that the gospel deals with the whole man," "his soul" and "body," "his material well-being" and "his spiritual well-being."[70] Professor Davis's insights into the truths of the Social Gospel helped give direction to King's preaching and his studies, for they "expanded King's understanding of the philosophical underpinnings of modern Christian liberalism, particularly the notion that God's reality" is "revealed through the historical unfolding" of God's "moral law."[71]

After reading Rauschenbusch, King shifted to "a serious study of the social and ethical theories of the great philosophers," from Plato and Aristotle down to Jean-Jacques Rousseau, Thomas Hobbes, Jeremy Bentham, John Stuart Mill, and John Locke.[72] Unfortunately,

King did not comment on exactly what he actually read in his "Autobiography of Religious Development" (1950),[73] written for one of Davis's classes, and his "Pilgrimage to Nonviolence" (1958),[74] which traces the trajectory of his academic pursuit of truth, and most of the class notes he took and papers he wrote on philosophy apparently no longer exist. There are occasional references, in some of the extant papers King wrote at Crozer, to Plato's idea of "God as the eternal Forms (or Ideas) of Justice, Truth, and Love" and to the Aristotelian concept of the "self-knowing, but not other-loving" God, and these philosophers obviously informed his thinking around "the great and eternal issues of reality." But interestingly enough, King found little "intellectual and moral satisfaction" in "the 'back to nature' optimism of Rousseau," "the social contract theories" of Hobbes and Locke, and "the utilitarianism of Bentham and Mill."[75] "All of these masters stimulated my thinking—such as it was," King conceded, "and, while finding things to question in each of them, I nevertheless learned a great deal from their study." King also quoted at times from all of these philosophical sources, during and after his years in seminary and graduate school, but their works seem to have been less important to him than those of Plato and Aristotle, which he always considered vital intellectual paths to truth.[76]

King also failed to find "intellectual and moral satisfaction" in "the revolutionary methods" of Karl Marx and Vladimir Lenin and in "the superman philosophy" of Friedrich Nietzsche, but these philosophers proved quite inspirational in his truth-seeking.[77] In order "to understand the appeal of communism for many people," King spent much of the Christmas holiday season of 1949 reading Marx, later turning to Lenin. He categorically rejected Communism's "cold atheism," its "materialistic and humanistic view of life and history," its "political totalitarianism," and its "ethical relativism." "Since there is no divine government, no absolute moral order," and "no fixed, immutable principles" in Communism, King declared, "almost anything—force, violence, murder, lying—is a justifiable means to the 'millennial' end."[78] King often singled out for special mention Communism's tragic reliance on the relativistic ethic when it came to matters of truth and untruth. But despite its "false assumptions and evil methods," King concluded that "communism had laid hold of certain truths which are essential parts of the Christian view of things," the most important among which are concern for social justice, protest against the injustices and indignities inflicted upon the poor, prophecy concerning the eventual collapse of capitalism, and emphasis on the classless society. King had been concerned about the poor, or what he would call "the least of these," from his early childhood, and reading Marx and Lenin significantly increased his awareness of the vast "gulf between superfluous wealth and abject poverty." King increasingly came to see the need to act on those "partial truths" he found in Communism, without subscribing to those "theories and practices which no Christian could ever accept."[79]

Nietzsche proved to be equally challenging for King, for he attacked the Hebraic-Christian ethic in ways reminiscent of Marx. King read Nietzsche's *The Genealogy of Morals* (1887) and *The Will to Power* (1901) at Crozer and later offered this assessment: "Nietzsche's glorification of power—in his theory, all life expressed the will to power—was an outgrowth of his contempt for ordinary morals. He attacked the whole of the Hebraic-Christian morality— with its virtues of piety and humility, its otherworldliness, and its attitude toward suffering—as the glorification of weakness, as making virtues out of necessity and impotence. He looked to the development of a superman who would surpass man as man surpassed the ape."[80] Like Marx, Nietzsche was an atheist, but King also knew that Nietzsche's writings on truth had greatly impacted Western philosophy and intellectual history generally, and this, perhaps more than anything else, sparked his interest in the German philosopher. Nietzsche argued vehemently that the present values of Christianity had nothing substantively to do with truth and reality. His critique of Hebraic-Christian values and his efforts to bring to vivid life his future ideal of the superman (Übermensch)—which, for King, evoked images of a Napoleon or a Hitler—brought King to the point of an intellectual and spiritual crisis.[81] King had already been exposed to a lecture in defense of pacifism at Crozer, delivered by A. J. Muste of the Fellowship of Reconciliation (FOR), and Nietzsche's claims led him to raise even more questions about the efficacy and/or practicality of that method.[82] King was compelled to struggle as never before with Jesus's admonitions to "love your enemies" and "turn the other cheek," thinking perhaps that such ethical teachings applied only to conflicts between individuals, and he almost despaired of the power of love for resolving social problems.[83] Although King's liberalism increasingly opened him to new ideas about life and the human condition, nothing in his background had prepared him for Nietzsche's radically alternative views concerning truth, morality, love, and power.

King discovered an answer to Nietzsche's tendency to reduce love to a resignation of power in the thought of Mohandas K. Gandhi, India's religious and political leader, who led his nation's independence struggle against British colonial rule. King had heard of Gandhi before enrolling in seminary—undoubtedly through his reading of the *Atlanta Daily World*, a local Black daily newspaper, and while listening to Benjamin E. Mays's Tuesday morning talks at Morehouse's Sales Chapel[84]—but his introduction to Gandhi came largely through a lecture given at the Fellowship House in Philadelphia, Pennsylvania, in early 1950 by Mordecai Johnson, the Black preacher, intellectual, and president of Howard University. Johnson, having just returned from India, spoke on Gandhi's life and teachings. His "message was so electrifying" that King "left the meeting and bought a half-dozen books on Gandhi's life and works."[85] From that point, Gandhi's thought struck a responsive chord in the heart and mind of King, who was ending his first year at Crozer and beginning "a serious intellectual quest for a method to eliminate social evil."[86] Of special significance for King was Gandhi's essential idea of *satyagraha* as "a way of life" or *satyagraha* as the guiding principle of all life, thought, and activity. *Satyagraha*, a term coined by Gandhi himself, denotes "holding on to Truth," and hence "Truth-force." According to Gandhi, *satya* derives from *sat*, which means "being," and it affirms that Truth is the only thing that exists in reality. Gandhi went on to assert that Truth is perhaps the most important name for God. The true *satyagrahi* devotes life to Truth, fully understanding that "holding on to truth" is an enduring pursuit. Gandhi regarded Jesus as "the prince of *satyagrahis*" because he not only "saw and expressed Truth" but taught that he who "first seeks Truth" will "also begin to achieve Beauty and Goodness."[87] Having studied the Gospels, the ideas of Rauschenbusch, and Platonic thought, it was not difficult for King to resonate with Gandhi's rich reflections on truth and to view them as a natural point of departure for further explorations. "Like Gandhi," he later explained, "I think we are all engaged in an experiment with truth."[88] King marveled at the fact that Gandhi "challenged the might of the British Empire and won independence for his people by using only the weapons of truth, noninjury, courage, and soul force."[89]

King shared Gandhi's conviction that truth-seeking and truth-telling are vital parts of liberation movements,[90] especially when rooted in love as expressed in a nonviolent ethic. But the agreement between the two leaders around a range of questions regarding the power of truth, or *satya*, had much to do with who King was and what he studied and believed before he embraced Gandhi. Gandhi made sense and appealed to King mainly because King had already discovered—at Ebenezer Baptist Church, Morehouse College, and in his studies of the life of Jesus and the early church at Crozer— that truth is always a potent force in personal and social transformation. In Professor Davis's Christian Theology for Today course, taken during his first semester at Crozer, King studied the gospel accounts and what Rauschenbusch said about "the Social Aims of Jesus" and "the Social Impetus of Primitive Christianity," and what he found in these sources further prepared him to accept Gandhi's idea of the ways of truth as being inseparable from the ways of love or the ways of nonviolent civil disobedience.[91]

By the time King reached his senior year at Crozer, he had become what he himself described as "a thoroughgoing liberal."[92] He was convinced at that point that liberalism afforded the only reliable path to truth. "A basic change in my thinking came," he later recalled, "when I began to question some of the theories that had been associated with so-called liberal theology."[93] This questioning process escalated when King, only months before graduating from

Crozer, seriously studied some of the writings of Reinhold Niebuhr, the American theologian and Christian realist who also became the nation's foremost authority in neoorthodoxy. The "prophetic and realistic elements" in Niebuhr's thought, along with his deep and insightful critique of liberalism, greatly impacted King, who had become "absolutely convinced of the natural goodness of man and the natural power of human reason." King wrote,

> I began to question the liberal doctrine of man. The more I observed the tragedies of history and man's shameful inclination to choose the low road, the more I came to see the depths and strength of sin. My reading of the works of Reinhold Niebuhr made me aware of the complexity of human motives and the reality of sin on every level of man's existence. Moreover, I came to recognize the complexities of man's social involvement and the glaring reality of collective evil. I realized that liberalism had been all too sentimental concerning human nature and that it leaned toward a false idealism. . . .
>
> I also came to see that the superficial optimism of liberalism concerning human nature overlooked the fact that reason is darkened by sin. The more I thought about human nature, the more I saw how our tragic inclination for sin encourages us to rationalize our actions. Liberalism failed to show that reason by itself is little more than an instrument to justify man's defensive ways of thinking. Reason, devoid of the purifying power of faith, can never free itself from distortions and rationalizations.[94]

King initially "became so enamored" of Niebuhr's social ethics that he "almost fell into the trap of accepting uncritically everything he wrote."[95] Clearly, he had made the very same mistake earlier with regard to the liberal tradition. Although Niebuhr's critiques of the liberal positions on the essential goodness of human nature and the natural power of human reason proved sobering and to some degree transformative for King, he continued to cherish liberalism's stress on the importance of the analytical and receptive mind, its openness to objective appraisal and critical analysis, its emphasis on the role of reason in theological reflection, its devotion to the pursuit of truth, and its unwavering support of the value of biblical criticism as a tool in scriptural interpretation.[96] A dialectical thinker of sorts long before enrolling at Crozer, King explained at great length how the search for truth demanded attention to both liberalism and neoorthodoxy:

> Although I rejected some aspects of liberalism, I never came to an all-out acceptance of neo-orthodoxy. While I saw neo-orthodoxy as a helpful corrective for a sentimental liberalism, I felt that it did not provide an adequate answer to basic questions. If liberalism was too optimistic concerning human nature, neo-orthodoxy was too pessimistic. Not only on the question of man, but also on other vital issues, the revolt of neo-orthodoxy went too far. In its attempt to preserve the transcendence of God, which had been neglected by an overstress of his immanence in liberalism, neo-orthodoxy went to the extreme of stressing a God who was hidden, unknown, and "wholly other." In its revolt against overemphasis on the power of reason in liberalism, neo-orthodoxy fell into a mood of antirationalism and semifundamentalism, stressing a narrow uncritical biblicism. This approach, I felt, was inadequate both for the church and for personal life. . . . So although liberalism left me unsatisfied on the question of the nature of man, I found no refuge in neo-orthodoxy. I am now convinced that the truth about man is found neither in liberalism nor neo-orthodoxy. Each represents a partial truth. A large segment of Protestant liberalism defined man only in terms of his essential nature, his capacity for good; neo-orthodoxy tended to define man only in terms of his existential nature, his capacity for evil. An adequate understanding of man is found neither in the thesis of liberalism nor in the antithesis of neo-orthodoxy, but in a synthesis which reconciles the truths of both.[97]

Niebuhr's challenge forced King into a more objective and critical reading of Walter Rauschenbusch and the whole structure of liberal theology and culture. Equally significant was Niebuhr's "critique of the pacifist position," which, in King's mind, raised certain questions about the realism of Gandhian nonviolence and, perhaps indirectly, about its identification with the ways of truth. Niebuhr himself had been a pacifist up to the early 1930s but abandoned that stance because of imminent world war and his conviction that it could no longer serve as a universally viable method in the struggle against injustice and oppression. King read Niebuhr's critique of pacifism in his *Moral Man and Immoral Society* (1932), and while agreeing with Niebuhr's views on the "unwarranted optimism" that drives many pacifists, King came to disagree with Niebuhr's claims that there is "no intrinsic moral difference between violent and nonviolent resistance," that it is irresponsible to rely on "nonviolent resistance when there" is "no ground for believing" it will successfully halt "the spread of totalitarian tyranny," and that "pacifism failed to do justice to the Reformation doctrine of justification by faith, substituting for it a sectarian perfectionism which believes 'that divine grace actually lifts man out of the sinful contradictions of history and establishes him above the sins of the world.'"[98] King felt that these claims showed that Niebuhr "interpreted pacifism as a sort of passive nonresistance to evil expressing naïve trust in the power of love." "My study of Gandhi convinced me," said King in contrast to Niebuhr, "that true pacifism is not nonresistance to evil, but nonviolent resistance to evil." "Between the two positions," King added, "there is a world of difference." King commented further: "True pacifism is not unrealistic submission to evil power, as Niebuhr contends. It is rather a courageous confrontation of evil by the power of love."[99] In Gandhian terms, pacifism had to do, as King had come to see, with the demonic structures of untruth being boldly challenged and ultimately dismantled by the crusading forces of truth.

When King graduated from Crozer Seminary in the spring of 1951, he was conversant on some levels with the thought and activities of Gandhi, perhaps the greatest self-proclaimed truth-seeker he studied during his academic odyssey. King began his doctoral studies in the fall of that year at Boston University's School of Theology, where he "had the opportunity to talk to many exponents of nonviolence, both students and visitors to the campus."[100] Dean Walter Muelder and Allan Knight Chalmers, the university's professor of preaching and practical Christianity, not only "had a deep sympathy for pacifism" but also had "a passion for social justice that stemmed, not from a superficial optimism, but from a deep faith in the possibilities of human beings when they allowed themselves to become co-workers with God."[101] A more stimulating environment could not have been imagined, for Boston University—much like Morehouse and Crozer—combined an emphasis on the academic, spiritual, and social dimensions of student life. Consequently, King—who had chosen systematic and philosophical theology as major areas of concentration[102]—was able to broaden his probing inquiry into streams of neoorthodoxy and liberalism while also continuing his search for a means to eradicate social evil and injustice.

"It was at Boston University that I came to see that Niebuhr had over-emphasized the corruption of human nature," King recounted. King went on to explain that "Niebuhr's pessimism concerning human nature was not balanced by an optimism concerning divine nature"—that Niebuhr "was so involved in diagnosing man's sickness of sin that he overlooked the cure of grace."[103] But significantly enough, Niebuhr deepened King's sense of those partial truths in both neoorthodoxy and liberalism, thus becoming one of his major intellectual sources:

> In spite of the fact that I found many things to be desired in Niebuhr's philosophy, there were several points at which he constructively influenced my thinking. Niebuhr's great contribution to contemporary theology is that he has refuted the false optimism characteristic of a great segment of Protestant liberalism, without falling into the anti-rationalism of the continental theologian Karl Barth, or the semi-fundamentalism of other dialectical theologians. Moreover, Niebuhr has extraordinary insight into human

nature, especially the behavior of nations and social groups. He is keenly aware of the complexity of human motives and of the relation between morality and power. His theology is a persistent reminder of the reality of sin on every level of man's existence. These elements in Niebuhr's thinking helped me to recognize the illusions of a superficial optimism concerning human nature and the dangers of a false idealism. While I still believed in man's potential for good, Niebuhr made me realize his potential for evil as well. Moreover, Niebuhr helped me to recognize the complexity of man's social involvement and the glaring reality of collective evil. . . . Many pacifists, I felt, failed to see this. All too many had an unwarranted optimism concerning man and leaned unconsciously toward self-righteousness. It was my revolt against these attitudes under the influence of Niebuhr that accounts for the fact that in spite of my strong leaning toward pacifism, I never joined a pacifist organization. After reading Niebuhr, I tried to arrive at a realistic pacifism. In other words, I came to see the pacifist position not as sinless but as the lesser evil in the circumstances. I felt then, and I feel now that the pacifist would have a greater appeal if he did not claim to be free from the moral dilemmas that the Christian nonpacifist confronts.[104]

King went to Boston University to study personalism, or personal idealism, a school of philosophy identified specifically with that institution and Borden P. Bowne since 1876. Perhaps even more appealing for King was the presence of Edgar S. Brightman, a second-generation personalist and philosopher of religion, to whom King had been introduced at Morehouse and whose ideas he had studied at Crozer with George Davis.[105] All personalists shared Brightman's views that the "person is 'the supreme philosophical principle,'" that reality is both personal and social in nature, that persons have intrinsic dignity and worth, that freedom is essential to authentic existence, that self-consciousness is of paramount importance, and that the universe is friendly to value.[106] These ideas were treated to some extent in a number of papers King wrote on personalism at Boston.[107] King studied personalism under both Brightman and L. Harold DeWolf, the professor of systematic theology at Boston, and DeWolf became King's PhD adviser when Brightman died in 1953. Of Brightman and DeWolf, King later stated, "Both men greatly stimulated my thinking. It was mainly under these teachers that I studied personalistic philosophy—the theory that the clue to the meaning of ultimate reality is found in personality. This personal idealism remains today my basic philosophical position. Personalism's insistence that only personality—finite and infinite—is ultimately real strengthened me in two convictions: It gave me a metaphysical and philosophical grounding for the idea of a personal God, and it gave me a metaphysical basis for the dignity and worth of all human personality."[108]

The idea of the personal God of love and reason and the inviolable dignity of persons had been taught to King in childhood, through what Rufus Burrow Jr. calls "the rudiments of a 'homespun personalism,'"[109] but King's studies at Crozer, and most especially at Boston University, provided him with the intellectual structure, the academic language, and the conceptual framework to articulate these ideas on paper and subsequently in interviews, sermons, and speeches. Personalism also profoundly influenced King's pursuit of truth. Burrow identifies its influences in this regard on at least four important levels. First, because personalism "as a philosophy is fundamentally metaphysics"—or "a way of thinking about the whole of reality and experience; of trying to see how all things hang together"[110]—it yielded endless possibilities for King's continuing ventures in truth-seeking. Second, King essentially agreed with the idea, embraced by Brightman and other personalists, that ultimately "truth is what is important, and we arrive at it through rational, coherent thought."[111] King suggested as much and more in a paper he wrote for Brightman. Contrasting Brightman's ideas with those of William E. Hocking, the well-known philosopher of religion and proponent of "objective idealism," King argued that Brightman "is much more sound philosophically" and that Hocking "fails to take seriously the fact that all truth, including religious, is based on the assumption that the human mind is valid and that the cosmos is rational." Brightman's "empirical method," King stated in that same paper, "is bound up with the idea of coherence as a criterion of truth."[112] Third, King invested in Brightman's personalistic method because it acknowledged the importance of "informal and nonintellectual sources and experiences" in "the quest for knowledge and truth." Finally, King fully subscribed to the idea, held by Brightman and other personalists, "that truth grows and that one should have the courage to alter one's views and practice in the face of new evidence and facts."[113] Thus, King joined Brightman in rejecting Hocking's position on "the rationalistic ideal of 'finished truth'" and on "the relevance and possibility of 'eternal truth' and certainty."[114]

At Boston, personalistic ideas increasingly became foundational, and indeed the point of departure, for King's engagement with and critique of other strands of philosophical, ethical, and theological thought. This was most certainly the case with Georg Hegel's dialectical method of analyzing not only history but truth as well. King had been introduced to Hegel at Morehouse and encountered him in his studies at Crozer and in a philosophy course at the University of Pennsylvania but studied Hegel more intensely at Boston under the guidance of Edgar S. Brightman and later L. Harold DeWolf and Peter A. Bertocci.[115] King read Hegel's *Phenomenology of Mind* (1807), *Philosophy of Right* (1820), and *Philosophy of History* (1837) and mentioned Hegelian dialectics and logic in many of his written assignments at Boston.[116] While rejecting Hegel's metaphysics on the grounds that it "was rationally unsound" and "tended to swallow up the many in the one," King nevertheless agreed wholeheartedly with Hegel's dialectical method of thinking.[117] To be sure, King had already been something of a dialectical thinker since his teens, for his very existence and sense of life were defined early on by the glaring opposites of segregation (white world) and community (Black world),[118] but Hegel brought more clarity, a broader focus, and an intellectual and conceptual structure to King's employment of the dialectical method of thesis, antithesis, and synthesis. Of Hegel, King wrote, "His contention that 'truth is the whole' led me to a philosophical method of rational coherence. His analysis of the dialectical process, in spite of its shortcomings, helped me to see that growth comes through struggle."[119] Thus, King's philosophy, theology, and ethics took on a dialectical quality. His thought, much like Hegel's, developed out of his encounter with two opposites—the thesis and the antithesis—and his effort to achieve a synthesis of the partial truths found in each,[120] as was shown previously in the discussion of his approach to neoorthodoxy and liberalism. The Hegelian dialectical approach became King's most useful intellectual tool for getting at truth and for explaining how such a quest is inevitably ongoing and ultimately endless, especially for the genuinely determined truth-seeker.

Hegel became King's favorite philosopher, but King was never unmindful of the importance of what personalists like Brightman, DeWolf, and Bertocci taught him about principal philosophical figures such as Heraclitus, Aristotle, and Kant and their thoughts about history, life, humanity, God, nature, knowledge, freedom, and other matters. Heraclitus, the ancient Greek philosopher, influenced both Plato and Hegel and, along with Hegel, taught King that humans have an amazing "capacity for rational development," that the nature of material and spiritual life arises out of "a tension of opposites," that "all things are in a state of change," that "justice emerges from the strife of opposites," and that growth comes "through struggle."[121] Significant from a different angle was Aristotle, whom King studied to some degree at Morehouse and Crozer and whose thought King found increasingly interesting as he read and studied with DeWolf. King agreed with DeWolf's critique of the Aristotelian concept of God as "unmoved mover"—of the "unchanging" and "self-knowing God" who "merely contemplates himself" while remaining "oblivious to human affairs"—insisting instead that God is "an other-loving God who forever works through history for the establishment of His Kingdom."[122] Although the German philosopher Immanuel Kant is more frequently mentioned in King's extant written assignments at Boston than both Heraclitus and Aristotle, it is an open question whether Kant's impact on King was significantly greater than theirs. King became somewhat familiar with Kant's political theory, his ideas on experience as a source of knowledge, his thoughts on the unity of all truth and reason, and his ethical emphasis on humans' rational nature and their freedom to establish moral law, but King was far more interested in what Kant said about "the worth of human personality as a *means* rather than an *end*."[123] In fact, personalist and Kantian ideas occasionally came together in King's mind when he addressed structures of injustice that targeted certain segments of humanity in society. For example, he held that segregation treated Blacks "as mere means," as "animated tools," rather "than as ends-in-themselves" or "as persons sacred in themselves."[124] In May 1955, a month before receiving his PhD from Boston University, King said essentially the same about patriarchy, gender inequality, and sexism, injustices he apparently opposed in principle but, ironically enough, largely tolerated in his own personal life and practices:

> Men must accept the fact that the day has passed when the man can stand over the wife with an iron rod asserting his authority as "boss." This does not mean that women no longer respect masculinity, i.e., strong, dynamic manliness; women will always respect that. But it does mean that the day has passed when women will be trampled over and treated as some slave subject to the dictates of a despotic husband. One of the great contributions that Christianity has made to the world is that of lifting the status of womanhood from that of an insignificant childbearer to a position of dignity and honor and respect. Women must be respected as human beings and not be treated as mere means. Strictly speaking, there is no boss in the home; it is no lord-servant relationship.[125]

King would have been among the first to concede that Kant's doctrine of treating persons "as *ends* and never as mere *means*" figured prominently into his path toward truth, but he, due to limited knowledge of Kant's political theory, mistakenly portrayed the philosopher as "a champion of the freedom and dignity of the individual."[126]

In Kant's "rational state," or his "kingdom of ends," one "had to be an adult male, to be his own master, and to have property—which could include a skill, trade, fine art, or science to support himself"—in order to "qualify as a citizen" with "the right to vote and to make laws through representatives."[127] Obviously, women were automatically excluded based on gender. Also, slaves, laborers, and others unable to "produce a commodity or sell their own property" would not qualify as citizens under such requirements. "Had King known about Kant's principle of *independence*," writes John J. Ansbro, "he would have been quick to denounce the contradiction between Kant's ethical emphasis on the freedom and dignity of the individual as a moral lawgiver and this justification of disfranchisement."[128] Of course, it is worth noting that King himself would also ultimately be criticized for the inconsistency between his philosophical stress on the dignity and worth of all human personality and his failure to seriously consider women's liberation as a part of his quest for the beloved community ideal.[129]

When King turned his attention to existentialism, he discovered yet another school of philosophical thinkers who "had grasped certain basic truths" about humanity and the human condition "that could not be permanently overlooked." King's introduction to existentialism came through his reading of Friedrich Nietzsche and Søren Kierkegaard and later Karl Jaspers, Martin Heidegger, Jean-Paul Sartre, and Paul Tillich.[130] Kierkegaard, Jaspers, and Tillich were theistic existentialists, and Nietzsche, Sartre, and Heidegger were atheistic existentialists. The fact that King, a Christian minister, had a deep interest in both camps affords additional proof of a life driven by not only a belief in the power of the intellect but, perhaps more importantly, a passion for truth. Knowing that individual existence was the highest and most fundamental truth in existentialism, King concluded that this philosophy, despite having become "all too fashionable," had contributed enormously to our understanding of humanity's "finite freedom," to our sense of the world as "fragmented," to our view of history as "a series of unreconciled conflicts," to the idea that humanity's "existential situation is estranged from" its "essential nature," and to our "perception of the anxiety," conflict, and meaninglessness "produced" in humans' "personal and social life by the perilous and ambiguous structure of existence."[131] In his doctoral dissertation, under the advisership of DeWolf, King highlighted "a common denominator between athe- istic and theistic existentialists" and asserted that, "like Kierkegaard and Heidegger, Tillich regards anxiety as directed toward 'nothing- ness.' Though ineradicable, it can be accepted and used creatively as a part of what it means to be human."[132] There are also references in King's papers to Kierkegaard's reflections on the "qualitative dif- ference between God and man," Nietzsche's thoughts on man as "a hammer or an anvil," Heidegger's views on "finite things" being "'thrown' into being," and what Tillich, Sartre, and Jaspers taught about the problems of "being" and "nonbeing." Tillich is discussed far more than the other existentialists in King's Boston papers, which is not surprising, since Tillich's concept of God is treated as a major topic in his dissertation.[133] Years after finishing his graduate work at Boston, King suggested that the existentialists' emphasis on certain truths about human beings, the state of human existence, and the human plight were "especially meaningful" for a time in which oppressed people worldwide were struggling for freedom.[134]

Paul Tillich's works draw together insights from the other existentialists, and thus he was primarily responsible for King's study of and engagement with the basic truths of existential- ism.[135] Tillich—the renowned preacher, teacher, philosopher, and theologian—also proved highly significant for King's exploration of certain ideas about God and the relationship between love, power, and justice. In his PhD dissertation, King attacked what he deemed to be Tillich's concept of the impersonal God, which contrasted with the personal God of his familial and church her- itage.[136] King held that Tillich's God, described as "Being Itself," was essentially "an Absolute devoid of consciousness and life" and was "little more than a sub-personal reservoir of power, some- what akin to the impersonalism of Oriental Vedantism."[137] But King, in an effort to define love, power, and justice as a "creative union" as opposed to "polar opposites," agreed with Tillich's idea that love and justice are indistinguishable as attributes of God, though King included power here as well. For King, then, love, power, and justice are dimensions of God's activity, and therefore, he could accept without hesitation Tillich's claim that "power at its best is love implementing the demands of justice," and "justice at its best is love correcting everything that stands against love." Tillich, like Gandhi, reinforced King's rejection of Friedrich Nietzsche's denunciation of the Hebraic-Christian love ethic "as a glorification of weakness."[138] However, King was far more indebted to Gandhi than Tillich when it came to his understanding of how love, power, and justice related to the ways of truth.

Other levels of meaning and depth to King's graduate studies tend to be either casually overlooked or mentioned fleetingly by his intellectual biographers. King studied philosophy extensively at the University of Pennsylvania and later at Harvard University, both first-rate institutions. It is not difficult to imagine how these studies, together with his classwork at Boston, might have contributed to his attitude toward truth and his truth-seeking. At the University of Pennsylvania, King took courses focused on aesthetics, Hegel, and Kant. Equally noteworthy was his study of the Platonic dialogues with Professor Raphael Demos at Harvard,[139] which extended beyond what he had covered in Professor Samuel Williams's classes at Morehouse. King was a more mature student by this time and thus almost certainly better equipped to discuss not only the Hegelian Dialectic and Kantian ethics but, more specifically, topics like beauty and truth in connection with what he would call "the chief quest of ethical philosophy" or as part of what Plato, Aristotle, the Stoics, the Epicureans, and other ancient Greek philosophers understood to be "the highest good," or "the *summum bonum* of life."[140]

As a supplement to philosophical training at Boston University, King and other graduate students occasionally met for informal discussion in the institution's cafeteria or dorm rooms. These gatherings morphed into a Dialectical Society, or Philosophy Club, composed of a dozen students who met monthly, usually in King's apartment, to discuss a paper presented by a participant. King often presided over the sessions and assisted in choosing topics and engaging guest speakers, such as his adviser, L. Harold DeWolf. A member of the club recalled that discussions usually centered around "certain philosophical and theological ideas" and how they applied "to the black situation in the country." On one occasion, King himself presented a paper in which he criticized "Niebuhr's notion of the inherent imperfectability of human nature." Although King, with a mind disciplined by years of study in philosophy, theology, and ethics, participated actively in the discussions, he apparently never gave the impression that what he said "had to be right" or that he was the authoritative bearer of truth around a particular topic.[141] Much of his habit of quoting from the great philosophers, theologians, and ethicists—in his writings, sermons, speeches, interviews, and in casual conversations—undoubtedly resulted from his exposure to and participation in that Philosophy Club. It was here that King developed a keener understanding of truth as the goal of both the philosophical-theological life and the socioethical quest.

There are some misconceptions about the trajectory of King's search for truth within the walls of academia. It has been suggested, for example, that King was not "a full-blown liberal in terms of biblical scholarship"—that despite his exposure to a range of liberal thinkers and intellectual sources at Morehouse, Crozer, and Boston, he exclusively turned to traditional, Bible-based Christianity for the fundamental truths that really mattered in his life as a Baptist clergyman. "While it is true that Dr. King would at times raise questions about such items as the virgin birth, the nature of the resurrection body," and a literal hell, the suggestion goes, "there are at least some of those who traveled with him or knew him well who believe that Dr. King was simply asking questions to sharpen the faith and apologetic skill of his friends."[142] The inference here is that those who knew and marched with King are in a better position to know his ideas and what he believed about basic scriptural truths and that they are convinced that he affirmed the inerrancy of the Bible, the virgin birth, Christ's bodily resurrection from the dead, the second coming, and other fundamentals of the faith. Ministers who had some association with King are especially susceptible to this viewpoint. Some even assume that because King was a preacher first and foremost, the church, and not the academy, afforded the primary and legitimate venue in which he engaged in truth-seeking. Hence, the conclusion is that when it came to biblical truths, King essentially accepted what Black Baptist preachers typically believed.[143] Those who make such claims are so grounded in the image of King as a Christian pastor that they forget he was also a polished intellectual who cherished liberalism's engagement with truth through objective appraisal and critical-analytical thinking, who deeply appreciated the fruits of biblical criticism, and who felt compelled to pursue truth in spaces far beyond the Christian church.

John J. Ansbro is right in saying that King had a "determination to accept truth from every position, no matter how antithetical to his own."[144] Convinced that no single sacred text, intellectual source, nor religious tradition exhausted truth, King—during his years at Morehouse, Crozer, and Boston—brought a sense of the value of total truth to an exploration of a range of topics in his research papers, including sacred and secular rituals, the significance of ancient Near Eastern texts for Old Testament studies, the Judaic origins of many of the great ethical principles of the New Testament, Mithraism and its stress on "Mithra as the defender of the truth," the influence of mystery religions on ancient Christianity, the limitations of scriptural literalism, the importance of reason and experience in understanding God, reconciling biblical truths and scientific facts, the use of the Bible in modern theological construction, the chief characteristics and doctrines of Mahayana Buddhism, atheistic tendencies in personalist and existentialist thought, and the categories of Hegelian logic.[145] Small wonder that King became such a staunch critic of academics—and of colleges, seminaries, or any other institutions for that matter—that claimed final, finished, ultimate, or absolute truth.[146]

Another misconception about King's evolving quest for truth is that he had ceased being a biblicist by the time he entered Boston University.[147] This was clearly not the case. Although King rejected claims of biblical inerrancy or infallibility, he still believed that much of Scripture was divinely inspired and that the Bible remains an authoritative source of truth. Some of his written assignments at Boston contain repeated references to the Old and New Testaments, and passages from Scripture continued to be the starting point for the framing and delivery of his sermons.[148] In a paper on "Contemporary Continental Theology," written for DeWolf's seminar in systematic theology at Boston, King strongly criticized the excesses of the liberal-critical approach to Scripture while showing that he remained, at least on some levels, something of a biblicist:

> The continental theologians call us back to the dimension of depth in the Bible. This is not to say that the critical approach to the study of Scripture must be disregarded. But it does mean that Biblical criticism must remain a means, not an end. Too many liberals have been so involved in "higher Criticism" that they failed to see the vital issues of the Christian faith. After one has gone through the whole process of Biblical criticism, he must be able to answer the question, "what then?" We must see the Bible as both the Word of God and the Word of Man. The Bible is more than a piece of historical literature, as many liberals would reduce it to; it is a personal word from a living God. We may wish to supplement Barth's exclusive emphasis upon God's self revelation in Scripture with a corrective emphasis upon tradition, reason or Christian experience, but we must agree that the Biblical revelation is classic and normative for Christian thought; it is the central pillar on which the whole structure of Christian theology must rest.[149]

It is equally misleading to assume that King's pursuit of truth in academic circles was essentially confined to the intellectual sources he discussed in versions of his "Pilgrimage to Nonviolence."[150] Even a cursory reading of King's papers at Morehouse, Crozer, and Boston exposes this misconception. The list of biblicists, philosophers, theologians, and ethicists King either discussed or quoted in those papers seems endless. King's thought was decisively eclectic and synthetic, which means that he drew from countless sources while combining much of the best of what he found in each into an intelligible whole, thus arriving at a system of thought he could accept with relative ease.[151] While it is important to have some sense of what these intellectual sources are and of why they were meaningful for King, it is not necessary to cover them all in order to grasp the essentials of King's truth-seeking. This can be achieved by focusing on some of the best-known intellectual sources or those that, by King's own admission, tremendously influenced his intellectual pilgrimage. This chapter suggests as much and more about King's paths to truth. King's "Pilgrimage to Nonviolence" offers important points of departure for exploring this subject, but it is beneficial to keep the range of his academic papers in mind and also his written documents such as "Autobiography of Religious Development" (1950) and "Letter from the Birmingham City Jail" (1963).

Yet another misconception surfaces in the assumption that King's search for truth in the academy ended when he received his PhD from Boston University in June 1955. When King finished his work at Boston, he had a free, analytical, and critical mind, and while he was no longer officially a student, he still maintained close contact to the culture of academia. This was only natural for one who never separated the "call for intelligence" from a "love for truth."[152] Never intimidated by great minds, King continued to read the works of the great theologians, philosophers, and ethicists. He remained abreast of developing trends in these fields of thought, especially philosophical theology, as evidenced by his frequent references to the Death of God theology of the late 1950s and 1960s.[153] In the fall of 1961, King and Samuel Williams, one of his former professors, team taught a course in social philosophy at Morehouse College in which they focused on metaphysics, ontology, epistemology, logic, and aesthetics. In his introductory lecture for the course, King defined philosophy as "the love of wisdom," provided "a broad overview of philosophy," made it clear that the focus would be on "connected truths about all available experience," and mentioned Socrates, Plato, Aristotle, Heraclitus, Thales, Parmenides, Zeno, Pythagoras, Empedocles, and Kant. The names of several other well-known philosophers and theologians were included in King's handwritten notebook for the course, including Rousseau, Niccolò Machiavelli, Goethe, Thomas Hobbes, John Locke, Spinoza, Francis Bacon, Augustine, Anselm, and Thomas Aquinas. All of these writers, in King's thinking, pursued some path to truth.[154] Although King never satisfied his love for teaching on a broader scale, for the remainder of his life, he either lectured or gave speeches at colleges, universities, divinity schools, and seminaries throughout the country and abroad. In short, King never surrendered that academic spirit that largely framed his passion for truth.

King was drawn to academic disciplines that encouraged, stimulated, and enhanced his pursuit of truth. In this context, Socrates's ultimate sacrifice for "academic freedom" became immensely important to him.[155] This concept of academic freedom explains in some measure King's choice of liberal Christian ethics and philosophical theology and also the levels of concentration and devotion he brought to his studies. Interestingly enough, after a long, arduous intellectual pilgrimage, King never arrived at a final or finished truth, and unresolved tensions remained in his thought.[156] But truth in final or finished form was never what King had in mind and was certainly not what he expected to achieve. On the contrary, by the time he completed his PhD, King had become unalterably convinced that seeking and engaging truth are lifelong, unending processes.

Truth-Seeking within the Sphere of Practical Action

Martin Luther King Jr.'s quest for truth progressed beyond an engagement with ideas in the world of academia to a protracted struggle for personal and communal liberation and empowerment. In December 1955, a few months after receiving his PhD in systematic and philosophical theology, he was catapulted to a position of leadership in the civil rights movement. From that point on, King sought to relate the truths he learned in the challenging confines of the classroom to the crusade against racial injustice, economic exploitation, violence, and human destruction. Such a path was not unexpected for a man who always believed in both speaking and living the truth and who had come to see that people are liberated and empowered only when the ethos of truth-seeking, truth-telling, and truth-sharing is valued as an imperative for action and change.

Truth and freedom became inseparable on King's own scale of values. He delighted in quoting Jesus's words: "Ye shall know the truth, and the truth shall make you free" (John 8:32).[157] Constantly facing the haunting specter of untruths about Jim Crow and its pervasive, devastating effects on people in the South, King reminded the oppressed and the oppressors that "it is time for all of us to tell each other the truth about who and what have brought the Negro to the condition of deprivation against which he struggles today." He continued, "In human relations the truth is hard to come by, because most groups are deceived about themselves. Rationalization and the incessant search for 'scapegoats' are the psychological cataracts that blind us to our individual and collective sins."[158] The interplay between truth and freedom, which gained some clarity in King's thinking when he read the words of Jesus, Henry David Thoreau, and Mohandas K. Gandhi, became starkly real to him in the context of his people's struggle. He increasingly came to realize that truth always matters in any legitimate movement for freedom and that without truth there is no freedom worthy of the name. Thus, every move King made to free his people would be done in the name of truth.

For King, the protest phase of the modern civil rights movement, which began with the Montgomery bus boycott in 1955–56, made possible what segregation had long prevented—namely, the unimpeded pursuit of truth in both theoretical and practical terms. Here he came to accept, as a matter of principle and practice, the nonviolent ethic embodied in the teachings of Jesus and Gandhi, for he knew that violence was not the means to propagate either freedom or truth. At this juncture, what King studied in classrooms came together in his consciousness with what he experienced in the context of struggle. King spoke about this in his "Pilgrimage to Nonviolence," noting, "The experience in Montgomery did more to clarify my thinking in regard to the question of nonviolence than all the books that I had read." He further explained, "When the protest began, my mind, consciously or unconsciously, was driven back to the Sermon on the Mount, with its sublime teachings on love, and the Gandhian method of nonviolent resistance. As the days unfolded, I came to see the power of nonviolence more and more. Living through the actual experience of the protest, nonviolence became more than a method to which I gave intellectual assent; it became a commitment to a way of life. Many of the things that I had not cleared up intellectually concerning nonviolence were now solved in the sphere of practical action."[159]

In a more general sense, the Montgomery bus protest reminded King that seeking and engaging truth is never merely about the life of the mind but involves the head and the heart—a commitment of the mind as well as the heart, soul, and body. As a result, King very early referred to the nonviolent movement as "a spiritual movement" while at the same time consistently urging all involved to get "the heart right."[160] The sheer significance of such a spiritual quest became increasingly and painfully real to King late one night in Montgomery, in January 1956, when he received a telephone call from a white supremacist who called him a "nigger" and threatened to kill him and bomb his home:

> I got out of bed and began to walk the floor. Finally, I went to the kitchen and heated a pot of coffee. I was ready to give up. With my cup of coffee sitting untouched before me I tried to think of a way to move out of the picture without appearing a coward. In this state of exhaustion, when my courage had all but gone, I decided to take my problem to God. With my head in my hands, I bowed over the kitchen table and prayed allowed. The words I spoke to God that midnight are still vivid in my memory. "I'm here taking a stand for what I believe is right. But now I am afraid. The people are looking to me for leadership, and if I stand before them without strength and courage, they too will falter. I am at the end of my powers. I have nothing left. I've come to the point where I can't face it alone. . . ." At that moment I experienced the presence of the Divine

as I had never experienced Him before. It seemed as though I could hear the quiet assurance of an inner voice saying: "Martin Luther, stand up for righteousness, stand up for justice, stand up for truth. And lo, I will be with you, even until the end of the world. . . ." Almost at once my fears began to go. My uncertainty disappeared. I was ready to face anything.[161]

King had undoubtedly heard his former Boston professor Edgar S. Brightman say at various times that "spiritual liberty is the result of a life in touch with the sources of truth and power"—that "the truth shall make you free"[162]—and this sense of the spiritual journey was most certainly reinforced by the kitchen vision. King brought to that experience a certain humility of mind and spirit that he, like Gandhi, considered essential to the quest for truth, and such a quality must have surfaced in his thinking whenever he spoke of being "pressed by the demands of inner truth."[163] The kitchen vision was as much about the inner King who opened his mind, heart, and soul to truth as the outer King who nonviolently challenged the structures of power while fighting for the full reali- zation of civil and human rights. King had a sense of being called by truth to pursue truth and knew that he had to become the embodi- ment of the truth that he struggled to make real in the lives of both the oppressed and the oppressors. Thus, he constantly spoke of the importance of the examined life while raising the inescapable need for self-criticism and for the nurturing of the best of life's intuitive convictions.[164]

King's leading of civil rights campaigns across the South in the 1960s—especially in cities like Albany, Birmingham, Saint Augus- tine, Selma, and Memphis—further clarified and developed his philosophy of nonviolence as the way of truth. On another level, nonviolence was most certainly a methodology or strategy for elim- inating racial injustice; it was also a personal and social ethic.[165] Furthermore, nonviolence was what William D. Watley calls "an ethic of exigencies" because it was refined in the midst of the conflict and crisis situations King and others confronted as they participated in boycotts and prayer vigils, marched in the streets, planned voter registration drives, staged sit-ins and kneel-ins, violated segregation laws and court injunctions, and engaged in other activities designed to eradicate the personal and institutional racism of white America.[166]

King's understanding of nonviolence as a way of truth has been almost entirely overlooked by his biographers and interpreters. Although King referred variously to nonviolence as "a creed," "a way of life," "the method of the strong," "the Christian way," and "the way of love,"[167] he, as was the case with Gandhi, was equally intentional about stressing its importance as a "weapon of truth."[168] This became quite evident after King's visits to Ghana in 1957, where he witnessed that nation's independence celebrations at the invitation of Prime Minister Kwame Nkrumah, and to India in 1959, where he talked at length with Africans as well as Gandhi's relatives and followers. Small wonder that King—before participating in a sweeping assault on segregation laws and structures in Albany, Georgia, in 1961—asserted that he and others who struggled and sacrificed for freedom and justice were, like Gandhi, experimenting with truth.[169] King echoed Gandhi's conviction that nonviolence is a necessary path to seeking and finding truth. Translating truth into a nonviolent crusade for constructive, meaningful, and lasting social change was among the high standards both men set for themselves.[170]

Gandhi and Henry David Thoreau were often mentioned by King when he considered civil disobedience, perhaps the most controversial dimension of his nonviolent practice, as truth in action.[171] Often attacked for disobeying segregation laws and the court injunctions designed to uphold them, King never hesitated to identify other models of such activism throughout human history. Drawing on the third chapter of the book of Daniel in the Old Testament (Hebrew Bible), he noted that civil disobedience "was seen sublimely in the refusal of Shadrach, Meshach and Abednego to obey the laws of Nebuchadnezzar because a higher moral law was involved."[172] The early Christians mastered "the art of civil disobedience," King argued, for they "were willing to face all kinds of suffering in order to stand up for what they knew was right even though they knew it was against the laws of the Roman Empire."[173] King was equally fascinated with the actions of Socrates, who was forced to drink hemlock because of his deep devotion to philosophical inquiry as a path to truth.[174] King also pointed to the noble example set by those who opposed Hitler's Nazi regime and its laws in Germany, the Hungarian freedom fighters, and antiapartheid activists in South Africa, all of whom sacrificed their lives for the ultimate triumph of freedom and truth.[175] And there were those who shaped what King called "the American tradition" of civil disobedience—the Boston Tea Party, the abolitionists, conductors on the Underground Railroad—in whose symbolic shadow he and other freedom crusaders stood in the 1950s and '60s.[176] For King, this long line of ethical nonconformists constituted living and historical proof that paths to truth are never safe, simple, and easy— that they are in fact risky and dangerous, oftentimes resulting in suffering and death. He felt nonetheless that "the world has always moved forward on the feet of its nonconformists."[177]

The cross event in the New Testament became immeasurably significant for King, symbolically and literally, as he pondered both the demands and risks involved in the search for truth. For King, the cross symbolized truth crucified and truth victorious,[178] but in more practical terms, it also meant love, forgiveness, reconciliation, and the healing of broken community. In both cases, the cross represented truth in action.[179] This became increasingly obvious to King as he met the range of his responsibilities as a pastor, civil rights leader, and world figure. In his pastoral roles at both Dexter Avenue Baptist Church in Montgomery and Ebenezer Baptist Church in Atlanta, King became more and more mindful of the relationship between parishioners participating in the sacrament of the Lord's Supper in commemoration of Jesus's willingness to die on the cross for truth and their determination to act on truth by putting their own lives on the line for the redemption and salvation of America's heart and soul.[180] In his capacity as a civil rights leader, King came to see "the cross of truth," cross-bearing, or "the cross of protest" as essential to social, political, and economic transformation.[181] As a global figure, he came to identify Christ's triumph over the cross and the grave with the elimination of all artificial human barriers to the full realization of the beloved community or the world house or, to put it in theological terms, the kingdom of God on earth.[182] In the vast landscape of the human struggle, it is evident that, for King, the cross ceased to be a mere symbol of truth; it became an actual experience with truth in the processes of daily living.

King ultimately envisioned making truth the basis of a large-scale, creative thrust for world community and peace. He saw this as the highest human and ethical ideal and felt that this pressing need would in time require moving beyond protest to both liberation and reconciliation.[183] King sought to advance this vision not only through his writings, sermons, and speeches but also by intersecting people of various races, classes, and religions in the civil rights movement and by encouraging interreligious dialogue and cooperative, concrete action aimed at the elimination of racism, poverty, and war.[184] Undoubtedly, King's witness for truth was both inclusive and unifying, and it had practical resonance as well as universal implications. For King, the global beloved community, or "the great world house," was about living and practicing truth, and those who worked against reconciliation, community, and universal wholeness in effect undermined truth. Truth is vindicated, King thought, when moral and rational persons unite and become coworkers with God. It is in this context that truth, like love, becomes something of a "regulating ideal."[185]

King's world vision had much to do with his rousing challenge to people of faith who claimed they had discovered and were therefore custodians or stewards of finished, fixed, or final truth. He did not make this claim for himself,[186] and this most certainly explains much of the problem he had with not only Christian fundamentalists and evangelicals but also adherents of other faith traditions in his time. As far back as King's Crozer years, when he became a complete liberal,[187] he seriously questioned the idea that any single religion at all could have a monopoly on truth, and he became more secure with that position as time passed.

When King became prominent as a pastor and civil rights leader, he actually expressed dissatisfaction with "Negro organizations," including some of the churches, for "warring against each other with a claim to absolute truth."[188] King's sharpest critique targeted the Vatican and the papacy, thus recalling, at least in some ways, the indictment made by the Protestant reformer Martin Luther back in the sixteenth century:

> I am disturbed about Roman Catholicism. This church stands before the world with its pomp and power, insisting that it possesses the only truth. It incorporates an arrogance that becomes a dangerous spiritual arrogance. It stands with its noble Pope who somehow rises to the miraculous heights of infallibility when he speaks *ex cathedra*. But I am disturbed about a person or an institution that claims infallibility in this world. I am disturbed about any church that refuses to cooperate with other churches under the pretense that it is the only true church. I must emphasize the fact that God is not a Roman Catholic, and that the boundless sweep of his revelation cannot be limited to the Vatican. Roman Catholicism must do a great deal to mend its ways.[189]

It is conceivable that King, who made this statement in 1956, softened his critique a bit as he lived through the Second Vatican Council (1962–65), when Pope John XXIII and the Catholic Church became more intentional about respecting the truths of, and pursuing unity and peace between, the various faith traditions and more especially reconciling Christian to Christian. In any case, in 1958, two years after launching his stinging critique of the Vatican and the papacy, King declared, "I believe that God reveals Himself in all religions." He went on to assert that "wherever we find truth we find the revelation of God, and there is some element of truth in all religions."[190] King made essentially the same comments in a letter to a Jewish questioner in September 1961, in a letter to the editors of the *Christian Century* in June 1962, and in a series of answers to questions posed by *Redbook Magazine* in November 1964.[191] But one of King's most extensive statements on the subject came in an interview with students and faculty at the Inter-American University in San German, Puerto Rico, in February 1962:

> I'm a Christian, and as a Christian I believe in the saving power of Jesus Christ for instance, but my Christianity has not led me to the point of believing that God has limited his revelation to Christianity. I think that God has revealed himself in some way in all religions, and even though I believe that Jesus Christ represents the most unique revelation of God, I believe firmly that God has revealed himself in other religions, and he has not left himself without a witness. And there are other sheep that are not of this fold, even the Christian fold. So that I'm not so narrow as to say that only within Christianity do you have ultimate truth. I would say that there are truths revealed in the other great religions of the world. Now, I'm sure that there are some people who would disagree with me at this point. There are many people who would, but I would hold the theory and the idea that there is an aspect of God's revelation in all religions.[192]

A few months later, King further clarified his position, noting, in terms quite unusual for most Christian pastors in that time, that he believed "that in some marvelous way, God worked through Gandhi, and that the spirit of Jesus Christ saturated his life." "It is ironic, yet inescapably true," King added, "that the greatest Christian of the modern world was a man who never embraced Christianity."[193] A more stunning conclusion, offered in an era when the exclusivity of salvation based on Christianity was preached widely in Black and white churches, is unthinkable, especially since Gandhi was a Hindu.[194] But here again, King emerges as a man who very early set himself to the task of exploring and embracing truth wherever he could find it.[195] This made him not only a driving force in interreligious dialogue and cooperation but also a towering influence in the quest for a more just, inclusive, and peaceful world.

2

Symphony of Truth

Meanings and Categories

A lie doesn't become truth, wrong doesn't become right, and evil doesn't become good, just because it's accepted by a majority.

—Booker T. Washington (1914)

Very few people have the toughness of mind to judge critically, to discern the true from the false, the fact from the fiction. Our minds are constantly being invaded by legions of half-truths, prejudices, and false facts.

—Martin Luther King Jr., *Strength to Love* (1963)

Throughout much of his life, Martin Luther King Jr. struggled with age-old, complex, and perennial questions concerning the meanings and categories of truth. In this regard, he stood in the tradition of the great philosophers, theologians, and ethicists.

55

Although he shared Georg Hegel's view that "truth is the whole,"[1] King conceded that truth comes in multiple forms and is therefore never reducible to a single definition, type, or category. King's engagement with truth over time evokes images of a mellifluous symphony—a range of different instruments playing collectively to produce elaborate, harmonious, and sweetly flowing sounds.[2] King had truth in mind, among other considerations, when he framed his dream in terms of "a beautiful symphony of brotherhood" and when he spoke of that "Personal Being" or "creative force that works to bring the disconnected aspects of reality into a harmonious whole."[3] This sense of truth as akin to a powerful and mellifluous symphony grounds much of the content of this chapter.

This chapter explores the ways in which King defined and categorized truth. It begins with King's thoughts on the meaning of truth, which must be understood in both definitional and descriptive terms. Some assessment of what King had in mind when he spoke of the coherence of truth with fact and reality; of the "different though converging truths" of religion and science; of relative versus absolute truth; of dialectical truth; of certain fundamental, immutable, and objective truths in the universe; and of the challenge of the concept of "final," "ultimate," or "finished truth" to the phenomenon of "new truth" is provided, for this, too, is central to the question of definition and/or meaning. The focus then shifts to a more serious and calculated treatment of the issue of categorization, taking into account what King said about truths that draw on the lessons of experience and history, biblical truths, theological truths, anthropological truths, philosophical truths, ethical truths, "truth in the natural law," and faith and reason as the driving forces in the advancement of truth.[4] From that point, attention is devoted to the differences King drew between truth and untruth, to what he shared concerning the enduring quality of truth, and to his convictions regarding truth's ultimate triumph over untruth.[5] The content of this chapter reveals, in startling clarity, not only the spirit of a preacher, pastor, and civil and human rights leader, with a vested interest in and genuine commitment to truth, but also the open and inquiring mind of a theologian, philosopher, and ethicist, deeply intrigued by the meaning, power, and complex nature of truth.

The Meaning of Truth: The Question of Definition

What is truth? Is there such a phenomenon as verifiable or indisputable truth? How is truth related to fact or reality? Is truth relative, or should it be viewed only in absolute terms? How does science and religion figure into the debate around truth and facts? What can be said about the lasting and triumphant quality of truth as a universal value? Martin Luther King Jr. undoubtedly had these and other questions in mind whenever he referred to problems that have "plagued the mind of man since the days of ancient philosophy." He knew that ascribing meaning to truth had been the central focus of philosophy, dating back to Plato, Aristotle, the Stoics, the Epicureans, and other classical Greek thinkers. Thus, King identified truth with what philosophers "over the centuries" had called "the highest good," or "the *summum bonum* of life," and he declared that affirming and standing on truth as a foundation is not only "the greatest thing in the world" but also "the end" toward which life should be directed. Further, King related truth to the divine design for humanity and the world, insisting that "the end of life is to do the will of God, come what may."[6]

King associated the Greek word *Phi* with "that thinking which seeks to discover connected truth about all available experience" and defined philosophy as "the love of wisdom," which he equated with a fidelity to truth.[7] Also in conformity with traditions rooted in ancient Greek philosophy, King apparently subscribed to some version of the Correspondence Model or Theory of Truth, which holds that truth is that quality that squares with fact and reality as they actually are, or as they can be verified.[8] For King, truth, fact, and reality overlapped at points in terms of their meanings. Thus, it is not surprising that he routinely used these words interchangeably to define *actuality* or to assign a definition to certain ideas, concepts, beliefs, statements, propositions, or events in their actual states.[9] But King never viewed truth, fact, and reality as completely synonymous. To the contrary, he realized that each of these phenomena could be defined separately and on its own terms. For the sake of further clarification, this point requires a more extensive and targeted discussion of how King related truth to fact and truth to reality.

Paraphrasing the words of Jesus, King often said that "man cannot live by facts alone."[10] Even so, he was never unconcerned about facts or about drawing conclusions or images of the real world "on a factual basis." "The toughminded person always examines the facts before he reaches conclusions" or prejudges, King maintained, as he drew a sharp distinction between "toughmindedness" and "softmindedness."[11] Unbiased fact-gathering processes remained a vital part of his life function, from the time he majored in sociology at Morehouse College through his years as a civil and human rights leader. King spoke a lot about being "true to the facts"—about not merely "stating a fact" but "telling the truth."[12] King suggested at times that truth is essentially a legitimate extension of the facts and that both truth and facts embody the power to change people, but he was equally clear in distinguishing truth from fact. A case in point was the address he delivered to the House of Representatives in the newly formed state of Hawaii in September 1959, when he reflected on progress made in the areas of racial justice and harmony:

> You see, it would be a fact for me to say we have come a long, long way but it wouldn't be telling the truth. A fact is the absence of contradiction but truth is the presence of coherence. Truth is the relatedness of facts. Now, it is a fact that we have come a long, long way but in order to tell the truth, it is necessary to move on and say we have a long, long way to go. If we stop here, we would be the victims of a dangerous optimism. We would be the victims of an allusion wrapped in superficiality. So, in order to tell the truth, it's necessary to move on and say we have a long, long way to go.[13]

For King, questions about the relationship between truth and fact extended into the worlds of religion and science. As far back as his Morehouse years, reconciling the truths of religion with "the facts of science" had been a real intellectual concern.[14] That concern became increasingly pressing in later years as King constantly thought of the importance of both religion and science in healing and eliminating barriers between people.[15] King knew that the periods of the Renaissance and the Enlightenment had done much "to free the mind of man"—"to lift us from the stagnating valleys of superstitions and half-truths to the sun-lit mountains of creative analysis and objective appraisal"—and this, he concluded, helped make the kind of intellectual quest he had long considered, with respect to science and religion, more possible and certainly achievable.[16] Although King said and wrote a lot about religious truths, "the unscientific dogmas of religion," the "many valuable facts" of science, and the limitations of a science-based approach to life and living, he—in a statement that merits extensive quotation—denied that religious truths conflicted in any inherent or measurable way with scientific facts:

There is widespread belief in the minds of many that there is a conflict between science and religion. But there is no fundamental issue between the two. While the conflict has been waged long and furiously, it has been on issues utterly unrelated either to religion or to science. The conflict has been largely one of trespassing, and as soon as religion and science discover their legitimate spheres the conflict ceases. Religion, of course, has been very slow and loath to surrender its claim to sovereignty in all departments of human life; and science, overjoyed with recent victories, has been quick to lay claim to a similar sovereignty. Hence the conflict. But there was never a conflict between religion and science as such. There cannot be. Their respective worlds are different. Their methods are dissimilar and their immediate objectives are not the same. The method of science is observation, that of religion contemplation. Science investigates. religion interprets. One seeks causes, the other ends. Science thinks in terms of history, religion in terms of teleology. One is a survey, the other an outlook. The conflict was always between superstition disguised as religion and materialism disguised as science, between pseudo-science and pseudo-religion. Religion and science are two hemispheres of human thought. . . . Both science and religion spring from the same seeds of vital human needs. Science is the response to the human need of knowledge and power. Religion is the response to the human need for hope and certitude. One is an outreach for mastery, the other for perfection. Both are man-made, and like man himself, are hedged about with limitations. Neither science nor religion, by itself, is sufficient for man. Science is not civilization. Science is organized knowledge; but civilization, which is the art of noble and progressive communal living, requires much more than knowledge. It needs beauty which is art, and faith and moral aspiration which are religion. It needs artistic and spiritual values along with the intellectual.[17]

Noting that "there may be a conflict between softminded religionists and toughminded scientists, but not between religion and science," King went on, in another statement, to further highlight what he called the "different though converging truths" of science and religion: "Science gives man knowledge which is power; religion gives man wisdom which is control. Science deals mainly with facts; religion deals mainly with values. The two are not rivals. They are complementary. Science keeps religion from sinking into the valley of crippling irrationalism and paralyzing obscurantism. Religion prevents science from falling into the marsh of obsolete materialism and moral nihilism."[18]

Although King affirmed the tremendous value of both religious and scientific truths for humanity and the world, he nonetheless insisted that there is no infallible religion or science.[19] He also concluded that, dialectically speaking, science and religion functioned as indispensable assets as well as potential threats to human wellness, growth, and progress. In his capacities as a clergyman and theologian, King was particularly concerned about religion as an essential discipline in the continuing quest for truth. While he labeled Christianity "a value philosophy"—in the sense that it affirmed the "eternal values of intrinsic, self-evidencing validity and worth" and embraced "the true and the beautiful" as "consummated in the Good"[20]—he still wondered if Christianity would remain a credible source for answers to both the proximate concerns and ultimate questions of life. Moreover, King lamented that the Christian church was too often caught in the type of dogmatic straitjacket and spiritual impotence—and indeed a rampart "softmindedness"—that kept it from experimenting with truth from one age to another, a problem that, if not corrected, virtually insured its ineffectiveness and irrelevance for future generations: "Softmindedness often invades religion. This is why religion has sometimes rejected new truth with a dogmatic passion. Through edicts and bulls, inquisitions and excommunications, the church has attempted to prorogue truth and place an impenetrable stone wall in the path of the truth-seeker. The historical philological criticism of the Bible is considered by the softminded as blasphemous, and reason is often looked upon as the exercise of a corrupt faculty. Softminded persons have revised the Beatitudes to read, 'Blessed are the pure in ignorance; for they shall see God.'"[21]

King was no less critical in his assessment of the adverse impact of the ever-growing body of scientific facts and knowledge on the individual and collective lives of humanity. He knew that science afforded no answers to the ultimate questions of life, that it provided no absolute or sovereign truths about the supernatural realm, and that it was not the sole and final authority on matters related to humanity and the physical world. He consistently warned against relying on "the false gods of science."[22] Mindful of the role of science in the explosion of nuclear tests, in the creation of atomic and nuclear weapons, in the spread of radioactive fallout in the atmosphere, and in the destruction of the environment generally, King found it increasingly difficult and at times impossible to reconcile the facts, knowledge, and wonders of science with the urgent and mounting demands and requirements for universal human dignity, welfare, security, and survival. In his celebrated sermon "A Knock at Midnight," he sadly declared,

> In the past when we have confronted midnight in the social order we have turned to science for help. And little wonder! Science has saved us on so many occasions. When we were in the midnight of physical limitations and material inconvenience it was science that lifted us to the bright morning of physical and material comfort. When we were in the midnight of crippling ignorance and superstition, it was science that brought us to the daybreak of objective appraisal and creative analysis. When we were caught in the midnight of dread plagues and diseases, it was science, through surgery, sanitation and the wonder drugs, that lifted us to the bright day of physical health, thereby prolonging our lives and making for greater security and physical wellbeing. So it is quite easy to understand why men turn to science when the problems of the world are so ghastly in detail and ominous in extent. . . . But alas! Science cannot rescue us this time, because the scientists themselves are caught in the terrible midnight of our age. Indeed, it was science that gave us the very instruments that can lead today to universal suicide. So modern man continues to face a dreary and frightening nightmare in the social order.[23]

In King's estimation, embracing truth was about accepting, affirming, and engaging reality in the face of unreality. To illustrate his thinking in this regard, he expressed deep disappointment that when it came to the world's greatest freedom fighters, who were so often maligned in the accounts of the press, most people failed to look beyond the "subjective appraisals" of the "headlines to the actual truth of the situation." Harking back on his own personal experiences with the mass media—especially radio, television, and the newspapers—King asserted that "advertisers have long since learned that most people are softminded, so they have developed special skill to create phrases and slogans that will penetrate the thin mind of the average reader or listener." "This undue gullibility is also seen in the tendency of many to accept the printed word of the press as final truth," King added. "They fail to see that even facts can be slanted and truth can be distorted."[24] King was absolutely convinced that it was impossible for truth to stand and flourish as a supreme human value when people live, consciously or unconsciously, in a clouded and perverted reality. He was undoubtedly thinking of this and much more when he spoke not only about bringing "reality into the very center" of human "existence" but also about injecting "new meaning and delight" into "the universe."[25]

Having studied Plato's aesthetics and theory of Higher Forms at various points in his life, King tended to include Truth among the fundamental properties of reality, along with Beauty, Goodness, Love, and Justice. He accepted the widely held view that in the ideal world of reality, Truth was intimately related to these other Platonic Forms.[26] Interestingly enough, all of these Forms came together in King's Nobel Peace Prize acceptance speech in Oslo, Norway, in December 1964, in which he envisioned some future ideal world of reality. In that short but powerful speech, he set forth a vision of the Good, spoke of "unconditional love" and "the blazing light of truth," highlighted the need for "a rule of justice," and accepted the award on behalf of "all those to whom beauty is truth and truth beauty—and in whose eyes the beauty of genuine brotherhood and peace is more precious than diamonds or silver or gold."[27] King understood Truth to be a prominent and indispensable aspect of reality in its most genuine and noble expression. The common essence Truth shared with Beauty, Goodness, Love, and Justice was always uppermost in his consciousness when he spoke variously, and in idealistic terms, of "the reality of the world," "the whole of reality," "the interrelated" and "interdependent structure of reality," "the beauty of the world," and "the moral order of reality."[28] King felt that the actualization of a higher and greater reality demanded some practical application and use of the Platonic Forms in human life.

King's spiritual sensibility and values contributed decisively to these and other penetrating observations concerning reality and truth. "I believe that there is a creative personal power in this universe who is the ground and essence of all reality," he wrote, "a power that cannot be explained in materialistic terms." He went on to make the point in more specific terms: "Reality cannot be explained by matter in motion or the push and pull of economic forces. Christianity affirms that at the heart of reality is a Heart, a loving Father who works through history for the salvation of his children."[29] King spoke similarly when addressing questions regarding the ultimate source of all truth. He thanked God for the "gifts of mind" that enabled humans "to rise out of the half-realities of the sense world to a world of ideal beauty and eternal truth."[30] He delighted in the liberal thinker who "finds God," not merely in truth as it unfolds in numerous "realms of life" from "age to age," but also "in the beauty of the world, in the unpremeditated goodness of men, and in the moral order of reality."[31] As Rufus Burrow Jr. points out, "King and the personalists who influenced him most were thoroughly theistic in outlook," and they "believed God to be the source of" all knowledge, truth, and reality.[32] Without hesitation, King held that any argument for God must simultaneously be an argument for truth and reality. He referred to God as not only "uncreated reality" and "the most certain Fact in the universe" but "truth" and the foundation "of all reality," and love, justice, goodness, and wisdom became for him limitless attributes of that ultimate reality that is God. Moreover, religion, in King's estimation, essentially amounted to "a universal phenomenon involving a set of beliefs about reality" and truth as lofty ideals or sovereign values.[33] Thus, he could speak and write with conviction about "this Hindu-Moslem-Christian-Jewish-Buddhist belief about ultimate reality" or "that force" that is "the supreme unifying principle of life."[34]

King stressed the importance of awakening self to reality and truth as expressed through the disciplines of theology, philosophy, history, and sociology and through music, poetry, and the full spectrum of the arts and sciences.[35] In his very last speech in April 1968, he took a "mental flight" back to ancient Greece and imagined himself watching Plato, Socrates, Aristotle, and other great philosophers "around the Parthenon" discussing "the great and eternal issues of reality" and truth, and he felt the same way about the many notable theologians, historians, sociologists, musicians, poets, and scientists who had made their special contributions to the development of the world of ideas and to the enrichment of the life of the human mind and spirit throughout the ages.[36] King was a firm believer in what the various disciplines, arts, and sciences taught humanity about the meaning, nature, and significance of reality and truth. This was consistent with both his claims regarding "the whole of reality" and his quest for truth as "the whole."[37] He also understood that the wisdom available across disciplines enabled humans' expanded conceptions of the world around them and a healthy and more inclusive sense of the range of God's created order. Moreover, acting in conformity with the moral order demanded, in King's opinion, a consciousness thoroughly informed, shaped, and molded by the loftiest ideals of reality and truth.

Although King acknowledged that truth is a part of reality and vice versa, he never meant to suggest that truth and reality are indistinguishable. He understood truth to be absolute and objective and reality to be essentially relative and subjective. In other words, truth is established by its own unquestionable validity and objectivity, or its own self-authentication, while reality is subject to the personal opinions, perceptions, and interpretations of the individuals who define or describe it. This distinction became immensely important to King as he attacked the values of individualism and ethical relativism to which all too many subscribed when it came to truth-telling and matters of right and wrong. King illustrated the point with references to Communists, whose quest for a higher ethical, human, and global ideal has always been tragically and heavily marred by both the absence of "fixed, immutable principles" and a confusion of "means and ends":

> Communism is based on ethical relativism and accepts no
> stable moral absolutes. Right and wrong are relative to the
> most expedient methods for dealing with class war. Com-
> munism exploits the dreadful philosophy that the end
> justifies the means. It enunciates movingly the theory of

a classless society, but alas! Its methods of achieving this noble end are too often ignoble. Lying, violence, murder, and torture are considered to be justifiable means to achieve the millennial end. Is this an unfair indictment? Listen to the words of Lenin, the real tactician of Communist theory: "We must be ready to employ trickery, deceit, lawbreaking, withholding and concealing truth." Modern history has known many tortuous nights and horror-filled days because his followers have taken this statement seriously.[38]

King feared that this disturbing tendency to view truth as relative rather than absolute had become increasingly more typical of the world's majority, thus threatening the moral and spiritual fiber of what he variously called "the great world house," "the worldwide neighborhood," "the human family," and "the emerging new world order." In a sermon entitled "Going Forward by Going Backward," preached in April 1954, King framed the problem in terms of an erosion of higher human values:

Most people today have adopted a sort of relativistic ethic. By this I mean that most people feel that right and wrong are relative to their taste and their customs and their particular communities. So that there is really nothing absolutely right and absolutely wrong. It just depends on what the majority of the people are doing. This philosophy has invaded the whole of modern life. Now I admit that there are certain customs and folkways which aren't right or wrong. They are simply amoral, they have no moral value. But on the other hand, there are certain things that are absolutely right and absolutely wrong. The eternal God of the universe has ordained it to be so. It's wrong to be dishonest and unjust; it's wrong to use your brother as a means to an end; it's wrong to waste the precious life that God has given you in riotous living, it is eternally and absolutely wrong; it's wrong to hate, it always has been wrong and it always will be wrong. It was wrong in two thousand B. C. and it's wrong in 1953 A. D. It's wrong in India, it's wrong in Russia, it's wrong in China, it's wrong in America. It always has been wrong and it always will be wrong.[39]

For King, any "relative attitude" toward truth or "right and wrong" constituted a revolt "against the very laws of God himself."[40] This explains in part the caution with which he approached the concept of dialectical truth, or the process of opposing truths set forth simultaneously. King alluded to dialectical truth in written assignments during his Boston years, when he studied Plato and Aristotle more intensely, and he was always mindful of its defects.[41] Interestingly, he was never apt to use terms like "opposing truths" or "contradictory truths" but did speak frequently of "partial truths" in "two opposites" or "opposing positions" (thesis and antithesis), which could in turn be brought together in a creative, meaningful, and effective synthesis to produce truth more valid and complete than the partial truths or truth as the whole. King understood, for example, that the partial truths in acquiescence (thesis) and violence (antithesis) could be combined in a synthesis (nonviolent direct action) to win social justice, while each of the opposing positions, "if considered in isolation from the other," had to "be rejected as extreme and immoral." King employed Hegel's logic, or the Hegelian dialectical process, in not only affirming the idea that "truth is the whole" but also concluding "that growth comes through struggle."[42]

Convinced that "some things in this universe are absolute," King, unlike many liberal thinkers, never abandoned his belief in absolute truth. He defended the concept to the greatest degree, arguing that some things in the universe are factually true, and not simply so in a specific time frame, from a particular perspective, or within a certain context. In other words, absolute truth remains essentially what it is in every age and in all circumstances and contexts. King's argument for absolute truth was predicated largely on the fact that there is a reality in existence that is immutable and that cannot be doubted, questioned, or disproved.[43] Also, and perhaps more importantly, the existence of God for King affirmed the existence of absolute truth, because God is absolute truth.[44] This is what King was thinking when he used terms like "absolute truth," "eternal truth," "categorical imperatives," "pure truth," "perfect truth," and "ultimate truth" interchangeably.[45] Living in an increasingly postmodern age and culture, he expressed deep disappointment that the very idea of absolute truth had become dubious and even outdated in all too many circles, for this had become his way of explaining so much of that reality that not only surrounded his existence as a Black man in America but defined all humanity.

King fully understood and appreciated the significance of the universal quality of truth. In many of his sermons, speeches, and writings, he highlighted truth as a fundamental and universal human value. Here he turned his attention more specifically to objective truths, or truths that are accepted as such by all human beings in every part of the world. For example, he felt that people everywhere agreed that love is the key that unlocks the door to ultimate reality, that hate corrupts and corrodes human personality, that endless wars can never result in world peace, and that evil embodies "the seeds of its own destruction," even if their actions suggest otherwise.[46] These are what King called "objective and unbiased truths"— truths that are also absolute and timeless or unchanging. At times, he variously referred to such truths as "basic," "fundamental," and "essential truths." He held that "the goal of true" and "complete education" should always involve a serious intellectual struggle with objective truth.[47] While studying at Morehouse College, and later in his role as a church pastor, he complained that "even the press, the classroom, the platform, and the pulpit in many instances do not give us objective and unbiased truths." For King, the great challenge in life is to always live in accordance with such truths, which are essential to any conception of "an honest universe."[48] When it came to the sheer power of objective and unbiased truth, he found a model in Mohandas K. Gandhi, whom many considered the quintessential truth-seeker, and who, as King put it, "embodied in his life certain universal principles that are inherent in the moral structure of the universe"—"principles" that "are as inescapable as the law of gravitation."[49] Although King was deeply interested in objective truth, or that which is universally held, he always had the sense that on a deeper level, what constituted truth for one individual or group is not necessarily truth for others. This kind of realism informed his conviction that "truth is the whole."[50]

King's disposition toward liberalism and realism was such that he viewed truth not as a static phenomenon but as a progressive and unfolding process. In other words, truth for him was determined by its tendency to grow and evolve in response to changing realities over time, or out of an interaction between the past, present, and future. This explains King's openness to what he called "new truth."[51] He was about enlarging both the definition and the reach of truth and was thoroughly disappointed with the failure of the Christian church, which he viewed as "the conscience" and "the moral guardian" of society,[52] to assume a leadership role in this regard. "At times it has talked as though ignorance were a virtue and intelligence a crime," King declared. "Through its obscurantism, closemindedness, and obstinacy to new truth, the church has often unconsciously encouraged its worshippers to look askance upon intelligence."[53] King turned his frustration directly toward fundamentalist and sectarian forms of Christianity, which arrogantly claimed to have "final," "ultimate," or "finished" truth; which absolutely refused to accept "new truth;" and which circumscribed truth while "placing obstacles in the path of the truth-seeker."[54] King urged ecclesiastical bodies to cease competing with one another over "the number of their adherents, the size of" their sanctuaries, and their "abundance of wealth" and to take more seriously the "moral demand for enlightenment." "If we must compete," he asserted, "let us compete to see which can move toward the greatest attainment of truth."[55] This was King's oft-repeated challenge not only to the Christian churches but to religious institutions generally.

Truth Deconstructed: Problems of Categorization

"Questions about truth are rarely as clear-cut as one might wish," writes Sophia Rosenfeld, "given that we are confronted immediately with problems of categorization," or exactly "what *kinds* of truth we are talking about."[56] This most certainly applies to Martin Luther King Jr., who stressed different categories or dimensions of truth. When discussing King along these lines, it is necessary to think in terms of the Pragmatic Theory of Truth, which shifts the focus away from simply how truth is defined toward its "broader practical and performative dimensions," thus highlighting the role truth serves in the shaping of certain disciplines and types of discourse.[57] Although King never spoke at length about this theory of truth, it corresponds to some degree with "the realistic position" he took when reflecting on the complex issues regarding human life and values,[58] including the phenomenon of truth itself.

King's earliest sense of truth was filtered through the lens of experience and history. This is not difficult to understand, since he was born Black in the American South, grew up under the scourge of white supremacy, and descended from generations of ancestors who suffered under the heavy yoke of slavery. Small wonder that truth for King was in some measure about lived experience, or that which people embody functionally each day of their lives. Truth entailed an accurate grasp of the human plight based not only on what is observed but also on what is experienced in the personal and collective lives of flesh and blood human beings.[59] In King's mind, this is what constituted experiential truth.[60] He was always quite clear about what was true in his own daily life and existence, about the experiential truths he came to know and accept, beginning with his earliest childhood. Even before he enrolled at Atlanta's Yonge Street Elementary School, he suffered some of the effects of white supremacy.[61] At age six, he witnessed his father, Martin Luther King Sr., being subjected to the verbal insults of a white policeman and store clerk. When he was "about eight years old," he was slapped "in one of the downtown stores of Atlanta" by a white woman, who accused the boy of being "the little nigger that stepped on my foot."[62] Before reaching adulthood, King was forced to accept certain painful, "unhappy," or "tragic" truths about the Black experience in a white world—truths that became unforgettable life lessons: "I had grown up abhorring not only segregation but also the oppressive and barbarous acts that grew out of it. I had passed spots where Negroes had been savagely lynched, and had watched the Ku Klux Klan on its rides at night. I had seen police brutality with my own eyes, and watched Negroes receive the most tragic injustice in the courts. All of these things had done something to my growing personality. I had come perilously close to resenting all white people."[63]

While in his teens, King worked two summers in a plant that hired both Blacks and whites in Atlanta. His experiences there, coupled with what he saw all around him in the South, convinced him that "the inseparable twin of racial injustice was economic injustice."[64] Consequently, he came to a greater sense of the shared experiences of people beyond the artificial barriers of skin color and was conceivably reassured in his view that humans should see their own "particular experiences in light of the totality of all experiences."[65] During his years at Morehouse College, Crozer Theological Seminary, and Boston University and throughout his adult life, King thought and wrote a lot about racial and economic injustice and how this, along with violence, impacted the lives of Blacks and whites in America—socially, economically, politically, culturally, religiously, and otherwise. Being "honest and realistic" about and having true knowledge of this broader context of core human experiences must have weighed heavily on his thinking whenever he referred to both education and social justice activism as critical aspects of any bold and persistent experimentation with truth. While recognizing that white supremacy kept both races from reaching their fullest stature and greatest potential as human beings, King held that, experientially, it was also true to say that "nobody in the history of the world has suffered like" Black people: "The central quality in the Negro's life is pain—pain so old and so deep that it shows in almost every moment of his existence. It emerges in the cheerlessness of his sorrow songs, in the melancholy of his blues and in the pathos of his sermons. The Negro while laughing sheds invisible tears that no hand can wipe away. In a highly competitive world, the Negro knows that a cloud of per-sistent denial stands between him and the sun, between him and life and power, between him and whatever he needs."[66]

Experiential truths of this nature were consequential not only in terms of King's own emerging self-concept, sense of existential reality, and thought processes but also for the social justice crusade he led, the ideal society he envisioned, and the methods he employed to translate his vision of the beloved community into practical reality. This point has been consistently made by King's associate Andrew Young, who acknowledges that King "saw leadership as a process of relating the daily plight of humankind to the eternal truths of creation."[67]

Any careful study of King's thought and approach to values suggests that experiential truths and historical truths cross-pollinate in terms of their meanings. Both have to do with existential reality and lived experience, but King viewed historical truths as more of a written record or a project of construction that tells exactly *what* happened and *how* and *why* it happened.[68] He felt that the proponent of historical truths had to be more intentional about honoring facts and events as they occur over specific time periods, or as they relate to the past and present. As a student of history, King also believed that such a proponent had to take seriously those truths that squared with the most reliable sources accessible to historians.[69] He exalted "historical truths," "the facts of history," "the lessons of history," or truths "vindicated by history"[70] because he knew that so much of what had been written, even by the most reputable scholars, celebrated the achievements of whites while denying the humanity and contributions of Blacks, thus giving credence to a blatantly false and deeply racist version of reality.

Undoubtedly, King received many lessons in historical truth during his childhood. His maternal grandmother, Jennie C. Parks Williams; his "Aunt Ida" Worthem; and his parents, King Sr. and Alberta Williams King, were the first truth-tellers he heard when it came to these and countless other matters. His vivid memories of the "many evenings" he heard "interesting stories" from "Mama Jennie" were telling enough, and so were the "stories of the 'old times'" shared by Aunt Ida, for storytelling in the Black South in the 1930s and '40s was never divorced from the facts of history.[71] The same might be said of young King's exposure to "the facts of life" as told by his parents, or his "Daddy King" and "Mother Dear," who gave him his first sense of the history of slavery and segregation as he sat quietly before them.[72] As pillars of influence in the King extended family, these elders were sources of both experiential and historical truth for King, and what they shared made sense in the sociocultural context in which he found himself. Sharing the historical reality of the Black experience was part of Mama Jennie's, Aunt Ida's, Daddy King's, and Mother Dear's own devotion to truth. Their efforts in this regard also advanced necessary and legitimate knowledge, for truth in this case became vital, fact-based knowledge. Moreover, the acts of truth-telling by these family-oriented and God-fearing elders contributed to that process of interpersonal bonding that had long grounded the Black struggle to survive. To be sure, they became part of that network of influences that set King on a lifelong search for and commitment to truth. Mama Jennie, Aunt Ida, Daddy King, and Mother Dear modeled for King the stewardship that all Black men and women, and especially mothers, had to assume as truth-tellers and communicators.[73]

Truth-telling for King had to do, first and foremost, with setting the record straight about the Black experience, because so much of what had been written and taught for generations did not meet the definition of truth. In his estimation, historically substantiated and accepted facts about people of African descent had to become the new and basic paradigm for a more legitimate and reliable reporting of both American and world history, especially since there was so much about the Black experience that distinguished it from the experiences of other human beings:[74]

Being a Negro in America means being scarred by a history of slavery and family disorganization. Negroes have grown accustomed now to hearing unfeeling and insensitive whites say: "Other immigrant groups such as the Irish, the Jews and the Italians started out with similar handicaps, and yet they made it. Why haven't the Negro done the same?" These questioners refuse to see that the situation of other immigrant groups a hundred years ago and the situation of the Negro today cannot be usefully compared. Negroes were brought here in chains long before the Irish decided *voluntarily* to leave Ireland or the Italians thought of leaving Italy. Some Jews may have left their homes in Europe involuntarily, but they were not in chains when they arrived on these shores. Other immigrant groups came to America with language and economic handicaps, but not with the stigma of color. Above all, no other ethnic group has been a slave on American soil, and no other group has had its family structure deliberately torn apart. This is the rub.[75]

King's essential message never changed: lessons from the past had to be framed in facts and truth if they were to be liberating and empowering for all people. In more specific terms, truth-seeking and truth-telling about the Black experience were indispensable in the struggle to achieve the fullness of freedom, human dignity, justice, equal opportunity, peace, and community. King's thinking on this issue owed much to the fact that his own personal experiences with discrimination and segregation connected him in mind and spirit with generations of his forebears. Richard W. Wills has this and more in mind when he says that King's mother, Alberta, interpreted his "earliest childhood encounter with race matters," and especially his rejection "at age six by a white playmate at the behest of his former friend's father," by "rehearsing the historical reality of slavery, its conclusion with the Civil War, and the subsequent forms of discrimination that Jim Crow assumed in an attempt to create and sustain a legalized system of racial segregation."[76] King was able to identify to some extent with the larger and more extensive history of Black oppression because the historical truths that confronted his slave ancestors were replicated on some levels in his own experiences. Put another way, what he read in the history books and what he heard from his parents, aunt, and maternal grandmother about slavery and segregation became real to him in the daily processes and routines of living. Thus, the reality of King's forebears became in some measure his own, making it possible for him to participate vicariously in the whole history of his people. King became more and more mindful of this in his specific jurisdiction of serving humanity, especially oppressed people. In those history-making moments that marked the freedom crusade he and others led, he always insisted that the story be told in ways that highlight and elevate truth. This was King's challenge to future historians as well. He declared that history should never be merely about great men or legendary figures and their achievements—that it should, perhaps more importantly, be about the struggles and contributions of "the least of these," or those who stand on a more solid foundation of truth.[77]

If there was a single source, aside from the Black experience, that figured most prominently in the genesis of King's interest in and quest for truth, it was by all accounts the biblical fundamentalism to which he was introduced as a child. Raised in an extended family and church culture in which Bible readings, along with music and instructions in right and wrong, were strongly and consistently encouraged, King was taught very early that the Old and New Testaments contained the inspired, authoritative, and inerrant word of God.[78] He sat at the feet of untrained Sunday school teachers who never doubted the veracity of the Scriptures, who were totally unfamiliar with biblical criticism, and who subscribed wholeheartedly and unambiguously to what was considered the five essential truths of the old-line biblical fundamentalism—namely, the virgin birth, the resurrection and deity of Christ, his substitutionary atonement, the second coming, and the authority and inerrancy of the Bible.[79] The rigidity and dogmatic character of this kind of scriptural literalism was evident to King at a very early age. By the time he reached his teens, King had already developed a critical and questioning attitude toward life and the established order of things. Before entering college, he had begun to approach certain biblical teachings with skepticism, and most certainly with a free and independent mind. King's questions regarding claims of scriptural authority and inerrancy grew substantially during his college, seminary, and graduate school years, as he was exposed more and more to biblical criticism, or historical-critical methods of studying and analyzing the Bible.[80] The impact of his studies was such that when he wrote his qualifying examinations for his PhD in systematic and philosophical theology at Boston University in 1953, he seriously challenged even those highly reputable "continental theologians" who affirmed that the Bible "is the norm and standard of truth."[81]

In contrast to old-line fundamentalists like his father, King Sr., King concluded that biblical criticism was a useful, necessary, and appropriate tool for studying and interpreting biblical revelation. While a student at Crozer Theological Seminary and Boston University, he wrote papers in which he applied historical-critical methods in evaluating the five essential truths of the Christian faith as understood and defined by biblical fundamentalists, suggesting that such truths could not be upheld logically and on historical and scientific grounds.[82] King categorically denied "the Virgin Birth of Christ as a literal fact," arguing that "the early Christians had noticed the moral uniqueness of Jesus," and "to make this uniqueness appear plausible," they "devised a mythological story of Jesus' biological uniqueness."[83] He went on to assert that the "Virgin Birth"—like "sin and salvation," "the divinity of Christ," his "bodily resurrection," and other points of traditional theology—is "peripheral" and that only "love is central"; it's "the essence of the Christian gospel."[84] Also in opposition to fundamentalist belief, King strongly rejected the concept of "hell as a place of a literal burning fire," insisting instead that "hell, to me, is a condition of being out of fellowship with God."[85] While conceding that there are "eternal" and "profound truths" behind "the legends and myths of the Book," he declared that "the modern critical method" makes it "plain to us" that "the Bible was not always historically accurate," that "every book in the Bible is not equally valuable," and that biblical revelation had to be interpreted and viewed in light of "reason," "the facts of experience," and "scientific knowledge."[86]

King described the Bible as "a spiritual guide," as "a sacred book of the Christian church," and as "the record of God's self-revelation, first to the people of Israel" and "afterward to the world in Jesus Christ." He went on to explain, "It tells us not only what men have thought of God and what they have done for God but what they have experienced of God. Thus, by bringing us in touch with the men and women who have found God before us, it encourages us to believe that we can find God for ourselves and it shows us how to do so." "The Bible helps us to realize afresh the perennial vitality of the central convictions of the Christian life," King added, "such truths as the love of God, the Lordship of Christ, the fact of sin, the need of redemption, the vitalizing influence of the Spirit of God, and the hope of immortality."[87] He concluded that the Bible must ultimately be seen as "a book of progressive revelation." "Notice the development of the great ideas in the Bible such as God, man, sin, and immortality," he wrote. "To understand how these great ideas progressed to their final culmination is to know the meaning of the Bible." Clearly, King was more apt to view the Bible as "progressive revelation" than as the "final revelation," which also set him apart from many Christian fundamentalists.[88] However, he did share with fundamentalists the belief that faith is the key ingredient in the proclamation and advancement of God's revealed truths in Scripture. But this sacred obligation, he felt, ultimately fell to the lot of the church universal, or the whole people of God (*laos*), and not to a chosen or righteous remnant or to some hierarchical structure centered exclusively in the clergy.[89]

Although King drew important distinctions between the Old and New Testaments,[90] he believed that both affirmed the relationship between truth and justice. In response to the many white southern fundamentalists who equated him and the struggle for equal rights and social justice with an out-of-control and dangerous extremism, King offered a direct rejoinder: "If employment, the franchise, education and brotherhood are extremists' demands, then the Old and New Testaments are wildly extremist documents."[91] Some discussion of how the wedding of truth and justice unfolds in each of these two parts of the Bible, beginning with the Old Testament, is needed here to further clarify King's thinking on the subject. The creation narratives, the exodus story, and the ancient Hebrew prophets are relevant to any thoughtful consideration of King's understanding of the truth-justice nexus in the Old Testament.[92] King found it impossible to reconcile the first two chapters of Genesis with historical and scientific facts, but he found there an affirmation of God's self-disclosure in creation and the image of God in persons (*imago Dei*)—concepts that, in his own mind, meant that all humans must be viewed as sacred and treated justly and respectfully.[93] Significantly, King accepted the factual basis for a belief in the exodus, or the Old Testament story of Moses and the Israelites being delivered from Egyptian bondage, and he maintained that "this is something of the story of every people struggling for freedom."[94] The exodus story as biblical, experiential, and historical truth found clarity in King's consciousness as he spoke in terms of his people moving "to the threshold of the Promised Land" of "racial justice" in his own time.[95] King declared that the Hebrew prophets, who routinely recalled the divine redemption of the exodus when rebuking Israel for her faithlessness and ingratitude, were imbued with the power and spirit of truth—that they rose up "amid religious idolatry and unjust power structures to declare the eternal word of God and the never-ceasing necessity of being obedient to His will."[96] The words of the prophet Amos, "Let justice roll down like waters, and righteousness like an ever-flowing stream" (Amos 5:24 NRSV), and of the prophet Micah, who declared that God requires "thee" to "do justly, and to love mercy, and to walk humbly with thy God" (Mic 6:8), were frequently quoted by King in the context of the freedom struggle.[97] "They were articulate, passionate and fearless, attacking injustice and corruption whether the guilty be kings or their own unrepentant people," said King of the prophets. "Without physical protection, scornful of risks evoked by their unpopular messages, they went among the people with no shield other than truth."[98]

King concluded that the teachings of Jesus, who stood squarely in the tradition of the Hebrew prophets, were the key to understanding how the themes of truth and justice flow throughout the New Testament.[99] By submitting "his will to God's will," Jesus, according to King, "had given himself to certain 'eternal truths'"—to "certain eternal" and "universal principles"—"that nobody could crucify and escape."[100] King found enduring inspiration in the fact that Jesus firmly established the inseparable link between truth and freedom and that he came "to preach the gospel to the poor," "to heal the brokenhearted," "to preach deliverance to the captives," "to set at liberty them that are bruised," and "to preach the acceptable year of the Lord" (Luke 4:18–19).[101] Jesus's Sermon on the Mount in the fifth chapter of Matthew, in King's view, communicated profound, timeless, and immutable truths about the power of love to achieve justice—truths that found practical expression in the Montgomery bus boycott and in the subsequent civil rights campaigns.[102] King was equally intentional about relating the idea of civil rights to the parables of Jesus, which he considered a vital part of God's revealed truth. He held that the parables, which constitute roughly a third of Jesus's recorded messaging, conveyed essential truths about "the divine reality," humanity, the problems of sin and evil, the meaning of love, altruism as "the first law of life," "the saving power of the Gospel," and the coming of the kingdom of God.[103] The kingdom of God ideal "was obviously implicit in everything" King "said and did" with regard to his vision of the beloved community, a fully integrated society based on truth, love, and justice. "Whenever you love truth, whenever you love justice, whenever you do right, the Kingdom is present," King declared.[104] The spiritual and eternal truths that fell from the lips of Jesus, and Jesus's willingness to suffer and die on the cross for the redemption and transformation of humanity, were such that King called this man from Nazareth "a Galilean saint" and "an extremist for love, truth, and goodness."[105]

Not surprisingly, King felt that genuine reverence for biblical truths is never based on blind faith and distorted reasoning. This explains much of his problem with Christian fundamentalism, especially in the white South. He had real problems with those who, driven by spiritual blindness, constantly misinterpreted and propagandized the Scriptures in defense of white supremacy, Jim Crow, and the oppression of people of color. King equated this proclivity with what he termed "softmindedness." He lamented the fact that all too many white preachers in various southern denominations were not free to speak the truth about truth in the Scriptures.[106] He was equally disturbed by Christian fundamentalists, white and Black, who taught that "ultimate" or "eternal truths" could be found only in the Bible. King argued that truth is not limited to any one period, to any single sacred book, to a specific set of human beings, or to a particular religion.[107] Because "God is continually working through history," truth can never be confined to the Scriptures and the times during which they were written. God's revelation is ongoing, and this means that "God is revealing Himself now."[108] The narrow-minded approach that many around King brought to the Scriptures possibly explains why he never accepted the image of the South as "the Bible Belt," especially since all too many of its residents merely had an enthusiasm for but no real devotion to living in accordance with biblical truths.[109]

Biblical truths and theological truths, to an extent, overlap in King's thought and language. He believed that theological truths should be consistent with, but certainly not limited to, the truths of the Scriptures. His definition of theological truth was premised on the convictions that God exists and that "God is truth" as well as the source of all truth.[110] When referring to essential theological truths, King emphasized God as being the Supreme Personality; by nature rational, loving, and sentient; omnipotent, omnipresent, omniscient, and omnibenevolent in character; the creator and sustainer of the universe and all life; the source of the moral order; both immanent and transcendent in humanity and the world; active in history; and a coworker with committed human beings in the ultimate triumph of good over evil and sin.[111] Here King conformed to much of what was standard Christian theological thought, despite his long-standing tendencies toward liberalism. All of these theological truths are covered to varying degrees in King's sermons, mass meeting speeches, and writings, but some seem to have figured a bit more prominently in his mind than others when he thought in terms of the day-to-day challenges of the movement. His beliefs that "God still reigns in history," that God is a "deity immanent in" and "working through" the "process of history," and that God "is able to subdue all the powers of evil" and sin constituted the basis for his hope and confidence that the struggle against social injustice would ultimately be won.[112] For King, the trajectory of the exodus story and Jesus's triumph over the cross virtually established that evil and sin cannot prevail indefinitely over the will, purpose, and plan of God.[113]

The person of Jesus Christ and his relationship to God was central to King's understanding of theological truth. While he took seriously Jesus's humanity—or the "historical Jesus" who experienced "growth, learning, prayer, and defeat"—and stopped short of referring to him as God in an absolute sense, King believed nonetheless in God's self-disclosure in Jesus Christ. Convinced that Jesus was in a sense both human and divine, King explained it in this manner: "I don't think anyone can be Jesus. He was one with God in purpose. He so submitted his will to God's will that God revealed His divine plan to man through Jesus. In this sense, Jesus was divine."[114] Referring variously to Jesus in terms of his "Lordship" and as "a new personality," "the spiritual genius," "divine Reality," and "the highest revelation of God," King concluded that there was "some uniqueness in the personality of the historical Jesus" that made him "divine." Jesus's "true significance," he further stated, lies not in "an inherent divinity" but "in the fact that his achievement is prophetic and promissory for every other true son of man who is willing to submit his will to the will and spirit of God."[115] This is all the more encouraging and inspiring since Jesus, King maintained, lived "in the closest detail the sublime philosophy which his lips had proclaimed," as evidenced by his willingness "to act on truth."[116] "Man's truth is always limited by the *Zeitgeist*," said King, "but the truth which Christ revealed is eternal," and Jesus wants us to be "his witnesses"—to give "verbal affirmation" to the cross, "the resurrection," and the fact that "the way of Christ is the only ultimate way to man's salvation," to "justice, goodwill," and "the power of the Kingdom of God."[117] Such an effort could not have been more sacred, meaningful, and demanding, especially since all too many in the churches were, in King's thinking, more committed to propagandizing Western Christianity than advancing "the way of Christ."[118] Only weeks before King was assassinated, as the threats against his person and safety escalated sharply, this call to witness to "the way of Christ" weighed heavier than ever before on his consciousness, prompting him to declare, "Yes, Jesus,

I want to be on your right side or your left side, not for any selfish reason. I want to be on your right side or your left side, not in terms of some political kingdom or ambition. But I just want to be there in love and in justice and in truth and in commitment to others, so that we can make this old world a new world."[119]

Uncomfortable with the very idea of what he termed a "set theology," King insisted that theological truth must grow with the progression of time and human experiences, with the best and most recent trends in rationality and scientific facts, and that it should "never be static." This was his special challenge to liberal theology, which he felt could, if left unchecked, possibly retreat into the kind of dogmatic rigidity so typical of much of fundamentalism. Also, this helps explain King's problem with the Apostles' Creed, the Athanasian Creed, and other great creeds or affirmations of faith, which too often made theological truths synonymous with immutable doctrinal truths.[120] King never considered theological truths to be perfect and timeless truths. As far as he was concerned, theological truth had to make sense in the world as it is, which means that it, too, is to some degree a continuously growing, evolving, or developmental process.[121]

The Bible and theology provided much of the basis for King's engagement with anthropological truths,[122] which he felt should also be subject to some degree to rational and scientific confirmation. For King, anthropological truths were about humanity as it is in terms of both individual and social life. Constantly faced with what he termed "man's inhumanity to man,"[123] he never hesitated to articulate his views on the subject. The key anthropological truths he affirmed are that humans are made in the image of God, or *imago Dei*; humans are biological beings with "a kinship to animate nature"; humans have a dialectical or paradoxical nature, as evidenced by their capacity for both good and evil; humans are creatures who possess "noble, spiritual powers, especially the power of reason"; humans have finite freedom; humans are subjects of self-estrangement, or their existential situation is estranged from their essential nature; human existence is by nature social; humans are interrelated and interdependent; and humans are prone to anxiety

and conflict in their "personal and social life" due to "the perilous and ambiguous structure of existence."[124] King's published and
unpublished sermons remain the best and most reliable sources
for tracing his views on these and other essential truths regarding
humanity, human relations, and the human relationship to the
supernatural realm.[125]

King believed that the point of departure for any penetrating study of humanity is the *imago Dei*, which he, according to
Richard W. Wills, considered "an immutable anthropological
and theological truth."[126] King urged Christians to embrace "a
realistic" conception of humanity by acknowledging that man
is "a biological being, injected with spirit, made in the image of
God"—that he is a unique embodiment of body, mind, soul, and
spirit. While emphasizing that "man is a being of spirit," King
insisted that he is also "less than divine," or "less than God," who
is "pure spirit."[127] This is what King conveyed when he, quoting the
psalmist, posed the question, "What is man?" noting that "thou
hast made him a little lower than the angels, and hast crowned
him with glory and honour" (Ps 8:4–5). To further clarify his
theological anthropology, King discounted the notion, advanced
by naturalists, that "man is a cosmic accident" whose "whole life
can be explained by merely matter in motion," or that man is
simply "an animal" with "a material" or "physical body" and "a
kinship with animate nature." He also disagreed with humanists,
who—impressed with humanity's "noble, spiritual powers," and
especially its "power of reason"—tended to "lift man almost to
the position of a god." Avoiding the extremes of what he termed
"a pessimistic naturalism" and "an optimistic humanism," King
approached the issue in true Hegelian fashion, or through the
process of dialectical thinking, asserting that humans are both
biological beings and spiritual beings.[128] Although "there is something within man that is god-like," which explains his "amazing
capacity for good," King reasoned, he can never be "pure spirit"
because "some of the image of God" in him was "scarred" due
to his "sinfulness." Thus, humans "are sinners in need of God's
grace—in need of repentance."[129]

But what did this image of humans as "beings of spirit" or "spiritual beings" mean in more specific terms for King, aside from the fact that they are "more than flesh and blood" and "crowned with glory and honor?" King answered this question on three levels. In the first place, "the spiritual element in man" firmly establishes "the dignity and worth," and indeed the sacredness, "of all human personality."[130] For King, this alone meant that there are no superior and inferior races, a myth thoroughly "refuted by the best evidence of the anthropological sciences." King lamented that this myth "lags around" in spite of the findings of "great anthropologists" such as Ruth Benedict, Melville J. Herskovits, and Margaret Mead. He found it even more disturbing that the Bible, religion, and philosophy had been put to the service of sanctioning and advancing such a myth:

> You know, there was a time when some people used to argue the inferiority of the Negro and the colored races generally on the basis of the Bible and religion. They would say the Negro was inferior by nature because of Noah's curse upon the children of Ham. And then another brother had probably read the logic of Aristotle. You know Aristotle brought into being the syllogism which had a major premise and a minor premise and a conclusion, and one brother had probably read Aristotle and he put his argument in the framework of an Aristotelian syllogism. He could say that all men are made in the image of God. This was a major premise. God, as everybody knows, is not a Negro; therefore, the Negro is not a man. And that was called logic.[131]

In his capacity as a theologian, King wrote and said a lot about the superior-inferior race argument, for he knew that "a false conception of man" invariably amounted to "a false conception of God." While conceding that "there may be intellectually superior individuals within all races," he vehemently denied that any one race is by nature or inherently superior to another, insisting that such an idea was both erroneous and detrimental to the human

84

struggle for freedom and empowerment. King bitterly complained that, in spite of evidence to the contrary, "the view still gets around somehow that there are superior and inferior races. The whole concept of white supremacy rests on this fallacy."[132] He strongly and consistently defended a biblically rooted kinship model of *imago Dei* that transcended the artificial barriers of race—that was anti-tribalistic in any fashion whatsoever.

King maintained that "the spiritual element in man" also recognizes "the solidarity of the human family," which suggested to him the need for "healthier ways of people being globally connected and integrated": "Integration seems almost inevitably desirable and practical because basically we are all one. Paul's declaration that God 'hath made of one blood' all nations of the world is more anthropological fact than religious poetry. The physical differences between the races are insignificant when compared to the physical identities. The world's foremost anthropologists all agree that there is no basic difference in the racial groups of our world. Most deny the actual existence of what we have known as 'race.'"[133]

The concept of an integrated human family in a global context squared perfectly with King's view of "the social nature of human existence," which means that humans are made to live together—that "the self cannot be the self without other selves." King further elaborated the point, explaining, "I can never be what I ought to be until you are what you ought to be, and you can never be what you ought to be until I am what I ought to be." He went on to point out that "self-concern without other-concern is like a tributary that has no outward flow to the ocean."[134] Because human beings are "caught in an inescapable network of mutuality, tied in a single garment of destiny," said King, "whatever affects one directly, affects all indirectly."[135] Thus, humans should treat one another "as persons" and not as "things," as "*ends*" in themselves and never as "mere *means*" to an end.[136] All of these ideas congealed and made even more sense when expressed within the framework of King's concept of "the interrelatedness of human life," or "the interrelated structure of all reality":

All men are interdependent. Every nation is an heir of a vast treasury of ideas and labor to which both the living and the dead of all nations have contributed. Whether we realize it or not, each of us lives eternally "in the red." We are ever-lasting debtors to known and unknown men and women. When we arise in the morning, we go into the bathroom where we reach for a sponge which is provided for us by a Pacific Inlander. We reach for soap that is created for us by a European. Then at the table we drink coffee which is provided for us by a South American, or tea by a Chinese, or cocoa by a West African. Before we leave for our jobs we are already beholden to more than half of the world.[137]

King further concluded that "the spiritual element in man" is "ultimately that which distinguishes man from his animal ancestry. He is in time, yet above time. He is in nature, yet above nature."[138] King went on to explain that unlike humans, other animals cannot write "a Shakesperian play," discuss "intricate problems concerning the political and economic structures of a society," speculate "on the nature and destiny of the universe," "think a poem" and commit it to paper, "think a symphony and compose it," or "imagine a great civilization and create it." In King's mind, "the spiritual element," "the human spirit," or the creative inner powers humans possess largely accounted for "man's amazing capacity for memory and thought and imagination" and his impressive ability to "leap oceans" and "break through walls," to "have communion with the past," to "rise above the limita-tions of time and space," to "entertain ideals" that "become his inspiration," to choose "his supreme end," to "embrace the uncer-tainties of the future," to "be a hero or a fool," and to "be true or false in his nature."[139] "The highest expression of man's spiritual quality," King concluded, "is freedom." Despite oppression—and though humans are limited by their finiteness, their past, the nat-ural world, and their powers of knowledge and imagination—King declared that "we are all free in the sense that freedom is the inner power that drives us to achieve freedom." He also framed this concept in terms of "a certain kind of inner hope," "an inner faith," or "an 'inspite-of' quality."[140]

King felt that humanity's spiritual element, or its essential inner nature, is reflected perhaps most importantly in its unique power and capacity to communicate and experience fellowship with God through prayer, fasting, meditation, and other means. He wrote, "Man is a spiritual being born to have communion with the eternal God of the universe"—"with that which is eternal and everlasting." "God creates every individual for a purpose—to fellowship with Him," King added. He elaborated on the point in more detail: "This is the ultimate meaning of the image of God. It is not that man as he is in himself bears God's likeness, but rather that man is designated for and called to a particular relation with God. The concept of the image of God assures us that we, unlike our animal ancestry and the many inanimate objects of the universe, are privileged to have fellowship with the divine."[141]

In King's opinion, fellowship with God affirmed in the loftiest terms the ultimate meaning of human life and existence. But the chief spiritual crisis of the modern scientific and technological world consisted, in his estimation, of humanity's common and seemingly inescapable tendency to turn against God and pursue the path of sin and evil. As far as King could determine, this increasingly led to man's self-estrangement, his estrangement from other selves, and most importantly, his estrangement from God. "Whenever a man looks deep into the depths of his nature," King exclaimed, "he becomes painfully aware of the fact that the history of life is the history of a constant revolt against God."[142] King believed that this revolt was the chief source of the nagging, ongoing spiritual hunger that had long haunted humankind. He felt that the great African church father, Saint Augustine, experienced this kind of hunger centuries earlier and that, "in his search for truth," he captured the deepest yearnings of the human heart when he declared that "we were made for God" and that "we will be restless until we find rest in Him," and also when he said, "Lord, make me pure but not yet." These words resonated with King because they spoke to his own lingering spiritual quest as a flawed and finite human being.[143] The sense of an intangible, divine, undying, "loving presence that binds all life" was both the basis of King's own spiritual security and the driving force behind his efforts to awaken in humans "a new spirit" and an unwavering desire to participate in "new levels of creative living."[144]

King knew that so much of what he said and wrote about human nature, life, and destiny fell into the category of not only anthropological truths but also philosophical truths. The lines of separation were not always so clear. King was drawn to the study of philosophy through deep, abiding questions he had about the universe, human existence, and the human condition. The answers he received came out of his encounter with philosophy and a range of other disciplines—including sociology, history, theology, anthropology, and ethics. But when it came to probing certain truths about the state of the known world and the meaning, purpose, and goal of human life, King's approach was largely that of a philosopher. He never abandoned the view, extending from many of the earliest Christian thinkers up to Thomas Aquinas, that philosophy, like theology, affords a necessary path to truth. Robert E. Birt is right in concluding that "King was not a systematic philosopher," but King was "a moral and social philosopher" whose ideas and activities were shaped by his academic training, his personal experiences and sense of the world around him, his view of the human condition, and the movement he led for freedom, social justice, human dignity, and peace.[145] He was always interested in truth as a philosophical principle and in philosophically based conceptions of truth.

In his approach to philosophy, King typically began with the philosophical idealism of Plato, Socrates, Heraclitus, Aristotle, and the other ancient Greek philosophers. Through this approach, he came to some understanding of truth as a classical philosophical concept before turning to the philosophical idealism of Kant, Hegel, and the personalists.[146] King believed that through their efforts "to discover the highest good," or "the *summum bonum* of life," the ancient Greeks, who were "very philosophical minded," emerged as the quintessential truth-seekers, thus setting the highest standard for the generations of philosophers who followed them. He noted that those who came later—such as Thomas Aquinas, one of the greatest philosophers and theologians of the medieval period—had cherished "the strength of mind" that conquers fear, anxiety, or "whatever threatens the attainment of the highest good."[147] The suggestion here is that "life is more than a physiological process with a physiological meaning"—that it is about advancing the powers of the mind "to achieve with increasing facility" life's "legitimate goals."[148] King spoke out of this tradition when he asserted that only by combining "intelligence and goodness" can man "rise to a fulfillment of his true nature" and "achieve the good life," when he described God as "perfectly good," and when he insisted that "noncooperation with evil is as much a moral obligation as is cooperation with good."[149]

"I think I have discovered the highest good," King repeatedly stated. "It is love." He added, "This principle stands at the center of the cosmos. As John says, 'God is love.'" Love in this case is not separate from a philosophical understanding of truth, as evidenced by King's interpretation of the Gandhian *satyagraha* principle, for the true *satyagrahi* cannot dedicate his life to truth without also committing life to love as expressed in nonviolent activism. King was thinking in these terms when he declared that his "whole philosophy of life and social action" was "one of love and nonviolence" and not "a reckless disregard of the lives and safety of persons."[150] Convinced that "love is the most durable power in the world," King, drawing on that larger philosophical tradition extending from the ancient Greeks to the Boston personalists, opened himself to other philosophical truths that established the significance of his thought as liberating and empowering discourse. These included the existence of a fundamental moral order in the universe, the world house metaphor as the ideal expression of global human community, dialectical analysis as the key to understanding and transforming social reality, the principle that "the end is pre-existent in the means," the concept that "growth comes through struggle," the redemptive and reconciling power of agape love and unearned suffering, the conviction that "the most meaningful life is a life whose center is a fixed point outside of" one's "own being," and the idea that it is not how long but how well one lives.[151] King credited the Western philosophical tradition with establishing reason as a useful and indeed indispensable tool in pursuing and assigning meaning to truth. He felt that all categories of truth had to be put to the test of reason.[152] Thus, he often turned to philosophy to put the problem of defining truth in proper perspective, but he never considered truth as a domain exclusive to philosophical inquiry and argumentation.

Even so, philosophy contributed perhaps as much as the Bible, theology, and the Christian faith to King's understanding of and approach to ethical truths, or those truths that fuse facts and values, that govern human conduct and actions, and that drive the total way of life. Philosophy and ethics were intrinsically related in King's thinking, which helps explain his belief that ethical truths are rooted in a keen sense of the existence of a moral order in the universe.[153] The "first principle of value" that humans needed "to rediscover," King often said, is "that *all* reality hinges on moral foundations," which in essence means "that this is a moral universe." For King, this translated into the idea that "some things" are absolutely right and "some things" are absolutely wrong, a point that reflected his belief that ethical truth is at its core objective truth. Mindful of Friedrich Nietzsche's blistering attack on basic Christian ethics and convinced that all human "conduct," at the individual and group levels, must conform to a "code of ethics," King lamented society's growing drift away from those ethical truths embodied in the Ten Commandments in the Bible, or those "ethical actions" and "laws" that "the God of righteousness" demands of his children:

> We have adopted a sort of pragmatic test for right and wrong—whatever works is right. If it works, it's all right. Nothing is wrong but that which does not work. If you don't get caught, it's right. That's the attitude, isn't it? It's all right to disobey the Ten Commandments, but just don't disobey the Eleventh, Thou shall not get caught. That's the attitude. That's the prevailing attitude in our culture. No matter what you do, just do it with a bit of finesse. You know, a sort of attitude of the survival of the slickest. Not the Darwinian survival of the fittest, but the survival of the

slickest—who, whoever can be the slickest is the one who is right. It's all right to lie, but lie with dignity. It's all right to steal and to rob and extort but do it with a bit of finesse. It's even all right to hate, but just dress your hate up in the garments of love and make it appear that you are loving when you are actually hating. *Just get by.* That's the thing that's right according to this new ethic.[154]

King held that "this new ethic," or "the ethic of midnight," constituted the greatest threat to lives lived in conformity with the demands and requirements of truth. Highly critical of "the mountain of moral and ethical relativism," which "we have been" in "long enough" and which "can lead only to moral degeneration," he called for "a new moral climate," a society established more firmly on "a moral foundation," a world in which "the moral and ethical ends for which" humans live are "abreast with the scientific and technological means by which" they live.[155] In King's opinion, this could happen only if persons, driven by moral sense and intuition, are determined to project "the ethic of love to the center" of their lives—love in the sense of seeking the good and well-being of others. Ethical truth by this standard is about wanting for other selves nothing less than what the self wants for the self. It is, in King's estimation, about a commitment to "higher values," or to truth in terms of the quest for a higher human and ethical ideal.[156]

Yet another point should be made as further clarification of King's view of and approach to ethical truths. King maintained that an ethos of truth and truth-telling becomes vital and meaningful only if it is translated or organized into a movement that liberates, uplifts, and empowers people, particularly those subjected to oppression and injustice. This was King's operating ethos as a social justice advocate and activist. He felt that it was in this manner that Jesus modeled ethical truth at its best. Like Jesus, King refused to embrace truth as only a matter of personal ethics, viewing it as also a call to communal accountability and responsibility. For him, the Christian faith, rooted in the life and teachings of Jesus Christ, was both ethical and communal in nature.[157]

King's idea of "truth in the natural law" was grounded in his study of not only ethics but theology and philosophy as well. Natural law for him consisted in those "things that" are "basic" and "structural" in "nature."[158] He reasoned that there were "some things" that are as "true," "basic," and "structural" in the "natural order" as in history. King identified "truth in the natural order," for example, with "the coming of the heat with the South wind" and "the rain with the gathering of the clouds."[159] Interestingly, he seemingly wrote and said less about truths in the natural law than other categories of truth, but this did not mean that the subject was less important to him. He opined that truth is indeed a power in nature and that the truths in the natural law are manifested in divine creation, activity, and providence; in the beauty of nature, the world, and its creatures; in those inherent rights that come to humans from God, nature, and reason; and in that intrinsic sense of right and wrong that governs human rationality and behavior. The truths that are inherent in the natural law, King believed, extended across time, human history, and geographical boundaries, and they embody a core of standards that human beings have in common. Undoubtedly, "truth in the natural law" was consistent with King's conviction that there are objective truths in the universe.[160]

This treatment of the various categories of truth in King's sermons, speeches, and writings brings more clarity to what he meant when he acknowledged that he subscribed wholeheartedly to the Hegelian "contention that 'truth is the whole.'" Clearly, when King referenced this idea, he was not simply thinking of the question of definition or meaning or referring to the Hegelian "analysis of the dialectical process."[161] He was demonstrating that truth is a powerful symphony and that getting a handle on truth is always a complicated and tedious intellectual undertaking.

Truth Vis-à-Vis Untruth: Marking the Boundaries

Martin Luther King Jr. reported that the religion he "grew up under" embraced certain "noble moral and ethical ideals" that he never abandoned. A vital part of that "inherited religion" was a belief in and commitment to truth vis-à-vis untruth. King's intellectual interest in and reflections on the clear and unequivocal boundaries between truth and untruth stretched at least as far back as his Morehouse College years, when he insisted, in essays published in the *Maroon Tiger*, that education "should enable one" to "discern the true from the false, the real from the unreal, and the facts from the fiction."[162] King came to see that there is no moral equivalency between truth and untruth and that those who thought or acted otherwise had fallen into the passionless and undisciplined depths of "softmindedness."[163] Deeply disturbed by the "softminded," or those who traffic in "distortions and half-truths," he raised the pressing need for the kind of "toughmindedness" that overcomes "downright ignorance," that "breaks the crust of legends and myths," and that "sifts the true from the false."[164]

King never subscribed to a Nietzschean, Leninist, or relativistic ethic when defining or assigning meaning to truth and untruth, and he was always distrustful of those who engaged truth and untruth as if they were identical or indistinguishable. As far as King was concerned, truth and untruth were really a matter of what is unquestionably right and what is unquestionably wrong. While conceding that both are forces in the universe and are means of communication with a place and a function in human life and history, he argued that truth differs in that it corresponds with fact or reality, or what is in actual existence. Untruth, by contrast, is an "illegitimate extension" and "perversion of the facts" and "reality."[165] King abhorred "untruthfulness," identifying it with "inferior methods" and "terrible sins" and labeling it as a form of deception, as a moral failing, and as ethically indefensible. He cherished truth, noting that it is more than merely what an individual thinks, feels, or believes, identifying it with "the highest ideals" or "higher values" and variously describing it as doing the will of God, as submitting to the "higher law" Jesus "eloquently affirmed from the cross," as civilized behavior, as an ethical principle, as an act of faith, as power, as love, as the foundation of the moral order, as "the most powerful thing in the universe," and as struggling for justice.[166]

Obviously, King considered truth and untruth to be by any reasonable standard irreconcilable. This explains to some extent his problem with Friedrich Nietzsche, Vladimir Ilyich Ulyanov Lenin and the proponents of Communism, Adolf Hitler, McCarthyism, and the architects and defenders of southern Jim Crow. King felt that in each of these cases, there were efforts to either conceal, distort, or devalue truth, or to wrap untruth in the garments of truth.[167] He declared that untruth can never become truth nor truth untruth. King further illustrated the point by bringing the philosophical question of means and ends to bear on the contrast between "the weapon of violence" and "the weapon of nonviolence." Violence always constitutes "untruthful means" and nonviolence "truthful means," he exclaimed. Nonviolence "is the relentless pursuit of truthful ends through moral means," he further noted, and it "seeks to" defeat or overcome "evil by truth"—"to resist physical force by soul-force."[168] Violence is the "sword method" that defeats, injures, humiliates, and kills, King concluded, and nonviolence is "a weapon fabricated of love"—"a sword" that transforms the "heart" and "heals."[169] Referring specifically to the campaign in Birmingham in 1963, he asserted that truth, or "the conviction that we were right," was "the most formidable weapon of all."[170] Living in times when the ruling elites routinely peddled and used lies as a means to desired ends and convinced that truth is the best barometer of what amounts to civilized and ethical conduct, King reasoned that he and other ministers of the gospel had "a mandate" to "lead men from the desolate midnight of falsehood to the bright daybreak of truth." This, he believed, was Jesus's message to every believer in every age and generation, and it was largely a matter of appealing to the heart and not simply the head.[171] King never lost that focus on Jesus's Sermon on the Mount in the fifth chapter of the Gospel of Matthew, which he interpreted as a call and commission to act on certain truths in the spirit of empathy, compassion, humility, and peace.

King never doubted the resiliency or the persevering spirit of truth in the face of untruth. He believed that truth embodies not only its own self-authentication but also its own power and enduring quality, especially since it, unlike untruth, rests on a solid and unshakable foundation. After all, he noted, God is the source of all truth.[172] Truth and untruth were for King a part of that tension at the very center of the universe. He often quoted from James Russell Lowell, whose poetic expression "'tis truth alone is strong" carried a message that exposed the rationale for Thomas Carlyle's declaration that "no lie can live forever."[173] King viewed untruth as part of that fount of evil that "carries the seeds of its own destruction."[174] Thus, he concluded that "we must never struggle with falsehood"—that, as moral and rational beings, humans should always resolve to be "led in the way of truth."[175]

The triumphant power and capacity of truth was a major, recurring theme in so much of what King said and wrote. He held that there is no version of truth that is subject to lasting failure and defeat and that untruth, though seemingly strong and victorious for a time, can never really succeed.[176] For King, truth had a way of exposing and eventually prevailing over untruth. "One day truth will rise up and reign supreme!" he proclaimed in an Easter Sunday message in 1957.[177] "The forces of evil may temporarily conquer truth," he said in another sermon some six years later, "but truth will ultimately conquer its conqueror."[178] King felt this contention was strongly borne out by the successful outcome of freedom struggles throughout human history, beginning with the exodus of the Israelites out of Egypt and their subsequent arrival in the Promised Land. The exodus account in Scripture was never a matter of fact or fiction for King but was a story of the triumphant quality of truth over untruth.[179] He felt similarly regarding Gandhi and his followers' successful struggle against British colonial rule, viewing it as essentially a victory for truth.[180] He called the Montgomery bus boycott, which succeeded under his leadership, "a victory for truth and justice, a victory for the unity of mankind." Recalling the struggle in Montgomery, King added, "We have seen truth crucified and goodness buried, but we have kept going with the conviction that truth crushed to earth will rise again."[181] Every victorious human struggle for liberation, uplift, and empowerment testified to his conviction that "somehow unarmed truth is the most powerful thing in the universe."[182] In this sense, the power of truth was akin to the power of spirituality; in fact, they were, in King's understanding, one and the same, at least on some levels.

The images of the scaffold and the cross appeared repeatedly in King's messaging, for they graphically symbolized for him the spirit, resilience, and victorious quality of truth and the fact that truth can never be fully subverted and conquered by untruth. Among his favorite quotations were these words from *The Present Crisis* (1844) by James Russell Lowell, the celebrated American romantic poet and literary critic:

> *Truth forever on the scaffold,*
> *Wrong forever on the throne,*
> *Yet that scaffold sways the future,*
> *And behind the dim unknown*
> *Standeth God within the shadows,*
> *Keeping watch above his own.*[183]

It is not difficult to imagine what "truth on the scaffold" meant for a Black man like King, who as a young boy had actually seen trees in Georgia on which members of his own race "had been savagely lynched."[184] In the context of that experience, "truth on the scaffold" became more than symbolic language about the unconquerable spirit of truth. To be sure, it became a commentary on the reality and meaning of American life and history and, more importantly, on what it meant to be Black in America. On the brighter side, it was also a striking reminder that the scaffold does not have the last word in the universe.[185]

The cross was equally important in this regard for King. In fact, the manger in which Jesus was born and the cross on which he died came together in King's consciousness as he proclaimed the inevitable triumph of truth over untruth. Drawing on what William Cullen Bryant, the American romantic poet and journalist, had written about truth and on what Thomas Carlyle, the British historian and philosopher, had said about untruth, King declared in "A Christmas Sermon on Peace," "Something must remind us of this as we once again stand in the Christmas season and think of Easter season simultaneously, for the two somehow go together. Christ came to show us the way. Men love darkness rather than light, and they crucified him, and there on Good Friday on the cross it was still dark, but then Easter came, and Easter is an eternal reminder of the fact that truth crushed to earth will rise again. Easter justifies Carlyle in saying, 'No lie can live forever.'"[186]

Untruth and truth were uppermost in King's mind whenever he spoke of the elements of tragedy and triumph on the cross. Good Friday symbolized tragedy and Easter triumph. Every time King thought of the cross, he was reminded of not only a blind and tragic submission to untruth, on the part of the Roman soldiers, but also "the majesty of unswerving devotion to truth," as exemplified in the unselfish spirit and the "sacrificial love" of Jesus Christ. For King, "there is a cross at the center" of every life, every human being comes to know "Good Fridays" and "Easters," and the vast and unbreachable gulf between truth and untruth shows that life itself "is not a great symphony with all of the instruments playing harmoniously together." If we "look at it long enough," King opined, "we will discover that there is a jangling discord in life that has somehow thrown the symphony out of whack. The nagging, prehensile tentacles of evil are always present, taking some of the meaning out of life."[187]

3

Strange Ambivalence

Truth and the Dialectical Nature of Persons and Society

Nations will always find it more difficult than individuals to behold the beam that is in their own eye while they observe the mote that is in their brother's eye; and individuals find it difficult enough. A perennial weakness in the moral life of individuals is simply raised to the *n*th degree in national life.

> —Reinhold Niebuhr, *Moral Man and Immoral Society:*
> *A Study in Ethics and Politics* (1932)

With all of her dazzling achievements and stupendous material strides, America has maintained its strange ambivalence on the question of racial justice.

> —Martin Luther King Jr., *Where Do We Go from Here:*
> *Chaos or Community?* (1967)

In an article published in the *Nation* in March 1962, Martin Luther King Jr. suggested that Americans should seek "our national

99

purpose in the spirit of Thomas Jefferson." King went on to quote those "majestic words of the Declaration of Independence," which Jefferson's pen etched "across the pages of history"—"words lifted to cosmic proportions": "We hold these truths to be self-evident, that all men are created equal, that they are endowed by their Creator with certain inalienable rights, that among these are life, liberty and the pursuit of happiness."[1] But what exactly did Jefferson's words mean to King, a Black man born and raised in the Jim Crow South? What use did he make of these words over time? Were they merely a part of King's rhetorical strategy, or did they serve a larger and more meaningful purpose in the context of the movement he led? How did King assess America's failure to live up to the Jeffersonian idea of "self-evident" truths? How did Jefferson's words figure into his understanding of the American dream and the ongoing quest for a more perfect union? Much of the discussion that follows takes seriously King's judgment and facility in engaging and answering these and other questions that form the basis of this chapter.

But the more general focus is on how King's ideas about America and its history and culture were grounded in his understanding of the dialectical or paradoxical nature of persons and society, a concept that, in his thinking, explained tendencies toward good and evil, truth and untruth.[2] The chapter begins with King's early struggles in a society steeped in contradictions—a society in which his humanity was affirmed by Blacks and denied by whites. From that point, the discussion moves in two directions. First, King's insights into humans as essentially creatures of contradiction are examined. Second, attention is devoted to King's lifelong challenge to a nation that claimed certain "self-evident" truths about human-ity and freedom in its founding and most sacred documents, the Constitution and the Declaration of Independence, while simul-taneously holding hundreds of thousands of Africans in slavery.[3] As this chapter explains, this coexistence of American democratic claims and the brutal oppression of Black people became clearer to King as he continuously experienced the pain of Jim Crow in the American South, as he studied and experienced the broad sweep of American life and culture over time, and as he increasingly applied W. E. B. Du Bois's dialectic of Black self-identity, Georg Hegel's analysis of the dialectical process, and Reinhold Niebuhr's insights into the behavior of individuals and groups to the human condition in the United States. King's subsequent use of the metaphors of "the ambivalent nation," "the American dilemma," and "the schizophrenic personality" are treated at some length, for they reveal a dialectical thinker judiciously describing a nation tragically "torn between selves"—a nation proudly proclaiming certain profound truths "on paper" while comfortably living a lie in its daily practices around race, poverty and economic injustice, and war and human destruction.[4] The chapter closes with King's thoughts on the relationship between the Declaration of Independence, the Constitution, and the Emancipation Proclamation and with some consideration of his oft-repeated calls for a renewed and uncompromising commitment to the full realization of the Jeffersonian idea of "self-evident" truths as an important step on the path toward a more perfect union.

Unreconciled Strivings: Truth and the Divided Self

Martin Luther King Jr. spent his childhood years in Atlanta, Georgia, at a time when the great W. E. B. Du Bois lived and taught there. A professor at the historically Black Atlanta University, Du Bois was widely known in the community for his impeccable scholarship and civil rights activism and was frequently mentioned in the local Black newspapers, including the *Atlanta Daily World*, to which the King family subscribed religiously. The young King undoubtedly felt the impact of Du Bois's presence in very personal and precise ways, for Du Bois had long written about the dialectic of Black self-identity, or the lens of "double consciousness" through which people of African descent in the United States were compelled to view themselves. In his classic piece, *The Souls of Black Folk* (1903), he wrote in poignant terms:

It is a peculiar sensation, this double-consciousness, this sense of always looking at one's self through the eyes of others, of measuring one's soul by the tape of a world that looks on in amused contempt and pity. One ever feels his twoness—an American, a Negro; two souls, two thoughts, two unreconciled strivings; two warring ideals in one dark body, whose dogged strength alone keeps it from being torn asunder. . . . The history of the American Negro is the history of this strife,—this longing to attain self-conscious manhood, to merge his double self into a better and truer self. In this merging he wishes neither of the older selves to be lost.[5]

Even before King understood Du Bois's concept of "double consciousness" in theoretical terms, he had some sense of the strange dualism that haunted his daily existence as a Black person in a white world. This would not have been surprising, for the situation the youngster faced in the South was in many ways so ambiguous, even anomalous, that no child could have survived it unscathed. Recalling his childhood, King spoke of the internal conflict he experienced living in a society that routinely raised the banner of freedom while oppressing people of color: "As I look back over those early days, I did have something of an inner tension. On the one hand, my mother taught me that I should feel a sense of somebodiness. On the other hand, I had to go out and face the system, which stared me in the face every day saying, 'you are less than,' 'you are not equal to.' So this was a real tension within."[6] This "inner tension" was reinforced and most certainly compounded as King was constantly exposed to teachings, in his home and in Black churches, that echoed Jesus's affirmation that "the truth shall set you free." But what could this possibly mean to a six-year-old Black child who lost his white playmate for reasons that defied logic, who was slapped and verbally abused by a white woman at age eight, who occasionally watched the Ku Klux Klan (KKK) on its night rides in his neighborhood, who witnessed police officers beating Blacks on the streets of Atlanta, who observed his own father insulted by whites, who saw Blacks receiving "the most tragic injustice in the courts," who "had passed spots" where Blacks had been brutally lynched, and who was restricted daily to segregated schools, theaters, parks, swimming pools, and lunch counters, all due to a vicious system of white supremacy? It is not difficult to imagine King struggling with Jesus's words about the relationship between truth and freedom and truth and self-realization, especially since he, at age fifteen, had already begun to question the relevance of Thomas Jefferson's declaration of "self-evident" truths regarding human equality and natural rights in a land in which "the finest Negro is at the mercy of the meanest white man."[7]

King's earliest life experiences contained a series of opposites that largely determined how he defined and distinguished truth from untruth. Rarely did he experience anything without also encountering its opposite. As a child, he sensed that he was fiercely hated by "the white man" and vowed to respond in kind, but his parents taught him that it was his "Christian duty to love him."[8] His own father, King Sr., preached and struggled against white supremacy while his white childhood friend's father prevented the boys from playing together because King was Black.[9] King had an economically secure and stable childhood, but his Black playmates lived in poverty and insecurity. He sat at the feet of Black teachers who consistently highlighted the importance of celebrating the great contributions of Blacks to the nation's history but faced a white society that insisted that Blacks had no history worthy of recognition.[10] King often heard Black men of the cloth proclaiming with moving fervor the need for a prophetic social gospel in the here and now and others who kept their people's minds riveted on "milk and honey," "silver slippers," and "mansions" in some great beyond.[11] He was taught to cherish the universal truths and egalitarian principles expressed in the Constitution and the Declaration of Independence but lived in a nation that lacked the moral imagination to do likewise.[12] Such experiences, which might have damaged the personality of the average sensitive and perceptive child, produced a youngster so driven to learn and think that King set upon himself the task of identifying and separating truth from the barrage of falsehoods that clouded his childhood world.

King was always interested in the human condition and wanted to know why people were prone to such twisted ways of thinking, feeling, and behaving when it came to certain basic truths concerning life, humanity, and race. His first extensive intellectual engagement with these issues occurred while he was at Atlanta's Morehouse College. He left that institution with the determination to bring as much clarity as possible to an idea that he felt explained the problem: that every human life is in reality a study in contradictions.[13] Later, when studying at Crozer Theological Seminary, King framed the discussion of humanity's enduring problem around a series of questions: "Why is it that from the same lips that truth falls lies also fall? Why is it that the same mother's heart that is overflowing with love is also overflowing with hate? . . . Why is it that good people are sometimes worse than the worst people and bad people sometimes better than the best people?" From that point, King ventured to answer these questions, or to make sense of the notion that there is "a tension" or "a strange dichotomy of disturbing dualism within human nature."[14] Drawing on modern psychology, he noted that "each of us is two selves" "split up and divided against ourselves"—"something of a schizophrenic personality."[15] This is much of what King was thinking when he highlighted the need to "see people in their true *humanness.*" He believed that anything less could only amount to a tragically limited and even false conception of both God and humanity, to say nothing of their relationship to each other.[16]

The explanations for this "conflict," or that which is dialectical or paradoxical about human nature, came gradually as King pursued his studies at Crozer and Boston University and as he observed human behavior across a broad spectrum. While at Crozer, he did not find complete intellectual satisfaction with the answers provided by neoorthodoxy or crisis theology, which was largely identified with Reinhold Niebuhr:

There is a modern school of theology which argues that the conflict resulted from the fall of man. They argue that at the beginning man was made in the image of God, but soon he rebelled against God which brought about the fall. And in the great fall the image of God was somewhat effaced, leaving man with a make-up that was predominantly evil. They argue that this conflict is a result of this evil nature that is in man forever fighting against the element of good that is left in him. Actually, I don't know what causes the conflict. But I do know that there is a conflict. There is something paradoxical and contradictory about human nature.[17]

King's reservations regarding neoorthodoxy at this juncture mirrored much of his critique of the Protestant Reformers, Martin Luther and John Calvin, who portrayed humans as so absolutely depraved that they could do no good without divine grace. King's struggle was ultimately between "the liberal doctrine of man," which upheld his "natural goodness," and the neoorthodox view, which highlighted "his capacity for evil." He finally reached the conclusion that each "represents a partial truth"—that humanity must be understood in terms of its capacity for both good and evil.[18] King must have been thinking along these lines when he, citing an unnamed French philosopher and Georg Hegel, spoke of humans bearing within their character "antithesis strongly marked," or "strongly marked opposites," though he was equally clear in maintaining that only "the strong man" achieves a proper "balance of opposites."[19] When it came to exploring the idea of the dialectical or dual self—and indeed achieving a realistic understanding of human nature—referencing Niebuhrian Christian realism and the Hegelian analysis of the dialectical process was for King the functional equivalent of invoking Du Bois's dialectic of Black self-identity, despite the different frames of reference these thinkers had in mind.

The fact that good and evil are perennially engaged in a struggle for the soul of human beings was never lost on King. King called this "a paradigm of life" in one sense but also likened the struggle within the human soul to "a civil war":

And there is something of a civil war going on within all of our lives. There is a recalcitrant South of our soul revolting against the North of our soul. And there is this continual struggle within the very structure of every individual life. There is something within all of us that causes us to cry out with Ovid, the Latin poet, "I see and approve the better things of life, but the evil things I do." There is something within all of us that causes us to cry out with Plato that the human personality is like a charioteer with two headstrong horses, each wanting to go in different directions. There is something within each of us that causes us to cry out with Goethe, "There is enough stuff in me to make me both a gentleman and a rogue." There is something within each of us that causes us to cry out with Apostle Paul, "I see and approve the better things of life, but the evil things I do."[20]

Explaining the problem from a different angle, King went on to assert that because of this perpetual war within the soul, humans find themselves "something like Dr. Jekyll and Mr. Hyde":

We discover that there is a private aspect of our lives forever in conflict with the personal aspect of our lives. We all have a private self that we don't want the public self to discover. There is a privacy about all of us that we are ashamed of, that we forever seek to hide, and that we would never want to become public. This is the sin of man. There is a Mr. Hyde in all of us that seeks at the night of life to go into being while pushing aside the day of life that is Dr. Jekyll, and then, the next morning it tries to become Dr. Jekyll again. Then, that night it becomes Mr. Hyde again. There is this conflict between the is-ness of our present natures and the eternal oughtness that forever confronts us. That comes in all lives.[21]

For King, this was the one central mystery about humanity, the enduring human conundrum. Even so, he was convinced that the conflict within the human soul is in reality "a tension between God and man," for "man is in eternal revolt against God." His stress on the idea of a civil war within the human soul, or "the war of spirit" within,[22] had everything to do with the contrast he drew between God and humanity, truth and untruth. King found further clarification of these matters in the existentialism he studied at Boston University, for the existentialists roundly agreed that there are contradictions and/or tensions in human life and existence that are irresolvable. As they put it, there is no good without evil, no love without hate, no life without death, and no truth without untruth. Although King acknowledged that existentialists like Søren Kierkegaard, Friedrich Nietzsche, Karl Jaspers, Martin Heidegger, and Jean-Paul Sartre had not discovered the "ultimate Christian answer" to many of life's questions, he concluded that Christian theologians could learn much from their insights into "the true state of human existence."[23]

As part of his extended explanation of the dialectical self, of why individuals behave as they do, King spoke more specifically in terms of "the higher" and "best self" and the "lower" or "worst self." "There is something high in us and there is something low in us," he maintained. In a sermon on "The Conflict in Human Nature," King was a bit more specific: "Whenever man seeks the high there is the grungy of the low. Whenever he seeks to commune with the stars, he feels the blinding gust of dust blocking his vision. Man's quest for the divine is interrupted by the nagging movements of the demonic."[24] King tried to convey this glaring dichotomy between the highest self and the lowest self when he, referencing the cross event in the New Testament, declared that "life somehow is a pendulum swinging between Good Friday and Easter, swinging between agony and triumph, swinging between darkness and light." At another point, he was more forthright: "The cross reveals two basic things it seems to me. On the one hand, it is a revelation of the amazing heights to which man can ascend by the grace of God. On the other hand, it is an expression of the tragic and demonic depths to which man can sink."[25] Put another way, "the conflict," according to King, is "between what we know we ought to be and what we actually are"—a conflict "that confronts us all." King lamented the adverse impact that such conflict too frequently has on the human personality, especially when it grows, illustrating his point with yet another reference to Scripture:

> The wider the gap is between our higher selves and our lower selves, the more disintegrated we are; the less meaning we find in life. The more we live up to our higher natures, the more integrated we are and the more meaning we find in life. No man can be permanently happy who lives on the low planes of existence. Any man who lives out of harmony with his higher nature, is living out of harmony with his true essence, and such a disharmony brings unhappiness and cynicism. Such with the plight of the Prodigal Son who had gone into a far country and wasted all, living on the low and evil planes of existence. But then one day out in a swine pasture he came to himself. He came to see that the life that God had given him was too precious to throw away in low and evil living, and he knew that so long as he remained there he would be frustrated and disillusioned, finding no meaning in life.[26]

The human capacity for evil, or to retreat to "tragic and demonic depths," was as intriguing for King as it was for the ancient Greek philosophers and early Christian thinkers like Saint Augustine. The personal racism white people had long practiced against people of color, perhaps more than anything else, supported King's assertion that "there are within all of us tides of evil which can rise to flood proportions," thus becoming "the slumbering giant."[27] "We don't have to go very far in life," he remarked, "to see that it is possible to live to our lowest and worst selves." Having experienced the brunt of the evils of white supremacy throughout his life, and sensitive to Reinhold Niebuhr's insights into "the complexity of human motives and the reality of sin on every level of man's existence," King wrote, "The more I observed the tragedies of history and man's inclination to choose the low road, the more I came to see the depths and strength of sin." "At many points it is quite understandable why it is difficult for us to have faith in man," he conceded. "Man has often made such a poor showing of himself. Within a generation we have fought two world wars. We have seen man's tragic inhumanity to man."[28] King further advanced his indictment of humanity, noting that violence always puts humans on a lower level of existence. "We live according to the philosophy that life is a matter of getting even and of saving face," King argued. "We bow before the altar of revenge." He opined that the lives of individuals often fall short of the lofty ideas they hold dear because they act out of "the wrong spirit" or yield "to low impulses or our worst inclinations."[29] "Wherever we discover life, somehow we discover this gone-wrongness," King declared. "Wherever there is a struggle for goodness, we discover, on the other hand, a powerful antagonism, something demonic, something that seems to bring our loveliest qualities to evil and our greatest endeavors to failure."[30]

King felt that "man's shameful inclination to choose the low road" is quite often discernible in the tendency to choose and embrace untruth over truth. "We stand amid the forces of truth and deliberately lie," he complained as he considered the depth of the ambivalence in the human spirit. In a sermon on "The Christian Doctrine of Man," he told his listeners that humans "know truth, and yet we lie. We know how to be honest, and yet we are dishonest."[31] King was not particularly surprised but nonetheless annoyed that all too many people, seemingly without any sense of probity or rectitude, turned to blindly rejecting truth, to spreading "evil rumors" and "lies," to lying by omission and commission, to morally defending falsehoods as long as they are told "with real finesse," to determining truth on the basis of a relativistic ethic, to confusing "the true with the false and the false with the true," and to making "the evil seem good, the ugly seem beautiful, and the unjust seem just."[32] King noted that some individuals, motivated by what he called "the drum major instinct," "lie about who" they "know sometimes," thinking that identifying themselves "with the big name people" enhances their own importance. He personally knew people in leadership positions and moral authority who were more committed to untruth than to truth, including clergy, politicians, and law enforcement officers.[33] Citing the "law of accumulation," by "which sin and goodness increase each after its own kind," King explained that "the more honest one is the easier it is to be honest" and "the more one lies the easier it is to lie."[34] He believed not only that lying revealed the darkest recesses of the human heart and soul but that it was all too frequently the source of other character deficiencies. "Jesus realized something basic," said King, as he reflected on the encounter between Jesus and Nicodemus, and that is "if a man will lie, he will steal." Always mindful of the complexities of the dialectical self, and with an eye toward the collective evils of humankind, King unequivocally insisted that "we must never come to terms with falsehood, malice, hate or violence."[35]

King's knowledge of the human situation was such that he clearly understood the potential danger of what he termed "ugly hypocrisy,"[36] or the human tendency to casually practice the antithesis of what is strongly, openly, and consistently professed in words. He grew up in a culture in which the adage "practice what you preach" was frequently heard in Black churches, and he always had difficulty with people who were not true to what they habitually expressed in testimonies. In King's estimation, this was tantamount to living a lie, and those who did so "exist according to this new ethic."[37] Struggling throughout his life with white supremacy and mindful of the impact of poverty and violence on the weak and helpless, he shuddered at the very thought of "a man" who "so consistently lived a lie that he lost the capacity to distinguish between good and evil."[38] Words are meaningful, King believed, only to the extent that they find substance in the right deeds. He was more interested in living and acting on truth than in proclaiming truth as a creedal statement. Convinced that "the test of belief is action," King held that Jesus was the ideal by which humans might assess the quality of their own lives, for Jesus matched "words and actions." In other words, "the magnanimity of Jesus' spirit" was such that he bridged "the gulf between practice and profession, between doing and saying."[39]

Of equal concern for King were those who wielded power and influence by exploiting the worst impulses or evil potential in human nature. He knew that much of the appeal of dictators like Vladimir Lenin, Adolf Hitler, and Benito Mussolini came not only from their shameless and excessive reliance on falsehoods but also from their ability to make people feel that their worst instincts were in fact their best instincts—that lies were actually the truth.[40] These tyrants epitomized for King the sheer depths to which humans could fall, especially when under the command of their "worst selves." King felt much the same about southern governors such as George C. Wallace, Ross Barnett, Orval Faubus, and Lester Maddox, all of whom claimed to be men of faith even as they appealed to the lowest human passions to appease and maintain the strong support of white supremacists and segregationists.[41] As far as King was concerned, these were men with dark and disfigured souls, and ironically enough, they ultimately brought out both the worst and the best qualities among certain sectors of humankind.

Despite King's desire and efforts to be the best person he could possibly be, he, too, must be understood in terms of his lowest self and highest self. Conventional wisdom has led some scholars to suggest that King was not being his "higher" or "best self" when he appropriated the words of others without proper acknowledgment, actions that negatively impact his standing and legacy as an intellectual and as a moral and spiritual leader.[42] Much the same has been suggested in response to the tabloid-style, jaw-dropping revelations regarding King's adulterous conduct.[43] King's actions as a plagiarist are difficult to explain in view of his oft-repeated declarations on "the content of character," his firm belief in "soul-searching honesty," and his insistence on operating "[at] the highest level of integrity." His behavior as an adulterer is indefensible given his expressed conviction that "without truth marriage is like a ship without a compass," let alone his willingness to offer women advice on the virtues of virginity, marital fidelity, and honest communication in marriage.[44] It is also difficult to conclude, based on what is known about King's character, that his plagiarism resulted from an intentional desire to deceive or to be dishonest, and he reportedly confessed his infidelity to his wife, Coretta, during the last year of his life.[45]

King was never the kind of person who easily and typically succumbed to his worst impulses. Even so, when his whole life is held in view, and not simply those moments of moral failings, it is obvious that he lived to both his lowest and highest self.[46] "I have no pretense to absolute goodness," commented King in an interview with the newspaper columnist Mike Wallace in 1961. The narrative King created about himself over time was never false and misleading. King denied that he was infallible, insisting that "that is reserved for the height of the Divine, rather than the depth of the human." "At every moment," he added, "I am conscious of my finiteness."[47] In his sermon "Unfulfilled Dreams," he was equally blunt in coming to terms with his worst self: "I don't know this morning about you, but I can make a testimony. You don't need to go out this morning saying that Martin Luther King is a saint. Oh, no. I want you to know this morning that I'm a sinner like all of God's children. But I want to be a good man. And I want to hear a voice saying to me one day, 'I take you in and I bless you, because you try. It is well that it was within thine heart.'"[48] Bearing this in mind, the question for those who study King is, as Frye Gaillard has noted, how to best juxtapose his humanity—"his frailties, doubts, and vulnerabilities, *and* his delights in the ordinariness of life—with his extraordinary gifts as a leader." As Gaillard suggests, it is ultimately about finding some way "to put the pieces together—the vulnerability and the greatness, the heroism and the feet of clay."[49]

Undoubtedly, the human tendency to be so often driven by the lowest rather than the highest motives and impulses was taken very seriously by King. As he struggled intellectually, morally, and spiritually with this tendency and with the larger dilemma of the self divided against the self on so many levels, he reached certain conclusions that were consistent with his mission to free and empower humanity. First, he determined that although "the evil potential of human nature" is real and inescapable, it should never lead individuals to define themselves based solely on the actions of the lower self—that developing a deep sense of self-worth, self-love, and self-acceptance is also essential for living a complete life:

Now it seems to me that that is the first way to overcome an inferiority complex—the principle of self-acceptance.

That's a prayer that every individual should pray: "Lord, help me to accept myself." Every man should somehow say, "I, John Doe, accept myself with all of my inherited abilities and handicaps. I accept those conditions within my environment which cannot be altered or which I cannot control. And after accepting these I go back to myself and see what I can do with myself." And this is a healthy attitude of life. So many people are busy trying to be somebody else, and that is what accounts for their frustration. There is within every man a bit of latent creativity seeking to break forth, and it is often blocked because we are busy trying to be somebody else. So this is the first way to overcome an inferiority complex: accept yourself. That means accept your looks. It means accept your limitations in every area. It means what it says: "Accept your actual self." And where the conflict really comes is that individuals find a sort of impassible gulf between their actual selves and their desired selves. And that is when an inferiority complex breaks out in morbid proportions— when individuals come to see that there is a tremendous gap between their actual selves and their desired selves. And the thing that every individual should pray to the Almighty God for is to give them that sense of acceptance of the actual self with all limitations and with all of the endowments that come as the results of our being born in this world.[50]

King felt that self-love, validation of self-worth, and self-acceptance were particularly important for his own people, whose individual and collective lives were defined, as W. E. B. Du Bois put it, by "warring ideals" and "unreconciled strivings" in dark bodies. "Too many Negroes are ashamed of themselves, ashamed of being black," King declared. "A Negro got to rise up and say from the bottom of his soul, 'I am somebody. I have a rich, noble, and proud heritage. However exploited and however painful my history has been, I'm black, but I'm black and beautiful.'"[51]

Second, King vehemently defended the enduring and critical need for creative and productive ways to curb the evil and sinful sides of persons and to ensure that they act in accordance with their better selves. Any notion to the contrary, he felt, defied logic. Although King commended Blacks for the amazing good they achieved as a creative minority within the context of the civil rights movement of the 1950s and '60s, he noted nonetheless that they, too, were subject to the same frailties as all other human beings. "No one can pretend that because a people may be oppressed, every individual member is virtuous and worthy," King reasoned. Although he repeatedly referred to humans' capacity for relatively decent, good behavior on the one hand and disturbingly indecent, evil conduct on the other, he evidently felt that the careful thinker always begins with the premise that no individual is all good and ends with the conclusion that some force is necessary to restrain his propensity for wickedness.[52] Man's "capacity for good makes persuasion a very powerful instrument," King observed, "but his inclination for evil makes coercion a necessity."[53] He went on to suggest in more specific terms, based on his reading of Reinhold Niebuhr, that government and laws are necessary because persons "inevitably corrupt their potentialities for love" and the good "by a lust" for power and "self-security that outruns natural needs." In other words, "men must be restrained by force lest they destroy their neighbors in a desperate attempt to make themselves secure."[54] Advancing his views further, King, using segregation to make his point, opined that "a great deal of our so-called race problem will be solved in the realm of enforceable obligations," or through the instruments of law, politics, and government:

> Let us never succumb to the temptation of believing that legislation and judicial decrees can play no major role in bringing about desegregation. It may be true that morality cannot be legislated, but behavior can be regulated. Judicial decrees may not change the heart, but they can restrain the heartless. The law cannot make an employer love me, but it can keep him from refusing to hire me because of the color of my skin. The habits if not the hearts of people have been and are being altered every day by legislative acts, judicial

decisions, and executive orders from the President. So let us not be misled by those who argue that segregation cannot be ended by the force of law. It is already being ended by legislative and executive acts presently in effect.[55]

Rejecting Henry David Thoreau's belief that humans would eventually reach a point of perfectibility, at which they would need "no government at all," King called "for an expanded role for government in the lives of individuals, so that the government as a moral agency could utilize its vast resources to provide the framework necessary for all individuals to develop as persons."[56] Also, King fully agreed with Niebuhr's contention that democracy is the best and "most desirable form of government mainly because 'it arms the individual with political and constitutional power to resist the inordinate ambition of rulers and to check the tendency of the community to achieve order at the price of liberty.'" Thus, when it came to the role of government as a force for good in "the life of man"—who embodies the "possibilities" of "the noble and base alike," who "can be true or false to his nature," and who "has within himself the power of choosing his supreme end"—King came down on the side of Niebuhrian Christian realism while rejecting the philosophical anarchism of Thoreau.[57]

Finally, King concluded that although individuals always face the possibility of living to the lowest self, this does not mean they are completely lost or beyond the possibility of redemption. Convinced that human personality is not absolutely fixed or static, that "it is dynamic, constantly growing and developing,"[58] King never surrendered a sense of the meaning of redemption and the fact that humans can be rescued from the vilest consequences of the worst in themselves, thus becoming more open to some greater good within themselves—a life of prosperity, abundance, and completeness. "But redemption can come only through a humble acknowledgment of guilt and an honest knowledge of self," King argued.[59] At another point, he noted that "salvation," which he often equated with redemption, "is an honest recognition of one's estranged and sinful condition" and that "one can never be saved until he recognizes the fact that he needs to be saved."[60] Here King had in mind what he called "a process of self-analyzation" grounded in truth:

> In this process we must ascertain what our weaknesses are. No one can ever make improvements unless he knows the points at which he is weakest. Before the wise physician gives a patient medicine he finds out where the sickness lies. The process of self-analyzation is of primary importance, for it is the open door which leads to the room of improvement. . . . After the individual has found his weakness through this process of self-analyzation he must admit that it is a weakness. Too often do we rationalize our sins by convincing ourselves that they are both healthy and normal. . . . One of the tragedies of human nature is that man has the power to adjust his mind to believe anything that he wants to. He has the power to convince himself that the wrong is right (William James), that the false is true, that the low is high, and that the bad is good. So, if we do not admit that our weaknesses are weaknesses the whole process of self-analyzation has no meaning.[61]

King here largely echoed Mohandas K. Gandhi, who believed that self-analysis is an essential path to truth about self and the relationship of self to the self, other selves, and the world and life generally.[62] But King pursued this line of thinking in his own terms, insisting that the "process of self-analyzation" is also the first in a series of steps that prepare humans to rid themselves as much as possible of the "dual personality," and especially the evil or worst self, that too often tends to define them. The other three steps King described are equally important in this regard, for they, together with the "process of self-analyzation," ultimately enable us to "actually master ourselves":

> Now that we have found our weaknesses we come to the point of getting rid of them. What procedures should we use? What steps should we take? Before answering this

question completely we must place it in a negative framework. We never get rid of our weaknesses by repressing them. This is the ringing cry of the psychiatrists. Repressed desires only lead to greater frustration and in the final analysis the problem isn't solved. . . . First, we must use the method of substitution. That is, we must find one good thing that we like to do as well as we like the evil thing, and every time we are persuaded to do the evil thing the good will overwhelm it. This means that we must not concentrate on the eradication of evil, but on the developing of virtue. To cast an evil habit out without replacing it by a good one is a purposeless procedure. . . . Secondly, we must find some profitable way to use our leisure time. We must learn to appreciate good books and learn to love great music. I'm not speaking of the type of popular books that we too often read nor the type of trashy music we too often learn to love. But I am here speaking of the type of books that have stood throughout the ages and the music that grew out of the hearts and souls of men. When we have reached this stage our lives will be well-rounded. And then we will no longer desire the evil things of life for our minds will be lost in those things which are high and noble. Finally, we may master our evil selves by developing a continuous prayer and devotional life. Through this process the soul of man will become united with the life of God.[63]

In setting forth these steps, King suggested once again that man's capacity to rise above his lowest self to a greater realization of the best within himself is ultimately a matter of getting both the heart and the head right. Convinced that "the real cause of man's problems" and "the world's ills" is traceable to "the hearts and souls of men," he predicted that "one day we will learn that the heart can never be totally right if the head is totally wrong." He continued, "This is not to say that the head can be right if the heart is wrong. Only through the bringing together of head and heart—intelligence and goodness—can man rise to a fulfillment of his true essence."[64]

As early as his student days at Boston University, King declared that humans had both a heart and head problem, and he repeatedly said in later years that this is why "we haven't learned how to be just and honest and kind and true and loving" with "all humanity."[65] Although he felt that education had a role in dealing with the head and religion the heart, he concluded that both are necessary for breaking down "the spiritual barriers" that keep individuals from overcoming the worst of the conflicted self.[66] King also reminded those who listened to his sermons that Jesus's timeless and wise words about truth and freedom were aimed at human minds and hearts and that his spirit had to pierce the darkness of both before humans could be transformed or made anew.[67]

King was thinking here about self-discovery as it relates to spirituality, or the inward journey of the self, which takes seriously truth as a vital dimension of "the spiritual ends *for* which we live."[68] For him, discovering truth about and within the person most certainly involved the head, but when exploring this in relation to the divided self, he tended to place more emphasis on the heart. Whenever King referred variously to "our entire inner life," "the inner law," "the inaudible language of the heart," "the inner voices of the soul," "an inner spiritual transformation," "an interior criteria of conduct," "the inner peace that the world can't understand," "a law written on the heart," or "the inner equilibrium" or "interior resources to confront the trials and difficulties of life," he, much like Gandhi, had in mind truth, or that spiritual power that can exude, deliver, and empower when humanity is at its worst.[69] Perhaps more than any other spiritual leader of his time, King brought the virtues of the interior life into a discussion of the steps humans might take in confronting and overcoming their lowest or worst selves.[70]

King consistently stated that the "great burden of life" is "to always try to keep that higher self in command." Drawing once again on the story of the Prodigal Son, he prayed God would "grant that" humans "will rise up out of the low, far countries of evil and return to the father's house"—"that under the spirit of Jesus the Christ" they "will choose the high way."[71] King held that this is what makes "life worth living." He also insisted that "living to our highest and best selves" is about falling in line with our "true essence" or "higher natures." While repeatedly acknowledging that "man has the capacity to do right as well as wrong," King asserted nonetheless that "his history is a path upward, not downward."[72] In other words, man's place is ultimately on the high ground, not "on the low planes of existence":

> Yet man is not made to dwell in the valleys of sin and evil; man is made for that which is high and noble. When I see how we fight vicious wars and destroy human life on bloody battlefields, I find myself saying: "Man is not made for that." When I see how we live our lives in selfishness and hate, again I say: "Man is not made for that." When I see how we often throw away the precious lives that God has given us in riotous living, again I find myself saying: "Man is not made for that." My friends, man is made for the stars, created for eternity, born for the everlasting. . . . Who this afternoon will rise out of the dark and dreary valleys of sin and evil, realizing that man's proper home is the high mountain of truth, beauty, and goodness.[73]

The core of the message King sought to get across was abundantly clear: that when it comes to the capacity to grow, develop, achieve, and be creative, humans should never limit themselves to the "'isness of today'"—that they should always push themselves toward the "'oughtness of tomorrow.'"[74] He believed "every man is capable of becoming more than he is," especially if he undergoes the proper self-examination, sufficiently disciplines himself, and lives a committed and sacrificial life. "Every man must declare war on himself," King maintained. "He must struggle to conquer his low evil and selfish nature and subject it to the higher nature." To further illustrate his point, he quoted Friedrich Nietzsche: "I look upon man as a fragment of the future."[75]

When King spoke in terms of "the dimensions of a complete life"—of the need "to rise to higher levels of self-completion"—he was far more specific about what it means to keep the "best" or "higher self in command."[76] Here King focused on the length, breadth, and height of life. The length of life for him was not about "its duration or its longevity"; rather, that dimension "in which every man seeks to develop his inner powers," with the goal of achieving his "personal ends and ambitions." While highlighting this as "perhaps the selfish dimension of life," King hastened to suggest that there is nothing inherently wrong with "moral and rational self-interest," for it can serve the best or higher self in numerous ways. An individual must first love and be concerned about himself before he can love and "be totally concerned about other selves." The proper self-concern leads the individual to discover "his calling," or "what he is made for," and this is praiseworthy to the degree that one gives "oneself to some great purpose that transcends oneself" and that one does "his job so well that the living, the dead, or the unborn could not do it better."[77] Reflecting back on the parable of the Talents in Matthew 25:14–18, King insisted that "the acme of the human spirit is for each of us to exploit our five talents, our three talents, or our one talent to his fullest potential." He could think of nothing greater than a person losing "himself in working for a great humanitarian cause," for "it is only when he loses himself that he will find himself."[78] Finally, King frequently stated that "moral and rational self-interest" is essential in "the forging of priceless qualities of character." As far back as his student days at Crozer Theological Seminary, he raised the need to "reestablish the moral and spiritual ends of living in personal character and social justice." Otherwise, he warned, "our civilization will ruin itself with the misuse of its own instruments."[79]

In underscoring character as a force in the cultivation and mastery of the best or higher self, King set forth a values argument while also calling for a commitment to basic moral and ethical norms. Here again, he assigned priority to what he termed "the essentials" or "internals of life," meaning self-respect, human dignity, love, selflessness, honesty, and integrity. He wrote, "It is tragic that so many of us make the mistake in life of being overly concerned with the externals of life, e.g., color, skin, hair, wealth, position, when really the essentials of life are the internals."[80] Most of what King said about character or life's internals related in some way to love and truth. He argued that "a higher law" is needed to produce both and that both are genuinely practiced only by those who "become possessed by that invisible, inner law" of the heart, which makes the faithful "obedient to unenforceable obligations." King turned to Harry Emerson Fosdick's "impressive distinction between enforceable and unenforceable obligations" to further clarify his point. "Enforceable obligations," which are "spelled out on thousands of law book pages," are those "which can be regulated by the codes of society and the vigorous implementation of law enforcement agencies," and "unenforceable obligations" deal "with inner attitudes, genuine person to person relations, and expressions of compassion which the law books cannot regulate and jails cannot rectify."[81] King believed that Jesus epitomized obedience to the "unenforceable" and that those who follow him must do likewise by committing themselves to the way of love and the way of truth. When man humbles himself, King thought, he opens himself to the power of love and truth, thus rising to "a fulfillment of his true nature" or to his highest or best self.[82]

Although King attached great significance to "the length of life," he was equally emphatic in asserting that this dimension alone cannot keep the best or higher self in command. Convinced that "there is nothing more tragic than to find an individual bogged down in the length of life," he encouraged an equal measure of devotion to "the breadth of life"—"that dimension of life in which we are concerned about others."[83] King found in Jesus's parable of the Good Samaritan, in Luke 10:25–37, perhaps the greatest description of this "other-regarding dimension" of life, for it tells of a man who, after encountering a Jew who had been beaten and robbed on the Jericho Road, "was moved by compassion," "administered first aid" to the wounded man, "placed him on a beast," "brought him to an inn," and "took care of him" without any desire for compensation. Noting that "the Samaritan was good because he made concern for others the first law of his life," King went on to declare that "an individual has not started living until he can rise above the narrow confines of his individualistic concerns to the broader concerns of all humanity."[84] By displaying an amazing capacity for "universal altruism," "a dangerous altruism," and "excessive altruism," the Good Samaritan, according to King, exemplified what it means to live the highest and best self and to keep that self in charge. Knowing that it was not enough to simply preach that "other-preservation is the first law of life,"[85] King, an unusually disciplined and structured man by any objective standard, desperately sought to model the Good Samaritan code of behavior he urged others to practice in their interpersonal and intergroup relations.

"The height of life," another dimension in King's sense of the triadic character of human life, is about reaching up and discovering God. He opined that establishing the dominion or supreme authority of the higher or best self invariably means breaking with "the rushing tide of materialism" and "the confused waters of secularism," making God "a power" in human life, submitting the human will "to God's will," and cooperating with God in the "divine purpose." While cautioning against "the deification of man," King himself never really doubted "man's better self being able to master his evil self." He also declared that "throughout his ministry, Jesus," too, "revealed his deep faith in the possibilities of human nature." "Jesus knew that God had given man certain creative powers and had endowed him with high and noble virtues," said King, "and that these virtues and powers could be made living realities in the life of man if he properly responded to the Grace of God."[86]

Convinced that "within the best of us, there is some evil, and within the worst of us, there is some good," King did not spend his life endlessly drawing distinctions between good and bad people.[87] This was wholly inconsistent with both his sense of mission and who he was as a human being. He never ceased to stress "the element of the good" or "the amazing potential for goodness within human nature," which makes it "possible for human beings to be transformed."[88] This firm belief in human "potentialities for goodness" was a product of King's theological and evangelical liberalism, and it was also consistent with his belief in the efficacy of nonviolence.[89] Nonviolence was a vital part of his tireless efforts to draw out the highest and best qualities in the human spirit—to appeal to people's better angels instead of their worst demons. He believed every person has "a moral imperative or a moral conscious-ness" with which he can live in harmony, and thus the capacity to respond in positive and constructive ways to the power and appeal of love and truth.[90] But when the whole of King's public life and activities are held in proper perspective, the irony is that his passion for truth and quest for the highest human-ethical ideal exposed both the best and the worst in people.

Ambivalent Nation:
The Conflicts over "Self-Evident" Truths

Martin Luther King Jr. was first introduced to America's found-ing and most sacred documents, the Declaration of Independence and the Constitution, while attending the segregated public schools of Atlanta. Mindful from childhood of the heritage of slavery in his family and sensitive to the vulnerability of Black people under the Jim Crow system in the South, he—even during those early years—was not likely to view these documents of freedom as mean-ingful and relevant for all Americans, let alone celebrate them. Undoubtedly, King's attitude toward the Declaration of Indepen-dence and the Constitution at that time was heavily influenced by the ever-present reality of white supremacy and its assault on his personal dignity and worth and by what he learned about the Black experience in American history from his teachers and elders in his family. It is also conceivable that King was impacted by his reading of the great abolitionist Frederick Douglass, his childhood idol,[91] who knew "firsthand the farce that history had made" of these cherished documents, who spoke of the Constitution at times as "a pro-slavery instrument,"[92] and who boldly declared, in his cel-ebrated speech on "The Meaning of July Fourth for the Negro" (1852), that "the great principles of political freedom and of natural justice" and the "rich inheritance of justice, liberty, prosperity, and independence bequeathed by [white America's] fathers" were not shared by people of African descent. Douglass never wavered in his conviction that the Declaration of Independence and the Constitution had been used, from their beginnings, to defend "the great lie" about the nation's stance on questions concerning humanity, freedom, natural rights, and representative democracy.[93] Many of his ideas about these matters filtered down through the generations of Blacks who followed him, for the conditions of oppression that inspired them and that insured their perpetuation remained essentially the same on many levels. Small wonder that much of the substance of what Douglass expressed regarding the country's founding documents, orally and on paper, can also be found in King's speeches and writings.

This was evident as far back as King's final year at Atlanta's Booker T. Washington High School, when he, at age fifteen, delivered a speech on "The Negro and the Constitution" (1944) at an oratorical contest sponsored by the Black Elks in Dublin, Georgia. Setting forth "a theme that would remain a major focus of his thought throughout his life," the youngster addressed the glaring "contradictions between the nation's biblical faith and constitutional values" and its enduring "problem of racial discrimination."[94] Bearing in mind the US Constitution and, more specifically, Thomas Jefferson's concept of "self-evident" truths in the Declaration of Independence, King asserted that "slavery has been a strange paradox in a nation founded on the principles that all men are created free and equal."[95] A single passage from thoughts shared in "The Negro and the Constitution" shows that he was thoroughly aware of the continuing legacy of slavery in the "land of the free," and of the conflicted notion of Blacks as American citizens:

> Black America still wears chains. . . . Even winners of our highest honors face the class color bar. Look at a few of the paradoxes that mark daily life in America. Marian Anderson was barred from singing in the Constitution Hall, ironically enough, by the professional daughters of the very men who founded this nation for liberty and equality. But this tale had a different ending. The nation rose in protest, and gave a stunning rebuke to the Daughters of the American

Revolution and a tremendous ovation to the artist, Marian Anderson, who sang in Washington on Easter Sunday and fittingly, before the Lincoln Memorial. Ranking cabinet members and a justice of the supreme court were seated about her. Seventy-five thousand people stood patiently for hours to hear a great artist at a historic moment. She sang as never before with tears in her eyes. When the words of "America" and "Nobody Knows De Trouble I Seen" rang out over that great gathering, there was a hush on the sea of uplifted faces, black and white, and a new baptism of liberty, equality and fraternity. That was a touching tribute, but Miss Anderson may not as yet spend the night in any good hotel in America. Recently she was again signally honored by being given the Bok reward as the most distinguished resident of Philadelphia. Yet she cannot be served in many of the public restaurants of her home city, even after it has declared her to be its best citizen.[96]

"The Negro and the Constitution" was essentially about making sense of the whole of the American story. Here King questioned the very idea of a nation founded and sustained on the bedrock of truth. In fact, the youngster brought his growing sense of right and wrong and of what constituted truth and untruth to bear on his reading and understanding of the content of the nation's founding documents. His yearning for a land devoted to the universal truths set forth in the Declaration of Independence and the Constitution echoes throughout "The Negro and the Constitution"—a yearning rivaled only by the personal indignation he felt after the oratorical contest, when he and his teacher, Sarah Grace Bradley, were forced to give up their bus seats to white passengers on the trip from Dublin back to Atlanta.[97] That anger carried over and found expression two years later in "Kick Up Dust," a letter King wrote to the *Atlanta Constitution*, the city's largest newspaper, in which he criticized whites who denied his people "the basic rights and opportunities of American citizens." A Morehouse College student at the time, King also published two essays in the *Maroon Tiger*, the campus newspaper, in which he strongly disagreed with those who felt that the true purpose of education is to "equip persons with the proper instruments of exploitation so they can forever trample over the masses,"[98] an observation perennially relevant to how he interpreted the country's founding documents in relation to the life experiences of his people over time. Furthermore, the experience of living in a society that proclaimed certain truths about human equality, life, and liberty while at the same time devaluing those very truths inspired King to engage in a serious intellectual search for answers. This quest was most certainly a part of the conversations he had with both his parents and professors. Given the nature of both his home and college training, he was apt to equate the lack of coherence between the values the nation cherished and how it treated people of color with blatant hypocrisy and rank untruthfulness.

While a student at Atlanta's Morehouse College, King began to engage, more intensely and in an intellectually honest manner, the question that would confront him, in one form or another, for the rest of his life: Are we as a nation who we say we are at the level of core constitutional, democratic, and Hebraic-Christian values? Already susceptible to the meaning and power of Jefferson's words—"We hold these truths to be self-evident, that all men are created equal, that they are endowed by their Creator with certain inalienable Rights, that among these are Life, Liberty, and the pursuit of Happiness"[99]—King began to probe and understand on a deeper philosophical level what had been painfully real to generations of his forebears; namely, that the United States of America was in essence a land of contradictions. King's thinking along these lines continued to evolve at Pennsylvania's Crozer Theological Seminary, where he studied the social contract theories of Thomas Hobbes and John Locke, for he found in the Enlightenment ideals of tolerance, reason, and natural law not only the language to extend his critique of the limitations of American democracy but also the conceptual framework he needed to articulate his growing appreciation of the Declaration of Independence and the Constitution.[100] At Crozer and later at Boston University in the early 1950s, King was exposed to two streams of thought that further clarified his thinking on these matters—personalism and Niebuhrian Christian realism. Personalism provided him with an angle of vision from which to assess, analytically and critically, the values of God-given human worth and dignity as expressed in the Declaration of Independence and the Constitution, and he discovered in the works of Reinhold Niebuhr insights useful for explaining America's lack of fidelity to her own sacred documents, for Niebuhr had argued as early as 1932 that "perhaps the most significant moral characteristic of a nation is its hypocrisy."[101] Although Niebuhr conceded that individuals also have tendencies toward hypocrisy, he, as King detected, made it clear that man as an individual is more prone than men as groups or nations to engage in relatively decent, moral behavior: "Individual men may be moral in the sense that they are able to consider interests other than their own in determining problems of conduct, and are capable, on occasion, of preferring the advantage of others to their own. . . . But all these achievements are more difficult, if not impossible, for human societies and social groups. In every human group there is less reason to guide and to check impulse, less capacity for self-transcendence, less ability to comprehend the needs of others and therefore more unrestrained egoism than the individuals, who compose the group, reveal in their personal relationships."[102] Due to his education, King was better prepared intellectually to understand America's historic failure to honor its promise, set forth in its founding documents, to promote civil and human rights. He was also able to bring more analytical depth and insight to his definition of America as essentially a dream deferred instead of a full-blown reality, a tendency reflected to a lesser degree in "The Negro and the Constitution."

King's most extensive critique of America's experiment in human equality, natural rights, and government of, by, and for the people—as expressed in the Declaration of Independence and the Constitution—came during his adult years, as he reflected more consciously and repeatedly on what the nation was to him as a Black man. Expanding on a theme raised much earlier in "The Negro and the Constitution," King—again evoking the image of "the schizophrenic personality"—boldly declared, "Ever since the signing of the Declaration of Independence, America has manifested a schizophrenic personality on the question of race. She has been torn between selves—a self in which she has proudly professed democracy and a self in which she has sadly practiced the antithesis of democracy. The reality of segregation, like slavery, has always had to confront the ideals of democracy and Christianity. Indeed, segregation and discrimination are strange paradoxes in a nation founded on the principle that all men are created equal."[103]

King traced this "schizophrenic personality" back to the founders of America, whose behavior around questions of race was far less than exemplary and whose politics largely accounted for "the state we are in now":

> Virtually all of the founding fathers of our nation, even those who rose to the heights of the presidency, those whom we cherish as our authentic heroes, were so enmeshed in the ethos of slavery and white supremacy that not one ever emerged with a clear, unambiguous stand on Negro rights. No human being is perfect. In our individual and collective lives every expression of greatness is followed, not by a period symbolizing completeness, but by a comma implying partialness. Following every affirmation of greatness is the conjunction "but." . . . George Washington, Thomas Jefferson, Patrick Henry, John Quincy Adams, John Calhoun and Abraham Lincoln were great men "but"—that "but" underscores the fact that not one of these men had a strong, unequivocal belief in the equality of the black man.[104]

The "ambivalent nation" and "the America dilemma" became immensely significant for King as he frequently used metaphorical language to explain the paradox of a nation aspiring "to the glories of freedom" while compromising "with prejudice and servitude." He focused in graphic terms on "the ambivalence of white America toward the Negro," an ambivalence that had grown out of its "oppressor status" and that had long "lurked with painful persistence," deeply impacting Black people over and beyond the period of slavery.[105] After suffering for centuries under "the bondage of chattel slavery," King wrote, Frederick Douglass and his people saw "all the beautiful promise" in "the Emancipation Proclamation," only to discover later that the American government had given them "abstract freedom expressed in luminous rhetoric." King went on to contrast the plight of some "four million liberated slaves"—"with no bread to eat, no land to cultivate, no shelter to cover their heads"—with that of "white settlers," who after the Civil War were granted "millions of acres of land in the West" free of charge, thus "providing America's new white peasants from Europe with an economic floor."[106] With this history in view, King would have readily agreed with W. E. B. Du Bois's eloquent description of the duality of "black self-recognition," which fluctuated "between being *in* America" but not *of* America, "from being black natives to black aliens."[107] King stated, "The inscription on the Statue of Liberty refers to America as the 'mother of exiles.' The tragedy is that while America became the mother of her white exiles, she evinced no motherly concern or love for her exiles from Africa. It is no wonder that out of despair and estrangement the Negro cries out in one of his sorrow songs: 'Sometimes I feel like a motherless child.'"[108] This slave spiritual took on a very personal meaning for King as he studied the long-term trajectory of the Black experience in America, especially the unfolding concept of Blacks as subhumans and noncitizens in the era of the Dred Scott Case (1857) as well as the disturbingly conflicted notion of Blacks as humans but second class citizens in his own time.[109]

King expanded his analysis beyond the Black experience to the broader issue of race, further illustrating his point that this same "ambivalence" has "been a constant part of our national heritage." With telling insight, he explained,

> In dealing with the ambivalence of white America, we must not overlook another form of racism that was relentlessly pursued on American shores: the physical extermination of the American Indian. The South American example of absorbing the indigenous Indian population was ignored in

the United States, and systematic destruction of a whole people was undertaken. The common phrase, "The only good Indian is a dead Indian," was virtually elevated to national policy. Thus the poisoning of the American mind was accomplished not only by acts of discrimination and exploitation but by the exaltation of murder as an expression of the courage and initiative of the pioneer. Just as Southern culture was made to appear noble by ignoring the cruelty of slavery, the conquest of the Indian was depicted as an example of bravery and progress.[110]

"Ambivalence," "hypocrisy," and "dilemma" became for King categories of social and cultural critique. King's reading of *An American Dilemma* (1944), authored by the Swedish economist Gunnar Myrdal, provided yet another source from which to denounce, in intellectual terms, the paradoxical coexistence of the American democratic creed and racial discrimination. King felt that Myrdal, due to his status as a foreigner, brought rich and unbiased insights to bear on the moral contradictions so characteristic of American democracy, thus showing that the nation's founding documents were essentially impractical in view of the problem. King repeatedly acknowledged Myrdal for identifying "the problem of race" as "America's greatest moral dilemma,"[111] and he used Myrdal's concept of "the American dilemma" to highlight the paradox of a nation that consistently professed a commitment to its highest ideals while making little or no effort to live up to those ideals.[112] King took Myrdal's analysis further, relating Myrdal's sense of "the American dilemma" to his own stirring and enduring critique of the American churches, particularly those that served what he termed "the false god of racial prejudice."[113] He also credited Myrdal with explaining how an American society conflicted about race had produced a conflicted Negro—the type of Negro who "looked to a professional life cast in the image of the middle-class white professional." According to King, this accounted for Myrdal's description of "the ambitious Negro as 'an exaggerated American.'"[114] Be that as it may, the influence of Myrdal's work was monumental from an educational standpoint, but the distinctiveness of its insights into the ambivalent character of the American spirit—and most certainly its impact on the advancement of Black rights in the decades after World War II—have probably been overstated, an issue King never really addressed.

When excoriating the "strange paradox" of American democracy, King was never interested in simply forging a narrative about the nation's past. In such instances, the past, present, and future always came together in his consciousness, as was the case with his famous "I Have a Dream" speech, delivered on the steps of the Lincoln Memorial in the nation's capital in August 1963. On that occasion, King spoke of Lincoln's signing of the Emancipation Proclamation, which "came as a great beacon light of hope to millions of Negro slaves" and "as a joyous daybreak to end the long night of their captivity"; of "the Negro" still languishing, "one hundred years later," in "the corners of American society" as an "exile in his own land"; and of his dream that "one day this nation will rise up and live out the true meaning of its creed—we hold these truths to be self-evident, that all men are created equal."[115] In King's estimation, this idea of America as "essentially a dream, a dream as yet unfulfilled"—"a dream of a land where men of all races, of all nationalities, and all creeds can live together as brothers"—had always stood in tension with the image of "an ambivalent nation" that "invoked and distorted" logic, natural science, and even the Bible and religion to give "moral sanction" and "academic respectability" to the myth that whites are inherently superior to people of color, and especially people of African ancestry. In 1967, a year before his death, King—disturbed by a government that passed civil rights legislation while refusing to implement it—acknowledged as much and more as he gave voice to his growing frustration:

Thus, through two centuries a continuous indoctrination of Americans has separated people according to mythically superior and inferior qualities while a democratic spirit of equality was evoked as the national ideal. These concepts of racism, and this schizophrenic duality of conduct, remain deeply rooted in American thought today. This tendency of the nation to take one step forward on the question of racial justice and then to take a step backward is still the pattern. Just as an ambivalent nation freed the slaves a century ago with no plan or program to make their freedom meaningful, the still ambivalent nation in 1954 declared school segregation unconstitutional with no plan to make integration real. Just as the Congress passed a civil rights bill in 1868 and refused to enforce it, the Congress passed a civil rights bill in 1964 and to this day has failed to enforce it in all its dimensions. Just as the Fifteenth Amendment in 1870 proclaimed Negro suffrage, only to permit its *de facto* withdrawal in half the nation, so in 1965 the Voting Rights Law was passed and then permitted to languish with only fractional and halfhearted implementation.[116]

It is therefore not surprising that King became increasingly doubtful that the citizenship rights of his people could be significantly advanced through the institutions or instrumentalities of the American government. He repeatedly sought to appeal to the best instincts and intentions of powerful figures in the executive, legislative, and judicial branches of government, who had taken oaths to defend the Constitution, only to discover that they lacked the moral courage to pursue and ensure freedom and justice for all through constitutional means. Noting that "the past record of the federal government" has "not been encouraging," King, in an interview in 1965, did not hesitate to criticize the US presidents with whom he had associated, especially Kennedy and Johnson. "No president has really done very much for the American Negro," King asserted, "though the past two presidents have received much undeserved credit for helping us." "The credit has accrued to Lyndon Johnson and John Kennedy only because it was during their administrations that Negroes began doing more for themselves," he continued. King referred specifically to Kennedy and Johnson's refusal to "voluntarily submit a civil rights bill" to Congress. While conceding that "Johnson did respond realistically to the signs of the times and used his skills as a legislator to get bills through Congress that other men might not have gotten through," King declared, "I must point out, in all honesty, however, that President Johnson has not been nearly so diligent in *implementing* the bills he has helped shepherd through Congress."[117] King was no less critical of congressional leaders, who, in his judgment, vacillated between their gaudy displays of patriotism and their unpatriotic stands on civil rights. He wrote, "The Negro has been betrayed by both the Democratic and Republican Party. The Democrats have betrayed us by capitulating to the whims and caprices of the southern Dixiecrats. The Republicans have betrayed us by capitulating to the blatant hypocrisy of conservative right-wing northerners." King went on to complain that "this coalition of southern Dixiecrats and right-wing northern Republicans defeats every move toward liberal legislation in Congress," thus forcing his people to choose "the lesser of two evils." Given this situation, he urged "the Negro" to "remain an independent voter, not becoming unduly tied to either party," and "to vote for the party which is more concerned with the welfare of all people."[118] With *Brown v. Board of Education Topeka* (1954) primarily in mind, King, in 1967, insisted that the Supreme Court, like the executive and legislative branches, had failed at the level of "implementation" when it came to legislation designed to guarantee civil rights: "Even the Supreme Court, despite its original courage and integrity, curbed itself only a little over a year ago after the 1954 landmark cases, when it handed down its Pupil Placement decision, in effect returning to the states the power to determine the tempo of change. This subsequent decision became the keystone in the structure that slowed school desegregation down to a crawl. Thus, America, with segregationist obstruction and majority indifference, silently nibbled away at a promise of true equality that had come before its time."[119]

King could never escape the glaring and painful reality that he, as a Black man, lived in a nation in which "false promises are daily realities" and "deferred dreams are nightly facts."[120] When he spoke of the continuing paradox of freedom in periods of human oppression and victimization, he riveted his attention not only on the race issue but also on poverty and economic injustice and war and human destruction. For King, the image of the "ambivalent nation" was applicable in these areas of human existence and experience as well. After quoting Jefferson's "self-evident" truths in the Declaration of Independence, King declared, "But if a man doesn't have a job or an income, he has neither life nor liberty nor the possibility for the pursuit of happiness. He merely exists."[121] In a similar vein, he—having observed firsthand "the gaping chasm between our proclamations of peace and our lowly deeds which precipitate and perpetuate war"—urged America to be forthright and honest rather than evasive, ambiguous, and inconsistent about her misadventure in Vietnam. "I think that it's absolutely necessary for me to extend my concern here, because at bottom I can't segregate my moral concern," King remarked. "I think we're committing a grave injustice in Vietnam," he added. "I think our policy is absolutely wrong, from a moral point of view, from a political point of view, from a practical point of view." King went on to assert, "We are engaged in a war where we are the aggressors, and I think it's necessary to say to the policy makers of our country that we are wrong. We should admit to the world that we made a tragic mistake in Vietnam."[122] He knew that America's acts of aggression and injustice against any segment of humanity, at home or abroad, undermined her claim of moral leadership in the world. "We are constantly asserting that we are on the side of angels," said King. "The world expects us to do good and to do right, since this is what we demand of everyone else."[123]

Ever mindful of America's failure to "bridge the gulf between practice and profession," between "promise and fulfillment," when it came to the edicts of her founding documents of freedom,[124] King felt that her history was essentially a tale of two societies. In other words, the nation had failed collectively and historically to live, function, and act on what he often called "hard" and "unbiased" truth. The United States of America had been founded, King believed, by white men who vacillated between proclaiming profound truths and living lives that contradicted those truths— who espoused certain "self-evident" truths about human dignity, freedom, natural rights, political equality, and the sovereignty of the people while owning and exploiting Black human beings.[125] The images of "the schizophrenic personality," "the American dilemma," and "the ambivalent nation" were King's prudent way of calling America's attention to its age-old lies about itself, its culture, its values, its history, and its heritage. Clearly, he was always cautious and indeed reticent to accuse the nation, forthrightly and publicly, of being in essence a lie—which was really what he felt in his heart and mind—because he thought this would undermine his efforts to appeal to the best in the American people.[126] Also, he did not want to risk alienating potential white allies, particularly those in power, who tended to be fierce advocates of American exceptionalism and who would not have responded graciously to such a bold, scathing, and sweeping indictment. Even so, King had his own pragmatic, skillful, and unoffensive way of explaining how Americans had long advanced a false narrative about who they have been and are as a people and of reminding them of their seemingly strange preference for easy and comfortable untruths over difficult and painful truths. He lamented the fact that white Americans particularly were too often consumed by their legions of fictional stories, half-truths, false history, wild exaggerations, and distorted myths, all of which led them to think of themselves as the messiahs of the world.[127]

King never hesitated to speak to the consequential nature of what not living up to time-honored and professed truths could be. He held that when a nation withholds truth from itself or chooses to live with or immerse itself in untruths, it loses touch with its history, its identity, and ultimately its sense of reality. In other words, it enslaves itself. Perhaps more importantly, King thought, becoming captive to falsehoods eventually corrodes the spirit and soul of a nation. He viewed hypocrisy and untruth as paths to "moral degeneration" and "a tragic death of the spirit" and "moral maturity" and "the forces of spiritual might" as fruits of unadulterated truth.[128] This view yields insight into King's oft-repeated proclamations about the need to "redeem" and "save the soul of America," for he regarded this as a precondition for the nation learning to live with its conscience.[129] As he studied the cultural and social land-scape of America, he saw a nation in precipitous decline, a nation in danger of becoming what he labeled "a soulless society,"[130] pre-cisely because she, in defiance of her own expressed constitutional ideals and values, was engaged in the subversion rather than the affirmation and advancement of participatory democracy. In King's opinion, if America continued to pursue such a path, it would become like many great nations that preceded her—nations whose "bleached bones" remained as a sad commentary on their refusal to hear "words of truth" about violence and humans' inhumanity to humans.[131] Always a sharp and perceptive critic of America's ambiv-alence, his message to his fellow citizens was quite simple, pointed, and marked by a deep sense of urgency—that God would not long tolerate lying words, let alone lying deeds.

When King turned to his native South, he witnessed some of the worst aspects of the American temperament in magnified form. He detected more than a trace of irony in the fact that white south-erners, whose history was heavily disfigured by their total invest-ment in plantation slavery and deep-seated white supremacy, had for generations contrasted themselves with the rest of the nation's population, confidently claiming to be the most patriotic, religious, and virtuous of the American people. King knew that such claims were starkly contradicted by the white South's posture of "interpo-sition and nullification" when it came to living out the terms of the nation's founding documents, by its insistence that federal inter-vention to assure constitutional rights for all violated states' rights, by its refusal to practice unequivocally New Testament–based con-ceptions of agape love and altruism in its behavior toward people of color, and by its ubiquitous and seemingly unashamedly embrace of what it considered to be a divinely ordained system of white supremacy and racial segregation.[132] King also understood that the South had scarred the nation with some of the greatest horrors in human history—from the deliberate break up of African fami-lies to slave breeding to countless incidents of violent lynching—and that it was probably more representative of the "ambivalent America" than any other region of the country.[133] Knowing that the South had long been infected with a homicidal poison due to white supremacy and that the region was awash with hypocrisy and, consequently, moral and spiritual perversion, King was more likely to consider it the gun belt or the lynching belt than the "Bible Belt."

The South figured prominently in much of what King said and wrote about truth, untruth, and the human condition.[134] For much of his life, he witnessed firsthand "closeminded reactionaries" throughout the region, who clearly lacked integrity, gaining "prominence and power by the dissemination of false ideas and by deliberately appealing to the deepest hate responses within the human mind."[135] Much of his sharpest critique of society targeted white southerners who "blindly believe in the eternal validity of an evil called segregation and the timeless truth of a myth called white supremacy."[136] To explain the self-imposed blindness and indeed the "spiritual myopia" that grounded such racially driven falsehoods, King turned to "the great philosopher-psychologist" William James's concept of "the stream of consciousness," which holds that "one of the unique things about human nature is that man can temporarily block the stream of consciousness and place anything in it that he wants to," thus convincing himself that "the wrong is right."[137] Challenging the widely held narrative about race among white southerners, King argued that it was "neither true nor honest to say that the Negro's status is what it is because he is innately inferior or because he is basically lazy and listless or because he has not sought to lift himself by his own bootstraps."[138] He opined that white supremacist and Jim Crow policies and practices—supercharged by the toxic and unhinged rhetoric of the likes of Ross Barnett, George Wallace, and Lester Maddox, who achieved folk hero status among the most vicious racists—revealed that the white South lived by the ethic of untruth rather than the biblical principle of *imago Dei* and the Jeffersonian idea of "self-evident" truths. Lies about race had been told for so long by white southerners, King reasoned, that they had become not only truth in the minds of the weak, thoughtless, and gullible but empowered and even weaponized against the best interest of the very society that had learned to accept and live with them.[139] He concluded that "the perpetuation" of the South's "archaic, dying order" was "hindering its rapid growth." "Yet they cannot speak this truth—they are imprisoned by their own lies," King declared. "It is history's rare paradox that when Negroes win their struggle to be free those who have held them down will themselves be freed for the first time."[140]

While deeply concerned about the white South's peddling or trafficking in untruth, King was even more disturbed by its use of falsehoods as a means to certain desired ends, which involved sustaining a master race ethos and a pervasive culture of Jim Crow "as the expression of a final truth."[141] He knew that in such a climate "justice is a lie," truth has no real meaning, and the ordinary conventions of participatory and representative democracy are undermined and even distorted. "I cannot cooperate with this evil system in any form," King asserted, as he cast a critical eye across the entire South. "I take this position because of my devotion to democracy, justice, and truth."[142] Perhaps he was even more repelled by white men, many of whom were "good church people" and even ministers, who defended the old order of the South on theological grounds, arguing that God was not only white but "the first segregationist." "The greatest blasphemy of the whole ugly process," King wrote, "was that the white man ended up making God his partner in the exploitation of the Negro." "What greater heresy has religion known?" he asked. Under such circumstances, King further noted, "ethical Christianity vanished and the moral nerve of religion was atrophied." He was convinced that "this terrible distortion sullied the essential nature of Christianity."[143] Knowing that there is no binary choice when it comes to speaking, living, and acting on truth, he could only conclude that the South, as it existed in his time, was ill-prepared to follow the path of truth—that it was in fact the classic study in profound contradictions.

King often said that unchecked evil is always contagious,[144] a statement that was quite meaningful, since Blacks, too, had been forced by circumstance to accept, live by, and even act on the South's ethic of untruth. Much like their slave forebears, southern Blacks in the era of Jim Crow often "had to lie to live."[145] King knew this as well as any student of American history. Based on his study of the period of slavery, the stories he was told as a child by his elders, and his own experiences with ex-slaves and their descendants while growing up and later struggling for freedom in Georgia and other parts of the South, King understood that his people had always confronted a certain tension between honoring the moral obligation to tell the truth while at the same time being forced, for the sake of their safety and survival, to be deceptive and even untruthful in their dealings with white people.[146] The sheer ingenuity displayed by Blacks in such encounters had been captured from slavery times in the endless cycle of trickster tales and especially the adventures of Brer Rabbit, in which the weak survive by taking advantage of the strong through shrewdness, deception, and lies.[147] Acquainted on a personal level with William J. Faulkner—the African American clergyman, educator, and major collector of the Brer Rabbit and other slave tales—King undoubtedly knew about these tales and valued them as both art and a record of the effects of slavery and Jim Crow on the behavior of Blacks.[148] Furthermore, the grinning and scratching associated with "the vacuous, happy-go-lucky Sambo image" during slavery also carried over into the age of southern Jim Crow, as Blacks themselves became in some ways reflections of an ambivalent South and, more generally, "an ambivalent nation."[149] Thus, King concluded that "the image of the Negro in American culture reflects a bewildering paradox."[150]

The "contradictory images" of Blacks under the yoke of oppression struck King as complex but not necessarily illogical, especially in view of his people's reptilian survival instinct, their awareness of the penalty for being truthful, and the absence of sufficient veils of protection. "To understand how two sharply contrasting images can exist," he explained, "requires an understanding of how truth and falsehood have been manipulated for centuries as a part of the unending conflict Negroes experienced in their quest for the attainment of human dignity."[151] Even so, King never meant to suggest that within the context of the "hard core" and "troubled South," Blacks had become carbon copies or pale facsimiles of whites. He could see that Blacks, unlike whites, were able to make sense of their need to lie as a survival strategy without establishing such behavior as the standard to follow in all instances or without fashioning what might be called a counter-Christian ethic.[152] Also, King recognized that Blacks and whites never developed a shared conception of what constituted truth, untruth, and reality and that lying and deceit gave Blacks some control over their immediate surroundings while allowing them to mask their true character and intentions in the face of adversity and the capriciousness of life. It is therefore not surprising that white southerners had mixed feelings about what Blacks really wanted, and some were led to believe that "the black man was content"—"that Negroes endure abuse without pain":

> For years, in the South, the white segregationist has been saying the Negro was "satisfied." He has claimed "we get along beautifully with our Negroes because we understand them. We only have trouble when outside agitators come in and stir it up." Many expressed this point of view knowing that it was a lie of majestic proportions. Others believed they were telling the truth. For corroboration, they would tell you: "Why, I talked to my cook and she said . . ." or, "I discussed this frankly with the colored boy who works for us and I told him to express himself freely. He said. . . ." White people in the South may never fully know the extent to which Negroes defended themselves and protected their jobs— and, in many cases, their lives—by perfecting an air of ignorance and agreement. In days gone by, no cook would have dared to tell her employer what he ought to know. She had to tell him what he wanted to hear. She knew that the penalty for speaking the truth could be the loss of her job.[153]

King brought to the question of Black behavioral patterns in the context of oppression a broad frame of understanding and insight. Although he refused to embrace deceit and lying as part of his own personal ethic, or of his sense of what amounted to the best norms of human conduct, he understood nonetheless that "the dilemma of the Negro,"[154] as he described it, left his people essentially no other choice. King believed the proper answer to the problems arising out of this dilemma was not only evident but incontrovertible, for there had to be a more genuine commitment to changing for the better the totality of those conditions that make persons untrue to themselves and others. He insisted, more specifically, that it was not enough to be merely "concerned with men being true and honest"—that society also had to be "concerned with the economic conditions that made them dishonest and the social conditions that make them untrue." King advanced this same argument in Hebraic-Christian terms, noting that the challenge ultimately involved changing both the souls of individuals and of the society in which they live and function daily. This was, as he put it, Christianity's "two-way road." King determined that there was no principled way to "be concerned with the souls of men" while remaining unconcerned "with the conditions that damn their souls."[155]

Perhaps the most glaring shortcoming of King's critical analysis of "the ambivalent nation" was his failure to bring into focus the problem of sexism and the historic plight of women. This failure on his part must be understood largely in the context of the times in which he lived and functioned, but it is clear nonetheless that it reflected not only the ambivalence of America but the ambivalent side of the freedom struggle King and others led as well. It is illogical to attribute the absence of women from King's critique of "the ambivalent nation" simply to an oversight on his part, for he evidently had a sense of the evils of female subordination,[156] and he even acknowledged the impact of earlier episodes of the women's liberation movement on the civil rights struggle of the 1950s and '60s.[157] The question remains: How could a normal, rational, and conscientious man completely overlook the ways in which the treatment of women over time conflicted with the nation's founding and most cherished democratic principles?

Being True to What Is Said on Paper: Reenvisioning America

Martin Luther King Jr. was always in a dialectical conversation between the nation's past and its present, and when it came to

America's refusal to honor the words expressed in the Declaration of Independence and the Constitution, he recognized how its past was also reflected in its present.[158] With the content of these founding documents of freedom in mind, he determined that the image America projected of herself as a nation had always been a strange mixture of truth and untruth; that truth and untruth had always functioned side by side in the American psyche. This invariably meant that even American exceptionalism, as articulated by many during King's time, had to be understood in view of what was both true and untrue about the nation. King was concerned that all too many Americans, and especially those who embraced an unenlightened and uncritical patriotism, were unwilling to come to terms with the gloomy side of American exceptionalism.

King had a very nuanced understanding of the complexities of American history and of the nation's founding documents of freedom. He knew that the framers of the Declaration and Constitution were, like all humans, creatures of contradiction and that the Constitution at the time it was written had declared that "the Negro was 60 percent of a person,"[159] but he valued certain ideas and ideals expressed in these treasured documents. They were, aside from the Bible, the sources he most often invoked to not only excoriate America for her hypocrisy but explain, validate, and advance a movement for freedom, justice, and human community.[160] In King's estimation, the movement he and others led affirmed, in both principle and practice, the "self-evident truths" proclaimed in the Declaration, and its goals were consistent with what the Constitution said about forming "a more perfect union," establishing "justice," insuring "domestic tranquility," providing "for the common defense," promoting "the general welfare," and insuring "the blessings of liberty to ourselves and our posterity." Thus, when it came to these documents of freedom, what mattered most to King was not so much the original intent of the founding fathers but rather the ways in which the principles embodied in those documents could best be universalized over time.[161] In other words, he, as Sylvester Johnson puts it, "made ambivalent but mostly positive recourse to these 'sacred' texts."[162] In repeatedly saying that "the goal of America is freedom," King evoked a particular myth that found expression not only in the Declaration of Independence and the Constitution but also in the Emancipation Proclamation. "Freedom," for King, became America's mythic meaning and ideal.[163]

King discovered in the Declaration and the Constitution the same basic values and norms that permeated Black religion, literature, and art and that were also consistent with what he termed "the sublime principles of the Judeo-Christian tradition."[164] Here he thought primarily of basic democratic norms and values such as freedom, justice, human dignity, and a natural rights tradition. In his appeal to the Declaration and the Constitution, he embraced a time-honored tradition that extended back to Frederick Douglass and countless other Black leaders. But King was seemingly more of a sentimentalist than a hardheaded realist at this point because the "all men are created equal" and the "certain inalienable rights" language of the Declaration, for example, included whites but not Black people. King conceded as much and more during the last year of his life, when he, having become increasingly radicalized, asserted that the Declaration of Independence "has never had any real meaning in terms of implementation in our lives."[165] Even so, King, mindful that both the Declaration and the Constitution had long been warped and stretched in the service of white supremacy, never felt that these most hallowed documents of freedom should be totally rejected by Blacks, nor that the democratic traditions they affirmed were irrelevant to his people's struggle for liberation and empowerment. He made this clear in his famous "I Have a Dream" speech, which was something more than a Kingian version of the Gettysburg Address. In that compelling moment in August 1963, King used his platform to, in Lincolnian terms, "appeal to the nation's better angels" instead of its worst demons: "When the architects of our republic wrote the magnificent words of the Constitution and the Declaration of Independence, they were signing a promissory note to which every American was to fall heir. This note was a promise that all men, *yes*, black men as well as white men, would be guaranteed the unalienable rights of 'life, liberty, and the pursuit of happiness.'"[166]

Interestingly, Thomas Jefferson's "self-evident" truths about "all men" being "created equal" and having "certain inalienable rights" such as "life, liberty, and pursuit of happiness" cut deeply into King's mind and soul, which explains why he quoted Jefferson's words more than any other part of the nation's founding documents.[167] When Jefferson penned these majestic words, King frequently stated, "the first government of the world to be based on" the "theory of natural rights," the "justification of revolution," and the "ideal of a society governed by the people" was "established on American soil."[168] Jefferson's words, according to King, also amounted to "a profound, eloquent and unequivocal expression of the dignity and worth of all human personality," thus affirming a concept King inherited from both Black church traditions and Boston personalism.[169] King went on to maintain that "the amazing universalism" and the "inviolable character of personal rights" expressed in the Declaration of Independence provided theoretical support for his practical quest for the beloved community, or the completely integrated society and world.[170] King had much more than a rhetorical device or strategy in mind when invoking Jefferson's affirmation of certain "self-evident" truths in the Declaration.

When it came to the ongoing quest to "enlarge the democratic vistas of our nation" or to extend the fruits of freedom, justice, and equality, King was particularly interested in how Jefferson's concept of "self-evident" truths informed not only the Constitution but also other cherished documents of freedom. This became increasingly apparent in 1962–63, as King called the nation's attention to the centennial of the Emancipation Proclamation. He made several speeches and wrote newspaper articles on the subject. Drawing on Frederick Douglass's insights on "the world significance of the Emancipation Proclamation," King called that document "the offspring of the Declaration of Independence" and reported that "it used the force of law to uproot a social order which sought to separate liberty from a segment of humanity."[171] He regarded the Emancipation Proclamation, signed by President Abraham Lincoln in 1863, as America's third major document of freedom and a document designed to redeem the truths and to reaffirm the notion of rights established earlier in the Declaration and the Constitution. "For King," writes Coleman B. Brown, "Lincoln's Emancipation Proclamation—confirmed and extended by the 13th, 14th, and 15th Amendments—was both integral and essential to the 'sacred' American obligation entered upon in the Declaration of Independence and the Constitution."[172]

But even as King extolled the values of the Emancipation Proclamation, he did not hesitate to point out that it was, much like the Declaration and the Constitution, yet another reflection of "America's chief moral dilemma"—of the character of "an ambivalent nation." "Morally, Lincoln was for black emancipation," King explained, "but emotionally, like most of his white contemporaries, he was for a long time unable to act in accordance with his conscience." King spoke "on the one hand" about "the spirit of Lincoln"—"that spirit born of the teachings of the Nazarene, who promised mercy to the merciful, who lifted the lowly, strengthened the weak, ate with publicans, and made the captives free"—but on the other, he labeled Lincoln "a vacillating president," noting that his "torments and vacillations" on slavery "were tenacious" and that his signing of the Emancipation Proclamation was driven more by political ambition and expediency than by moral convictions and considerations.[173] King further elaborated,

A civil war raged within Lincoln's soul, a tension between the Dr. Jekyll of freedom and the Mr. Hyde of slavery, a struggle like that of Plato's charioteer with two headstrong horses each pulling in different directions. . . . But Lincoln was basically honest and willing to admit his confusions. He saw that the nation could not survive half slave and half free; and he said, "If we could first know where we are and whither we are tending, we could better judge what to do and how to do it." Fortunately for the nation, he finally came to see "whither we are tending." On January 1, 1863, he issued the Emancipation Proclamation, freeing the Negro from the bondage of chattel slavery. By this concrete act of courage his reservations of the past were overshadowed. The conclusion of his search is embodied in these words: "In giving freedom to the slave, we assure freedom to the free,—honourable alike is what we give and what we preserve."[174]

As far as King was concerned, the Emancipation Proclamation became as much an act of disappointment as a symbol of hope, for it accepted Black people as a legal fact while not embracing them as human beings and first-class citizens with the same rights as white Americans. "What the Emancipation Proclamation proscribed in a legal and formal sense," King complained, "has never been eliminated in human terms."[175] While he agreed that the centennial anniversary of this historic document should be celebrated, he, quoting President Lyndon B. Johnson, reminded America that "Emancipation was a Proclamation but not a fact": "But one hundred years later, the Negro still is not free. One hundred years later, the life of the Negro is still sadly crippled by the manacles of segregation and the chains of discrimination. One hundred years later, the Negro lives in a lonely island of poverty in the midst of a vast ocean of material prosperity. One hundred years later, the Negro is still languished in the corners of American society and finds himself an exile in his own land."[176]

King was never naive nor romantic when considering the significance of the Emancipation Proclamation, or any other national document of freedom for that matter, in the lives of Black people. Drawing on biblical imagery, he acknowledged that "the Emancipation Proclamation" brought his people "nearer to the Red Sea, but it did not guarantee" their "passage through parted waters" and ultimately into the Promised Land.[177] In King's thinking, the power and efficacy of that document had been woefully undermined as far back as the Supreme Court's "separate but equal" doctrine in *Plessy v. Ferguson* in 1896. Furthermore, its essential meaning and significance, he held, had been continuously ignored since that time by leaders at the highest levels of the nation's political life, and especially by "the pharaohs of the South," who turned to "legal maneuvers, economic reprisals, and even physical violence to hold the Negro in the Egypt of segregation."[178] Consequently, King could logically speak of "the Negro revolution" as a protracted and sustained effort to actualize the promises made in America's greatest political documents. "It was courageous" and "epic," said King of the freedom movement, and he reasoned that it fitted squarely "in the American tradition, a much-delayed salute to the Bill of Rights, the Declaration of Independence, the Constitution, and the Emancipation Proclamation."[179]

King's appeals to the Declaration of Independence, the Constitution, and the Emancipation Proclamation were heavily informed by his religious faith. His rhetoric of freedom, of civil and human rights, was designed to bring the nation in line with the truths set forth in not only these cherished texts but the Bible as well. "All we say to America," commented King in his very last speech, is "be true to what you said on paper."[180] At other points, he, thinking and speaking more consciously as a clergyman and a theologian, put his hope for America in the form of a prayer: "God grant that America" will "hold true to her dreams" and "ideals."[181] He acted here largely in a priestly capacity, as he spoke to the heart and soul of a nation afflicted and wounded by racial strife, economic disparities, militarism, and violence and human destruction. His was a call to conscience and high ideals, to a more genuine sense of loyalty and tradition, and to honesty, decency, and rationality, all of which were, in his opinion, keys to reshaping the narrative about a nation whose history was steeped in contradictions, hypocrisy, and the lack of a shared commitment to truth.

It was King's wish that all freedom-loving Americans would join him in "continuing the noble journey toward the goals reflected" in America's founding principles, which he almost always identified with the Jeffersonian definition of "self-evident" truths.[182] He understood that America's story was still unfolding toward the ideal of a more perfect union but that the obstacles and challenges ahead would not be easily met and surmounted. This was a vital part of his public messaging strategy. Convinced that truth was essential to the workings of democracy, and especially to America's survival as a democratic republic, King urged American citizens of every background and persuasion to recommit themselves to "the Founding Fathers' dream"—to find new and creative ways to struggle for a more perfect union, because he knew that "the honor of the nation which we love" is at stake.[183] The age in which King lived yielded hopeful signs of the rise of a true Americanism—a national spirit consistent with what Jefferson asserted in the Declaration of Independence. Thus, King could believe in the possibility that "America will be truly America." To those who doubted that such would be the case, he offered an unequivocal and resounding affirmation of what he envisioned as "a new birth of freedom": "We will win our freedom because the sacred heritage of our nation and the eternal will of God are embodied in our echoing demands."[184]

4

Courageous Maladjustment

Speaking Truth to Power

History still has a choice place for those who have the moral courage
to be maladjusted. The salvation of the world lies in the hands of the
maladjusted. The challenge to you is to be maladjusted; as maladjusted as the prophet Amos, who, in the midst of the injustices of his day,
could cry out in words that echo across the centuries, "Let judgement
run down like waters and righteousness like a mighty stream . . ."

—Martin Luther King Jr.,
"The Cause of the 'Maladjusted'" (1956)

Sometimes it seem like to tell the truth today is to run the risk of
being killed. But if I fall, I'll fall five feet four inches forward in the
fight for freedom. I'm not backing off.

—Fannie Lou Hamer,
"Sick and Tired of Being Sick and Tired" (1968)

Martin Luther King Jr. was a man driven and guided by the blazing and penetrating light of truth. Truth empowered the words he

149

spoke in pulpit and on platform, saturated the thoughts he committed to books and essays, and animated the most heartfelt concerns he shared in public interviews and in letters he exchanged with dignitaries and supporters. Truth permeated the conversations he had with family, friends, comrades in the struggle, and the common, ordinary people he encountered daily. King's spirit was sustained by the range of his encounters and involvements with people at all levels of society—people who respected the humility with which he pursued truth, who admired the depth of his commitment to truth and truth-telling, and who shared his belief that truth should always find expression in word, thought, and deed. King lived as if any serious engagement with truth as a universal and all-pervading force required meaningful connections to and associations with people of all backgrounds. Thus, he was equipped—intellectually, morally, spiritually, and psychologically—to more effectively deal with much of the loneliness that so often haunts the avid seeker and proclaimer of truth.[1]

This chapter extends the discussion in chapter 3 by exploring King's messaging strategy as it unfolded around truth and truth-telling from a different angle. The primary focus is on King as an ethical prophet who felt divinely called and inspired to speak truth to institutions and structures of power and evil in high places.[2] The chapter opens with some attention to King's roots in a family and church tradition that affirmed, in word and deed, the critical need to witness to truth in any form and at all costs—a tradition grounded in the Black experience and in a certain reading of the ancient Hebrew prophets, the life of Jesus, and the apostolic church.[3] King's emergence as a church pastor and civil rights leader in Montgomery, Alabama, in the mid-1950s is considered, especially since that was the point at which he was compelled to ask himself the question that essentially defined his role as an ethical prophet: when and how to speak truth to power that is fundamentally evil and untruthful.[4] The kitchen vision King experienced in the early stages of the Montgomery bus boycott—during which "an inner voice" told him to "stand up for truth, and God will be at your side forever"[5]—is treated here as the critical spiritual leap toward an answer to this and other probing questions regarding his own prophetic leadership and the prophetic role in general. His constructive critique of powerful forces such as mass media outlets, white supremacist organizations, political advocacy groups, governmental officials, the judicial system, and Christian churches around their failure to pursue truth as a guiding principle is discussed. Of special significance is King's understanding of the prophet's role as "a witness for truth" and as involving the shouldering of a cross,[6] which developed largely out of a careful reading of parts of both the Hebrew Bible and the New Testament. The chapter ends with some attention to King's challenge to the people of God around the need to reclaim "the prophetic way"[7] as the key to much-needed church renewal and the revitalization of the spiritual life.

Answering a Call: Becoming an Ethical Prophet

Martin Luther King Jr.'s determination to speak truth to power firmly established him in "the prophetic strand of the black Christian tradition."[8] He was the descendant of a long line of clergymen and leaders whose passionate regard for truth and truth-telling as a sacred duty led them to courageously challenge the powers that be in the interest of freedom, justice, human dignity, equality of opportunity, and peace. King's maternal grandfather, Adam D. Williams, who pastored Atlanta's Ebenezer Baptist Church from 1894 to 1931, personified this prophetic spirit in ways that inspired his son-in-law and King Jr.'s father, Martin Luther King Sr., who followed Williams as Ebenezer's pastor. In an age when Blacks were mercilessly lynched, Williams called for racial justice and fought for the rights of his people under the auspices of organizations such as the Georgia Equal Rights League (GERL) and the National Association for the Advancement of Colored People (NAACP). He participated in voter registration rallies, led Atlanta's Black community in a boycott of local stores and businesses that used racial epithets when referring to Blacks, and spearheaded efforts to halt a municipal bond issue because it lacked provisions for Black high school education. It is not difficult to imagine how Williams was viewed and treated by whites, but he persevered in his assault on injustice and refused categorically to allow himself or Ebenezer Baptist Church to become a tool of the status quo and the white power structure.[9] Although Williams died in 1931, when King Jr. was only two years old, memories of him lingered in family circles,[10] and he conceivably figured into his grandson's later reflections on what it meant to be an ethical leader and indeed a prophet.

King Sr., known widely as Daddy King, closely followed the same prophetic path his father-in-law tread when it came to speaking truth to power and challenging ruling elites, and he too was known and highly regarded for his devotion to "moral and ethical principles."[11] Like Williams, King Sr. served as president of the Atlanta branch of the NAACP and used that position, Ebenezer Baptist Church, and other platforms to attack southern Jim Crow boldly at all levels and to challenge structures and institutions that marginalized and excluded Blacks. Constantly threatened by the forces of raw white power, King Sr.'s sermons were always saturated with righteous discontent and anger and at times prophetic fury. Reflecting on his father's activism in 1961, years later, King Jr. stated, "He has had an actual interest in civil rights across the years"—"he has always stood out in social reform."[12] He said on other occasions that Daddy King "had wielded great influence in the Negro community, and had perhaps won the grudging respect of the whites."[13] Daddy King's habit of stating truth in an unvarnished manner and of leveling with people, including racist and powerful white southern politicians and law enforcement officers, left a lasting impression on his son. "I have rarely ever met a person more fearless and courageous than my father," King Jr. reported, "notwithstanding the fact that he feared for me." Of Daddy King, King Jr. went on to note, "He never feared the autocratic and brutal person in the white community. If they said something to him that was insulting, he made it clear in no uncertain terms that he didn't like it." King Jr. was often amazed that his father was never physically attacked by the Ku Klux Klan (KKK) and other white supremacists groups, "a fact that filled my brother and sister and me with wonder as we grew up in this tension-packed atmosphere."[14]

He came to see that truth had been the animating factor in the life and social justice activism of his father, and he also recognized in him the very qualities he would later identify with and expect of great prophets.[15]

But the larger prophetic tradition intrigued King from his Morehouse College years forward—that tradition that stretched back to Amos, Jeremiah, Isaiah, and the other ancient Hebrew prophets. Undoubtedly, King's father occasionally preached about these legendary figures, and there was much in his own personal history to remind the younger King of the Hebrew prophets. While at Morehouse, King studied the Hebrew prophets at great length with Professor George D. Kelsey for the first time, and what he learned about these visionaries of ancient Israel—along with influences such as his father, Kelsey, and Benjamin Mays—significantly shaped his life and his concept of ministry at its best.[16] King wrote most of his papers on the prophets during his seminary and graduate school years. At Crozer Theological Seminary, where he took a course on the Hebrew prophets with Professor James B. Pritchard, King wrote a paper on Jeremiah's "public pietism"—placing special emphasis on the prophet's sense of "social responsibility," "his public exposure," and "the extreme isolation in which he experiences the transforming encounter with the divine"—but he appeared to be most interested in Jeremiah's commitment to truth and his denunciation of religious hypocrisy and false religion. There is some indication here of how King read the Hebrew prophets in general, especially in terms of their great ethical principles.[17] On note cards and in examinations at Boston University, he focused on ethical insights derived from Amos and Hosea. Highlighting Amos's stress on "the deep ethical nature of God," King declared that for the prophet, "God is a God that demands justice rather than sacrifice; righteousness rather than ritual." "For Hosea," he wrote, "God is a God of love, and even his justice is but an expression of his love."[18] The impact of King's father and the Ebenezer Church tradition, mentors such as Kelsey and Mays, and Walter Rauschenbusch and the Social Gospel on this approach to the Hebrew prophets was unmistakable.

The Hebrew prophets took on added significance for King after he emerged to prominence as a civil and human rights activist, for they were among the intellectual and spiritual sources he needed most to explain, justify, and legitimate a crusade for a better nation and world. The prophets undoubtedly came to mind whenever King thought of persons who faced the inadequacies of the old established orders throughout human history with what he termed "a divine dissatisfaction," or "a sort of divine discontent."[19] Referring to the prophets as "ethical giants," as "those most extraordinary men of history," King explained how they were driven by the dictates of conscience to cry out against the "evils" and "hypocrisy" of Hebrew society, to declare that its "disobedience" would lead to its downfall, and to transform God's people for the better, even under the risk of attack and the threat of death. Of the Hebrew prophets, King further noted, "They did not believe that conscience is a still small voice. They believed that conscience thunders or it does not speak at all." "They were bold, courageous, and uncompromising," he added, "attacking injustice and corruption" with "unpopular messages" grounded in truth.[20]

Amos seems to have been King's favorite among the Hebrew prophets, or the prophet he most frequently quoted. References to Amos 5:24, quoted at other points in this volume, appear repeatedly in his sermons and speeches. As with the other Hebrew prophets, King most certainly appreciated Amos's attack on the neglect of divine laws as they related to social justice and social responsibility, but he was most intrigued and inspired by Amos's concern for the widening disparity between the excessively rich and the extremely poor. Amos epitomized ethical leadership, and he, like the other prophets, reminded King that when it came to speaking truth to power, there was no essential distinction between ethical leadership and prophetic leadership.

King was thoroughly impressed with the Hebrew prophets' refusal to mince words and with their impeccable reputation as faithful and fearless bearers, tellers, and sharers of truth. In King's judgment, the prophets were harbingers of divine revelation, of the truths of Old Testament prophecy. He felt that nothing could have prevented "Amos and Hosea, Ezekiel, Isaiah and Jeremiah from standing up amid forces of religious idolatry and unjust power structures and declaring with prophetic urgency the eternal word of God, and the never ceasing necessity of being obedient to his will."[21] Although King was equally generous at times in praising the ancient Greek philosophers as messengers of truth, the prophets for him were different because they were divinely called and inspired with the task of revealing the demanding truths of God's message to the people and because they majored in the rhetoric of discontent and judgment. In King's thinking, prophetic rhetoric was always the rhetoric of discontent and judgment, but never to the exclusion of the rhetoric of hope and redemption.

The rhetorical content, style, and strategy of the Hebrew prophets had long established them as aberrant, marked figures in human history. King understood this, but in his opinion, this only heightened their significance as proclaimers of truth. King described the prophets as "transformed nonconformists" and "extremists" for "justice" and "truth"—and he used terms like "creative nonconformity" and "courageous maladjustment" in characterizing their refusal to bow to the seductive power of the status quo.[22] But in his letter to the eight Alabama clergymen in 1963, King dismissed any suggestion that "the prophets of the eighth century B.C." were "outsiders," insisting that they were justified in carrying "their 'thus saith the Lord' far beyond the boundaries of their hometowns."[23] They paid a steep price for their unwavering devotion to truth, he argued, for the "same religious community that produced the prophets also produced the conservative religious forces which stoned the prophets to death." They were "crucified men," King added, "because they stood up for right."[24]

King felt there was a certain timelessness about the values to which the Hebrew prophets committed their lives. Although he understood the specific links between the prophets and the Jews' spiritual, moral, and cultural commitment to social justice concerns down through the ages, he, in a speech at the Synagogue Council of America in New York in December 1965, spoke at great length about the relevance of these ancient voices of truth for humans everywhere in his own time:

The Hebrew prophets belong to all people because their concepts of justice and equality have become ideals for all races and civilizations. Today we particularly need the Hebrew prophets because they taught that to love God was to love justice; that each human being has an inescapable obligation to denounce evil where he sees it and to defy a ruler who commands him to break the covenant. . . . The Hebrew prophets are needed today because decent people must be imbued with the courage to speak the truth, to realize that silence may temporarily preserve status or security but to live with a lie is a gross affront to God. . . . The Hebrew prophets are needed today because we need their flaming courage; we need them because the thunder of their fearless voices is the only sound stronger than the blasts of bombs and the clamour of war hysteria. . . . The Hebrew prophets are needed today because Amos said in words that echo across the centuries, "Let justice roll down like the waters, and righteousness as a mighty stream"; because Micah said, in words lifted to cosmic proportions, "They shall beat their swords into pruning hooks, nation shall not lift up sword against nation, neither shall they learn war anymore." Because Isaiah said, "Yea when ye make many prayers, I will not hear; your hands are full of blood. Wash you, make you clean; put away the evil of your doings from before mine eyes. Cease to do evil. . . ." I think the Hebrew prophets are among us today because although there are many pulpits that are empty while ministers physically occupy them there are others from which the passion for justice and compassion for man is still heard. In the days to come as the voices of sanity multiply we will know that across thousands of years of time the prophet's message of truth and decency, brotherhood and peace survives; that they are living in our time to give hope to a tortured world that their promise of the Kingdom of God has not been lost to mankind.[25]

Kenneth L. Smith and Ira G. Zepp Jr. contend that "the Hebrew prophets influenced King more than any other part of Scripture with the exception of the Sermon on the Mount."[26] Much of that influence filtered down to King through Jesus and the early Christians, for King shared Rauschenbusch's view that Jesus Christ and the apostolic church stood squarely in the tradition of the Old Testament prophets.[27] King held that Jesus and the early Christians, much like the prophets, were "nonconformists" or "maladjusted personalities" and that they were also "extremists" for justice, righteousness, and truth.[28] While King's deep indebtedness to these Hebraic-Christian sources and traditions was undeniable, his tendency to equate prophetic leadership with ethical leadership made it possible for him to draw on other largely unrelated influences as well, the most important among which was the Hindu leader Mohandas K. Gandhi. King included Gandhi among the great prophets of the ages and apparently agreed that he was also one of the "major prophets" of what Louis Lomax called "the new gospel of the American Negro."[29] King's understanding of ethical prophecy and of the image of the prophet was broad enough to include God's messengers of truth from a range of different religious traditions.[30]

When King referred to himself as a prophet, he had this broader and more inclusive concept of what this role meant in mind, but he still viewed himself, first and foremost, as a product of traditions associated with the ancient Hebrew prophets. The values and examples of the Hebrew prophets, Jesus, and the apostolic church came together in King's consciousness with Black church traditions, liberal Christian theology and ethics, and Gandhian thought and praxis whenever he felt the need to explain his own prophetic role. But it was his determination to speak truth to power, in his own time and in his own manner, that established his place among history's greatest prophets, as those closest to him readily admitted at times.[31] King realized that he too, like the prophets of old, was "an extremist" for truth, love, and justice.[32] He internalized God's revealed truth and was thus able and willing to tell it to everyone, even those ill prepared to hear and receive it, as he proclaimed in a sermon at Ebenezer Baptist Church in June 1966:

> You called me to Ebenezer, and you may turn me out of here, but you can't turn me out of the ministry, because I got my guidelines and my anointment from God Almighty. And *anything* I want to say, I'm going to say it from this pulpit. It may hurt somebody, I don't know about that; somebody may not agree with it. But when God speaks, who can but prophesy? The word of God is upon me like *fire* shut up in my bones, and when God's word gets upon me, I've got to say it, I've got to tell it all over everywhere.[33]

King's sense of himself as an ethical prophet initially surfaced in Montgomery, Alabama, in the mid- to late 1950s when he was the pastor of the Dexter Avenue Baptist Church and a leader in the boycott against the city's segregated bus system. His memorable kitchen vision, which occurred in early 1956, was the critical spiritual leap in his coming to terms with his prophetic role as "a witness for truth." During that encounter with God while praying, King "experienced the presence of the Divine" as never before, an "inner voice" urging him to "stand up for righteousness" and "for truth."[34] This calling to be a witness and a credible voice and purveyor of truth was very much in the structure and pattern of experiences stretching back to the ancient Hebrew prophets. Be that as it may, from that point on, King understood his own role to be that of an ethical prophet—a human vessel chosen and anointed by the God of the universe to speak truth to institutions and structures of power that were fundamentally evil and untruthful. In his estimation, this constituted the very essence of freedom.[35]

As "the leader of a new movement in the American Negro's struggle for dignity and equality," and indeed the quintessential prophet of twentieth-century America,[36] King was compelled to speak truth to the nation and the world about the problem of race. Since his maternal grandfather and father had taken on this same prophetic responsibility decades before him, he carried the weight of both history and tradition on his shoulders. King confronted America with a rather blunt and fact-based challenge about its long-standing and unchecked falsehoods about communities of color and its continuing failure to eliminate racism. He asserted, "It is an unhappy truth that racism is a way of life for the vast majority of white Americans, spoken and unspoken, acknowledged and denied, subtle and sometimes not so subtle—the disease of racism permeates and poisons a whole body politic. And I can see nothing more urgent than for America to work passionately and unrelentingly—to get rid of the disease of racism."[37] King consistently outlined the immeasurable and unspeakable acts of cruelty done in the name of race and the scars left on the nation over time by that history. He advanced his analysis within a larger global context, noting that "in country after country we see white men building empires on the sweat and suffering of colored people."[38] Pressed for his own response to racism in the United States, the impact of which knew "no geographical boundaries," King called for sustained positive action and resistance, acknowledging that he "would rather be a man of conviction than a man of conformity."[39] Any serious discussion of the role of ethical leadership in race relations, he felt, had to "ultimately emphasize the need for prophecy." "May the problem of race in America soon make hearts burn so that prophets will rise up saying, 'Thus saith the Lord,'" he bellowed.[40] In a moment of stern prophecy, he declared, "If Western civilization does not now respond constructively to the challenge to banish racism, some future historian will have to say that a great civilization died because it lacked the soul and commitment to make justice a reality for all men."[41]

The tragic conditions confronting the world's poor and the needy, or what King called "the least of these," fell within the purview of his prophetic challenge and vision as well. "Like a monstrous octopus," said he of poverty, "it projects its nagging, prehensile tenacles in lands and villages all over the world." King lamented the hardships faced by the poor in the United States, especially since they were "surrounded by a vast ocean of material prosperity," and he attributed the "shared misery" of the poor in Africa, Asia, the Caribbean, and Latin America to "years of exploitation and under-development." He chided "the well-off and secure," who were too often "indifferent and oblivious to the poverty and deprivation in their midst" and who routinely acted dishonestly, unjustly, and disrespectfully toward the poor.[42] King offered a trenchant critique of the evils and abuses of capitalism, and he insisted that to know God is to do justice toward the "*have-nots.*" He dreamed of a time when humans everywhere would have "food and material necessities for their bodies, education and culture for their minds, and freedom and dignity for their spirits." Convinced that "the agony of the poor diminishes the rich, and the salvation of the poor enlarges the rich," he held that "it is obvious that if man is to redeem his spiritual and moral 'lag' he must go all out to bridge the economic gulf between the *haves* and the *have-nots* of the world."[43] Anything short of economic justice for the poor, he argued, would ultimately bring the judgment of God upon the heads of wealthy and powerful elites.

King was always in his best element as an ethical prophet when he took on the issues of militarism and war. He denounced his own country as being too obsessed with violence and with "the quagmire of military programs and defense commitments" and repeatedly proclaimed, "I believe that the Lord told me to say it to the United States of America, that it's sick with militarism"—"sick with excessive militarism."[44] By the mid-1960s, King had begun to boldly challenge what he believed to be America's false narrative about her military adventure in Vietnam. He vividly recalled the rising tide of questions and opinion that greeted him as his thinking evolved on and against the Vietnam War:

> As I moved to break the betrayal of my own silences and to speak from the burnings of my own heart—as I called for radical departures from the destruction of Vietnam—many persons questioned me about the wisdom of my path. At the heart of their concern, this query has often loomed large and loud: "Why are you speaking about the war, Dr. King?

Why are you joining the voices of dissent?" "Peace and civil rights don't mix," they say. And when I hear them, though I often understand the source of their concern, I nevertheless am greatly saddened that such questions mean that the inquirers have not really known me, my commitment, or my calling. They seem to forget that before I was a civil rights leader, I answered a call, and when God speaks, who can but prophesy. I answered a call which left the spirit of the lord upon me and anointed me to preach the gospel. And during the early days of my ministry, I read the Apostle Paul saying, "Be ye not conformed to this world, but be ye transformed by the renewing of minds." I decided then that I was going to tell the truth as God revealed it to me. No matter how many people disagreed with me, I decided that I was going to tell the truth.[45]

Noting that he was "a minister of the Gospel" and "the pastor of a church"—both of which he took "very seriously"—King declared that in those capacities his role was not merely that of a priest, or ritual leader, who prays, administers the sacraments, and ministers to the grief-stricken. He explained, "I have not merely a priestly function but a prophetic function, and I must ever seek to bring the great principles of our Judeo-Christian heritage to bear on the social evils of our day."[46] As a priest, he felt compelled to comfort the afflicted, but his calling as a prophet demanded that he speak truth to the comfortable and indifferent—to those who were not particularly interested in truth and fact-based information and decision-making and who misused and exploited power for personal and political reasons. King felt that Vietnam fell squarely into the field of his moral vision as a prophet.[47]

King's appearance at the historic Riverside Church in New York on April 4, 1967, exactly a year prior to his assassination, was a monumental and particularly pointed moment in his public messaging around the Vietnam War issue. He began his speech in the true spirit of an ethical prophet, reminding his hearers that he could never be silent and noncommittal. "I come to this magnificent house of worship tonight because my conscience leaves me no other choice," he asserted. He acknowledged that "even when pressed by the demands of inner truth, men do not easily assume the task of opposing their government's policy, especially in time of war," but went on to firmly establish that he and other like-minded "religious leaders" had moved "beyond the prophesying of smooth patriotism to the high grounds of a firm dissent based upon the mandates of conscience and the reading of history."[48] Without flinching, King denied that the American soldiers were authentic "liberators" of Vietnam, and he referred to "my own government" as "the greatest purveyor of violence in the world today." He sadly admitted that "we have destroyed" the Vietnamese people's "two most cherished institutions—the family and the village," that "we have cooperated in the crushing" of "the unified Buddhist church," that "we have supported the enemies of the peasants of Saigon," and that "we have destroyed their land and crops."[49] Convinced that he was among those "called to speak for the weak" and "the voiceless," in both Vietnam and the United States, King later outlined in more graphic and gruesome detail his country's crimes against the Vietnamese people:

When I see our country today intervening in what is basically a civil war, mutilating hundreds of thousands of Vietnamese children with napalm, burning villages and rice fields at random, painting the valleys of that small Asian country red with human blood, leaving broken bodies in countless ditches and sending home half-men, mutilated mentally and physically; when I see the unwillingness of our government to create the atmosphere for a negotiated settlement of this awful conflict by halting bombings in the North and agreeing unequivocally to talk with the Vietcong—and all this in the name of pursuing the goal of peace—I tremble for our world. I do so not only from dire recall of the nightmares wreaked in the wars of yesterday, but also from dreadful realization of today's possible nuclear destructiveness and tomorrow's even more calamitous prospects.[50]

Saddened and frustrated to the core, and filled with moral outrage, King was disarmingly truthful when lifting his voice against war generally, and he was the nation's one true voice of reason when it came to Vietnam. Message coherence and consistency were always uppermost in his mind, for he believed that it was morally wrong for him to preach nonviolence in his own country while supporting and condoning the violence of the American government in Vietnam or anywhere else in the world.[51] As far as King was concerned, the evidence of America's misadventure in Vietnam was overwhelming and uncontestable, and he warned of God's impending judgment: "I can hear the God of History saying to America, 'You're too arrogant. And if you don't change your ways, I'll rise up and break the backbone of your power. And I'll put it in the hands of a nation that doesn't even know my name. Be still and know that I'm God.'"[52]

At times, King—who had long been called "a traitor," "an outsider," and the "Nation's No. 1 Troublemaker"[53]—felt like the lone dissenting voice crying in the wilderness when the subject of Vietnam was raised. He occasionally spoke about those "moments of loneliness" that sometimes stalk the path of the ethical prophet, even when he is not alone.[54] By speaking fearlessly and prophetically on the Vietnam War, King opened himself to criticism, persecution, and ultimately martyrdom. "When I first took my position on the war in Vietnam," he recalled, "almost every newspaper in the country criticized me. It was a low period in my life." He further explained, "Some of my friends of both races and others who do not consider themselves my friends expressed disapproval because I had been voicing concern over the war in Vietnam. In newspaper columns and editorials, both in the Negro and general press, it was indicated that Martin Luther King Jr., 'is getting out of his depth.' I was chided, even by fellow civil rights leaders, members of Congress, and brothers of the cloth for 'not sticking to the business of civil rights.'"[55]

King became increasingly radicalized during the last three years of his life (1965–68).[56] He angered friends and foes alike when he linked the violence in Vietnam to the violence of white supremacy, poverty, and economic injustice and when he called on young men who found the war "objectionable, abominable, and unjust" to "file as conscientious objectors."[57] The Vietnam War was the one issue on which King publicly broke with Roy Wilkins of the NAACP, Whitney Young of the Urban League, and other moderate civil rights leaders and sided with militants such as the late Malcolm X and Black power advocates like Stokely Carmichael and Willie Ricks of the Student Nonviolent Coordinating Committee (SNCC). This was not insignificant, since *Time*, a highly reputable magazine, had previously portrayed King "as a prophet of moderation and reason when compared with the radicals of Black Power."[58] Disturbed by Roy Wilkins's claim that he was, by "advocating the fusion of the civil rights and peace movements," making "a serious tactical mistake," King responded, "I have always insisted on justice for all the world over, because justice is indivisible. And injustice anywhere is a threat to justice everywhere."[59] When Whitney Young "cornered King in public and reprimanded him" for his position on Vietnam, King reacted passionately: "Whitney, what you are saying may get you a foundation grant but it will not get you into the kingdom of truth."[60] At such times, King's sense of himself as an ethical prophet interfaced in his thinking with "the meaning" of his "commitment to the ministry of Jesus Christ" and to the early church's "radical gospel" and "clarion call for truth."[61]

The challenges and criticisms King endured due to his stance on the Vietnam War question, and the doubts and uncertainty that occasionally gnawed at his conscience, repeatedly reminded him of the sheer magnitude of the demands, inner struggles, and obligations that weigh heavily on the shoulders of the ethical prophet. As time passed, he came to see himself more clearly as a mouthpiece for God, commissioned to speak clearly and boldly concerning arrogance, greed, pride, misplaced loyalty, racism, war, and other individual and collective sins and evils that kept people alienated from themselves, from one another, and from God. King increasingly recognized in himself exactly what he had come to know as the classic definition of a prophet—"a maladjusted personality," "a transformed nonconformist," "a transgressor," "a disturber of the status quo"—one who "combined a tough mind and a tender heart."[62] Thus, he refused to take back the uncomfortable truths he proclaimed about Vietnam merely for the sake of remaining in a good standing with people, maintaining white liberal philanthropy, and pleasing powerful and misguided politicians, even when pressured by representatives of the news media to do so:

> I remember a newsman coming to me one day and saying, "Dr. King, don't you think you're going to have to change your position now because so many people are criticizing you? And people who once had respect for you are going to lose respect for you. And you're going to hurt the budget, I understand, of the Southern Christian Leadership Conference; people have cut off support. And don't you think that you have to move now more in line with the administration's policy?" That was a good question, because he was asking me the question of whether I was going to think about what happens to me or what happens to truth and justice in this situation.[63]

King was never driven by the forces of cognitive self-interest. He was never overly concerned about his popularity. He lost so many Black and white friends and supporters during those thirteen years of active involvement in the human struggle because he chose courage, conviction, and truth over untruth, expediency, and convenience. When the flow of financial support for King's civil rights activities diminished in 1967–68, he held firmly to the belief that there is no substitute for speaking truth to a nation that needs so desperately to hear it. King received numerous letters from concerned citizens who withdrew their support from him because of his public statements on Vietnam and especially the Riverside Church address. In response to one of those letters, he left no doubt about where he stood:

> I have been strongly influenced by the prophets of old and those who place the search for truth above expediency.

I would like to hope that I am not a consensus leader, constantly determining what is right and wrong by taking a sort of Gallup poll of the majority opinion. Ultimately, a genuine leader is not a searcher of consensus, but a molder of consensus. On some positions, cowardice asks the question, is it safe? Expediency asks the question, is it politic? Vanity asks the question, is it right? There comes a time when one must take a stand that is neither safe, nor politic, nor popular, but he must take it because it is right. This is where I find myself today.[64]

"Where does moral religious leadership in America come from today? . . . Where does God dwell in America today? . . . Where in America today do we hear a voice like the voice of the prophets of Israel?" asked Rabbi Abraham Joshua Heschel, who was introducing his friend Martin Luther King Jr. to the delegates at the sixty-eighth annual convention of the Rabbinical Assembly in Kiamesha Lake, New York, in March 1968. Heschel, who had marched with King during the voting rights campaign in Selma three years earlier, went on to essentially answer his own questions:

Martin Luther King is a sign that God has not forsaken the United States of America. God has sent him to us. His presence is the hope of America. His mission is sacred, his leadership of supreme importance to every one of us. The situation of the poor in America is our plight, our sickness. To be deaf to their cry is to condemn ourselves. Martin Luther King is a voice, a vision and a way. I call upon every Jew to harken to his voice, to share his vision, to follow his way. The whole future of America will depend upon the impact and influence of Dr. King. May everyone present give his strength to this great spiritual leader, Martin Luther King.[65]

The Bible provided the primary model for King's own prophetic role, and for how he understood that role historically and in various contexts. His sense of the prophetic mind and posture

166

largely came from his reading of Amos, Micah, Isaiah, Hosea, Jeremiah, and other Hebrew prophets in whose tradition Jesus, the apostles, and the early church stood. Although King spoke out of a twentieth-century American orientation, and particularly out of the Black experience, the social and political message he shared with America and the rest of the world called to mind the prophets. Like the prophets, King was a public figure concerned about public affairs.[66] In Hebrew society in the eighth century BCE, prophets such as Amos, Hosea, Jeremiah, and Micah recognized the problems of social dislocation, of the mistreatment of the poor and humble by the powerful and the privileged, and of idolatry, and they urged the people to seek God and not evil in the face of the coming judgment. King discovered in these prophets echoes of his own concerns as he spoke out courageously and consistently against America's racism, her economic exploitation of the poor, her idolatry, her militarism, and her overall mistreatment of communities of color.[67]

Religion in the United States in King's time was similar in some ways to religion in Hebrew society during the age of the prophets. In both cases, it appeared to be healthy and vital in all its externals but was rotten to the core. This explains King's frequent quoting of Amos 5:24. Generally, the message that the Hebrew prophets and King so eloquently proclaimed was essentially threefold. First, God would not continue to tolerate the silence, cowardliness, and inactivity of those who enabled and empowered structures of social injustice. Second, God would not long endure the cruelty and destructiveness of people against people. Third, God would not continue to allow otherwise devoted people not to practice what they affirmed in creeds and ceremonies, because there had to be continuity between what was affirmed and celebrated in worship and what was practiced in daily life.[68]

The ways in which the Hebrew prophets and King turned their attention inward to keep themselves true to their calling and mission also highlight their similarity. They knew that they, too, stood under the judgment of what they proclaimed. They constantly subjected their lives to introspection or self-analysis, keeping at a bare minimum the gulf between their public and private selves.[69] They presented their messages forcefully, knowing that they were bearers and sharers of God's holy and prophetic word for their respective times and that they had to apply their concerns for truth, justice, and righteousness to their own specific contexts. Furthermore, the Hebrew prophets' claim that God had chosen Israel to be a comforting, liberating, redemptive, and empowering community for herself and other nations clearly corresponded to King's notion that God had assigned a messianic role to Black Americans to be a positive, transforming force in America and the world.[70] Blacks in America, then, had become in a sense the new Israel, and the spirit of the Hebrew prophets continued to live and speak through King.[71]

Although the Hebrew prophets were not always in complete agreement about exactly what constituted the divine will and purpose, they were hopeful for Israel and the world. They knew that a just, wrathful, and yet merciful God was at work in history and the world to bring some purpose to full realization and that this God would in due course find vindication. King shared this hope, which largely explains his willingness to endure suffering without hatred and retaliation. When he expressed a deep and abiding faith in the ultimate triumph of the moral order and when he sang "We Shall Overcome" and "Free at Last, Free at Last, Thank God Almighty I'm Free at Last," he affirmed the existence of a power in the universe that would not be denied—that punishes the wicked, rewards the virtuous, and ultimately replaces evil with good.[72]

The Hebrew prophets and King were also similar in that they died before accomplishing their missions, which involved calling and bringing their respective nations back to God—to redemption and transformation. During their life pilgrimages, they experienced one failure after another, were often unpopular, and routinely suffered verbal insults and physical attacks, but they were sustained by the belief that though they had failed at times, God would not fail.[73] On April 3, 1968, the night before his assassination in Memphis, Tennessee, King dramatically expressed this conviction in words inspired by the legacy of Moses and the Hebrew prophets:

Well, I don't know what will happen now; we've got some difficult days ahead. But it really doesn't matter with me now, because I've been to the mountaintop. And I don't mind. Like anybody, I would like to live a long life— longevity has its place. But I'm not concerned about that now. I just want to do God's will. And He's allowed me to go up to the mountain. And I've looked over, and I've seen the Promised Land. I may not get there with you. But I want you to know tonight, that we, as a people, will get to the Promised Land. And so I'm happy tonight; I'm not worried about anything; I'm not fearing any man. Mine eyes have seen the glory of the coming of the Lord.[74]

Witnessing to Truth: A Vocation of Agony

Martin Luther King Jr. declared that "the calling to speak is often a vocation of agony, but we must speak."[75] He referred here to the demands and the cost involved in witnessing to truth against individual and collective evil, and more specifically against the powers that be or evil and corruption in high places. When King spoke of witnessing to truth against institutions and structures that so often trafficked in deception, falsehoods, half-truths, misinformation, and propaganda, he clearly had in mind certain elements in the press; white supremacist organizations such as the KKK and the Nazi Party; governmental officials at the local, state, and national levels; political advocacy groups such as the White Citizens Council (WCC) and the John Birch Society (JBS); and religious leaders of considerable influence in their various churches and denominations. Convinced that the truth about the events of his time needed to be told from all quarters, King discovered that he needed enormous resources of love and grace as he clashed with representatives from these various sources over what was truthful and untruthful about himself, about the movement he and others led, and about what was happening in the United States and on the world stage.[76]

From the very beginning of the Montgomery bus protest in 1955–56, King felt that print and broadcasting media outlets could potentially become a rich and indispensable asset in explaining and bringing widespread exposure and support to the civil rights cause. Although King and the freedom movement were outrageously misrepresented and subjected to a barrage of outlandish attacks and outright untruths by various southern media sources from the outset of the boycott, the accounts that appeared in magazines such as *Time*, *Newsweek*, and *Jet* were initially far more positive and favorable, thus reinforcing King's feeling about the media as a potential ally and valuable resource. *Time* variously referred to King as "a prophet of moderation," "a spiritual architect," and "a prophet of brotherhood" and featured his face on its cover in February 1957; *Newsweek* labeled him "a defender of justice"; *Jet* called him "a kind of modern Moses" for Black southerners; and these magazines depicted the boycott as a necessary, useful, and effective weapon for Black southerners against Jim Crow policies and practices. But as King increasingly became more radical and devoted to causes widely viewed as controversial, both *Time* and *Newsweek*, like countless other media sources, came to regard him with suspicion.[77]

By the late 1950s, King had begun to speak openly and consistently about many of the irresponsible claims and misstatements of the press concerning events at home and abroad and about its tendency to misrepresent the facts and the truth to "the average reader or listener," all too many of whom were victimized by the kind of "softmindedness" that degenerated into "unbelievable gullibility":

> This undue gullibility is also seen in the tendency of all too many readers to accept the printed word of the press as final truth. . . . So President [Kwame] Nkrumah of Ghana is considered a ruthless dictator by many because the American press has carefully disseminated this idea. The great statesman and scholar, Prime Minister [Jawaharlal] Nehru of India, is often considered a non-committed ingrate because some segments of the American press have given the impression that his policy of non-alignment is at bottom a [vacillating] commitment to nothing. Many social revolutions in the world growing out of the legitimate aspirations

of oppressed people for political independence, economic security and human dignity are all too often believed to be Communist inspired because the conservative element of the American press reports them as such. . . . Very few people have the toughness of mind that drives them to look beyond the inevitable biases and subjective appraisals of the newspaper headlines to the actual truth of the situation.[78]

King knew early on that he and the movement were always under a microscope, and especially the watchful glare of enemies and detractors. Frequently blindsided by false allegations and untruths that were obvious, checkable, and verifiable, he had to consider whether to dignify these with responses or to simply remain silent. In February 1960, a press release falsely claimed that King "purchased an $85,000 home," a charge obviously designed to buttress the myth that his foremost concern was personal enrichment.[79] In a letter to a concerned citizen and fellow clergymen written in November 1960, King denied press reports that he would endorse Senator John F. Kennedy for president of the United States and that he was "being used by the Democratic Party 'as a tool for their selfish designs.'" After explaining where he and his Southern Christian Leadership Conference (SCLC) stood on political endorsements, King reminded the writer of the letter of his endless experiences with the press. "It has been my policy all along to follow a nonpartisan course," he reported. "If this letter appears rather blunt, please forgive me," he continued, "but I am sure that you know that a person in my position is constantly misquoted by the press and misrepresented."[80] In October 1961, false reports that King would take on a minor role as a southern senator in "Advise and Consent," an upcoming movie, surfaced and received more than passing attention in certain corners of the press, including the *New York Times*. Tom Roland, a white Congress of Racial Equality (CORE) supporter, accused King of trivializing the "Negro's problems" and "publicity seeking," and King, understandably shocked, called Roland's criticisms "misconceptions" so "groundless that," as he put it, "I need not take the time to answer them."[81] King's reaction was equally sharp and candid whenever the press sought to "willfully put certain statements" in his mouth; when it spread "rumors of disunity" between the SCLC, the NAACP, and other civil rights organizations; and when its releases suggested that he and other civil rights leaders had, for money or some other benefits, simply "sold out."[82] King regarded "being constantly misrepresented, misquoted, and misconstrued" as "one of the perils of being a leader," and he longed for the day when media sources would be free to witness to truth based on conscience, despite the consequences. He deeply believed that tendencies toward distortion and sensationalism had to be vehemently and consistently discouraged and that a climate more conducive to truth-telling and truth-sharing had to be created for all media outlets. When Alabama governor John M. Patterson and other Alabama officials filed libel suits against the *New York Times* in the spring of 1961 for criticizing their opposition to the protest movement, King declared that if the judgments rendered in their favor "are not reversed, no newspaper can publish truthful accounts of injustice without risk of bankruptcy and without hazard to its reporters of criminal indictment."[83]

Throughout the early and mid-1960s, the misinterpretations and criticisms of King's activities and ideas continued unabated among certain segments of the press. Conservatism and fear of ostracism and reprisals led many southern newspaper and magazine editors and journalists either to ignore King and the movement altogether or to provide false and negative coverage of the events associated with them. In December 1961, on a television program called "Open Circuit" in Cleveland, Ohio, King predicted that "if the problem of racial discrimination" was not solved soon, "some Negroes, out of frustration, discontent, and despair," would "turn to some other ideology," and he fleetingly mentioned Communism and Black Muslimism as possibilities. Shortly thereafter, in an editorial entitled "Dr. King Does His Cause a Dis-Service," Edward D. Ball of the *Nashville Tennessean* gave the impression that King "had advocated that the Negro turn to a new ideology in his struggle for freedom and human dignity—the ideology being either Communism or the Muslim Movement." Several news channels joined the effort to distort the meaning of King's comments. The charge shook King to the core, driving him to respond to Ball in a two-page, single-spaced letter. "Such an idea" was "so far out of harmony with" his "general thinking" that he wondered how anyone even casually familiar with his thought and work could propagate such misinformation. "Suffice it to say," King declared, "that I can see no greater tragedy befalling the Negro than a turn to either Communism or Black Nationalism." He went on to explain the problem he had with both ideologies: "It is my firm conviction that Communism is based on an ethical relativism, a metaphysical materialism, a crippling totalitarianism, and a denial of freedom which I could never accept. Moreover, Black Nationalism is based on an unrealistic and sectional perspective that I have condemned both publicly and privately."[84]

King's standing with both the print and broadcasting media increasingly declined as he and his SCLC launched campaigns in Albany in 1961–62 and Birmingham in 1963, in part because he had become more vocal in blaming these sources for false reporting and misinformation. It was in Birmingham that his differences with media outlets across the spectrum publicly surfaced on a level not previously witnessed, mainly over the question of "timing," the issues of breaking laws and exposing rising racial tensions, and the use of children on the front line in demonstrations.[85] King was widely viewed as "an outside agitator" who incited racial tensions in Birmingham at a time when the city's newly elected city council, under the moderate Mayor Albert Boutwell, promised positive change, and his decision to invite the active participation of children in the struggle was deplored. The *Birmingham News* and the *Birmingham Post Herald* occasionally featured editorials and commentaries from concerned citizens questioning King's decisions and motives. Local news channels and radio broadcasters joined in, as did major media sources from across the country. But King stood his ground, insisting that the time to do right for right is always right, declaring that prophets are morally obligated to break unjust laws and to carry their "thus saith the Lord" wherever injustice exists, and maintaining that a constructive, nonviolent tension was "necessary for growth" in race relations.[86] King was particularly rankled by those in the print media who attacked his "introduction of Birmingham's children into the campaign." Speaking to the dishonesty and hypocrisy he felt had long been reflected in the media's critique of himself and the movement, he lashed out: "Where had these writers been, we wondered, during the centuries when our segregated social system had been misusing and abusing Negro children? Where had they been with their protective words when, down through the years, Negro infants were born into ghettoes, taking their first breath of life in a social atmosphere where the fresh air of freedom was crowded out by the stench of discrimination?"[87] For much of the mass media, King had moved from being what *Newsweek* called an "apostle of nonviolence" in Albany, who followed "the way of moderation and sweet reason," to being what both *Newsweek* and *Time* described as "a prophet of Old Testament mien whose strategy was to press his adversary to the wall—nonviolently, to be sure, but to the wall."[88] This shifting image of King became indelibly etched in the public imagination in the mid- to late 1960s as his demand for action on voting rights in Selma, his mounting attacks on capitalism, his growing calls for a radical redistribution of economic power, and his relentless assault on US involvement in Vietnam reflected his growing militancy.

When King clashed with younger, more militant activists in the SNCC over movement plans in Selma in 1965 and later the use of the Black power slogan, elements of both the print and broadcast media exploited the rift in what seemed to some to be a classic example of a divide and conquer strategy. When King turned back the march involving some three thousand on Selma's Edmund Pettus Bridge two days after "Bloody Sunday," on March 9, 1965, in order to avoid what would have been another violent attack on demonstrators by Alabama's state troopers, SNCC's participants were both surprised and outraged, and they were led by certain news reports to believe that King had made a secret agreement with state officials and the federal government to abort the march. King was "very concerned about this perversion of the facts" and about other false reports put out by the media about his meetings with state and federal authorities.[89] His frustration with media outlets increased as the nation's press distorted the meaning of Black power, heralding it as a repudiation of the ideal of the integrated society and "as an end of the Negro's reliance on nonviolence as a means of achieving freedom."[90] For King, this was typical of the kind of propaganda, of the untrue and irresponsible claims, for which media sources had become increasingly and widely known in Black circles. He strongly "criticized the press for diverting attention from white southern injustice to internal divisions within the movement." Mindful of the press's love for "the sensational," King also denounced its effort to create "heroes and villains, something that had worked so well for him in Birmingham and Selma." "In every drama there has to be an antagonist and a protagonist," he stated, "and if the antagonist is not there the press will find and build one."[91] For the sake of those interested in an accurate reading of Black power, King insisted that "one must look beyond personal styles, verbal flourishes, and the hysteria of the mass media to assess its values, its assets and liabilities honestly."[92]

The nation's media outlets seemingly turned completely against King during the last three years of his life as he brought a more enlightened, explicit, and radical perspective to bear on his critique of capitalism, economic exploitation, and the Vietnam conflict. King's attacks on capitalism and the US military venture in Vietnam further convinced his enemies that he was a Communist and a traitor—and indeed "the most dangerous and effective Negro leader in the country"—and there was virtually no support for him on news channels, on radio talk shows, or from newspaper and magazine editors.[93] Even Black newspapers like the *Pittsburgh Courier*, which had previously criticized King's leadership style and his relationship to other civil rights organizations,[94] raised serious questions about his growing radicalization around economic justice and international peace issues. The experience compounded King's feeling of being alone and abandoned. Witnessing to truth proved to be an agonizing experience for King partly because he had to deal with a mass media that too often compromised and wavered when confronted with truth and that often straddled the line between truth and untruth. He knew that the print and broadcasting media were a vital part of the powers that be and that when forces of this kind shirk the moral duty of truth-telling and truth-sharing, reputations, careers, and even lives are potentially destroyed. It must have been difficult at times for King to avoid the conclusion that the mass media was part of the larger effort to marginalize and ultimately silence his prophetic voice.

This was most certainly the case with white supremacist groups such as the KKK, the Nazi Party, and the National States Rights Party (NSRP), all of which derived great pleasure from attacking and putting out false reports about King. As far back as his college years, King had described the KKK as a "secret order" or "society" deeply "committed to a philosophy of 'one hundred percent Americanism', white supremacy and nationalistic isolation."[95] The Klan were among those advocates of white supremacy who worshipped at what he called "the shrine" of "the false god of nationalism."[96] The frequency with which Klansmen, Nazis, and States Righters resorted to violence to silence and keep Blacks "in their place," so to speak, became all too familiar to King. The images of Klansmen violently assaulting students involved in the sit-ins and freedom rides in 1960–61, captured on television screens across the country and world, shimmered before him. He was punched in the mouth by Roy James of the American Nazi Party in Birmingham in September 1962, hit and kicked by Jimmy George Robinson of the NSRP in Selma in January 1965, and was quite aware of Klan involvement in numerous church bombings and the deaths of countless civil rights workers in his time. King blamed white supremacists for what he described as this "tragic reign of violence and terror" in "the Southland." He lamented the fact that there was essentially no recognition of the value of Black life, noting, "In some of our states and counties in the deep South, the murder of a black man by a white mob is still a popular pastime." In a moment of somber reflection, he remarked, "We've known our Good Fridays in the fact that so often we have had to live with the Ku Klux Klan marching on outside of our doors."[97]

From the time of the Montgomery bus boycott, King and his associates struggled around fierce opponents who dared to compare their actions with those of Klansmen who paraded in the streets of southern cities. Dumbfounded by such jaw-dropping comparisons, King always responded swiftly and adamantly: "There will be no crosses burned at any bus stops in Montgomery. There will be no white persons pulled out of their homes and taken out on some distant road and lynched for not cooperating. There will be nobody amid, among us who will stand up and defy the Constitution of this nation. We only assemble here because of our desire to see right exist."[98] In cities throughout the South, King was exposed to the grotesque ignorance and lunatic rumblings of Klan leaders, but he was never intimidated by the toxicity of their rhetoric and their racially charged appeals to violence. "I don't worry about a thing," he asserted. "They can bomb my house. They can kill my body. But they can never kill the spirit of freedom that is in my people."[99] King knew that Klansmen, Nazis, and States Righters epitomized the tyranny of white supremacy; that they lived and functioned in an *us versus the other* reality; that they were not "guided by the highest principles of law and order"; that they dealt primarily in falsehoods, nonsense, rumors, and propaganda; and that they wielded more influence than they deserved—but he still affirmed their human-ity and their right to dignified treatment as God's children. King refused to allow these "close-minded extremists" to stifle his gospel of truth concerning race and humanity, and he was, at the same time, open-minded enough to accept whatever truths fell from their lips about him and his people. "Whenever we are objects of criti-cism from white men, even though the criticisms are maliciously directed and mixed with half-truths," King said, "we must pick out the elements of truth and make them the basis of creative recon-struction. We must not let the fact that we are victims of injustice lull us into abrogating responsibility for our own lives."[100]

Political advocacy groups such as the WCC and the JBS pre-sented another formidable challenge for King around the need to speak truth to power. Both groups emerged to prominence in the 1950s and became part of the evil powers ranged against King and the freedom cause. King described the WCC—a loosely connected conglomerate of local groups that arose across the South in protest of the Supreme Court's *Brown v. Board of Education* desegregation decision in 1954—as "a modern version of the Ku Klux Klan," and he spoke of its "dark and agonizing story" in the following terms:

> Since they operate on a higher political and economic level than the Klan, a halo of respectability hovers over them. But like the Klan, they are determined to preserve segregation and thereby defy the desegregation rulings of the Supreme Court. They base their defense on the legal maneuvers of interposition and nullification. Unfortunately for those who disagree with the Councils, their methods do not stop with legal tactics; their methods range from threats and intimidation to economic reprisals against Negro men and women. These methods also extend to white persons who will dare to take a stand for justice. They demand absolute conformity from whites and abject submission from Negroes.[101]

To highlight the sheer danger of the WCC, King quoted "a man down in Mississippi" who "said that God was a charter member of the White Citizens Council." "And so God being the charter member means that everybody who's in that has a kind of divinity, a kind of superiority,"[102] King explained. When a Montgomery newspaper editor suggested that the bus boycott was an example of Blacks using "the same approach to their problems as the White Citizen Councils used," King responded with frustration: "Our purposes were altogether different. We would use this method to give birth to justice and freedom, and also to urge men to comply with the law of the land. Our concern would not be to put the bus company out of business, but to put justice in business." Noting that the WCC's methods included "open and covert terror, brutal intimidation, and threats of starvation to Negro men, women, and children," King argued unequivocally that this group scarred "the dream of our democracy" with its "fanatical acts and bitter words," "its apathy and hypocrisy," and "its betrayal of the cause of justice"—that it in fact stood "against the Constitution of the United States."[103] King offered the same assessment of the JBS, a conservative group purportedly dedicated to limited government and the crusade against Communism. He labeled the JBS an "ultra-white right-wing" group and declared that when it came to "tyranny over the mind of man," it was as "dangerous" as "McCarthyism" and "White Citizen Councils."[104] When reminded by an interviewer that the "literature of the John Birch Society" roundly accused him of counseling "hatred and demagoguery" and of being "a conscious agent of the Communist conspiracy," King fired back:

> As you know, they have sought to link many people with Communism, including the Chief Justice of the Supreme Court and a former president of the United States. So I'm in good company, at least. The Birchers thrive on sneer and smear, on the dissemination of half-truths and outright lies. It would be comfortable to dismiss them as the lunatic fringe—which, by and large, they are; but some priests and ministers have also shown themselves to be among them. They are a very dangerous group—and they could become even more dangerous if the public doesn't reject the un-American travesty of patriotism that they espouse.[105]

King realized that support from wealthy, powerful political and religious figures was the key ingredient that made the JBS and the WCC such influential, seductive, and driving forces in American life and culture. He was particularly disturbed by "the status of respectability given" the WCC, which was the most active in its resistance to racial integration, "by law officers, elected public officials, and 'solid citizens' of the South."[106] Knowing that sound reasoning did not figure into the equation for the WCC and the JBS when it came to matters of race, King longed to see persons of conscience and goodwill challenging these and other ultraconservative political advocacy groups with the kind of truths that set captives free. Perhaps his greatest contribution as a moral and spiritual leader, and indeed as an ethical prophet, consisted in his determination to reach those for whom the truth about race and oppression appeared to be a phantasm to be ignored, even disputed and casually dismissed. King always sought ways to communicate unmitigated truth clearly and more effectively.

The moral component of King's life and thought was such that no persons or groups that abused or misused power in the service of unethical ends could escape his indictment. This applied especially to those in positions of public trust, the most notable of whom were politicians at the local, state, and federal levels who opposed much-needed social change while majoring in false promises, divisive rhetoric, and reckless hyperbole. From the time King was catapulted to leadership in the bus boycott in Montgomery, he and others in the Montgomery Improvement Association (MIA) sought to engage in good-faith negotiations with local white political leaders who were not interested in objective truth, who were not held accountable, who used "the power of their offices to defy the law of the land," and who redefined truth to defend the status quo. King's repeated calls for deliberations that were "honest and fair" fell on deaf ears, and "false rumors" were spread by city officials and others in the white community to discredit King, to divide Black leadership, and to frustrate and ultimately throttle the Black community's demands for justice.[107] King met the same hostility and resistance from Police Chief Laurie Pritchett in Albany in 1961–62, Commissioner of Public Safety Eugene "Bull" Connor in Birmingham in 1963, and Sheriff Jim Clark in Selma in 1965, all of whom sought desperately to defeat the civil rights cause by distorting the truth and confusing the issues.

As the civil rights movement progressed, King had to deal with even more powerful figures in state governments who used their authority and resources to maintain segregation. In May 1960, when King and other Black leaders criticized Alabama governor John M. Patterson and his associates for greeting "peaceful protests with intimidation and violence," Patterson demanded that King "publish a retraction of" what he termed "'false and defamatory' statements." King refused and Patterson and other state officials filed libel suits, which were upheld by the decision of state courts but later overturned by the Supreme Court "in a landmark free speech case."[108] King's experiences with powerful politicians across the South—with Alabama governor George C. Wallace, Arkansas governor Orval Faubus, Mississippi governor Ross Barnett, Georgia governor Lester Maddox, and others—convinced him that when it came to addressing issues of equal rights and social justice, they were more prone to acts of political calculation and expediency than to acts of conscience.[109] Undoubtedly, King thought of public servants like these when he excoriated politicians for "choosing between truth and votes," likening them to "the businessman choosing between truth and some sharp business practice which means more money."[110] Quite accustomed to politicians who bent and twisted truth to fit their desired ends, King at times found it impossible to conceal his indignation, and he made his feelings known in no uncertain terms. "Through their irresponsible actions, their inflammatory statements, and their dissemination of distortions and half-truths," he wrote concerning southern local and state officials, "they have succeeded in arousing abnormal fears and morbid antipathies within the minds of underprivileged and uneducated whites, leaving them in such a state of excitement and confusion that they are led to acts of meanness and violence that no normal person would commit."[111] King's close friend and associate Stanley D. Levison, a Jewish lawyer, defended his fearlessness in witnessing to truth against such glaring abuses of power, asserting, "Fortunately, facts are more eloquent than words, and our nation can well be proud of a man whose courage of conviction and deed is unequalled in our day."[112]

As King waded into the murky, complex, and controversial issues of economic justice and international peace in the mid- to late 1960s, he met people in government throughout the country who held significant power but did not share his vision of a just and peaceful society. King emphatically addressed this reality in 1966 as leaders of the various civil rights organizations, threatened with disunity due to differences over Black power, prepared to continue James Meredith's "Freedom March" against fear in Mississippi. "You see, to change Mississippi we've got to be together," King argued. "We aren't dealing with a force that has a little power." He went on to declare, "We are dealing with powerful political dynasties, and somehow we must set out to be that David of Truth sent out against the Goliath of Injustice."[113] The wisdom of these words became quite evident that same year as King and his SCLC staff met a herculean challenge from Mayor Richard J. Daley as they moved against segregated housing and slum conditions in Chicago. The Daley political machine was significantly more powerful than any King had encountered in the South, and Daley used that power against the Chicago Freedom Movement. Although a "Summit Agreement" was reached with Mayor Daley and other Chicago leaders in August 1966, in which the real estate board and other agencies pledged access to open housing without regard to race, King, referring to himself as "an honest man," was later reminded of a lesson that he had learned from the earliest days of the struggle— namely, that so much of what politicians said had to be entertained with a certain degree of skepticism:

> It was clear to me that city agencies had been inert in upholding their commitment to the open housing pact. I had to express our swelling disillusionment with the foot-dragging negative actions of agencies such as the Chicago Housing Authority, the Department of Urban Renewal, and the Commission on Human Relations. It appeared that, for all intents and purposes, the public agencies had reneged on the agreement and had in fact given credence to the apostles of disorder who proclaimed the housing agreement a sham and a batch of false promises. The city's inaction was not just a rebuff to the Chicago Freedom Movement or a courtship of the white backlash, but also another hot coal on the smoldering fires of discontent and despair that are rampart in our black communities. For more than a month during the marches we were told to come to the bargaining

table, that compromise and negotiation were the only ways to solve the complex, multi-layered problems of open occupancy. We came, we sat, we negotiated. We reached the summit and then nearly seven months later we found that much of the ground had been cut out from beneath us.[114]

With the experience in Chicago on his mind, King later commented on how "the children of darkness" are usually "shrewder" and more "zealous and conscientious" than "the children of light"—how "they use time to spend big money, to disseminate half-truths, to confuse the popular mind" with the goal of defeating fair housing bills.[115]

During this same period, King complained that "in several Southern states men long regarded as political clowns had become governors or only narrowly missed election, their magic achieved with a witches' brew of bigotry, prejudice, half-truths and whole lies."[116] From his time in Montgomery, he had regarded with suspicion those "high places where men are willing to sacrifice truth on the altars of their self-interest,"[117] where they pursued a Machiavellian approach to governing, and his push for economic justice, through his involvement with the unfolding Poor People's Campaign and the Memphis Sanitation Strike in 1967–68, exposed such tendencies in glaring proportions. The rich and powerful turned against King when he became more vocal about the evils of capitalism and more intense in his calls for a radical restructuring of economic resources in the interest of the poor, but he, having toiled in the prophetic wilderness for some thirteen years, refused to buckle under the pressure. He publicly criticized Mayor Henry Loeb and other city officials in Memphis for their failure "to be fair and honest" in their "dealings with" their "public servants, who happen to be sanitation workers."[118] In his dealings with politicians at all levels and around any issue, King had always stressed "honest compromise" and the need for "a climate of decency and fair play." Also, he often said that "the basic thing in determining the best candidate" for public office "is not his color but his integrity."[119]

The challenge King presented for various branches of the federal government, the chief centers of the nation's power, revealed, perhaps more than anything else, the sheer depth of his commitment to the prophetic role. Always hopeful that the executive branch of the federal government would become a strong ally of civil rights, King met, talked, and tried to work with three US presidents—Dwight D. Eisenhower, John F. Kennedy, and Lyndon B. Johnson—and he was never intimidated in their presence. Convinced that conscience demanded fearless truth-telling, King spoke to these men in carefully honed language but firmly and directly, sharing the truth about white supremacy, poverty, and violence and repeatedly urging them to use executive orders, moral suasion, and other powers of the office to defeat segregation and enforce integration policies. King discovered that "all three" espoused the civil rights cause "in principle" but that they were too often voices of caution and compromise rather than voices of conscience and conviction.[120] What King shared in the following statement about his conversations with Johnson is equally revealing in terms of how he related to Eisenhower and Kennedy:

> I followed a policy of being very honest with President Johnson when he consulted me about civil rights. I went to the White House when he invited me. I made it very clear to him why I had taken a stand against the war in Vietnam. I had a long talk with him on the telephone about this and made it clear to him I would be standing up against it even more. I was not centering this on President Johnson. I thought there was collective guilt. Four presidents participated in some way leading us to the war in Vietnam. So, I am not going to put it all on President Johnson. What I was concerned about was that we end the nightmarish war and free our souls.[121]

King did not hesitate to acknowledge the personal qualities, gifts, and talents of all the US presidents with whom he had connections, but he was just as blunt in speaking truth to and about them. He suggested that these men too often valued the status quo and politics more than the nation's most vulnerable and oppressed people,[122] but he was still hopeful because, in his estimation, no man—not even the leader of the so-called free world—was powerful enough to block the advance of freedom. To those who believed otherwise, King, referring to the exodus story in the Hebrew Bible, promptly recalled the fate of "the Pharaohs" who sought to "hold God's children in the clutches of their political power."[123]

Not surprisingly, much of King's critique of the federal government targeted the legislative side, the only branch with the power to make, repeal, and amend acts and laws. He knew and publicly acknowledged that all too many in the House of Representatives and the Senate lacked honor, character, and integrity—that they were hardly serious-minded, factual, and truthful when considering the kind of legislative and public-policy initiatives designed to promote desperately needed social change. King was thinking primarily of "southern Dixiecrats" and "conservative right wing northern Republicans" who had consistently betrayed his people. In a speech in 1966, he complained, "Many of the key committees in our Congress are headed by men like Richard Russell of Georgia and James Eastland of Mississippi, and the decisions of peace on earth, good will toward men are too often subject to their power." King was relentless in his criticisms of Dixiecrats like Russell and Eastland, who were cloaked in the disgrace of their support for rigid patterns of Jim Crow in the South. King also denounced the politics of influential figures like Senator Barry Goldwater of Arizona, declaring that his "right wing conservatism sometimes [made] him a bed-fellow with the southern racist."[124] These public officials frequently responded with harsh and insulting language about King, but King's independence of mind and autonomy of voice were such that he never apologized to or fell under the influence of anyone in Congress. His determination to speak truth to and about congressmen in a resounding and pronounced manner sprang from his keen sense of mission and values, but it also owed much to the firm imprint of his father's character on him.

King moved to the crux of the federal government's feeble and less encouraging record when he "sincerely questioned the effectiveness of the" Federal Bureau of Investigation (FBI) "in racial incidents, particularly where bombings," the murders of civil rights workers, "and brutalities against Negroes" were "at issue."[125] Shortly after the inauguration of President Kennedy, in February 1961, King "published an article in *Nation* magazine that made a parenthetical reference to the" FBI. "If, for instance, the law-enforcement personnel in the FBI were integrated," he stated, "many persons who now defy federal law might come under restraints from which they are presently free."[126] In comments made later, King was more specific, noting, "One of the great problems we face with the FBI in the South is that the agents are white Southerners who have been influenced by the mores of the community." He observed that "in order" for such agents to "maintain status," they had "to be friendly with the local police and people who [were] promoting segregation." To deal with the problem, King recommended that nonsoutherners be appointed to FBI offices in the Deep South, for he felt that "if an FBI man agrees with segregation, he can't honestly and objectively investigate."[127] Viewing these and numerous other criticisms by King as unwarranted attacks on "his beloved bureau," the FBI director J. Edgar Hoover, who made no secret of his fear and hatred of the civil rights leader, questioned King's moral leadership and dubbed him "the most notorious liar in the country."[128] "I was appalled and surprised at your reported statement maligning my integrity," said King in response to the charges, adding, "What motivated such an irresponsible accusation is a mystery to me." King concluded that Hoover's attacks on him showed that the FBI director was "under extreme pressure"— that he had "apparently faltered under the awesome burden, complexities, and responsibilities of his office."[129] The FBI was the one agency within the federal government whose behavior toward the movement King found almost totally unacceptable. Speaking from the heart concerning this and other matters was his authenticity, and many of his people were further strengthened, morally and spiritually, by his example in standing up and speaking his mind to the leader of the most powerful law enforcement agency in the country without flinching.

Much the same might be said of King's challenge to the American judiciary. In the early days of the bus boycott in Montgomery and beyond, his frustrating experiences with local and state courts in the South, in which white judges and lawyers too often took a cavalier and even indifferent attitude toward what was manifestly true, left him with little or no faith in their capacity to administer justice. King made this abundantly clear in the pulpit and in his published writings. "Many Americans are aware of the fact that on the crooked scales of 'Southern Justice,'" he wrote, "the life, liberty and human worth of a black man weigh precious little." "The segregated character that pervades southern justice," he added, "runs all the way through the judicial system, extending from the lowest municipal courts all the way up to the federal bench."[130] For King, a kind of permissive judicial system explained the "police state" bureaucracy that existed virtually unchallenged throughout the southern landscape.[131] He initially had more reasons to see the Supreme Court, the nation's most powerful judicial body, as the movement's strongest and most trustworthy and supportive ally, especially after its decisions rendering school segregation unconstitutional in 1954 and striking down bus segregation in 1956.[132] But the Supreme Court's increasing tendency to surrender its powers of judicial oversight and review and its appellate jurisdiction over state courts when confronted with southern defiance and resistance frustrated King, causing him to ultimately doubt the effectiveness of that body as a support mechanism in the struggle. He was deeply saddened by the high court's practice of rendering decisions while either retreating from them or allowing them to languish with only half-hearted implementation and sometimes none at all. According to King, this explained why some twelve years after *Brown v. Board of Education*, "barely 12 percent school integration existed in the whole South, and in the Deep South the figure hardly reached 2 percent":

It is an unadvertised fact that soon after the 1954 decision the Supreme Court retreated from its own position by giving approval to the Pupil Placement Law. This law permitted the states themselves to determine where school children might be placed by virtue of family background, special ability and other subjective criteria. The Pupil Placement Law was almost as far-reaching in modifying and limiting the integration of schools as the original decision had been in attempting to eliminate segregation. Without technically reversing itself, the Court had granted legal sanction to tokenism and thereby guaranteed that segregation, in substance, would last for an indefinite period, though formally it was illegal.[133]

The failures of the American judiciary in the crusade for justice for his people reminded King of the actions of Pontius Pilate, the governor of the Roman province of Judaea, who, as Jesus stood innocently before him, presided over the latter's trial and later condemned him to crucifixion. "And one cannot leave that point without weeping for Pilate," King declared, "for here is a man who sacrificed truth on the altar of his self-interest. Here was a man who crucified justice on the cross of his egotism."[134] Evidently, the Supreme Court's actions after *Brown* reminded King of that arrogance of power that had infected the nation's major institutions and structures for too long, thus rendering them impotent and ineffectual in the face of human needs. He could not remain silent. He gradually engaged in the violation of court injunctions at all levels as part of the demonstrations he led, for he knew that these instruments were routinely used to thwart the momentum of civil rights campaigns, thereby preserving the established social, political, and economic order.[135] Such actions on King's part were probably the best indication of his declining confidence in the American judiciary as an ally in the struggle against human oppression.

King felt similarly regarding the Christian church universal, another bastion of power and influence which had too often disappointed him. He accused that institution of leaving humans stranded "at midnight" when "they seek the bread of social justice."[136] He never had a messaging problem with holding the church and its leadership accountable for their moral and spiritual failures.

Convinced that the church at its best functioned as a prophetic community, King consistently denounced churches and their galaxy of pulpit giants, in America and in places like South Africa, for their refusal to unmask and challenge the power of white supremacy and other social evils with the truths of the gospel.[137] He viewed the pulpit as a powerful "communications media"—as a platform from which to speak "objective and unbiased truth" to and about evil in high places—but he sadly admitted that it was difficult to accept much of what church leadership said in his times as holy writ, largely because it too often lied by commission and omission and too few were prepared to take what he called "risks of faith and the divine adventure."[138] Instead, the church had become a part of that "tragedy of the modern world" known as the "age of jumboism," an age in which "we worship that which is big—big buildings, big cars, big houses, big corporations." Living the gospel with integrity and courage, King opined, was eminently more significant than maintaining ecclesial structures of power and wealth. "Have we ministers of Jesus Christ sacrificed truth on the altar of self-interest and, like Pilate, yielded our convictions to the demands of the crowd?" King asked.[139] He believed that the judgment of God was upon the church:

> And you know it seems that I can hear God saying this morning, "I will not hear your eloquent sermons. Get out of my face. I will not listen to the glad outpourings, the general sighs, the beauty of your anthems, and your hymns. I will not hear your long prayers. Get out of my face because your hands are full of blood. You don't know what I require. What I require is that you will do justly, that you will love mercy, and that you will walk humbly with your God." This is what God is saying today to a dead church, that leaves men and women disappointed at midnight.[140]

When King repeatedly raised the need for leaders with integrity, the church was uppermost in his thinking—that institution in which pastors testified every Sunday morning to the truths of the biblical revelation. Josiah Gilbertt Holland's famous words regarding the need for "leaders who will not lie" became King's rallying cry.[141] In his famous "Letter from the Birmingham City Jail" (1963), which stands in the tradition of the apostle Paul's letters to the early churches, King urged the Christian church to reclaim its prophetic role in the world.[142] His persistent challenge to the Christian church, and especially his stress on speaking and acting on truth as a matter of conscience, stirred powerful emotions and triggered some opposition among even men of the cloth, most of whom were literally married to the status quo. White and Black clergy targeted King with falsehoods,[143] he was accused of perverting "the Christian message,"[144] and it was widely reported on one occasion that he had become a part of a society that "represented a dangerous turn toward a humanistic secularism with Gandhi replacing Christ as a central figure."[145] King frequently responded kindly but firmly when he was falsely and unjustly accused by religious leaders whom he respected, or who he felt would listen to and seriously engage his concerns. On such occasions, he typically explained the problem with the charges, made his feelings known, and called for either a public retraction of the charges, an apology, or a promise to desist from making them.[146] Undoubtedly, King's determination to speak unfettered truth to and about the church and its leaders, including powerful ecclesial forces like the papacy and the Vatican,[147] revealed so much about his credibility as an ethical prophet, for he believed that there was no room in what he described as "the kingdom of truth" for the weak, the unprincipled, and the faint of heart.[148]

King blamed the powerful and wealthy, and especially those who appeared to have no belief in the power of truth, for the unrest of mind and spirit that pervaded so much of the nation's life and culture. He was convinced that this problem would be corrected only when the emotional, spiritual, and moral dimensions of life were given primacy over the lingering and seemingly insatiable thirst for power, materialism, and supremacy over other nations:

> And I would say that there is a restlessness in the land because the land doesn't seem to have a sense of purpose, a proper

sense of policy, and a proper sense of priority. This is the basis for this restlessness. The words of Jesus are still applicable. "What does it profit a generation. What does it profit a nation" to own the whole world of means—television, automobiles, electric lights—and in the end lose the soul. And the words of Jesus are still true in another sense. Man cannot live by the bread of color television alone, but by every word—the word of love, the word of justice, the word of truth—every word that proceedeth out of the mouth of God. And the problem is that all too many people in power are trying to get America to live on the wrong things.[149]

King's insistence on telling the truth in the face of the powers of evil—of those intellectually, morally, and spiritually unwilling to hear and function in accordance with it—essentially explains why his popularity declined toward the end of his life. He had always been controversial in the minds of most white Americans, and it is not surprising that he had become anathema by the time of his death. President Johnson's decision not to include King on the Kerner Commission, the eleven-member presidential commission appointed to investigate the causes of race riots in July 1967, was telling enough, for it was a metaphor for what those at the pinnacle of power in the United States thought of the civil and human rights leader. The Communist charge had long been "the big lie" that the rulers of America used to justify and rationalize their attacks on King and to ultimately surveil and sabotage his efforts, but when that did not work, the decision was to literally isolate and destroy him. King's adversaries realized that if ever there was a Black man prepared to risk all in defense of truth, it was King. Speaking and acting on truth had become part of his agonizing quest, and nothing could have caused him to shrink from his prophetic task. It is also important to note that his habit of speaking truth to power, as much as anything else, endeared him to so many of the common, ordinary people he met daily.

The terrible cost King had to pay led him to think of witnessing for truth as "a vocation of agony."[150] "The word 'witness' means being willing to die for the cause of Jesus Christ," he declared, and for him, this entailed freedom.[151] "Freedom is not free," he frequently asserted. "It is always purchased with the high price of sacrifice and suffering."[152] King spoke of the need to stand for "some great truth" even "till death," insisting that "we must believe that there is something so dear, something so precious, something so eternal, that we'll die for it." "And if you haven't discovered something you will die for," he added, "you aren't fit to live."[153] King reasoned that no sacrifice was too great to eliminate white supremacy, economic injustice, war, and other social evils, and he called upon dedicated people of goodwill—irrespective of race, gender, class, and nationality—to be prepared, if necessary, to die for the freedom cause. His sense of the prophetic task was such that he, like Gandhi, expected of others only what he demanded of himself. Having internalized a kind of spiritual nonviolence, King was always "willing to talk and seek fair" or "creative, honest compromise." He was equally emphatic in declaring his and his followers' willingness to make the ultimate sacrifice. Variously, he notes, "We are ready to suffer and even risk our lives," "to present our very bodies" as "witnesses to the truth as we see it."[154] "I say to you this afternoon that I would rather die on the highways of Alabama," he commented during a march in Selma in 1965, "than make a butchery of my conscience."[155] King also expressed these thoughts in dramatic fashion through references to the ancient Greek philosopher Socrates, who was told by his friend Crito "that he can leave and everything can be all right and he need not face the tragedy of the hemlock": "Socrates looks back and said to him, 'I must stand on what I consider to be right and true, even if it brings death to me.' And now he said at the end of the *Apology*, 'I go to life and, you—I go to death, and you go to life. Which of us goes to the better life, nobody knows but God. But I go because I believe finally in truth.'"[156]

In more specific terms, King's idea of witnessing to truth was about "taking up" or "bearing the cross."[157] Speaking truth to power was for him an expression of radical love, of truth being on the cross, of "a dangerous and costly altruism." His Good Friday and Easter sermons always focused on instances in which untruth or "evil" sits temporarily "on the throne," while truth or "the good" hangs momentarily on a cross, scaffold, or lynching tree.[158] King spoke graphically of "wounded truth and love lying prostrate on the rugged hills of nameless Calvaries."[159] "The cross is something that you bear and ultimately that you die on," he declared. Convinced that truth by its very nature bears a cross, he went on to assess, on a very personal level, the suffering or privation typically endured by those who struggle for truth and justice:

> No, it isn't easy to stand up for truth and for justice. Sometimes it means being frustrated. When you tell the truth and take a stand, sometimes it means that you walk the streets with a burdened heart. Sometimes it means losing a job. It means being abused and scorned. It may mean having a seven or eight-year-old child asking, "Daddy, why do you have to go to jail so much?" I've long since learned that to be a follower of Jesus Christ means taking up the cross. My Bible tells me that Good Friday comes before Easter, and before the crown we wear there is a cross that we must bear. Let us bear it. Bear it for truth. Bear it for justice. Bear it for peace.[160]

In the context of the struggle for equal rights and social justice, the cross was never merely symbolic for King—it became an actual personal experience in the routines and processes of daily living. This became quite evident during a critical moment in Birmingham on Good Friday in 1963, when the movement was threatened by a lack of sufficient funds and much-needed vitality and when city officials resorted to a court injunction to cease civil rights activities until the right "to demonstrate had been argued in court." King stated publicly, "We cannot in all good conscience obey such an injunction which is an unjust, undemocratic, and unconstitutional misuse of the legal process." He and his associates thought of the meaning of the cross as they boldly violated the injunction and were promptly arrested. King later wrote, "We decided that, because of its symbolic significance, April 12, Good Friday, would be the day that Ralph Abernathy and I would present our bodies as personal witnesses in this crusade."[161] His description of demonstrators marching and singing on that Good Friday must have reinforced in his mind the image of Blacks as the creative, cross-bearing minority struggling to save a sin-sick nation from impending doom.[162]

By highlighting truth-telling as a form of cross-bearing that can result in martyrdom, King saw himself standing firmly in the tradition of the Hebrew prophets, Jesus of Nazareth, and the early church. He held that ethical prophecy involved bearing a cross and that the prophets themselves were "crucified because they stood up for right."[163] Jesus could have gone back to Nazareth to "become merely an insignificant figure in history," King opined, but he, envisioning a higher and much more noble ideal, "said to himself": "Oh no, I cannot follow this way. I must be true to what I know is truth and what I know is right. What I know will eventually be a part of the structure of the universe." "And this," King proclaimed in an Easter sermon, "is what the cross says to us this morning . . . [that] greatness in life comes when we are obedient to the unen-forceable."[164] King concluded that "sin and evil blotted out the life of Christ"—that his crucifixion was a case of truth and love being "nailed to a tree by hate."[165] Thus, taking up the cross, he felt, is about "being true" to Christ, or following "the example and spirit of Jesus Christ himself."[166] The word "service" took on a special meaning for King in relation to the cross, for it helps explain why he had no real problem comparing himself to Jesus at certain points in his own life. "If it sounds like I am comparing myself to the Savior," he told an interviewer on one occasion, "let me remind you that all who honor themselves with the claim of being 'Christians' *should* compare themselves to Jesus."[167] King felt essentially the same about the early Christians, who were brutally persecuted and left a powerful legacy as martyrs for truth.[168] By risking his own life for truth, he participated vicariously in the suffering of the Hebrew prophets, Jesus of Nazareth, and the apostolic church.

Although King denied that he had a "martyr complex," he was always clear in stating his willingness to die if necessary for the transformation of himself and the healing of others, and indeed for the realization of the highest human and ethical ideal.[169] He proudly included the names of Emmett Till, Medgar Evers, those four little girls killed in Birmingham, the three murdered civil rights workers in Mississippi, lesser-known civil rights figures such as George Washington Lee and Mr. and Mrs. Harry Moore, and countless others on that long list of those whom he called "sacred martyrs" and "martyred heroines of a holy crusade" for the cause of truth and justice.[170] In contrast, King denounced those who, driven by fear and indifference, substituted "a cushion for a cross"—those who typically asked, "If I take a stand for truth, what will happen to me?"[171] He demonstrated by his own life that the ethical prophet is never deterred by the potential for spilled blood. King repeatedly stated that "when you have" truth, love, and justice "in your hearts, a cross can't stop you."[172] The failure to stand up for such values was, he argued, tantamount to "a death of the spirit":

You may be thirty-eight years old, as I happen to be, and one day, some great opportunity stands before you and calls upon you to stand up for some great principle, some great issue, some great cause. And you refuse to do it because you are afraid. You refuse to do it because you want to live longer. You're afraid that you will lose your job, or you are afraid that you will be criticized or that you will lose your popularity, or you're afraid that somebody will stab you or shoot at you or bomb your house. So you refuse to take the stand. Well, you may go on and live until you are ninety, but you are just as dead at thirty-eight as you would be at ninety. And the cessation of breathing in your life is but the belated announcement of an earlier death of the spirit. You died when you refused to stand up for right. You died when you refused to stand up for truth. You died when you refused to stand up for justice.[173]

King believed that those who risked all for truth could rest assured that "God suffers with us"—that "he leaves us not alone in our agonies and struggles." "Don't ever think you're by yourself," he said to the faithful. He continued, "Go on to jail if necessary, but you never go alone. Take a stand for that which is right, and the world may misunderstand you, and criticize you. But you never go alone, for somewhere I read that one with God is a majority. And God has a way of transforming a minority into a majority. . . . He'll be with you even until the consummation of the ages."[174]

King held firmly to the conviction that suffering and dying on the cross for truth would ultimately be redemptive. "Many quiet afternoons I have walked into this Sanctuary and looked meditatively at the illumined Cross above the altar," King declared while preaching at Ebenezer, his home church in Atlanta. "Every time I look at the Cross I am reminded of the greatness of God and the redemptive power of Jesus Christ."[175] This was the basis of King's hope for the future. His wife, Coretta, reported that "Martin sometimes placed himself in the historical context of Jesus, especially when he said he would be 'crucified for his beliefs.'" Coretta went on to recount, "As he told me, 'If I am crucified, remember to say, 'He died to make men free.'"[176] "If you are cut down in a movement that is designed to save the soul of a nation," King often remarked to foot soldiers in the demonstrations, "then no other death could be more redemptive."[177] His great love for the hymn "When I Survey the Wondrous Cross" revealed that he was part of that church tradition that Black liberation theologian James H. Cone describes in making the connection between the cross and the lynching tree— that tradition that affirms how Jesus's crucifixion transformed "a 'cruel tree' into a 'Wondrous Cross.'"[178]

Confronting the powerful with truth was for King the ultimate sacrifice, or the very essence of the cross. Cone is right in saying that "King lived the meaning of the cross and thereby gave an even more profound interpretation of it with his life."[179] This is what made him such an epic figure, a model and inspiration for those who faced hardships and tragedies for their involvement in the human struggle. King knew that challenging the powers of evil with truth could eventually cost him everything, including his life, as he occasionally acknowledged in private conversations with family, friends, and his closest associates. Years before his death, King told his wife,

Coretta, that longevity was not an option for him, and at times he predicted that he would not reach age forty. "I probably won't live a long life," he often said.[180] He was murdered when he was only thirty-nine years old. He lived by the belief that truth-telling in the most genuine sense is a revolutionary act, an act of ethical non-conformity and of the maladjusted personality, and his devotion to truth was eventually sealed by his own blood. But what is truly remarkable—from the perspective of the philosopher, theologian, and ethicist—are the ways in which King wove intellect, imagination, and experience into his reading of the meaning of the cross.

Reclaiming the Prophetic Way: A Challenge to the People of God

Martin Luther King Jr. believed that the ever-present reality of sin and evil at every level of human existence highlighted the absolute necessity for prophets and prophecy in every age and generation. He held that any serious discussion of the role of the church, religion, and religious leadership in the twentieth-century world ultimately emphasized this need. Although King associated prophets and prophecy with all the world's great religions, as a pastor in the Christian church, he most often focused his attention primarily on that institution and its leaders when speaking of the prophetic model as vital, workable, and durable for the future.[181] This is clear from even a casual reading of his many sermons, mass meeting speeches, and writings—and especially his widely acclaimed "Letter from the Birmingham City Jail." King was deeply concerned that vast segments of the church and its leadership in his time had lost a sense of the prophetic,[182] that too many Christians valued creedal affirmations far more than the prophetic posture, and he felt the need not only to reaffirm the essentiality of the prophetic role but also to exemplify its power in his own life to the benefit of all of Christendom.

King sensed that the credibility and relevance of the church as a prophetic community in the future, and the reach of interest in the faith itself, hinged on the ability of Christians to open themselves to a continuous process of self-analysis and self-renewal and revitalization. Only in this manner would they be prepared not only to "hear the words of prophecy" in the face of the societal ills of the age in which they found themselves but also "to follow" what King termed "the prophetic way."[183] King routinely called upon clergypersons to lead the way in bearing "witness to the prophetic faith of our Judeo-Christian tradition":

> Who is it that is supposed to articulate the longings and aspirations of the people more than the preacher? Somehow the preacher must have a kind of fire shut up in his bones, and whenever injustice is around he must tell it. Somehow the preacher must be Amos, who said, "When God speaks, who can but prophesy?" Again with Amos, "Let Justice roll down like waters and righteousness like a mighty stream." Somehow the preacher must say with Jesus, "The spirit of the Lord is upon me, because He hath anointed me, and He's anointed me to deal with the problems of the poor."[184]

At the same time, King was ever sensitive to the need for Christian leaders who majored in the priestly role as well. "Not every minister can be a prophet," he wrote, "but some must be prepared for the ordeals of this high calling and be willing to suffer courageously for righteousness."[185] King was equally clear in defining the essential role of the prophet in the United States, a nation he felt would remain sharply divided over the superficialities of race for generations to come:

> The prophet must remind America of the urgency of now. The oft-repeated cliches, "The time is not ripe," "Negroes are not culturally ready," are a stench in the nostrils of God. The time is always right to do what is right. Now is the time to realize the American dream. Now is the time to transform the bleak and desolate midnight of man's inhumanity to man into a glowing daybreak of justice and freedom. Now is the time to open the doors of opportunity to all of God's

children. Now is the time to change the pending national elegy into a creative psalm of brotherly love.[186]

King insisted that truth, and truth alone, should always be the only messaging option for the ethical prophet. He believed this was established for all times in the words and actions of the Hebrew prophets themselves, and most certainly in the teachings of Jesus. According to King, "Jesus is calling upon his disciples" everywhere to always "be true propagandizers" of his word, which is in essence truth: "He is saying in effect propagandize my word, spread it, disseminate it, push it into every nook and crook of the universe, carry it to every tribe and race, every nation and every village; propagandize my word to the uttermost part of the earth. This command comes to every generation of Christians. Jesus is saying to Christians everywhere, ye shall be my witnesses, ye shall be my propaganda agents, ye shall be the spreader of my truth in all the world."[187] For King, this meant in part giving "verbal affirmation" to "the resurrection"—to the triumph of truth over the cross and the crucifixion.[188] "In these days of worldwide confusion," King argued, "there is a dire need for men and women who will courageously do battle for truth."[189] At another point, he declared that "the prophetic words 'Thus saith the Lord' must be spoken in the United Nations no less than in the legislature of the State of Mississippi."[190] King had problems with Christians who routinely highlighted the need "to preach the true gospel," or to proclaim the triumphant power of the cross over evil, while avoiding any "talk about social issues," a problem he insisted led "to a dangerously irrelevant church." Although King understood the problem that led many among the faithful to see "the Christian gospel as only concerned with the individual soul," he, as an ethical prophet, categorically rejected such a position. "But every now and then," he asserted, "people must hear the truth. America must hear the truth. If we are going to survive as a nation, somebody has got to have vision, somebody must be willing to stand up and be criticized and called every bad name, out of love for this country."[191]

Intrigued by Søren Kierkegaard's emphasis on "the value of suffering," especially for those who live the faith devoid of self-ish pursuits, King consistently declared that truth is the cross that the ethical prophet should willingly bear with love. This he knew from personal experience, for he, as Andrew Young put it, "had lived his life in the shadow of the cross." King did not think it was possible to be a Christian in his time, or at any other time in human history for that matter, without taking up the cross. For him, truth was not simply about bearing the cross—it was in fact the cross itself. In other words, the cross is always about the crucifixion of truth. King frequently said that "Good Friday is a fact of life."[192] Thus, the voices of prophetic Christianity must be ever aware of how truth-telling invites persecution from the forces of evil and untruth. King's enduring message to ethical prophets was that standing "for truth and justice" often means being "called an impractical idealist or a dangerous radical," and that "it might even mean physical death."[193]

Always a visionary with amazing powers of foresight and dis-cernment, King concluded that church renewal and the revital-ization of the spiritual life ranked among the greatest challenges confronting humankind in the future. He felt that this challenge could be met only if the Christian church and its leadership were prepared to draw heavily on the wellsprings of those sources that gave Christianity power in its infancy, when the faithful held firmly to an ethic of no surrender in the face of the edicts of Roman impe-rial power. In other words, they had to reconnect—morally, spiri-tually, and practically—with that tradition that took its cues from the apostle Paul and others in the New Testament church, who "told Caesar they would not fight war," who refused to "follow the patterns of the Roman world that gave them no power or capacity to worship the God of their salvation," who "were persecuted," and who went "to the chopping block" and "into the dens of lions" with "a hymn on their lips," "singing about the glory of God" and their determination to "stick to what" they believed "is right."[194] "If today's church does not recapture the sacrificial spirit of the early church," King wrote, "it will lose its authenticity, forfeit the loyalty of millions, and be dismissed as an irrelevant social club with no meaning for the twentieth century."[195]

Despite the pervasive presence of sin and evil in the world, on both individual and social levels, King found in the Hebraic-Christian traditions of ethical prophecy a basis for a message of hope. For him, that hope was grounded ultimately in an omnipotent, omnipresent, and omniscient God who is both judgmental and loving, wrathful and merciful—a God who "is at work in the universe" and who will in time bring down the powerful and evil while liberating and empowering the weak and the downtrodden. King witnessed this God at work in the human struggle for freedom, justice, human dignity, and peace. He saw the walls of injustice gradually crumbling in the face of courageous and determined resistance on the part of committed human beings. Even so, King warned against what he described as "magic hope" or "superficial optimism," which leads persons "to conclude that the death of a particular evil means that all evil lies dead upon the seashore." He felt the story of the children of Israel's successful crossing of the Red Sea, after which the Egyptian soldiers drowned, graphically illustrated this point because they still had to suffer greatly due to a cruel and howling wilderness. "All progress is precarious, and the solution of one problem brings us face to face with another problem," King declared. He added, "The Kingdom of God as a universal reality is *not yet*. Because sin exists on every level of man's existence, the death of one tyranny is followed by the emergence of another tyranny." And yet King, imbued with the hopeful spirit of prophets down through the ages, was fully convinced that evil eventually "dies on the seashore, not merely because of" humans' "endless struggle against it, but because of God's power to defeat it."[196]

5

The New Advancing Truth

The Spirit of a Movement

I feel safe in the midst of my enemies, for the truth is all powerful and will prevail.

—Sojourner Truth (1863)

The historic achievement is found in the fact that the movement in the South has profoundly shaken the entire edifice of segregation. . . . The persistence of segregation is not the salient fact of Southern experience; the proliferating areas in which the Negro moves freely is the new advancing truth.

—Martin Luther King Jr., *Where Do We Go from Here: Chaos or Community?* (1967)

Martin Luther King Jr. variously referred to the freedom crusade of the 1950s and '60s as "a spiritual movement," "a spiritual

203

explosion," "a spiritually rooted movement," "a movement depending on moral and spiritual forces," "a great and creative spiritual venture," "the burning spirit of this new period," "this righteous struggle," and "a movement of essentially revolutionary quality." He understood and viewed the movement not from the standpoint of the significance of his own leadership but primarily in terms of the spirit of the people of different faiths and divided allegiances who comprised, defined, and launched it.[1] In a 1967 lecture entitled "Youth and Social Action," King described the movement as an "awakening" that had grown in breadth and focus since the mid-1950s, as young people injected it with a new, more energetic spirit of resistance and as the forces of progression clashed with the forces of stagnation, gradualism, tokenism, and retrogression.[2] King's stress on the spiritual and/or sacred quality of what unfolded during those years calls into question any interpretation of the movement that explains it essentially in sociopolitical terms.

This chapter explores the meaning and dimensions of the civil rights movement as yet another episode in what King called not only "experiments with truth" but also "the new advancing" or "unfolding truth."[3] It begins with King's persistent efforts to refute the lingering myth that the South and the North were two vastly different regions of the United States when it came to matters of race. The discussion then turns to his insistence on viewing the civil rights movement in historical context, and especially his tendency to see that phenomenon as yet another example of "truth marching on."[4] Of special significance are the ways in which King highlighted truth as the guiding principle of a creative, concerted, and protracted thrust to bring the beloved community into being or a completely integrated human family in the forms of "a new South," "a new America," and "a new world."[5] The content provided lends credence to the Black psychologist Kenneth B. Clark's contention that nonviolent direct action in pursuit of the beloved community was for King "not just a strategy" but "a truth"—an "assertion of the philosophical position that one cannot differentiate means from ends."[6] Considerable attention is given to King's perspective on leadership in the human struggle, and especially to the messianic role he conferred upon "the non-myth" or "new Negro" as "a creative minority"—a vanguard role that owed much to his own reading of history and the works of Henry David Thoreau, Mohandas K. Gandhi, Reinhold Niebuhr, and Arnold Toynbee.[7] In short, this chapter captures the ways in which King gave expression, in theory and practice, to his beloved community ideal in regional, national, and global terms.[8]

South and North: The Myth of Two Vastly Different Americas

Martin Luther King Jr. was quite familiar with the white South and its long-standing and persistent efforts, through a set of myths rooted in idealized and romanticized versions of its history, to create an identity separate from the North. He saw this firsthand during his own time, as the movement for freedom forced white southerners to vigorously reaffirm the age-old myths of superior and inferior races, of the South as the epitome of a godly and orderly society, and of states' rights as more consistent with representative democracy than national sovereignty.[9] With this and more in mind, King, in an essay in 1963, described the South as "a hostile nation," thus calling into question the notion, put forth later by the historian Charles R. Wilson, that its dream of becoming a separate political nation had died with General Robert E. Lee's surrender at Appomattox:

> The South in walling itself off from the application of laws and judicial decrees behind an iron curtain of defiance, becomes a law unto itself. It is an autonomous region whose posture toward the central government has elements as defiant as a hostile nation. Only the underdeveloped or primitive nations of the world tolerate regions which are similar, in which feudal autocrats or military governors have supremacy over the federal power. It is a condition unknown to modern industrial societies except for our own. This is the source of the scorn expressed by African and Asian states

when we lecture them on government while our own suffers from a glaring defect of sovereignty.[10]

King wondered how the South could continue to defy the Supreme Court's 1954 decision on school desegregation and other laws of the nation without consequences. "Southern states continue to make a mockery of justice in an attempt to maintain their hold on political power and the special privileges which go with it," he complained in 1966.[11] But for King, the white South's audacious and troubling "declarations of defiance" and resistance to much-needed positive change on the racial front could not be explained solely on the basis of an insatiable desire to maintain power and privilege. He held that "the treatment of Negroes [was] a basic spiritual problem," which, in his opinion, proved, unmistakably, that the South had a heart problem. "Dixie has a heart all right," King declared, "but it's having a little heart trouble right now."[12] This "heart trouble" translated into a "spiritual," "intellectual," and "conscientious blindness" that largely explained all too many white southerners' inability to engage in "honest thinking" when confronted with the evils of white supremacy and racial segregation.[13] Thus, King agreed with the novelist and new South advocate Lillian Smith, who suggested that the complete elimination of the old societal order would be possible only after the minds of hate-filled southerners had been cleared "of the myths and fantasies which the demagogues have for so long substituted for truth."[14]

The facts of both history and life established for King the tragic connection between his native South and the myth of white supremacy. Mindful of how both truth and logic had been manipulated and distorted to create and sustain this myth, he explained its origins and advancement over time in these terms: "The South was the stronghold of racism. In white migrations through history from the South to the North and West, racism was carried to poison the rest of the nation. Prejudice, discrimination and bigotry had been inextricably imbedded through all the institutions of Southern life—political, social, and economic. There could be no possibility of life-transforming change anywhere so long as the vast and solid influence of Southern segregation remained unchallenged and unhurt."[15] King felt that white supremacy prevented the South—a society "rich in natural resources, blessed with the beauties of nature, and endowed with a native warmth of spirit"—from realizing its "marvelous possibilities."[16] "In her unwillingness to accept the Negro as a human being," he argued, "the South has chosen to remain undeveloped, poorly educated and emotionally warped." Despite its assets, King reasoned, the region had essentially chosen to languish in cultural, educational, political, and economic backwardness. "The South is retarded by a blight that debilitates not only the Negro but also the white man," King lamented. "Poor white men, women, and children, bearing the scars of ignorance, deprivation, and poverty, are evidence of the fact that harm to one is injury to all." King went on to assert, "Segregation has placed the whole South socially, educationally, and economically behind the rest of the nation."[17] This explains his abiding interest in bringing "the South culturally, politically and socially up to the level" of other regions in the country.[18]

Even as King consistently chided the South for its miserable record in race relations, he never wanted to leave the impression that white supremacy was "just a Southern problem" or that the South and the North were two radically different Americas when it came to the realities and challenges confronting Black and white people. Always careful to address situations involving the movement "in the light of truth," King repeatedly urged his people to be both realistic and cautiously optimistic when assessing their continued status as the most oppressed group in every region of the country. "Let's not fool ourselves," he said. "We are far from the promised land, both North and South."[19] "Negroes, North and South, still live in segregation, are housed in slums, eat in segregation, pray in segregation, and die in segregation," he wrote. "The life experience of the Negro in integration remains an exception even in the North."[20] King found it problematic that whites in the North tended to think otherwise:

Well, the northern white, having had little actual contact with the Negro, is devoted to an abstract principle of cordial interracial relations. The North has long considered, in a theoretical way, that it supported brotherhood and the equality of man, but the truth is that deep prejudices and discriminations exist in hidden and subtle and covert disguises. The South's prejudice and discrimination, on the other hand, has been applied against the Negro in obvious, open, overt and glaring forms—which make the problem easier to get at. The Southern white man has the advantage of far more actual contact with Negroes than the northerner. A major problem is that this contact has been paternalistic and poisoned by the myth of racial superiority. Many southern whites, supported by the "research" of several southern anthropologists, vow that white racial superiority—and Negro inferiority—are a biological fact.[21]

King acknowledged in 1966 that the civil rights movement up to that point had been essentially a Southern phenomenon. "In these recent years our struggle has centered largely in the Southern states which make up the stronghold of the old Confederacy, where the dark clouds of racial injustice had cast their longest shadows," he noted. He knew that such an organized and sustained effort in nonviolent direct action was also needed in the North. Thousands of Blacks had left the South to settle in the North in the first half of the twentieth century, King recounted, "seeking a Promised Land of plenty which they had glimpsed fleetingly during the prosperity of two world wars," but "instead of the Promised Land they experienced a lot replete with poverty, another Egypt of denial, discrimination, and dismay." This meant that Blacks had "nowhere to turn, North and South," as "the brief hope of a new era" was "threatened by rapidly increasing technology." "Both farms and factories are now automated to a large extent," King pointed out, "and the recent progress in the political and legal status of the Negro is threatened by economic forces that may throw us back into a more serious crisis in race and class relations than ever before." Faced during that time with the brutal murder of "unarmed, nonviolent civil rights workers in Mississippi and Alabama," with "violent, futile riots in Los Angeles" and other major cities, and with "millions of my black brothers slowly perishing on an island of poverty in the midst of a sea of affluence," King sadly admitted that his "dream" for both the North and South had gradually turned "into a nightmare." The fact that "the hundred years of one party, racist domination had given the South virtual control of the United States"—a situation in which "Southern Senators controlled the key committees and presided over our total national appropriations"—compounded the problem for King.[22] Even so, he insisted that "the prodigious mountains of adversity cannot blot out our vision of a truly great society." He refused to completely abandon his dream that every region of the country would, "day by day," "awaken from the nightmares of chaos and hostility and begin to fashion a new reality of love and brotherhood amid the rubble of hatred and bitterness."[23] But the pragmatist in King was such that he sensed the enduring and intense battles ahead.

As King and his Southern Christian Leadership Conference (SCLC) turned their attention to segregated housing and slum conditions in Chicago in 1965–66, they encountered white resistance that was as strong as and, in some cases, more intense than in the South. Strangely enough, much of the pushback came from northern politicians who supported the freedom movement in the South. The irony of the situation was not lost on King, who stated, "Here, too, the North reveals its true ambivalence on the subject of civil rights. When, in the last session of Congress, the issue came home to the North through a call for open housing legislation, white Northern Congressmen who had enthusiastically supported the 1964 and 1965 civil rights bills now joined in a mighty course of anguish and dismay reminiscent of Alabama and Mississippi. So the first piece of legislation aimed at rectifying a shocking evil in the North went down to crushing defeat."[24] Even more telling and disheartening were the racial epithets and mob violence King and other movement foot soldiers endured as they marched through the lily-white Gage Park, Belmont-Cragin, Bogan, and Jefferson Park communities in Chicago. Recalling the "screaming white hoodlums" who lined "the sidewalks," throwing bricks and bottles,

King declared that he had not seen that level of hostility and violence "even in Mississippi."[25]

In highlighting white supremacy as a national rather than a regional problem, King was merely stating the facts of American history, life, and culture. To be sure, the growing consciousness concerning the national character and impact of racism and race relations was part of the "new advancing" or "unfolding truth" in King's time, and he and the civil rights campaigns he led figured most prominently in that development. Based on history and personal experience, King knew that neither the white South nor the white North were prepared to play a major, collective role in Black liberation, but he had more faith in the capacity of white southerners to change for the better. In other words, he believed that white southerners had a capacity for honesty and commitment to principle that surpassed that of their counterparts in the North—a capacity that, if properly cultivated, could contribute to a transforming impulse:

> You know, when you can finally convert a white southerner, you have one of the most genuine, committed human beings that you'll ever find. Did you ever notice that? You see, what the white South has going for it that the North doesn't have is that the average white [s]outherner has at least had individual contact with Negroes. It hasn't been person-to-person contact, but he's at least had individual contact with Negroes. Now, the thing to do is to transform that Lord-servant relationship into intergroup, interpersonal living. And when that happens, do you know that I really feel that the South is going to get ahead of the North. Because one thing about this brother down here is that he doesn't like us, and he lets us know it. . . . You do at least know how to deal with it. I've been up North, and I've found that you don't know how to deal with it, because you can't quite get at your target. He'll (white northerner) sit up there and smile in your face. You go down to see the officials and they'll serve you cookies and tea, and shake

your hand and pose for pictures with you. And at the same time, keeping Negroes in ghettoes and slums. But down here, they won't take no pictures with us, they won't give us no tea and cookies, and they tell us on television that they don't like us. They don't hide it.[26]

King's belief in the capacity of white southerners for growth around the race question increased over time as he detected in some of them a genuineness of spirit despite their apparent commitment to white supremacy and Jim Crow. In May 1960, after an all-white Alabama jury acquitted King of the charge of perjury for signing a false state income tax return, King, "stunned by the verdict," declared, "This represents to my mind great hope, and it reveals what I have said on so many occasions, that there are hundreds and thousands of people, white people of goodwill in the South, and even though they may not agree with one's views on the question of integration, they are honest people and people who will follow a just and righteous path."[27] In an interview five years later, King predicted, "If the South is honest with itself, it may well outdistance the North in the improvement of race relations."[28] On yet another occasion, King assured his listeners, in a speech at a mass meeting in Alabama, that he was convinced that even die-hard, violent white supremacists in the South could be shown a better path in life: "I want to tell you this evening that I believe that Senator Engelhardt's heart can be changed. I believe that Senator Eastland's heart can be changed. I believe that the Ku Klux Klan can be transformed into a clan for God's kingdom. I believe that the White Citizens Council can be transformed into a Right Citizens Council. I believe that."[29] King left no doubt about his hope for and faith in the South over the long hall. "I am convinced that in our time the South can be a peaceful and integrated society," he declared.[30]

King was "more optimistic about the South than the North," believing that the South could in the long run prove the better environment for the kind of ideal society he envisioned.[31] Recognizing that race relations in the South were not characterized by the kind of hypocrisy, pretentiousness, and false sympathy so typical of the

North, King felt that white southerners, when finally convinced that they, too, had much to gain from the civil rights crusade, would be more inclined to confront their bigotry and intolerance while also opening themselves to much needed social and cultural change. "The South has a problem and knows it," said King as he considered different strategies for creating a genuinely interracial society. He concluded that the South, despite its rigid patterns of Jim Crow, had much to teach the North about human communication between the races.[32] Although such sweeping declarations reflected King's belief in the capacity of white southerners to ultimately undergo a radical change in attitude and behavior, they were more indicative of his faith in what he called "the essence of the Gospel."[33]

Much of King's hope for a transformed South was also grounded in the fact that "the legislative and judicial advances" of the 1950s and '60s—from the Supreme Court's *Brown* decision of 1954 to the Civil Rights Bill of 1964 and the Voting Rights Act of 1965—had a greater impact on the region than in the North:

> Now these legislative and judicial developments gave a great deal of hope to the Negro, and it is very important to see that they rectified longstanding evils of the South but they did very little to improve conditions for the millions of Negroes in the teeming ghettoes of the North. In other words, it did very little to penetrate the lower depths of Negro deprivation, and I think that we must see that the North finds itself in that position now, of seeing retrogress and not progress. At least in the South, the Negro can see pockets of progress, but this isn't true of the Negro in the northern ghetto. He sees retrogress in the sense that the masses of Negroes find themselves in a worst economic situation now, and the progress that we've made economically has been mainly on the professional level, middle-class Negroes, so I think we have to see that these things did not apply in the northern ghetto, and this makes for a great deal of despair.[34]

But it became increasingly evident to King that the South of the 1950s and '60s was not monolithic. This, too, was part of the new emerging truth of that period. He often stated that "there is no single 'solid' South"—that, in his words, "the South is not today one whole." He identified "at least three" Souths "geographically speaking": "There is the South of compliance—Oklahoma, Kentucky, Kansas, Missouri, West Virginia, Delaware, and the District of Columbia. There is the wait-and-see South—Tennessee, Texas, North Carolina, Arkansas, and Florida. And there is the South of resistance—Georgia, Alabama, Mississippi, Louisiana, South Carolina, and Virginia."[35] King offered an interesting and seemingly more perceptive assessment of how these "several Souths" broke down in terms of attitudes:

> A minority in each of these states would use almost any means, including physical violence, to preserve segregation. A majority, through tradition and custom, sincerely believe in segregation, but at the same time stand on the side of law and order. Hence, they are willing to comply with the law not because they feel it is sound but because it is the law. A third group, a growing minority, is working courageously to implement the law of the land. These people believe in the morality as well as the constitutionality of integration. Their still small voices often go unheard among the louder shouts of defiance, but they are actively in the field. Furthermore, there are in the white South millions of people of good will whose voices are yet unheard, whose course is yet unclear, and whose courageous acts are yet unseen. These persons are often silent today because of fear—fear of social, political, and economic reprisals.[36]

King felt that the phenomena of "several Souths" were not necessarily unhealthy or problematic—that this situation actually afforded potential opportunities for the kind of healthy dialogue around race not possible in the white North, a region that seemingly approximated more closely one whole. This explains

King's conviction that "extending the frontiers of democracy in the South" constituted the first step in any genuine effort to democratize the entire nation. "Since the largest segment of the Negro population lives in the South," he opined, "the problem must be solved in the South or it cannot be solved anywhere." King also prophesied that "the future of America may well be determined" in southern states like Mississippi, for it was there "that democracy faces its most serious challenge."[37] Perhaps more importantly, he felt that God was using the South "to bring some of the most creative advances for the black man in the United States of America."[38]

There were certain hopeful signs that continuously reinforced King's thinking along these lines. "We are convinced that the great majority of white Southerners are prepared to accept and abide by the Supreme Law of the Land," he said in 1957, at the risk of overstatement.[39] By the early 1960s, he remarked that "the simple and arresting truth that became clear" was that "significant elements of the South" had "come to see" that "the whole region" could not prosper "socially, educationally, and economically" without "rectifying racial wrongs."[40] "More and more southerners are speaking out, telling plain truths to the bitter and blind," King claimed. "Enlightened self-interest makes them accept the Negro's drive for freedom as an ally rather than an enemy."[41] King asserted, perhaps naively, that "even the segregationists [knew] in their hearts" that segregation was "morally wrong and sinful." "If it weren't, the white South would not be haunted as it is by a deep sense of guilt for what it has done to the Negro," he reasoned, "guilt for patronizing him, degrading him, brutalizing him, thingifying him; guilt for lying to itself. This is the source of the schizophrenia that the South will suffer until it goes through its crisis of conscience."[42] At another point, King elaborated further on this "guilt complex": "Psychologists would say that a guilt complex can lead to two reactions. One is repentance and the desire to change. The other reaction is to indulge in more of the very thing that you have the sense of guilt about. And I think we find these two reactions. I think much of the violence that we notice in the South at this time is really the attempt to compensate, drown the sense of guilt, by indulging in more of the very thing that causes the sense of guilt."[43]

Although King found it difficult at times to believe in the fundamental pragmatism of white Americans, he was unalterably convinced that the forces of truth and justice would ultimately triumph in both the South and North. However, he was concerned that aside from "the obvious methods of defiance," white supremacists were increasingly turning to "the subtle and skillful method of truth distortion" in an effort "to influence the minds of northern and southern liberals," the best hope for a transformed white America, with cleverly disseminated half-truths.[44] Although King was certain that such attempts would not succeed in the long run, he knew nonetheless that they virtually assured that the struggle to transform the hearts and minds of white America for the better would continue to be difficult and even tedious. This became painfully obvious to King toward the end of his life, as much of the optimism he had about the creation of a New South and a new North, and indeed a new America, faded under the weight of the white backlash that greeted the cry for Black power. In an essay entitled "A Testament of Hope," published posthumously, King sadly acknowledged, "If we look honestly at the realities of our national life, it is clear that we are not marching forward; we are groping and stumbling; we are divided and confused." "Our moral values and our spiritual confidence sink," he said, "even as our material wealth ascends."[45] Apparently, King was wrestling anew with the spirit of a nation that seemed hopelessly fragmented over what was true and untrue, real and unreal, rational and irrational, acceptable and unacceptable. This could not have been more challenging and perhaps even disheartening for one who thought not only of the liberation and empowerment of his own people but of the collective needs, well-being, and survival of all Americans.

Truth Is Marching On: Characterizing the Movement

Martin Luther King Jr. felt that the freedom crusade, much like the church and academia, constituted legitimate space in which to affirm, engage, and exalt truth. The ways of truth became strikingly evident to him, in the practical realm, through love and nonviolence. Love expressed through nonviolence, he maintained, was "a new idea, more powerful than guns and clubs."[46] Through the method of nonviolence, he and his followers forced America to engage in a serious reckoning with truth relative to itself, its past, its present, and its future. "I'm concerned about truth," King declared, noting that such a person "can never advocate violence." He went on to state, "Through violence you may murder the liar, but you cannot murder the lie, nor establish the truth. Through violence you may murder the hater, but you do not murder hate. Darkness cannot put out darkness. Only light can do that."[47] "The beauty of nonviolence is that in its own way and in its own time it seeks to break the chain reaction of evil," said King on another occasion. "With a majestic sense of spiritual power, it seeks to elevate truth, beauty and goodness to the throne."[48] King's interest in and continuing search for truth became a commitment not only to a particular personal and social ethic but to a persistent struggle for personal and communal liberation and empowerment.

From the time of the Montgomery bus protest, King used cultural, biblical, and theological rhetoric to describe "a Negro revolution" launched and sustained in the name of truth. The freedom movement of the 1950s and '60s, he held, was about "truth marching on" or "God's truth marching on." Of the march toward freedom in Montgomery, King remarked, "We're walking because we're tired of being suppressed politically. We're walking because we're tired of being suppressed economically; we're walking because we're tired of being segregated and discriminated. Freedom is the just claim of all men. As we walk we're going to walk with love in our hearts." "When Dr. King called upon us to march," wrote John Lewis, "we marched knowing that truth was on our side." The image of crusading freedom fighters armed with the weapon of truth, substituting "tired feet for tired souls," became indelibly etched in King's mind as he offered his own descriptions of the movement as it unfolded from Montgomery to Memphis.[49] Marching in the streets and along the highways in the South was for him an important visual message about not surrendering to the machinations of evil and untruth. Convinced that "nothing could stop the marching feet of a determined people,"[50] King and other freedom fighters translated truth into a crusade for much-needed, meaningful, and lasting social change and, in the process, challenged the might of the richest and most powerful country in the world. "Now, there is nothing wrong with marching in this sense," King opined as he explained his people's continuing journey toward "the land of freedom."[51] He likened "the patter of their feet as they walked through Jim Crow barriers in the great stride toward freedom" to "the thunder of the marching men of Joshua," noting that "the world rocks beneath their tread." This explained King's appreciation for the old slave spiritual "Joshua Fit the Battle of Jericho," which he insisted "was given to us" by some "unknown, long dead, dark-skinned originator" and "yet with empathetic pertinence for all of us today." King declared that "the Bible tells us that the mighty men of Joshua merely walked about the walled city of Jericho and the barriers to freedom came tumbling down." While recognizing that the story of Joshua was about a "simple yet colorful depiction of that great moment in biblical history," King insisted nonetheless that it was indeed still meaningful or relevant for the movement's foot soldiers, especially as they responded to "the call to higher ground to which the new directions of our struggle summon us."[52]

King had no problem drawing spiritual connections between the civil rights campaigns he led and certain events and revelations in Scripture, even as he was accused of being nonbiblical in the tactics and strategies he brought to the freedom struggle. Unlike all too many of his white Christian adversaries, who reduced much of the Bible to pro–Jim Crow propaganda, King employed Scripture in ways that enabled and empowered foot soldiers in the movement. Using biblical language both figuratively and literally, he described the freedom movement as a more contemporary exodus from "the Egypt of segregation":

We have left the dusty soils of Egypt and crossed a Red Sea whose waters had for years been hardened by a long and piercing winter of massive resistance. But before we reach the majestic shores of the Promised Land, there is a frustrating and bewildering wilderness ahead. We must still face prodigious hilltops of opposition and gigantic mountains of resistance. But with patient and firm determination we will press on until every valley of despair is exalted to new peaks of hope, until every mountain of pride and irrationality is made low by the leveling process of humility and compassion; until the rough places of injustice are transformed into a smooth plane of equality of opportunity; and until the crooked places of prejudice are transformed by the straightening process of bright-eyed wisdom.[53]

This statement from King, like the old Negro spiritual "Go Down Moses," reveals that King and his people were not simply students of the Bible who read about the exodus but actual participants in that event. King's many references to Joshua's army, Moses and the exodus, and countless other scriptural narratives and accounts put the lie to the claim, made widely by southern white clergy, that the civil rights movement was not in line with biblical teachings, that it had no sound basis in theology, and that it was inconsistent with the demands and requirements of the Christian faith.[54]

The need to defend the indispensability, integrity, and legitimacy of the freedom cause was pressing and indeed inescapable for King, especially in view of that maze of misinformation commonly and widely perpetrated regarding it. The "new advancing" or "unfolding truth," in his manner of thinking, had much to do with constantly explaining and clarifying the meaning, values, tactics, strategies, and goals of the civil rights movement to a questioning and often hostile people, many of whom had no interest in or desire to know the truth. A strange and complex web of fictional narratives about the movement contributed in the long run to a climate in which King spent as much and perhaps more time teaching and promoting a messaging strategy as leading demonstrations, boycotts, acts of civil disobedience, and other forms of nonviolent direct action. He let it be known, as a point of departure in any serious conversation, that it was his devotion to truth, and not an insatiable need for publicity and personal fortunes, that drove him into the sphere of civil and human rights. King also clearly noted that the movement was never about him personally but was the people's movement, an admission of immense significance, since a considerable amount of the misinformation and misconception had to do with him and his leadership role:

> And one of the prayers that I pray to God every day is: "O God, help me to see myself in my true perspective. Help me, O God, to see that I'm just a symbol of a movement. Help me to see that I'm the victim of what the Germans call a *Zeitgeist* and that something was getting ready to happen in history; history was ready for it. And that a boycott would have taken place in Montgomery, Alabama, if I had never come to Alabama. Help me to realize that I'm where I am because of the forces of history and because of the fifty thousand Negroes of Alabama who will never get their names in the papers and in the headlines. O God, help me to see that where I stand today, I stand because others helped me to stand there and because the forces of history projected me there. And this moment would have come in history even if M. L. King had never been born." And when we come to see that, we stand with a humility. This is the prayer that I pray to God every day, "Lord help me to see M. L. King as M. L. King in his true perspective." Because if I don't see that, I will become the biggest fool in America.[55]

King's sense of the freedom movement as a product of "the forces of history" and of the zeitgeist, or "the spirit of the times," constituted a direct and forceful challenge to those southern whites who used the myths of "the satisfied Negro" and "time" to denounce the need for such a movement. White segregationists had long argued that "the Negro was 'satisfied'" with his place in society, that whites understood him well, that Blacks should be patient and thankful for what they already have, and that the races got "along beautifully" as long as "outside agitators" stayed away and did not interfere. Thus, they accused King of "bringing trouble where" they had "always had peace."[56] King engaged such myths forthrightly and firmly. He determined that the myth of the "satisfied Negro" simply revealed the extent to which the Negro had been successful in developing "the pretense of self-deprecation" and "satisfaction," of playing "the fool" while making "a fool of his oppressor," especially in a climate in which "speaking the truth" could have led to a loss of livelihood and even life itself.[57] Race relations over generations, King held, were anything but beautiful, for they were indicative of "a negative peace," which is "the absence of tension," rather than "a positive peace, which is the presence of justice." Convinced that "innate in all life and all growth is tension" and that "growth comes through a struggle" between the forces of progression and the forces of retrogression, King insisted that the movement was designed to precipitate not unhealthy tension and violence but a healthy, nonviolent tension that exposed the violence already endemic to the system, thus forcing society to confront and to deal honestly, creatively, and constructively with it.[58] He delighted in the fact that because of the movement, "the South's negative peace was rapidly undermined."[59] In King's opinion, "a type of constructive, nonviolent tension" was an essential part of any social movement grounded in truth and geared toward better and more harmonious relations between humans.[60]

Nothing frustrated King more than segregationists who lived "by a mythical concept of time," constantly urging "the Negro to wait for a 'more convenient season'" for his freedom. He illustrated the point by recalling a letter he received from "a white brother in Texas," who wrote, "All Christians know that the colored people will receive equal rights eventually, but it is possible that you are in too great a religious hurry. It has taken Christianity almost two thousand years to accomplish what it has. The teachings of Christ take time to come to earth." King wondered about any person of seeming goodwill "who paternalistically believes he can set the timetable for another man's freedom," but perhaps more disturbing for him was the shortsightedness of those white persons of faith who embraced "the myth concerning time in relation to the struggle for freedom":

> Such an attitude stems from a tragic misconception of time, from the strangely irrational notion that there is something in the very flow of time that will inevitably cure all ills. Actually, time itself is neutral; it can be used either destructively or constructively. More and more I feel that the people of ill will have used time more effectively than have the people of good will. Human progress never rolls in on the wheels of inevitability; it comes through the tireless efforts of men willing to be co-workers with God, and without this hard work, time itself becomes an ally of the forces of social stagnation. We must use time creatively, in the knowledge that the time is always ripe to do right.[61]

In King's judgment, the "white brother in Texas" was living proof of the validity of Henry A. Wallace's assertion that "there have been times in history when new and creative ideas appeared on the scene, but they ended up unaccepted because the very historical atmosphere at that time was not sufficiently new and strong to contain them." A creative movement, like a creative idea, King held, "needs something new and strong to hold it." But despite those whites who took shelter behind the myth of time, King was convinced that he was living in an age, or what he called "the *Kairos*," when history was "ready to accept a new event." He felt that this conviction was vindicated in the 1950s and '60s by the "marching feet" of freedom's foot soldiers:

> When Negroes marched, so did the nation. The power of the nonviolent march is indeed a mystery. It is always surprising that a few hundred Negroes marching can produce such a reaction across the nation. When marches are carefully organized around well-defined issues, they represent the power which Victor Hugo phrased as the most powerful

force in the world, "an idea whose time has come." Marching feet announce that time has come for a given idea. When the idea is a sound one, the cause a just one, and the demonstration a righteous one, change will be forthcoming. But if any of these conditions are not present, the power for change is missing also.[62]

But such logic regarding time was not likely to lead to understanding on the part of the average white southerner, who had "not suffered unduly from the disease of segregation."[63] The white South was, for the most part, impervious to what King had in mind when he asserted that the time is always right to do what is right. Instead of heeding his words, many accused him of rank hypocrisy—of failing abysmally to match words with deeds, especially when it came to his own movement tactics. Since the King-led Montgomery Improvement Association (MIA) and the White Citizens Council (WCC) made use of "the boycott method" during the mid- to late 1950s, it was suggested by some whites that King was in no moral position to criticize the white supremacist group. But King maintained that the WCC resorted to the boycott tactic to force Blacks and whites to conform to Jim Crow policies and practices, while the MIA used the same tactic to achieve an integrated society or to further ethical and Christian ends. Moreover, King noted that he and his fellow protesters launched the bus boycott "not to put the bus company out of business, but to put justice in business."[64]

King employed essentially the same logic when repeatedly asked how he could "advocate breaking some laws and obeying others," or how he could urge southern whites to obey the legal decision of the Supreme Court "outlawing segregation in the public schools" while he violated local laws and court injunctions in street demonstrations. King explained, "The answer lies in the fact that there are two types of laws: just and unjust. I would be the first to advocate obeying just laws. One has not only a legal but a moral responsibility to obey just laws. Conversely, one has a moral responsibility to disobey unjust laws." "All segregation statutes are unjust because segregation distorts the soul and damages the personality," said King as he further revealed the rationale for his resistance to such laws in the South.[65] Also, "knowing well what the consequences would be and prepared to accept them," King only broke court injunctions that were used "to block the direct-action civil-rights drive" and to preserve segregation.[66] At the same time, he adamantly insisted that his acts of civil disobedience were not to be confused with the "uncivil disobedience" of white supremacist groups like the Ku Klux Klan (KKK), who bombed churches and homes and killed civil rights workers under the cover of darkness, with no desire to answer for their criminal actions. "In no sense do I advocate evading or defying the law, as would the rabid segregationist," King wrote. "That would lead to anarchy." He went on to state that "one who breaks the law must do so openly, lovingly, and with a willingness to suffer the penalty."[67]

The widely held misconceptions and misinformation about the tactics and strategies used in King-led civil rights campaigns were challenging enough, but there was also the myth, emanating from the press, that the goals of the movement were significantly hampered due primarily to King's and his SCLC's failure to conform to clearly and well-established norms of bureaucratic behavior and routine. King knew that such fabrications resulted almost entirely from media sensationalism, for representatives of both the print and broadcasting media eagerly seized upon opportunities to characterize much of SCLC's leadership as inept and inefficient and to make the movement appear more chaotic, disorganized, and unstructured than it actually was.[68] King expected no less from the media, and he spent surprisingly little time debunking its exaggerated accounts about SCLC and the movement. "I believe we are being victimized," he declared as he spoke of media-driven myths as part of that growing pattern of attempts by the larger society to undermine the spirit and reach of the civil rights cause.[69] Functioning in a culture in which the SCLC was variously called "a church," "a faith operation," "the social action arm of the black church," and "the black church writ large," King would have been the first to admit that that organization did not conform to the traditional Western model of the bureaucratic organizational structure.[70] But it would have been difficult for him to see how such a model would have made SCLC a more effective organization, especially in its activities among people who were not particularly interested in, and who had long suffered due to, bureaucratic structures. A close adherence to the Black church model is what SCLC needed to be most appealing to the masses of Blacks or people at the grassroots level. Adam Fairclough makes the point at some length, noting how the SCLC was successful in ways untypical of the more bureaucratic National Association for the Advancement of Colored People (NAACP):

> In the turbulent, fast-moving, and unpredictable world of the civil rights movement, organizational hardness was a liability rather than an asset. Thus, the NAACP, the most bureaucratic of the civil rights organizations, found it difficult to adapt and respond to the rapidly changing circumstances of the early 1960s, when crisis followed crisis and the situation changed from day to day. SCLC, by contrast, had the capacity to make quick decisions, to think on its feet. Too great a concern with bureaucratic routine would have undermined this ability. King himself was keenly aware of this, consciously neglecting internal structure so that SCLC's staff could move quickly as the circumstances changed and opportunities presented themselves. What appeared to outsiders as chaos and inefficiency was often the inevitable consequence of flexibility, spontaneity, and a capability for swift decision making and mobilization. As Eugene D. Genovese was one of the first to suggest, SCLC's loose, informal structure was probably the best way—perhaps the only way—of effectively mobilizing Southern blacks.[71]

King readily admitted that the movement reflected essentially the same shortcomings so typical of social movements throughout American history. "It necessarily has weaknesses and the people who lead it have faults," he maintained, but he insisted, "We are creative and intellectually bold enough to reach in new directions."

224

In the final analysis, then, what hurt the SCLC most, in King's estimation, was not the lack of a strong bureaucratic structure but sustained white resistance and the seemingly endless struggle to secure the necessary manpower and financial resources to fulfill its mission and reach its goals. Even so, "this movement," King proudly concluded, "has meant more to America than even its civil rights objectives."[72]

King felt that critics too often overlooked the fact that the movement was "vibrant with idealism, with goodwill, with honest zeal," and with a set of principles and values that "inspired tens of millions."[73] SCLC was unstructured bureaucratically, but certainly not in terms of the idealism, the vision, and the principles and values that grounded and drove its outreach and activism. This was most evident in the "four basic steps" and "six principles" that comprised its nonviolent philosophy. The "four basic steps" are (1) the "collection of facts to determine whether injustices exist," (2) attempts at "negotiation," (3) "self-purification," and (4) "direct action."[74] The "six principles" are listed here in a similar fashion: (1) "nonviolent resistance is not a method for cowards; it does exist"; (2) this method "does not seek to defeat or humiliate the opponent, but to win his friendship and understanding"; (3) its "attack is directed against forces of evil rather than against persons who happen to be doing the evil"; (4) it rests on "a willingness to accept suffering without retaliation, to accept blows from the opponent without striking back"; (5) "it avoids not only external physical violence but also internal violence of spirit"; and (6) "it is based on the conviction that the universe is on the side of justice."[75] When these "steps" and "principles" are viewed as an amalgam, it is quite evident that they provided a powerful set of ideas and ideals, and indeed a vision, around which to structure and organize a social movement. King argued that "the principles," which reflected the influence of both Jesus of Nazareth and Mohandas K. Gandhi, provided both "a way of disarming the opponent" and "a creative force through which men can channelize their discontent." Although King knew and always said that the march to freedom required multiple paths, he vehemently denied "the myth" that "nonviolent direct action is a weak and ineffective method that lulls people to sleep":

> How this idea ever emerged is strange indeed. Can one honestly refer to the fifty thousand Negroes of Montgomery, Alabama, the thousands of sit-inners and the hundreds of freedom riders as weak and asleep? Of course not, and so this method is for the strong and well-disciplined. It does not overlook the need for court action; only the misinformed and short-sighted would seek to minimize the importance of litigation. Many of the current breakthroughs have come because of the groundwork laid by the diligent work through the courts across the years, and so nonviolent direct action should not minimize work through the courts. But it recognizes that legislation and court orders can only declare rights; they can never thoroughly deliver them. Only when the people themselves begin to act are rights on paper given life blood. A catalyst is needed to breathe life experience into judicial decisions by the persistent exercise of the rights until they become usual and ordinary in human conduct.[76]

The persistent efforts, by figures at the highest levels of the nation's political and religious life, to place into public consumption the myth that the civil rights movement was essentially devoid of spiritual and moral values always evoked sharp but measured responses from King. This supposed lack of a spiritual and moral core was rooted in the erroneous claim that the movement was infiltrated, inspired, and financed by Communists who were atheists and ethical relativists, who embraced no moral absolutes, and who subscribed to a "materialistic and anti-spiritualistic world view." King categorically rejected the Communist label and strongly maintained that he was involved in a movement that, from its earliest stirrings, was deeply rooted in "moral and spiritual forces" and led largely by ministers of the gospel of Jesus Christ.[77] From a morality standpoint, King insisted that SCLC's freedom campaigns were driven by clearly defined, coherent values in terms of how notions of truth and untruth, right and wrong, and good and evil were conceived and practically applied. He was equally emphatic in asserting that he was a part of "a spiritual movement"—a movement that reflected not a "godless communism" but "the spirit of mature adults, young people, and children."[78] King wholeheartedly agreed with W. E. B. Du Bois's contention that this spiritual dynamic constituted much of the gift of Black folk to America. He declared, in 1966, that during "the past ten years" the "masses of" his "people across the Southland have translated the songs and prophecies of their forefathers into stirring campaigns of action, and have taken the Old Testament call for righteousness and justice flowing down like waters in a mighty stream and merged it with the New Testament call to love one's enemies and to bless one's persecutors and formed the most creative and constructive revolutionary force that our world has known for many decades."[79] This is much of what he had in mind when he spoke of "the spiritual grandeur of our struggle."[80]

King had reasons to carefully explain the spiritual and moral character of the civil rights movement, over and beyond any desire or need to refute what he considered to be the myth of Communist infiltration, influence, and support. He wanted to make it clear, first and foremost, that the movement revealed the strange workings of the God of the universe, "a God of revolution," who embodies and personifies by nature that which is spiritual and moral in absolute form. The idea of this God being active in history, collaborating and suffering with humanity in a protracted struggle to subdue and ultimately conquer "the powers of evil," gave King and other freedom fighters the "interior resources" they needed "to confront the trials and difficulties of life." This affirmation also gave them "courage to face the uncertainties of the future," as King himself confidently proclaimed in his sermon "Our God is Able": "Let this affirmation be our ringing cry. It will give our tired feet strength as we continue our forward stride toward the city of freedom. When our days become dreary with low-hovering clouds and our nights become darker than a thousand midnights, let us realize that there is a great benign Power in the universe whose name is God, and

He is able to make a way out of no way, and to transform dark yesterdays into bright tomorrows. This is our hope for becoming better men. This is our mandate for seeking to make a better world."[81]

King also felt that the movement answered the need for a much-needed "spiritual and moral reawakening in America."[82] He sensed that there was a distinctly spiritual and moral initiative in the movement that the nation badly needed, despite the fact that this remained undetected by those determined to distort its meaning or to reduce it to something other than what it really was. King knew that the nation had long suffered from what he called an "ethical infantilism" or a "spiritual or moral lag," which accounted for its oppression of people of color, and also for its stubborn refusal to face its moment of reckoning around the issues of race, class, violence, and militarism.[83] "Any nation or government that deprives an individual of freedom is in that moment committing an act of moral and spiritual murder," he commented.[84] Thus, America needed a heavy dose of spiritual and moral cleansing. Under the leadership of figures like King, a loyal son of the Christian church, the civil rights movement brought the nation to a greater awareness of this vital need and challenged Americans of all races and creeds to forge fresh standards of right and wrong, good and evil, that would significantly enhance the spiritual and moral fabric of the country. In other words, the goal was, according to King, "to re-establish" the spiritual and "moral ends of our lives in personal character and social justice," thus creating a more spiritually and morally enlightened and functioning society. "Without this spiritual and moral reawakening," he concluded, "we shall destroy ourselves in the misuse of our own instruments."[85]

For King, reestablishing life's moral and spiritual ends was in essence about "the growth of the soul" or giving primacy to intuition and feeling over "enlarged material powers" and the need to use technological advances to conquer nature and to subjugate people, which can only "spell enlarged peril."[86] This outlook had significant implications for how King viewed the human struggle, particularly in an era marked by the lingering paranoia and hysterical intolerance wrought by McCarthyism, the geopolitical tensions associated with the Cold War, and the evils of Jim Crow-ism. It was also quite revealing in terms of the methods King and his SCLC used in dealing with centers of power and systems of oppression at all levels of American society—local, regional, and national. Viewing himself as "a fighting pacifist" involved in "a spiritual war" and "a war of ideas" for the nation's soul, King tried "to awaken the slumbering national conscience" and "to teach the world how to fight for justice" with "moral force" and with "weapons of the spirit."[87] He held that nonviolence was "active" and "aggressive spiritually" and that it "appeals not to physical might but to moral right" by making one "cognizant of the evil" that exists.[88] "Soul force" for him was spiritual and moral force that can triumph over "physical force," which is not only ethically intol-erable but symptomatic of "a sort of poverty of the spirit."[89] Armed with such convictions, King brought the Christian church and the world of protest together in new and unprecedented ways, target-ing that ethic or mode of behavior that redefined spirituality and morality in ways that affirmed violence and the status quo. In the summer of 1966, he marched with gang members in Chicago who honored his request not to strike back even as they were pelted with bricks and bottles by "screaming white hoodlums,"[90] an expe-rience that reminded him, perhaps more than anything else, of the sheer spiritual and moral dynamism of nonviolence. "We don't need our guns, we don't need any ammunition," he maintained. "All we need is the very power of our souls and our commitment and our determination to be free."[91] King came to see successes in the nonviolent movement as moral and spiritual victories.[92]

A stronger and more reasoned defense of the movement, from the standpoint of its spiritual and moral vitality, would not have been possible in that time. King's roles as interpreter and leader of the civil rights program assumed more impressive dimensions as he continued to challenge and refute accounts and descriptions of the movement that had no basis in facts. A case in point was his constant debunking of the myth that the movement, due largely to its ties to Communism, was essentially un-American and most certainly a threat to American democracy. This myth became a favorite topic for white southerners at all levels of society from the very beginning of the bus boycott in Montgomery in 1955, for they were determined to delegitimize the movement, or to convince themselves and others that it was motivated by something other than a sincere desire to advance the cause of democracy. King pushed back occasionally in a calm and thoughtful manner and at times out of sheer frustration. At the very first mass meeting held in connection with the Montgomery bus boycott, he called the boycotters "stalwart fighters for democracy and for citizenship" and declared, "We are here also because of our love for democracy, because of our deep-seated belief that democracy transformed from thin paper to thick action is the greatest form of government on earth." King went on to assert that "the great glory of American democracy is the right to protest for right." He acknowledged that he and his associates would not have had this right if they "were incarcerated behind the iron curtains of a Communistic nation" or if they "were dropped in the dungeon of a totalitarian regime."[93] King's explanations proved totally unconvincing over time to the most passionate opponents of civil rights, and as students actively engaged in the sit-ins and freedom rides in 1960–61, he sensed that the charge of Communist influence had possibly surfaced within the ranks of the federal government. In a news conference in Ithaca, New York, in April 1960, former president Harry S. Truman reported "that the southern lunch counter demonstrations were engineered by Communists." Knowing that Truman had established the President's Committee on Civil Rights and desegregated the US armed forces in the late 1940s, King expressed deep disappointment and admonished the former president at length in a letter:

> For many years I have admired you. Like many other Negroes I have deeply appreciated your civil rights record. But I must confess that some of your recent statements have completely baffled me, and served as an affront and disappointment to millions of Negroes of America. Your statement that appeared in the morning paper affirming that the

"sit-ins" were Communist inspired is an unfortunate misrepresentation of the facts. The more you talk about the sit-ins the more you reveal a limited grasp and an abysmal lack of understanding of what is taking place. It is a sad day for our country when men come to feel that oppressed people cannot desire freedom and human dignity unless they are motivated by Communism. Of course, we in the South constantly hear these McCarthy-like accusations and pay little attention to them; but when the accusations come from a man who was once chosen by the American people to serve as the chief custodian of the nation's destiny then they rise to shocking and dangerous proportions. We are sorry that you have not been able to project yourself in our place long enough to understand the inner longing for freedom and self-respect that motivate our action. We also regret that you have not been able to see that the present movement on the part of the students is not for themselves alone, but a struggle that will help save the soul of America.[94]

Constantly looked upon as and called "anarchists"; "rabbler-ousers"; "seditionists"; "professional, outside agitators"; "traitors"; "aliens"; "Reds"; "Communists"; and invading hordes of Black "outsiders," foot soldiers in the movement typically looked to King, who suffered the brunt of such attacks, to provide cogent and reasonable explanations for what was unfolding.[95] King, in his classic pushback against the false images of participants in the movement, asserted, "And those people who are working to bring into being the dream of democracy are not agitators. They are not the dangerous people of America. They are not the un-American people. They are people who are doing more for America than anybody that we can point to."[96] King assured those whom he felt were thoughtful and well-meaning that "the Negro is American in culture, language, and loyalty." "The present integration struggle is based on Democratic principles and an abiding love for America rather than the faults and misguided principles of Communism," he declared. "I think we have a great tradition, ideally, the democratic creed is a marvelous one," he argued, "and my work is simply an attempt to say to America that you have a marvelous ideal and you should live up to it." King opined that it was "amazing that so few Negroes have turned to Communism in the light of their desperate plight." "I think it is one of the amazing developments of the twentieth century," he contended, "how loyal the Negro has remained to America in spite of his long night of oppression and discrimination."[97] King felt that his people's patriotism had been more than sufficiently demonstrated by their willingness to fight in wars for America despite being denied the right to its most precious democratic tool: the right to vote. "That the Negro remains a patriotic American while deprived of this sacred right," said King, "is a tribute to his deep allegiance to his nation, its ideals and its promise of democracy." Convinced that "men and women who cannot vote are forcibly exiled from their national heritage," he set out to, along with other genuinely patriotic Americans, "bring into full realization the ideals and dreams of our democracy."[98]

King concluded, "In one sense the civil rights movement in the United States is a special American phenomenon which must be understood in the light of American history and dealt with in terms of the American situation."[99] He viewed the history of America as "the history of a long and tireless effort" to extend the boundaries of democracy, going back to the Boston Tea Party, the abolitionist movement, the Underground Railroad, the Niagara Movement, the work of civil rights organizations such as the NAACP and the Urban League, and the great effort "made by women to obtain the franchise," which led to "the Nineteenth Amendment to the Constitution" and "opened a new chapter in the lives of women and in the life of our nation."[100] King insisted that in the struggle for a more participatory and representative democracy in the 1950s and '60s, he and his people were employing some of the same protest methods as the women suffrage activists, from whom they had learned important lessons:

When the women decided the time had come for them to vote, they were far from submissive or silent. They cried out in the halls of government. They agitated in their homes. They protested in the streets. And they were jailed. But they pressed on. Their voices were vigorous, even strident, but they were always effective. Through their courage, their steadfastness, their unity and their willingness to sacrifice, they won the right to vote. From these women we have learned how social changes take place through struggle. In this same tradition of determination, of confidence in the cause of justice, Negroes must now demand the right to vote. And these qualities of courage, perseverance, unity, sacrifice plus a nonviolence of spirit are the weapons we must depend upon if we are to vote with freedom.[101]

King repeatedly stated that those "unknown heroes," male and female alike, who risked their well-being and even their lives marching for freedom throughout the nation were part of that historic continuum for a greater flowering of democracy. These were "the real saviors of democracy," he held. Speaking more specifically of Fannie Lou Hamer, Victoria Gray, Annie Devine, Hazel Palmer, and others, who organized the Mississippi Freedom Democratic Party (MFDP) in 1964 to challenge the power and right of the all-white Mississippi Democratic Party to represent Blacks and who were jailed and physically and verbally attacked for their activities, King declared, "For it is in these saints in ordinary walks of life that the true spirit of democracy finds its most profound and abiding expression. These are the true heirs of the tradition of Jefferson and Hamilton."[102]

It was evident to King that the real threats to the welfare and survival of the nation, and indeed to the essence and meaning of America, were the KKK, the White Citizens Council, and other misguided, misinformed, and hate-filled white people who opposed the foundational principles of democratic living. These people, King noted, were always apt to choose whiteness, white supremacy, and white privilege over democracy based on truth. Instead of grasping the true meaning and significance of the boycotts, demonstrations, sit-ins, freedom rides, voter registration drives, acts of civil disobedience, and other forms of nonviolent direct action, they saw the struggle as an assault on their preferred way of life, which was a segregated society rooted in a master-race ethos. King was all too familiar with their tendencies toward the use of violence, which undermined and threatened the very core of democracy. He referred to the assassination of Mississippi's NAACP leader Medgar Evers in June 1963 as "this dastardly act on the part of those who are against democracy,"[103] and he applied this same logic in describing the brutal beating and murder of countless other civil rights workers. Describing such conduct as "America's shame," or as "un-American outrages," King reminded oppressed communities across the country that "our common fight" is not only "against these deadly enemies of democracy" but also against those seeking to annihilate truth.[104] "Every situation, no matter how trying," he remarked, "helps us to understand the truth that God has urged us to seek."[105] He also warned that the American experiment in democracy could not be sustained on the basis of hatred, violence, hypocrisy, and falsehoods. A pragmatist when engaging such matters, King would have found it impossible to rationalize how the House Un-American Activities Committee (HUAC) could be more concerned about identifying Blacks with Communist ties than about the terrorist acts of groups like the KKK.[106]

The lack of logic about what constituted the greatest threats to American democracy was evident among whites across the socioeconomic and political spectrum, and this made the challenge before King and the movement all the more daunting. Convincing the most ardent white supremacist that the civil rights movement was about addressing the contradictions in and redeeming the promises of democracy would continue to be difficult if not impossible. "The land of the free and home of the brave" had long been a vital part of the nation's principal narrative, but how could people who seemed so deficient in moral and ethical sensibilities be made to see that this was an ideal to be continuously pursued instead of a reality to be accepted, affirmed, and celebrated? Was it possible to convince them that the movement was not about destroying America but about giving an honest accounting of where America was and where America needed to go to actually become America? What would it take to make them understand that America would be at her best only when all of her citizens resolved to live out the true meaning and terms of her democratic creed? These and other probing questions shimmered before King as he desperately and persistently sought to convince even God-fearing and Bible-believing white Americans that the prophet Amos's declaration—"Let justice roll down like waters" (Amos 5:24 NRSV)—was not only a mandate for truth but a mandate for democracy, for fairness, and indeed for life.[107]

Moving from the premise that even the worst human being can at times be rational and sensitive to notions of right and wrong, King insisted that the civil rights movement should never surrender its critical role as a source of enlightenment around the meaning of democracy and what it requires or demands. The movement demonstrated, in his estimation, that democracy at its best is about absorbing, embodying, and acting on truth. King argued for the continuation of the movement on the grounds that "it has done a great deal to add to the vitality of American democracy."[108] In 1967, as he reflected on events as they had developed from the time of the Montgomery protest, he saw that the challenge of marching feet had forced whites to a new point in their thinking about core American values and ideals, a development he felt was difficult to overstate: "The role of the Negro has been significant, forcing a re-examination of the true meaning of American democracy. The whole nation has for a decade given more inquiry to the essential nature of democracy, economically and politically, as a consequence of the vigorous Negro protest. Without writing books or articles, and by taking to the streets and there giving practical lessons in democracy's defaults and shortcomings, Negroes influenced white thought significantly."[109] Clearly, King believed that the mission of his people was historic in the sense that they were demonstrating to the nation and indeed the world the practical power of democracy. In other words, they were showing what it meant to have a practical commitment to, and not simply a theoretical assessment of, democratic norms and values. "The Negro, in his struggle to secure his own rights," King opined, "is destined to enlarge democracy for all people, in both a political and social sense."[110] Moreover, he exclaimed that the movement's foot soldiers taught by example that democracy requires not only discipline, struggle, sacrifice, and suffering but "responsibility, courage and the will-to-freedom for all" people.[111] This helps explain why the civil rights movement was such a critical and defining moment in American life and culture.

King and other civil rights activists were compelled to contend with yet another myth, which held that the civil rights movement in America was an "isolated struggle" or phenomenon—that beyond the Gandhian influence, it had no real, definitive, and identifiable links to movements for freedom and independence abroad. King always insisted that the movement was "a relatively small part of a world development"—that it was inseparable from "the worldwide movement for freedom and human dignity."[112] "The people of the Third World are now rising up," he declared in May 1956, "and at many points I feel that this movement in Montgomery is a part of this overall movement in the world in which oppressed people are revolting against the imperialism and colonialism that have too long existed."[113] "The Negro of America has been caught up in the *Zeitgeist*," he stated on another occasion, "and with his black brothers of Africa and his brown and yellow brothers of Asia, South America and the Caribbean, he, too, is on the move."[114] Speaking specifically of the struggle within the United States, but with much of the world struggle in mind, King concluded that "a Christian movement in an age of revolution cannot allow itself to be limited by geographic boundaries."[115] Here he was calling for a new global spirit.

This sense of the civil rights movement as part of a larger struggle of the oppressed throughout the globe for liberation was consistent with King's concepts of "the social nature of human existence," "the indivisibility of justice," and "the interrelated structure of all reality."[116] Noting that "in a very real and compelling sense, no man, no nation and no part of the universe is an island unto itself," he maintained that even giant steps toward racial justice and equality in the United States would not solve the problems of either Blacks or whites as long as millions across the globe were haunted by the scourge of white supremacy, grinding poverty, and the threat of "extinction by war."[117] For King, this necessarily meant that "our loyalties must become ecumenical rather than sectional"—that America and every other nation had "to develop an overriding loyalty" to humankind "as a whole in order to preserve the best in their own individual societies."[118] On a practical level, King gave expression to this conviction by speaking out against the mistreatment of Jews in Russia, by condemning human oppression and war in his writings and public addresses, by signing numerous statements with activists worldwide condemning nuclear testing and the stockpiling of weapons of mass destruction, by denouncing America's military intervention in Vietnam, by lending moral and financial support to the struggle against apartheid in South Africa, and by attacking patterns of paternalism, colonialism, and neocolonialism throughout Africa and Asia. Even in his most depressing moments, King found inspiration in the fact that the oppressed were no longer bowing or yielding to the power and will of their oppressors. He noted, "All over the world formerly oppressed people are making it palpably clear that they are determined to be free."[119]

The failure of most Americans to understand the interconnectedness of the human struggle troubled King, for this showed that they were oblivious to the nature of the times—that they failed to see that they stood at the end of one period in human history and at the beginning of a new age.[120] The civil rights revolution became inextricably linked in his thinking with the "human rights revolution" worldwide, and he called upon all Americans to come to the aid of their oppressed brothers and sisters everywhere because they faced a common enemy. To be sure, King recognized a sort of symbiotic relationship between the oppressors and the oppressed of the human family, which suggested that both stood in need of liberation and that one could not be truly free without the other. Since the challenge to get on the right side of the world revolution was seemingly more evident and formidable at home than abroad, King spoke with urgency of the need for Americans to abandon "the heavy crosses of narrow, national self-interest" while developing "the world perspective."[121]

This was particularly important, since advocates of American exceptionalism too often celebrated the nation's self-proclaimed leadership role in the continuing efforts to democratize the world. But King frequently said that "the American government" had never really practiced democracy—that it "must begin the struggle for democracy at home."[122] "Can we preach freedom and democracy in Asia, Africa and Latin America if we refuse to give voice and vote to the only democratically constituted delegation from Mississippi?" King asked as he defended the right of representatives of the Mississippi Freedom Democratic Party to represent their state at the 1964 Democratic National Convention in Atlantic City, New Jersey. He went on to point out, "The extension and preservation of freedom around the world depends on its unequivocal presence within our borders."[123] He was convinced that "the shape of the world" in his times did "not permit America the luxury of an anemic democracy." "The democratic ideal of freedom and equality will be fulfilled for all," he prophesied, "or all human beings will share in the resulting social and spiritual doom."[124]

Convinced that the civil rights movement was a necessary and vital chapter in the continuing march toward the democratic ideal, King hoped for a successful outcome for the nation and the world. Much of that hope hinged on the fact that America was made up of people from virtually every part of the globe, which he felt was a driving factor in the stride toward positive change. "This Grand Experiment is now being waged quite successfully within the borders of the United States," he estimated, "for America has been both blessed and challenged by the presence of every conceivable racial and ethnic group."[125] Although the triumph of democracy was certain, King thought, many obstacles remained. "Somewhere along the way men of goodwill must come to see that we are struggling against a stubborn and unyielding adversary," he explained. "Its massive resistance must be met with massive resistance." King was especially concerned about those "lovers of democracy" who were "still all too silent and timid" when confronted with the demands of the oppressed,[126] for he knew that they were potentially more of a problem than the sworn enemies of the civil and human rights struggles. He wanted it to be known that extending the full benefits of democracy to all Americans was not about competing with or defeating Communism but about taking steps that were consistent with "the ethical demands of the universe."[127]

As King turned more consciously toward the final phase of the civil rights movement—the quest for economic justice and international peace—in the mid-1960s, he was even more emphatic in proclaiming that truth was the key to America moving forward as a democracy. In his dynamic speech at the Alabama state capitol building at the end of the Selma to Montgomery march in March 1965, he declared that not only democracy but truth was "on the move," and those who held high the banner of both could not be stopped even by the most despicable acts of evil and terror:

> Today I want to tell the city of Selma, today I want to say to the state of Alabama, today I want to say to the people of America and the nations of the world: We are not about to turn around. We are on the move now. Yes, we are on the move and no wave of racism can stop us. We are on the move now. The burning of our churches will not deter us. We are on the move now. The bombing of our homes will not dissuade us. We are on the move now. The beating and killing of our clergymen and young people will not divert us. We are on the move now. The arrest and release of known murderers will not discourage us. We are on the move now. Like an idea whose time has come, not even the marching of mighty armies can halt us. We are moving to the land of freedom.[128]

King challenged his hearers to continue the struggle against all forms of injustice and inequality, prefacing each statement with the phrase "Let us march on . . ." He ended by quoting his favorite lines from "The Battle Hymn of the Republic": "His truth is marching on. . . . Our God is marching on."[129]

The Beloved Community Ideal:
In Pursuit of Truthful Ends

When Martin Luther King Jr. spoke of "an unfolding truth" or "the new advancing truth," he thought of the larger issue of the pursuit of "truthful ends" through "truthful means." Here the ideal of the beloved community always surfaced and became his main focus.[130] Beloved community for King meant a "truly integrated society" characterized by "true inter-group, interpersonal living," "mutual acceptance," and "shared power." "I think too often people have thought of integration in kind of romantic or aesthetic terms," he remarked, "where you add a little color to a still predominantly white power structure. I think of integration in political terms, or in the sense that it is shared power."[131] At other points, King defined integration in terms of "the welcomed participation" of persons "into the total range of human activities."[132] Segregation and oppression are forms of social evil and theological heresy because they are inconsistent with four basic principles that formed the essential core of King's vision of the beloved community: (1) the impartiality of God in creating and dealing with human beings; (2) a sacramental idea of the cosmos as echoed by the Psalmist—"the earth is the Lord's, and the fulness thereof; the world, and they that dwell therein" (Ps 24:1); (3) a belief in the dignity and worth of all human personality; and (4) a solidaristic conception of society and the world, which holds that each individual is a distinct ontological entity who finds growth, purpose, and fulfillment through personal and social relationships based on the *agape* love ethic.[133] In the discussion that follows, the beloved community is treated as a sort of overarching telos that embraces the essential elements of King's vision of "a new South,"[134] "a new America,"[135] and "a new world."[136] It also reveals the significant interplay among the South, the nation, and the world in King's consciousness, which was evident from the period of the Montgomery protest but became more informed and explicit over time, especially during the last three years of his life.[137]

The vision of a new South and the persistent efforts to bring this ideal into practical reality did not begin with King and the civil rights movement. New South rhetoric first surfaced almost a century earlier, after the defeat of the Confederacy, when white newspaper editors, businessmen, politicians, and religious leaders advocated a rejection of the attitudes, values, and mores of the Old South and its plantation-based economic system in favor of a more modernized South defined by increased industrialization and urbanization, enlightened agricultural practices, improved educational opportunities, harmonious race relations, and national reconciliation.[138] Henry W. Grady of the *Atlanta Constitution* is credited with coining the phrase *New South* in 1874 and popularizing it through his writings and speeches. Grady, Francis W. Dawson of the Charleston *News and Courier*, Richard H. Edmonds of Baltimore's *Manufacturer's Record*, Henry Watterson of the Louisville *Courier-Journal*, and Daniel A. Tompkins of the Charleston *Observer* are usually considered the "prime movers" and the "chief advocates" of the new South cause. Important contributions were also made by businessmen such as James Duke, politicians like Virginia governor William Mahone, and church leaders such as the Southern Methodist Bishop Atticus G. Haygood.[139] During the early decades of the twentieth century, another generation of New South idealists rose to prominence, which included newspapermen such as W. J. Cash in Charlotte; Mark Ethridge in Louisville; John Temple Graves in Birmingham; Hodding Carter in Greenville, Mississippi; Virginius Dabney in Richmond; and a number of Black educators, activists, and newspaper editors, among whom were W. E. B. Du Bois, Booker T. Washington, and Ida B. Wells-Barnett of the Memphis *Free Speech and Headlight*. These figures also brought their own unique perspectives to bear on "the idea of a New South of economic, educational, and racial progress."[140] Martin Luther King Jr. shared some of the ideas of these earlier generations of thinkers and activists as he set forth his own vision of the New South in the 1950s and '60s, but he also differed with them on certain matters, particularly with respect to Black-white relations and the issues of racial justice and equality.[141]

The industrialization and urbanization that the previous generations of New South thinkers envisioned for the southern United

States had occurred on some levels by the time King emerged to prominence in the late 1950s. Even so, King continued to push the notion of increased industrialization and urbanization for the region, but for reasons not strongly considered by most of the thinkers who preceded him—thinkers who were mostly white, who were committed to laissez-faire capitalism, and who were not favorably disposed to any development that would have eliminated white power and supremacy. King fully embraced the idea of an increasingly industrialized and urbanized South not simply for the sake of modernization but because he felt that this would help eliminate many of the physical, social, educational, and economic barriers that separated the races: "If the South is to grow economically it must continue to industrialize. We see signs of this vigorous industrialization, with a concomitant urbanization, throughout every Southern state. Day after day, the South is receiving new multi-million-dollar industries. With the growth of industry the folkways of white supremacy will gradually pass away. . . . This growth of industry will also increase the purchasing power of the Negro, and this augmented purchasing power will result in improved medical care, greater educational opportunities, and more adequate housing. Each of these developments will result in a further weakening of segregation."[142] Here King, in both a theoretical and practical sense, came closer to positions held earlier by Black New South thinkers such as Du Bois, Wells-Barnett, and to some extent Washington, all of whom supported the ideal of an industrialized and urbanized South to the degree that it meant greater economic benefits for all of its residents, irrespective of race. Although Washington—unlike Du Bois, Wells-Barnett, and King—essentially capitulated to the forces of segregation, all of these leaders agreed that expanded economic power for all southerners was foundational in any serious quest for a new South.[143]

The matter of enlightened agricultural practices presented a similar challenge for King as far as his place in the tradition of New South advocates was concerned. Like the New South visionaries who came before him, he supported the idea of economic growth and prosperity through manufacturing facilities and free trade, but he also knew that despite the increasing industrialization and urbanization of the South, most southerners, white and Black, still resided on and worked the land as farmers. King agreed with the development of more automated or mechanized agricultural means, but enlightened agricultural practices for him also included equal rights and opportunity for Black farmers, a concern never seriously addressed by the previous generations of white New South advocates. He strongly denounced the exploitation of Blacks through sharecropping and tenant farming practices. In 1961, as he did on numerous occasions, King challenged the Department of Agriculture to stand up for the rights of Black farmers. "The department could be of tremendous assistance to Negro farmers who are denied credit simply because of their desire to exercise their citizenship rights," he declared. "To wipe out this kind of discrimination would be to transform the lives of hundreds of thousands of Negroes on the land." King went on to point out, "A department zealous to implement democratic ideals might become a source of security and help to struggling farmers rather than a symbol of hostility and discrimination on the federal level."[144]

Improved educational opportunities for Blacks and whites were also a priority for any meaningful movement toward a new South. This was as true for King as it was for the generations of New South idealists who preceded him, but King's predecessors had little or no vision beyond basic education with some emphasis on moral and spiritual values as well. While not particularly opposed to such an approach, King was thinking more of the type of education that not only encouraged critical consciousness and thinking but also humanized persons and enhanced the practice of freedom and community.[145] This is what he wished for both white and Black southerners. King knew that the widespread acceptance and defense of Jim Crow policies and practices on the part of the white South resulted primarily from the total lack of critical thinking around issues of race. In his opinion, this is why all too many white southerners—trapped in guilt, ignorance, and irrational fears—accepted the age-old myths that Blacks were innately inferior, lazy, unclean, irresponsible, and prone to thievery, sexual assault, and other types of indecent and criminal behavior. The fact that many Blacks accepted such images of themselves, consciously and unconsciously, compounded the problem, leading King to repeatedly insist, "We must no longer allow our physical bondage to enslave our minds." He reminded all southerners that "the fact that so many Negroes have made lasting and significant contributions to cultural life in spite of crippling restrictions is sufficient to refute all the myths and half-truths disseminated by segregationists."[146]

King concluded that a powerful and carefully designed process of reeducation was necessary to free southern whites "of artificially contrived restraints," of their "intellectual and moral blindness," and to instill in southern Blacks a deeper and more genuine sense of their essential dignity and worth and of group identity and unity.[147] It was in this connection that King highlighted the educational value of the civil rights movement, which taught lessons in human relations, "social responsibility," "discipline," "courage," "self-sacrifice," and other "priceless qualities of character" that could not be learned in the classroom, or in what he called "the ivory towers of learning."[148] Referring specifically to the energy that students brought to the movement, King noted that they moved beyond "the one dimensional quality of learning," which is about "one's own advancement alone," and which "is inevitably self-defeating," to "become an instrument of social advancement," which "has always been a keystone of achievement." According to King, "It is this quality at the heart of the student movement today which guarantees the additional dimension of wisdom accompanying knowledge." "The type of education that the students are gaining as a result of this movement," he believed, would "assure a meaningful transition" from an "unjust" to a just "social order." King was convinced that the student activism component of the movement, in and of itself, had much to teach about "life's lessons," about being "socially aware," about being "unafraid of experimentation," and about being "imbued with the spirit of service and dedication to a great ideal."[149]

It was around the issue of harmonious race relations that the contrast between King and most of the earlier New South thinkers appeared most glaring and evident. The earliest New South advocates, beginning with Henry Grady himself, confronted the issue of race at a time when memories of slavery were still fresh and strong, and when newly freed Blacks were exercising their recently achieved right to vote and hold public office, thus sparking fear, uneasiness, and anger among many southern whites.[150] The first-generation New South idealists encouraged whites and Blacks to work together and seemingly accepted the idea of the South as a biracial society and culture, but their writings and speeches never seriously questioned or critiqued the culture and folkways of the Old South, or the ways in which white and Black southerners related to one another socially, economically, politically, religiously, and otherwise in that era. Even their image of the biracial southern society, which was shaped and nurtured exclusively in the context of white culture, was not nearly as inclusive and interdependent in nature as King's beloved community vision would be, for they called for racial harmony and goodwill only within the confines of white supremacy and the segregated system, a position upheld by the ethos of "separate but equal" as defined by the Supreme Court decision in *Plessy v. Ferguson* in 1896.[151]

King categorically rejected the racist ethos and the us versus them edict embodied in *Plessy v. Ferguson*, which had too long determined the relationship between the races in the South, insisting that it was not based on sound judgment, reasoning, and a recognition of the power of human community. "The minute you allow race to become a factor in your relationship with another person, you've lost the *agape* quality," said King.[152] He directed his message squarely at southern whites who distorted the meaning of integration or who defended racial segregation as if it was a divinely ordained order or the highest ethical ideal. "So many half-truths and false ideas have been disseminated concerning integration that many white people sincerely feel that it is a design of the devil so to speak," he complained.[153] Mindful of the haunting echo of claims often made by whites in the KKK and the WCC, King noted, "They say we want integration because we want to marry white people." "Well, we know that is a falsehood," he added. "We know that.

We don't have to worry about that."[154] Perhaps more frustrating for King were those seemingly well-meaning whites in the South who pointed to the glaring problems caused largely by segregation—such as the Negro's crime rate and his not being "culturally ready for integration"—in arguing for the continued existence of segregation.[155] "We must decide that in a new era," he contended, "there must be new thinking." He repeatedly explained how white supremacy "separates not only bodies, but minds and spirits"—that it inevitably "descends to inflicting spiritual or physical homicide upon the out-group." For King, this situation virtually assured the continuation of a distorted sense of self-identity on the part of the segregationist. The white segregationist "will never" really "know himself," King surmised, "until he knows that every Negro, however dark his skin may be, is his brother."[156]

When King stated, "The end is the creation of the beloved community," he meant, in regional terms, the new South. Words like "desegregation," "integration," "interconnection," "mutuality," and "shared power" are key concepts that must be considered within the larger frame of what he envisioned as the beloved community. He was thinking not of "a romantic mixing of colors" but of Black and white southerners living together as a single people, of them having "physical proximity" with "spiritual proximity," or "elbows" and "hearts" that were "together."[157] Beloved community for King involved the races relating on terms of equality—an unfolding process in which both Blacks and whites contributed something vital in terms of values and institutions. In other words, King was not talking about Blacks assimilating into white southern culture or being shaped in the image of white people. He maintained that historically Black institutions, for example, would not necessarily be eliminated in what he termed "the transition from segregated to integrated living," a point he clarified in response to a questioner who expressed an inability to reconcile his belief in integration with support for funding Black colleges:

> I feel that you are wrong in your feeling concerning the United Negro College Fund. There is no contradiction in believing

in integration and supporting the United Negro College Fund. You must remember that although Negro colleges are by and large segregated institutions, they are not segregating institutions. If these colleges are properly supported they will survive in an integrated society. Many of these colleges already have white students. It is not true to feel that as soon as integration becomes a thoroughgoing reality the so-called Negro private colleges will close down. In supporting these Negro colleges we are only seeking to make sure that the quality and caliber of these schools are of such nature that they will be appealing to all people.[158]

Toward the end of his life, as he realized that most whites were unwilling to integrate with the masses of poor Blacks, King began to think in terms of "temporary segregation"—the idea that "there are times when we must see segregation as a temporary way-station to a truly integrated society." Although he opposed segregation as an ultimate goal for the races, his concern about being "integrated *out* of power" led him to conclude that "temporary segregation" was necessary to allow his people time to accumulate some power to bring to the integration process. "We will eventually achieve this, but it is going to be much more difficult for us than any other minority," King explained. "After all, no other minority has been so constantly, brutally and deliberately exploited." "We want to be integrated *into* power," he declared, which meant that Black and white power had to intersect and be shared in any genuine expression of the beloved community. "Integration is meaningless," he asserted, "without the sharing of power."[159]

King's beloved community vision was radically different from the race relations model proposed by white New South thinkers before him, but it was shared on many levels by white and more liberal New South idealists who were his contemporaries. He respectfully mentioned these idealists in a very brief but important essay entitled "Who Speaks for the South?" (1958) and in his famous "Letter from the Birmingham City Jail" (1963). They included James McBride Dabbs Sr., Lillian E. Smith, Ralph McGill, Harry

Golden, Sarah Patton Boyle, Harry S. Ashmore, and Anne M. Braden, all of whom, like many of the earliest New South advocates, ranged from journalists to newspaper writers to authors and social critics of the Old South. King thought of them as New South prophets, and he rejoiced in the fact that some of these figures had "not only written about our struggle in eloquent and prophetic terms" but also "grasped the meaning of this social revolution and committed themselves to it."[160] King further noted, "Others have marched with us down nameless streets of the South. They have languished in filthy, roach-infested jails, suffering the abuse and brutality of policemen who view them as 'dirty nigger-lovers.' Unlike so many of their moderate brothers and sisters, they have recognized the urgency of the moment and sensed the need for powerful 'action' antidotes to combat the disease of segregation."[161] Although these New South advocates recognized white supremacy and Black oppression as core problems of southern life and culture and supported integration in principle and practice, they were not as vocal and active as King when promoting the idea of a radical redistribution of economic power as an important step in the direction of the beloved community.

Models of genuine interracial community were difficult to find in the white South during King's time. He did discover in Myles Horton's Highlander Folk School and Clarence Jordan's Koinonia Farm rare examples of southern-based interracial communities. The Highlander Folk School—a unique embodiment of unionism, democracy, and Christian socialism—had been organized by Horton in Monteagle, Tennessee, in 1932, and it became "an interracial training center for labor, socialist, and religiously oriented community organizers in the South."[162] King called it "one of the most significant institutions in the South." From a practical standpoint, the Highlander Folk School approximated on some levels what King envisioned when he thought of the beloved community in a southern context, for it "provided an interracial living and learning experience."[163] King felt similarly regarding the Koinonia Farm, a racially integrated expression of Christian community, which was established by Clarence Jordan in Americus, Georgia, in 1942.

King fully supported what he termed "the noble work that [was] being done there," especially since its approach, much like his own, pitched the beloved community as a truthful end to be pursued through the truthful means of nonviolence.[164]

King assigned a special place to his home city of Atlanta in this quest for the beloved community in the South, or the new South, probably because he came to see it as the mecca of both Black education and civil rights activity. After all, Atlanta was the only city with several Black colleges and seminaries, and the headquarters of the SCLC was located there, where plans for civil rights campaigns throughout the South were always debated and often finalized. But King apparently had other reasons, apart from a deep sense of place, to highlight Atlanta's importance for the whole South, for it had long claimed to be "a shining city of civility and tolerance" in the region. As early as 1959, King wrote, "Atlanta is a city with vast potentialities and great promise. It is unique, and economic and cultural prominence places it in a position to stand as a beacon light of hope to the whole South. If Atlanta succeeds, the South will succeed. If Atlanta fails, the South will fail, for Atlanta is the South in miniature."[165] King could see that, aside from its significance in the cultural and educational arena, Atlanta was already leading the South in terms of industrialization and urbanization, and this clearly figured into his conception that this city was the key to the full realization of the new South.

But King never meant to suggest that the burden of creating a South more consistent with his beloved community ideal should be borne by southerners alone. Here he differed somewhat from some of the white New South advocates in his generation, such as Lillian Smith, who advised him to "keep the northern do-gooders out"—to accept their assistance with publicity and money but not to "let them come down and ruin what you are doing so well." Smith, like Ralph McGill, was uneasy about the emergence of militancy within the ranks of the civil rights movement, especially Black power elements, and she tended to blame both King's "lack of toughmindedness" and "intruders" or "outsiders" from the North.[166] Convinced that integration would "not be some lavish dish that the white man will pass out on a silver platter while the Negro merely furnishes the appetite," and that "the problems of the South are bigger than the South," King argued, "We need the concerted efforts of the whole nation to revolt against the evils of injustice which are so rampart in our society." He saw no other way to "liberate all southerners, Negro and white."[167] "The new South which is emerging is not something that will come into being devoid of human effort,"[168] he often said, and he called for a broad cadre of leadership—an "alliance" or "coalition of conscience"—that would include southern white moderates and liberals, northern white liberals, the federal government, and Black Americans.[169] Although King opined that "the darkness of the soul of the South will never fully be dissipated until the passion for justice" first "grips the white southerner," he held nonetheless that a thorough transformation of the region demanded that all of these potential sources of leadership had to develop a more broadly based humanitarian ethic, to become more progressive, to boldly speak and act toward truthful and effective ends, and to make sacrifices if necessary for what they deemed to be right—morally, socially, politically, and otherwise.[170] What they refused to repudiate, he maintained, they in effect enabled, empowered, and sustained.

King believed that "the new Negro of the South" had a special obligation to assume a vanguard role in the redemption and transformation of the region. The "new Negro," according to him, had been "freed from the paralysis of crippling fear" and had "a new self-respect," "a deeper sense of dignity and destiny," and "a new determination to achieve freedom." King often said that "the Negro people of Montgomery"—"stung into action by the decisively defiant stand of Mrs. Rosa Parks"—actually "provided the prime impetus for this psychological change."[171] But the change in the southern Black, as far as King could determine, was not only psychological but moral and spiritual as well, for this figure had "a new determination to tell the truth":

> And all of these factors come together to make what seems to me to be the new Negro. I think I would like to mention

this growing honesty which characterizes the Negro today. There was a time that the Negro used duplicity, deception too, rather as a survival technique; although he didn't particularly like conditions he said he liked them because he felt that the boss wanted to hear that. But now from the housetops, from the kitchens, from the classrooms and the pulpit, the Negro says in no uncertain terms that he doesn't like the way he's being treated. So at long last the Negro is telling the truth. And I think this is also one of the basic characteristics of the new Negro.[172]

For King, southern Blacks demonstrated that truth-telling as an act of conscience was indispensable for anyone who took on the mantle of leadership in the quest for a new South. By pursuing "truthful ends," in the form of the beloved community, through the "truthful" or "moral means" of nonviolence, the Black southerner was, to use King's words, "helping" his white counterpart "to know himself"—to know that he "will never know himself until he knows" that he has a special kinship to all other humans, including Blacks.[173] King concluded that the new Negro was able to provide most of the energy around the prospects for a new South, or to lead in the crusade for integration "in the external society," precisely because he was "powerfully integrated within."[174] He was careful at this point, however, to distinguish between the "new" or "non-myth Negro" and those comparatively few Black southerners who represented the extremes of "Uncle Tomism," or who were driven by self-interest and opportunism to become traitors to the cause of their people and to the New South ideal. King openly attacked such individuals who, like Judas, squandered their credibility for a few pieces of silver, declaring that they were fundamentally unfit for leadership in the struggle. "We must gird up our courage and stand firm for an integrated society," he declared. "We must tell our white brothers that the few Uncle Toms who will sell their souls for a mess of economic pottage do not speak for the Negro."[175] King witnessed Uncle Toms being used daily by the white power structure to obstruct much-needed social change, and he urged his people not to be discouraged by such behavior. "Protest until the walls of segregation have been finally crushed by the battering rams of surging justice," he cried. It was largely because of the "new" or "non-myth Negro," not the polished Uncle Toms or stubborn white bigots, he maintained, that "the old South is a lost cause" and was "passing away," and "a new South is being born." He was convinced that "legal segregation is on its death-bed, and the only thing uncertain about it is how costly the South will make the funeral."[176] King sounded an even more hopeful note in January 1966 as he and his SCLC extended their operations from the South into Chicago: "Factories are moving South, employment and opportunities are on the increase, and recent civil rights legislation is rapidly disintegrating the cruelties of segregation. The South is now a land of opportunity while those who generations ago sang, 'going to Chicago, sorry but I can't take you', now sink into the depths of despair."[177]

Obviously, the vanguard role of the "New Negro" was enormously significant for King as he envisioned a new South, but it was never meant to undermine his expressed belief in the group or team model of leadership as suggested in his concept of an "alliance" or "a coalition of conscience."[178] He insisted that the "New Negro," due to his history and suffering, was better equipped to assume the primary leadership role but not the sole leadership role in transforming the segregated South into an integrated South. The problem with King's proposed and preferred leadership model was not that it excluded or limited the involvement of potential male sources but that it encouraged the subordination of women. King said on paper that "the women of the nation and the South have a tremendous role to play in this tense period of transition." Referring to Ella Baker, he further explained, "This is one of the reasons we employed a woman as associate director of the Southern Christian Leadership Conference. We felt the need of bringing together this vast wealth of latent potential." King also conceded that "in every age there have been a group of men and women whose contributions have been equally significant,"[179] but these thoughts did not translate into an advocacy of the full leadership potential of women in the crusades for "a new South," "a new America," and "a new world." Simply put, women were not allowed to enter and function freely in that world of male leadership, irrespective of their ambitions, qualifications, gifts, and talents.[180]

Most of King's thinking, writings, and activities were devoted to the struggle for "a new South" because he knew that bringing it to realization was an immensely important and necessary step in the direction of "a new America" and "a new world." An important shift in focus occurred during the march on Washington in August 1963 as King thought more consciously about making the connection between his dream for the South and his dream for the nation. He described his widely publicized speech at the Lincoln Memorial on that occasion as his "dream for a new America."[181] Widely known by this time as "a Negro rights general" and "the American Gandhi," King knew that white supremacy still symbolized the nation's sickness and her ambivalent spirit and that the movement had to increasingly "address itself to the question of restructuring the whole of American society."[182] His respect for the spiritual capacity of his people led him to propound a messianic role for them in this process.[183] King's thinking at this point owed much to his own reading of history and to insights he gleaned from his reading of Henry David Thoreau, Mohandas K. Gandhi, Reinhold Niebuhr, and Arnold J. Toynbee. American Negroes constituted for King that "creative minority" that Thoreau had highlighted, those who served the state by resisting and even suffering to make it stronger and better.[184] King was undoubtedly intrigued by Gandhi's observation that "it may be through the Negroes that the unadulterated message of nonviolence will be delivered to the world."[185] Niebuhr's prediction that the oppressive condition of the Negro awaited the emergence of a nonviolent leader—one who could "fuse the aggressiveness of the new and young Negro with the patience and forbearance of the old Negro"[186]—was most certainly known to King, but King' spirit of humility was such that he never claimed to be the fulfillment of that prophecy. He frequently referenced Toynbee's idea that "it may be the Negro who will give the new spiritual dynamic to Western civilization that it so desperately needs to survive."[187] The insights from Thoreau, Gandhi, Niebuhr, and Toynbee came together in

King's mind as he imagined and reimagined his people's role in the crusade for a new America, as he sought to inspire and motivate them in the darkest days of the struggle, and as he challenged them around the rare opportunity they had to demonstrate "to the world the practical power of Christianity" and "the unmatched vitality of a nonviolent, loving approach to social protest."[188] But even as King stressed the significance of his people's leadership role, he continued also to appeal to a sense of shared commitment and sacrifice on the part of all Americans. He believed that Americans had to meet the challenges before them as a nation, not in a fragmented manner, but in the form of "multiracial alliances," sealed by a covenant of mutual respect and trust.[189]

King insisted that the path to a new America involved, perhaps more than anything else, a coming to terms with the truth about humanity and race. Mindful of the fact that superficial but exaggerated racial and ethnic differences constituted the chief obstacle to the beloved community, he maintained that "the basic thing about a man is not his specificity but his fundamentum, not the texture of his hair or the color of his skin, but his eternal dignity and worth." King expressed the point at greater length in a statement he sent to parents in Chicago to read to their children in the schools, reminding them that what humans share is eminently more important than what they do not share:

A friend is a friend whether his hair is brown or black or blonde. What makes him your friend is how he feels about you and how you feel about him. This is not influenced by whether he is Spanish or East Indian or whether he is light or dark or brown or black. Friendship does not come in colors or skin or hair or nationality. It is the result of what happens when two personalities meet in harmony. Most of the things in life are not what they seem to be. The color white only looks that way. In reality it is all colors combined. We must learn to look into and beyond to find the truth. Whether a boy is short or tall, stout or thin, white or black does not reveal what is in his soul, mind and heart.

This can only be learned and understood by experience. The natural tendencies to reduce the mysteries of life to simple terms presents one of the greatest problems of civilized existence. It is not true that all fat boys and girls are "jolly"; that all Italian boys "talk with their hands"; that all Jewish boys and girls want to grow up to be "storekeepers"; that all Negro boys and girls want to "fight and make trouble." It is easy to accept this way of thinking but it is not truthful. Each person must be judged by what he is. The human race is in reality a brotherhood of man. Among us are many things which differ, race, language, culture. Underneath these differences is a similarity. We possess hearts and minds and souls. By comparison with these the differences are of minor importance.[190]

This statement was indicative of how King routinely addressed the false notions and stereotypes that kept people of different backgrounds from understanding and living peacefully and harmoniously with one another over generations. Much of his effort in this regard had to do with refuting the many biased and uninformed perceptions that made whites, "fearing property devaluation," so resistant to the idea of living in the same neighborhoods with Blacks:

We must expunge from our society the myths and half-truths that engender such groundless fears as these. In the first place, there is no truth to the myth that Negroes depreciate property. The fact is that most Negroes are kept out of residential neighborhoods so long that when one of us is finally sold a home, it's *already* depreciated. In the second place, we must dispel the negative and harmful atmosphere that has been created by avaricious and unprincipled realtors who engage in "blockbusting." If we had in America really serious efforts to break down discrimination in housing, and at the same time a concerted program of government aid to improve housing for Negroes, I think many white people would be surprised at how many Negroes would choose to live among themselves, exactly as Poles and Jews and other ethnic groups do.[191]

But King also knew that meaningful strides toward a new America, or the beloved community in the larger American context, required greater contact between people of different races, ethnic backgrounds, and classes, and this largely explained his fierce opposition to separate Black and white residential areas. He was disturbed by those white supremacists who, when confronted with demands for integration, angrily pulled back on the phrase "It's America, love or leave it," and he denounced the idea of a separate white homeland promoted by the KKK and other white supremacists. King was equally critical of the Black Muslims for scolding others in the community for not living up to their ideal of Blackness and for rejecting the possibility of "an interracial society" in favor of a separate Black nation. In response to a question raised by the Jewish rabbi Everett Gendler in March 1968, King, with the Black Muslims in mind, reiterated his objection to the kind of Black separate state long envisioned by political nationalists in the Negro community: "As I said, most Negroes do not believe in black separatism as the ultimate goal, but there are some who do and they talk in terms of totally separating themselves from white America. They talk in terms of separate states, and they really mean separatism as a goal. In this sense I must say that I see it as a negative because it is very unrealistic."[192] King used different language, with a touch of humor, to make a similar point about racial separatism in a sermon to a Black congregation in Los Angeles:

> And I want you to get the message across to our white brothers who are not here this morning, that we are here to stay. We ain't going nowhere. It's about 22 million that they admit of, and that's just what the census bureau got. When you deal with the thousands and millions that ran when the census man came around because they thought it was somebody to collect a bill, then it adds up to about 30 million Negroes in America. And we're here to stay. We ain't going

anywhere, and white folks just as well need to learn to live with us. And that's a good message to get across.[193]

The only workable alternative King saw was the type of integrated society that completely dismantled the myth of white supremacy, the economic roots of racism, and various forms of violence. "I believe in the rebirth," he exclaimed as he considered how this process might advance from protest to reconciliation and ultimately to community.[194] He felt that the challenge of redefining community beyond considerations of race, ethnicity, and class was such that a "Secretary of Integration" should be named as part of the cabinet of the president of the United States. This was not at all surprising considering King's emphasis on the need to open more vital "channels of communication between the races," his belief that "complete integration" required the extension of democracy, and also his deep concern that "token integration" was too often being promoted as the societal ideal. "Anyone who feels that our nation can survive half segregated and half integrated is sleeping through a revolution," King noted as he reflected on the immense amount of work that still needed to be done before "American life" could "be an integrated life," or a life "integrated racially and culturally as well as economically."[195] He believed that the Christian church at its best could contribute to this transition with resources that were unavailable to government or any other institution, but only to the degree that it remained receptive to the ways in which "the blessings of God's Kingdom" might "become incarnate in the institutions of our society."[196] After all, the church, in King's opinion, was the custodian of the moral and spiritual values the society needed to change course from a perceived Black versus white reality to humans of different shades united, living, and functioning as one nation under God. King wanted the church, like the civil rights movement itself, to truly symbolize the kind of society he and others hoped to bring into being.[197]

An America moving away from both white supremacy and capitalism toward "cooperative interracial nation building" and democratic socialism was what King himself ultimately had in mind. This obviously required a fundamental altering of the character and spirit of the country, a development that the masses of Black people, whom King called "the least of these" or "the disinherited of this land," were more apt to embrace than whites. By translating their "degradation into resistance," Blacks had already shown themselves to be America's renaissance people, a "people reborn with the spirit of a new age" and unyielding in their pursuit of the type of structural change that made for what King called "a new society."[198] King was able to take center stage in this venture because he lived and operated in a different reality from that of most white Americans—because he lived the beloved community and reflected this higher ethical ideal in his civil rights campaigns. He fully understood that the search for the beloved community in the United States was essentially about keeping "the moral and ethical ends" for which its citizens lived "abreast with the scientific and technological means" by which they lived.[199] Thus, the civil rights activist John Lewis was right in identifying King as "one of the founding fathers of the New America."[200]

An incurable optimist at heart, King was convinced that progress was being made toward "the promised land of integration," though hardly at a sufficient rate.[201] The passage of the Civil Rights Bill of 1964 and the Voting Rights Act of 1965 inspired new hope, but the letdown came when it was clear that the federal government had little or no intention of seriously implementing these very important pieces of legislation. But King constantly reminded foot soldiers in the movement not to grow weary in well doing, for their willingness to suffer for the actualization of the beloved community in America—for reconciliation, community, and universal wholeness—not only affirmed and exalted truth but also had "tremendous educational and transforming possibilities."[202] King was certain that "when the blazing light of truth is focused on this marvelous age in which we live—men and women will know and children will be taught that we have a finer land, a better people, a more noble civilization—because these humble children of God were willing to suffer for righteousness' sake."[203]

Much of King's optimism regarding the possibility of a transition from the old to the new America was severely tested in the late 1960s, as the cry of Black power and riots in the urban ghettoes were greeted with a white backlash.[204] Attacked by white mobs in Chicago in 1966 as he and others in SCLC led demonstrations against slum conditions, King witnessed yet another side of the depth of white supremacy and its economic roots. "My dream for a new America turned into a nightmare," he reported, "as I watched millions of my black brothers slowly perishing on an island of poverty in the midst of a sea of affluence." "I watched in horror as Ku Klux Klan violence reared its ugly head," he continued, "brutally murdering unarmed, nonviolent civil rights workers in Mississippi and Alabama."[205] King came to see vividly that white racism ran much deeper into the fabric of American life and culture than he initially thought. He was compelled to think more intensely and analytically not only about systemic white supremacy but also about the myth of the "Great Melting Pot" in America and what that possibly meant for the shift from an old to a new world:

> America was called the Great Melting Pot of the world and yet as we look into her pressurized cauldron we see that the blocks are not melting, but side by side English and Irish, French and German, Greek and Italian, African and Oriental have created ethnic subcultures which contribute to the whole but somehow manage to preserve and perpetuate their own identities. And so one might look upon America as the world in miniature, and the significance of the American experiment becomes apparent, for if men and women of differing backgrounds cannot learn to live in harmony with many years of close proximity, then the outlook for the rest of the world is indeed dim.[206]

The illusiveness and apparent failure of the Great Melting Pot experiment in the United States only heightened King's sense of the challenges and difficulties that obstructed the path toward the creation of a new world.[207] But he found some hope in the "world-shaking revolution" taking place in his time, in which the "disinherited masses" throughout the globe were freeing themselves of the yoke of colonialism and imperialism. This "human rights revolution" or "freedom explosion" compelled King to put before humans everywhere a challenge around the question of their collective moral obligation. He denounced silence and neutrality as options, especially for moral and rational persons. He urged all Americans to "achieve the new mental attitudes which the situations and conditions [demanded]." Recalling Washington Irving's "familiar story" of Rip Van Winkle, who "slept through a great revolution," he warned, "There would be nothing more tragic during this period than to allow our mental and moral attitudes to sleep while this tremendous social change takes place."[208] Moreover, he challenged America to develop "a revolution of values to accompany the scientific and freedom revolutions engulfing the earth"—a more vital set of values that cherished human beings more than "things," that stressed community over individualism, and that assured that humanity's past and present would not also be its future.[209]

King identified "three groups of people in the world." The first group is "the lawless people," who "break laws," who serve time in prisons, and who "never follow the codes of society, whether they are written laws or customs." The "second group" is "the law-abiding people," whose "standards of conduct come mainly from without," from "the man-made law, the law written on the book, or the customs and mores of society." The "third group," which represented for King humanity at its best, "are law-abiding" but also "committed to an inner law," or "an inner criteria of conduct," which makes them "obedient to the unenforceable." "These are people who are obedient to something that the law without could never demand and could never write for you to do," King explained. "These are people who change history and who make history." King felt that those who were "obedient to the unenforceable," or to "an inner criteria of conduct," embodied the best potential for leadership in the struggle against global systems of oppression, for they were also willing to disobey laws and customs that conflicted with the higher law and with the highest human and ethical ideal. In other words, they were "nonconformists" or "maladjusted personalities." As King considered and reconsidered the problems of the oppressed at home and abroad, and as he advanced his obligations as "a citizen of the world," he concluded that "it may well be that the whole world is in need of the formation of a new organization, the International Association for the Advancement of Creative Maladjustment."[210]

As was the case with the "new South" and the "new America," King insisted that people of African descent in America had a messianic role to play in the shaping of "a new world." Here his views, from a global standpoint, might be considered from essentially three angles. First, he asserted, "The hard cold facts today indicate that the hope of the people of color in the world may well rest on the American Negro and his ability to reform the structure of racist imperialism from within and thereby turn the technology and wealth of the West to the task of liberating the world from want."[211] King assigned this messianic vocation to American Blacks because he considered them perhaps the most well-educated and materially affluent group among the world's peoples of color during that time, because they were strategically situated within the confines of the most powerful country in the Western world, and, perhaps more importantly, because of their commitment to nonviolence as demonstrated in the context of the civil rights movement. Put another way, King thought that Blacks in America were in a position to do for other people of color what they were ill-equipped to do for themselves:

> I don't think it can work the other way around. I don't think the non-whites in other parts of the world can really be of any concrete help to us, given their own problems of development and self-determination. In fact, American Negroes have greater collective buying power than Canada, greater than all four of the Scandinavian countries combined. American Negroes have greater economic potential than most of the nations—perhaps even more than *all* of the nations—of Africa. We don't *need* to look for help from some other power outside the boundaries of our country, except in the sense of sympathy and identification. Our challenge, rather, is to organize the power we already have in our midst.[212]

On another level, King believed that God had "entrusted his black children in America to teach the world," and especially white people, "to love, and to live together in brotherhood." "Everywhere we look, things are confused and messed up," he declared, "and it's all because our white brothers have not learned how to be just. And we've got to make them just."[213] For all the shortcomings of American Blacks, many of them born of oppression, King concluded nonetheless that history had shown them to be generally more humane than their white oppressors. In other words, he detected in the great mass of Negroes in America certain values and virtues—a vital and genuine spirituality, a humanitarian spirit, a prophetic vision of democracy, an incurable optimism, a great toleration for human differences, and an amazing capacity to forgive—values and virtues he considered rare in the great mass of white people. In King's opinion, the preoccupation of the great mass of white Americans with racism, materialism, war, and the quest for power and domination over peoples of color had resulted over time in an incalculable loss of genuine spirituality, moral sensitivity, and higher human values within the group. Consequently, whites, he felt, were generally less congenial than Blacks to the idea of creative, meaningful, and communal living among the various peoples of the world. King himself had countless experiences with white Americans that reinforced his thinking along these lines, but there were also genuinely positive experiences with certain whites, including Europeans, that gave him the impression that considerable numbers of them were prepared to listen and learn from Black Americans. While in Berlin in 1964, he discovered not only that "the Court of World Opinion" was "the most powerful ally that the Negro struggle has" but also the fact that many Europeans looked to the Negro for leadership and for lessons about the indomitability of the human spirit in the face of oppression—observations he shared widely with Blacks upon his return to America: "These people were not there just to hear me speak. They were there to hear me tell your story. This interest confirms my belief that the Negro is now in a position to lead the world. As the Negro goes, so goes the world. We are the conscience of the Western World.

We represent the problems of democracy, not just the problems of the Negro."[214] But this challenge to lead in the struggle for a new world, King believed, was not limited to these considerations. Thus, he urged his people to insist on "a role in international affairs," thus undermining "the assumption that foreign policy is a white man's business."[215] He also asserted that "the Negro people, because of their peculiar experiences with oppression through the use of physical violence," had "a particular responsibility to not participate in inflicting oppressive violence on another people." "This is not a privilege," King wrote, "but an exceptional moral responsibility, the weight of which is far from a happy burden."[216]

At yet another level, King attributed the messianic role in the world to the "colored peoples" across the globe, which included Black, brown, red, and yellow peoples. He believed that due to their history and experiences with oppression, they had nurtured certain values, particularly in the spiritual realm, that could possibly save the planet from "drifting rapidly to its doom."[217] Such an opinion had much to do with what King knew about the struggles for independence in countries like Ghana, India, and South Africa, where peoples of color had embraced and employed nonviolent principles. But even as King spoke to the leadership potential of peoples of color in transfiguring and shaping the destiny of humanity, it is certain that, when his ideas are plumbed at a depth dimension, he also understood that the new world he envisioned could not find full realization without the resources and input of all well-meaning and freedom-loving peoples everywhere, irrespective of race, class, religion, and nationality. This position was consistent with King's concept of the "interdependent structure of mankind" and with his conviction that all humans are global citizens with a moral obligation to act "in a spirit of international brotherhood, not national selfishness."[218]

King's vision of the new world, and the steps required to bring it into existence, was set forth with Socratic clarity and thoroughness. For him, the reality of "the great world house" already existed in the form of "geographical oneness" or "togetherness,"[219] and the challenge was to work toward the ideal of a globalized beloved community, or a totally integrated world society grounded in truth and governed by the law of love. He categorically rejected the notion of separate humanities and urged the peoples of the world to explore new ways of viewing and relating to the diverse segments of the human family, to forge a unifying conception of humanity, and to reframe what it meant to live as one humanity. King's analysis began with the problem of racism, especially in the form of white supremacy, which was organized and institutionalized on a global scale, and which stood as one of the greatest barriers to world peace and community.[220] He noted that "two-thirds of the people of the world," numbering "one billion six hundred million," are "colored," and he longed for the time when bringing people of different hues, backgrounds, and persuasions together would no longer be viewed "as a problem, but as an opportunity to participate in the beauty of diversity": "I still have a dream that one day black men and white men, brown men and yellow men, Protestant, Catholic and Jew, believer and unbeliever, will coexist in a world where men are judged only by the content of their character rather than the color of their skins or the nature of their heritage. And where brotherhood is more than a meaningless word at the end of a prayer, but the first order of business on every legislative agenda."[221]

King essentially envisioned a globalized beloved community when he spoke of "a world of ideal beauty and absolute truth." "World brotherhood is no longer a beautiful ideal," he stated on one occasion, "but an absolute necessity for civilization's survival."[222] Although America claimed to be the leader of the free world, King knew well its tragic history of dealing with race, and he questioned whether it had the "moral posture" to lead the world in eradicating white supremacy. During the last week of September 1960, in a speech to the North Carolina branch of the NAACP, he commented,

> We must face the painful fact that we are losing out in the struggle to win the minds of the uncommitted peoples of the world. Just this week the most eloquent spokesman of the Communist bloc, Nikita Khrushchev, suggested in

his speech to the U.N., among other things, that the head-quarters of this great organization be moved from the United States. The American press generally was very careful to conceal one of the reasons Mr. Khrushchev gave for suggesting the move. His direct words were: "Facts are known . . . of representatives of young African and Asian states being subjected to racial discrimination in the United States." While we are used to Mr. Khrushchev's intemperate and sometimes irresponsible words, we cannot dismiss these as totally false. The hour is late. The clock of destiny is ticking out. We must act now! It is a trite yet urgently true observation that if America is to remain a first-class nation it cannot have second class citizens.[223]

King feared that the depth of white supremacy as a corrosive force in the world was such that a race war was not an unimaginable scenario. He said as much and more in an interview in London during the winter of 1968, as he saw his dream of an integrated society and world increasingly fading into something of a nightmare:

I think we have to honestly admit that the problems in the world today, as they relate to the question of race, must be blamed on the whole doctrine of white supremacy, the whole doctrine of racism, and this doctrine came into being through the white race and the exploitation of the colored peoples of the world. I think that this is ultimately going to depend to a great extent on the white peoples of the world. The fact is that the colored races have been terribly exploited, and trampled over with the iron feet of oppression, and this exploitation is not going to exist any longer. The cup of endurance has run over, and there is a deep determination on the part of the peoples of color to be freed from all of the shackles that they faced in the past. Now if the white world does not recognize this and does not adjust to what has to be, then we can end up in the world with a kind of race war, so it depends on the spirit, and the readjusting qualities of the white peoples of the world, and this will avoid the kind of violent confrontation between the races if it is done properly by the white peoples.[224]

King could have said much the same about poverty and economic injustice, which he considered another major obstacle to the creation of a new world, or to integrated, creative, and productive living in the form of the beloved community. But he understood that the evils of capitalism—which bred poverty, hunger, homelessness, disease, and death—extended across racial, national, and cultural boundaries, greatly impacting millions of whites and even more peoples of color. King blasted the rich and powerful of the world, who not only lived extravagantly at the expense of the poor but seemingly had little or no interest in dismantling unjust economic structures or sharing the fruits of their wealth. "This is the question that is now challenging the world," King declared during a speech in Paris in October 1965. "Which side are you on?" He went on to ask, "Are you on the side of change and growth and new opportunity for the underprivileged peoples of the earth, or will you stand in fear, seeking to conserve the bits and pieces of value and virtue which you can hold to your bosom?"[225] King's enduring message was "We must be as concerned about the poor in India as we are about the poor in Indiana," and he repeatedly called for "an all-out world war against poverty."[226] Although he favored multiracial alliances of conscience to address poverty in America and abroad, he wondered about the extent to which race and other factors of human difference might render this improbable and perhaps even impossible. In any case, King concluded that by developing new modes of thinking and action around poverty and economic justice issues, the peoples and nations of the world, and especially the affluent and powerful, could "go a long way toward conquering" these "ancient" enemies.[227] The failure to do so, he believed, would ultimately be catastrophic as far as the prospects for a new world were concerned.

The looming and enduring threat of war and human destruction was yet another pressing concern for King as he increasingly committed himself to the shaping of a new humanity and world. He knew that war, or violence on a mass scale, constituted the most colossal of all social evils, for it threatened the very health and existence of all life-forms. He reminded the nation that in the first half of the twentieth century, "we fought two world wars." "And I'm sorely afraid that the clouds of a third war are hovering mighty low," King remarked. "And if this war comes," he continued, "it will be the war to end all wars, because it's going to end the whole of mankind."[228] "The civilized world stands on the brink of nuclear annihilation," he sadly conceded.[229] "Not only in the South, but throughout the nation and the world," said King in a moment of somber reflection, "we live in an age of conflict, an age of biological weapons, chemical warfare, atomic fallout and nuclear bombs. It is a period of conflict between the mammoth powers. It is an age of conformity. It is a period of uncertainty and fear. Every man, woman and child lives, not knowing if they shall see tomorrow's sunrise."[230]

Having lived through and studied the calamities and casualties of war, King opined that "there is no excuse for the kind of blind craving for power and resources which provoked the wars of previous generations."[231] His strongest and most persistent denunciation of war targeted the United States, his native land, which he felt routinely used military might to assert and maintain its Machiavellian advantage in the world. King frequently turned to the Vietnam conflict to make his point, insisting that the American government had long been untruthful in its claim that "we are there blocking Communist aggression." "American boys are being sent to Asian soil to perpetuate a war that is at bottom perpetuating white colonialism," King argued. "And we are criminals in the war." "We have committed more war crimes almost than any other nation in the world, and I'm going to continue to say it," he added. "And we won't stop it because of our pride and arrogance as a nation."[232] He predicted that his country's cause in Vietnam would never be vindicated, especially since truth was absolutely essential to any successful effort to build bridges of peace and goodwill between the United States and the rest of the world, let alone a new world order.

"We will not build a peaceful world by following a negative path," he exclaimed.[233]

King reasoned that the time had come for peoples of every nationality to "in concert proclaim that war is wrong, that war is obsolete," due mainly to "the potential destructiveness" of modern weapons. The challenge, then, was for them to also "develop a common conception of what a world at peace looks like."[234] The nations of the world, King estimated, had to take three important steps in transitioning from "an arms race" to "a peace race." First, they had to end the "bitter colossal contest for supremacy." Second, in order "to avoid the drudgery of war," or "being plunged across the abyss of atomic destruction," they had to "transcend the narrow confines of nationalism." "Nationalism," King argued, "must give way to internationalism." Finally, King insisted that "the nations of the world must get together" at a "Summit Conference" in Geneva "to bring an end to the armament race"—"to bring about universal disarmament and set up a sort of world police force."[235]

These steps could only be taken, according to King, in a world in which peoples everywhere took seriously their global citizenship— in which they are endowed with both a deep global consciousness and a keen sense of global responsibility around issues of war and peace: "The challenge confronting the global citizen even in this latter half of the twentieth century is to break down the dividing walls of hostility, freeing men of all nations that they may face one another without protective devices and defense mechanisms in confidence that men can live together in love and that the family of man can encompass many nations, extend beyond oceans and overcome the historic, racial, political and economic factors which have perennially plunged man into the depths of dissension and divided him into warring factions."[236]

To Americans who supported the freedom movement within their own country but appeared uncongenial to the kind of drastic action needed to develop new forms of freedom and peace on a global scale, King declared that "no sane person can afford to work for social justice within the nation unless he simultaneously resists war and clearly declares himself for nonviolence in international relations."[237] Having witnessed "the possibilities of its use in Western civilization," he advocated resolving human ills internationally through nonviolence, which was for him the force of truth and also a form of countervailing power. Nonviolent resistance provided, in his words, "a creative force through which" humans everywhere could "channelize their discontent" as well as their desire to be free and independent. King thought here of the "nonviolent affirmation of the sacredness of all human life," and of a method that brought a more civilized quality to the struggle for a globalized beloved community.[238] He hoped that human beings of goodwill would exhibit "moral courage of a high order" by moving "forward in a nonviolent but resolute spirit to achieve rapidly proper standards of humanity and justice in our swiftly evolving world."[239]

King recognized in the different faith traditions worldwide an indispensable resource for advancing such a global ideal within history, for he found in their "noble creeds and ethical insights" precepts fundamentally essential to the kind of inner transformation humans had to undergo to live in peace and unity. He held firmly to this conviction, despite the fact that "the adherents of the particular religions" had long failed to follow their "ethical systems."[240] Although King felt that the struggle for a new world rose above any particular religious tradition and would not be defined by any particular ideology, culture, or nationality, he believed nonetheless that "God has intended through all religions to keep intact the brotherhood of man."[241] In other words, the world's religions constituted limited and fragmentary pointers to that noble end to which God had planned for all segments of the human family. King held that this kingdom of God, which for him was the theological equivalent of the ethical ideal of a global beloved community,[242] already existed as "a universal reality" in the hearts, souls, and minds of those who sacrificed uncompromisingly and untiringly for it—and most certainly "in such isolated forms as in judgment, in personal devotion, and in some group life." But King also spoke of the kingdom in terms of the *now* and the *not yet*, the *present* and *future*, or the *real* and the *ideal*. He himself envisioned the ideal of the kingdom of God—or the new world order or globalized beloved community—as "a time when God would reign supreme in all life, and love, brotherhood, and right relationship would be the order of society." "We seek new ways of human beings living together," King maintained, "free from the spiritual deformation of race hatred—and free also from the deformations of war and economic injustice." "And this vision does not belong to Negroes alone," he added. "It is the yearning of mankind."[243]

6

A Distorted Legacy

Remembering Martin Luther King Jr. in a Post-truth Age

I believe that unarmed truth and unconditional love will have the final word in reality. This is why right, temporarily defeated, is stronger than evil triumphant.

—Martin Luther King Jr., "Acceptance Address for the Nobel Peace Prize" (1964)

In many ways, the key risk of our post-truth era is not that facts really will disappear and never be heard from again, despite much recent hand-wringing on the subject. It is that the particular, old-fashioned mythology around truth, which remains central to the modern liberal democratic imaginary, will turn out to have outlived its relevancy and its appeal, and we will have nothing to put in its place.

—Sophia Rosenfeld, *Democracy and Truth: A Short History* (2019)

Martin Luther King Jr. challenged the nation and the entire Western world to think in new ways about what constitutes truth

271

in word and practice.[1] Although he knew that no human being embodies truth in pure or absolute form—that that prerogative rests only with God—he nonetheless defended truth as an absolute, foundational, and universal concept and was never afraid nor hesitant to speak, witness to, stand for, and act on truth in ways that changed humanity and the world for the better. Those who study King should feel compelled to do no less, for this, as King so often said, is the essential purpose and goal of human life. For King, valuing, pursuing, and acting in the service of objective truth was never merely about accumulating knowledge and wisdom, stating facts, or slavishly adhering to certain doctrinal or dogmatic formulations. King thought on a much deeper level and had in mind truth as a life force, truth as a guiding principle and regulative ideal, truth as the coherence of means and ends, and truth as a commitment to the highest good or the most noble human and ethical ideal. Unfortunately, this side of King's life often gets lost in the intellectual wrangling of King interpreters, including those who specialize in philosophy, theology, and ethics.

This concluding chapter breaks with the pattern of the previous chapters. It highlights the problems involved in reconciling the historical King, or the King in context—who thought, spoke, and acted on truth in his own time—with the transhistorical King, or the King beyond context, whose birthday is recognized and celebrated worldwide and to whom so many continue to appeal for some sense of what amounts to truth about human life, the human condition, and human destiny. The content of this chapter unfolds on three levels. First, it explores how King is remembered, viewed, and appealed to in contemporary times, or in what some cultural and social critics variously call "the post-truth age," "the age of lies," "the post-truth era," "the post-truth society," or "the post-truth world." The twenty-first-century reality of "alternative facts," "the crisis of truth," "deliberate deception," "fake news," "half-truths," "conspiracy theories," "disinformation campaigns," and "the war on truth"—a reality in which the lines between truth and untruth are too often blurred and distorted[2]—is taken seriously, particularly from the standpoint of its impact on how King is understood, how his legacy is interpreted and appropriated, and how certain elements on the political and religious right assess their own obligation in terms of advancing his image as "a transhistorical prophet of truth."[3] Second, the chapter treats the challenge presented to the King model of ethical leadership and to the King legacy by the presidency of Donald J. Trump and Trumpism, which has escalated the assault on truth to unprecedented levels and remains one of the major manifestations of "post-truth politics."[4] Finally, the chapter provides an assessment of the relevance and implications of King's ideas and activities for a society and culture in which a relentless attack on truth has become the new normal, even with the blessing of all too many political and religious leaders. Because King always cherished, advocated, and practiced objective truth-telling as part of a larger culture of basic moral and ethical norms, he yields insights, and indeed some of the answers, about how truth might be rescued and reclaimed in this age of social media.

The Man and the Myth: Recalling and Appealing to King in Post-truth Times

Much has been said and written over the last three decades about the emergence of post-truth as a defining cultural, philosophical, and political experience of contemporary times. The term "post-truth" describes a climate in which science, evidence, and even objective facts and truths are no longer influential in the shaping of public opinion and public perceptions of the world. Terms like "alternative facts," "alternative reality," "truth decay," "the crisis of truth," "anti-truth-telling," "deliberate deception," "fake news," "credibility crisis," and "conspiracy theories" are frequently used in media, academic, and political circles, suggesting that the lines separating truth from untruth, reality from unreality, and rationality from irrationality are no longer so clear and distinct.[5] Former president Donald J. Trump is largely associated with this trend toward "a post-truth reality," and some view him as "the standard bearer for this strange new world."[6] But the question driving the discussion that follows is What is the impact of post-truth on our understanding of the life of Martin Luther King Jr. and on our celebration and appropriation of his legacy?

It is evident that post-truth contributes to widespread tendencies to further distort the meaning and message of King, thus influencing how many in our society and world memorialize him. This much and more can be derived from the African American scholar and social justice advocate Vincent Harding's discussion of "the ambiguous message surrounding the official celebration of King's birthday." Harding has written in poignant terms about "the profound sense of national amnesia that has distorted so much of America's approach to Martin Luther King, our national hero." Convinced that Americans are "still unclear about who he was, what we expect of him as a hero, and what he might expect and demand of us," Harding concludes that King can only be regarded as "the inconvenient hero"—as one whose "unfettered, loving truth to hubristic American power" is badly needed but no longer remembered nor desired in these contemporary times:

> Ever since we began talking about establishing a national holiday honoring King in this country (U.S.), it's been very clear to me that there has been a great tension. Many of those who, out of the best intention, wanted to see the country honor Martin, knew, or at least they felt they knew, that the country could not take Martin as he was. Somehow Martin would have to be somewhat domesticated in order for the country to deal with him because he was both a prophet seeking to speak the truth to the country, and a lover seeking to grasp the country in his great affection for the country. There is always a temptation to want to ask the prophet to back off some and not be so demanding on us and not to keep calling us to our best possibilities.[7]

Harding highlights "the forgotten legacy" of King and how this informs the annual national celebration of his birthday.[8] But it could be argued that most Americans, especially white Americans,

274

have never really understood King or his legacy in the first place, and so it becomes a matter not of what is forgotten but what has never actually been known and accepted about King. King's life has been reduced in large measure to a series of myths created by those who are determined either to destroy his heroic image or to make him a convenient and useful symbol in a carefully orchestrated effort to promote their own agenda for America and the world.

King the man and the mythical King have always existed side by side, and in tension with each other, from the beginning of King's rise to national and international fame up to the present time. Images of King in the public imagination have always been a mixture of fact and fiction, as is the case with any great figure in human history. This is not surprising given the complexity of forces surrounding King's memory and legacy and since people the world over have always come at him from different backgrounds and viewpoints. The best one can do, then, is to wade through the layers of images to get to know or understand the "real" or "true" King better.[9] While this is not impossible, it most certainly becomes more of a challenge in this post-truth era. Perhaps the only point about King on which humans everywhere can agree is that the historical King was a product of his circumstances and times.

Perhaps the best example of mythmaking targeting King in this post-truth age is Clarence B. Jones's *What Would Martin Say?* (2008). Jones—a close friend, legal adviser, and confidante of King—actually attempts the impossible: to establish what King would say about many of the human welfare, social justice, and public-policy issues currently confronting the nation and the world. Writing less than a decade after the term "post-truth era" was coined and launched into common usage, Jones declares that King would be bitterly disappointed with the misguided, disingenuous, and self-serving actions of present-day Black civil rights leaders such as Jesse Jackson and Al Sharpton; that he would advocate the abolishment of affirmative action as we know it; that he would oppose those "illegal aliens" who violate the country's immigration laws, threaten its border security, and take jobs from native-born citizens; that he would denounce anti-Semitism as the most insidious and virulent form of world racism; that his attack on anti-Semitism would be aimed specifically at the anti-Semitic statements of Black leaders like Jackson, Sharpton, and Louis Farrakhan; and that he would ultimately support the use of violence as the most practical means of eliminating Islamic terrorism. Jones bases his right to speak as an authoritative voice for King on the claim that he put words in King's mouth when King was alive and that he is therefore in a position to speak to what King would say today.[10] The resulting image of King is that of a figure who fits well into the world of right-wing conservatism[11] and perhaps even into the post-truth reality world of Trumpism. The best and only evidence of what King would say about the issues Jones raises is what King said about them when he was alive. King was always reluctant to attack fellow Black civil rights leaders,[12] he called for affirmative action in the form of "compensatory measures" to atone for injustices inflicted upon his people over time,[13] he urged the nation to extend a welcoming hand to immigrants and denounced the preferential treatment given to white immigrants from Europe,[14] he attacked anti-Semitism while denying that it was a serious and enduring problem in the Black community,[15] he identified white supremacy as the world's worst and most glaring form of organized and institutionalized racism,[16] and he always opposed violence in interpersonal, intergroup, and international relations.[17] Jones's accounts of what King would say about the human condition and how best to improve it are nothing more than mythology masquerading as truth.

It is also important to note that Jones's revisionist appropriation of King for right-wing, conservative purposes is part of a much larger and more disturbing trend in what has gradually become an anti-truth-telling culture. In 2006, Carolyn Garris, a research associate with the Heritage Foundation, opined that it was "time for conservatives to lay claim to the legacy of the Rev. Martin Luther King, Jr." While admitting that "King was no stalwart conservative," Garris argued nonetheless that King's "core beliefs, such as the power and necessity of faith-based association and self-government based on absolute truth and moral law, are profoundly conservative."[18] In a 2012 issue of the *National Black Republican Association Newsletter*,

King's niece, Dr. Alveda C. King, erroneously reported that "Martin Luther King, Jr. was a Republican." "It should be no surprise that Dr. King was a Republican," she wrote. "Why? Because it was the Democrats who Dr. King was fighting and he would not have joined the Democratic Party."[19] Alveda King's claims about her uncle tinkled sweetly on the ears of representatives of the "New Right," for they had, as far back as the 1980s, used King as a kind of sacred aura for their own political ends. His nonviolent principles and praxis and right-to-life advocacy remained morally and politically relevant for right-wing forces that opposed abortion and what they perceived as attacks on family values. The Jewish rabbi Yehuda Levin and "others in the pro-life movement" declared that "their protests follow in the tradition of Martin Luther King, Jr.'s civil rights movement."[20] The conservative political consultant and lobbyist Ralph Reed found King's legacy useful on several levels. He used the name of King's Southern Christian Leadership Conference (SCLC) "to justify the name *Christian* Coalition," the political action group he and Pat Robertson founded in 1989. As the first director of the Christian Coalition, serving up to 1997, Reed also turned to King as a model when setting the blueprint for the organization:

> During his speech at the 1995 "Road to Victory" conference, Reed distributed a seven point "Christian Coalition Pledge Card." This pledge was supposedly based on one drafted by Martin Luther King, Jr. for the Southern Christian Leadership Conference. Citing the seventh point of the pledge, Reed urged CC members to "Refrain from the violence of fist, tongue, or heart." Reed argued that King's healing and inclusive rhetoric was crucial for the success of the civil rights movement. According to Reed, the pro-family movement has needed a similar rhetoric. "The American people," wrote Reed, "need to know that we do not desire to exclude our political foes, only to gain our own place at the table."[21]

Finally, Reed "appealed to the precedent" of King's "religiously-based civil rights movement to justify the political activism of religious conservatives," especially in response to liberals who questioned the conservative right's wedding of faith and politics. One of the major complaints Reed and other right-wingers had was that they were being criticized for doing essentially what King and religious liberals had always done; namely, mixing religion with politics. King, they argued, went from the pulpit to the streets to the polling booths, and he took ideals rooted in the Bible, evangelical piety, and the US Constitution and made them the foundation of a crusade for social and political justice. In the opinion of Reed and other right-wingers, then, those liberals who celebrate King while denouncing the religious and political right were merely "using a double standard when it comes to conservative faith-based political activism."[22] World-renowned ethicist and social analyst Daniel C. Maguire brilliantly exposes the deception and false notion behind this claim:

> The issue is not whether religion has its legitimate place under the political sun. Surely it does. The question is: *how is religion being used?* To disempower and disable or to empower and enable? The former use of religion is antipolitical and subversive. People get hurt when the power of religion is thus abused. There is all the difference imaginable between what Martin Luther King, Jr., brought to the political order and what the Falwells and LaHayes bring. When King left his pulpit and ceased his political activism, many who had lacked rights before had come to possess those rights. People were voting who could not vote before, were getting hired and educated who would have known only rejection, and were finding decent housing who could not before. In short, King's interventions in politics were *enabling* and *empowering*. However, when the Falwells of the New Right leave their pulpits and end their political activism, inasmuch as they are successful, people who had rights will have lost them. Their interventions are *disabling* and *disempowering*. Also, depending on their success, the most wholesome elements of the American dream will have been undermined.[23]

Viewing King through the distorting lens of right-wing extremism, and especially partisan Republican politics and Christian conservatism, has gradually become commonplace in America—a nation that delights in celebrating heroes, and that thrives under the twin yoke of capitalist greed and cultural arrogance. Throughout the 1990s and the first two decades of the twenty-first century, voices on the conservative right shrewdly and deceptively used some of King's most famous words in arguments against government-sponsored public-policy initiatives designed to benefit communities of color and the poor and marginalized as a whole, maintaining, for example, that King's calls for a nation in which persons are judged by character rather than skin color suggest that he would oppose affirmative action. Notorious and rabid anti–affirmative action advocates such as Newt Gingrich, Dick Armey, and Clint Bolick invoked "King's struggle in support of their specious arguments." The outright distortion and manipulation of King's words are not surprising given his status as a celebrated national hero. This remains simply another indication of how representatives on the right are desperately trying to reshape King's image and legacy, thus making him a more convenient symbol—a symbol useful in their protracted campaign to advance a conservative social and political platform.[24]

Alveda King's claims about her uncle's ties to the Republican Party and right-wing conservatism must be understood in this context. They must also be considered in light of her own close association with Donald Trump and the era of Trumpism, during which the nation and the world were bombarded daily with alternative facts, disinformation, misleading statements, conspiracy theories, and lies told on an unprecedented scale by a US president and his spokespersons. In any case, Alveda's claims do not pass the credibility test. King was highly critical of the failures of both the Democratic and Republican Parties to take a strong stand on civil rights,[25] his SCLC was "a nonpartisan organization,"[26] and he followed "a policy of not endorsing candidates" publicly.[27] Even so, King, beginning with Senator John F. Kennedy, the presidential candidate, routinely voted for Democrats. King explained his preference in an interview in Atlanta in March 1961, after Kennedy's inauguration as the new commander in chief: "But on the whole, when we look at the Democratic Party as a whole and its basic philosophy, it has advocated policies that are more helpful to not only the Negro but to the common man in general. And I'm sure that this is the reason that the vast majority of Negroes still vote the Democratic ticket in this area."[28] By 1967, King insisted, "The future of the Democratic Party, which rests so heavily on its coalition of urban minorities, cannot be assessed without taking into account which way the Negro vote turns."[29] He was equally emphatic in saying that his people should not become preoccupied with party labels— that they should instead always support political leaders who "are committed to a higher manifesto of justice and love."[30]

Vincent Harding's recognition of society's need for a domesticated King has become all too obvious in these post-truth times. Each year on the third Monday in January, people worldwide are exposed to carefully selected excerpts from King's 1963 "I Have a Dream" speech, which are meant to reinforce the false and misleading image of him as a harmless, gentle, southern Black Baptist preacher who localized nonviolence, redemptive love, and suffering as the core of the Christian faith. Harding is right in saying that we have frozen King on the steps of the Lincoln Memorial and in reminding us that "there is no honest way to honor King that does not call us beyond our gentle, convenient memories of the March on Washington and thrust us—with him—into the burning cities of Newark, Detroit, Los Angeles, Danang, and Baghdad."[31] As the high and mighty gather annually and take center stage during demonstrations and at worship services at Atlanta's Ebenezer Baptist Church on King Day and as military guards join some of the parades honoring King, the radical prophet who highlighted the evils of white supremacy, exalted "the least of these," decried violence and militarism in all forms, advocated democratic socialism, and shed blood fighting for a living wage and union recognition for garbage workers somehow gets lost. All too many in this nation and the world are afraid of the radical King because he reminds us of our moral obligation to always speak truth to power and that spilled blood is inevitably the price for doing so. In some strange fashion, the King who epitomized the voice of powerful and uncomfortable truths in his own context has been transformed into the post-truth King in ours. In other words, the King who sought, spoke, and acted on truth in the twentieth-century era of revolutionary change has become, strangely enough, the target of so much untruth in this twenty-first-century age of conspiracy theories, deliberate deception, disinformation campaigns, and fake news. We have done this to King in order to protect ourselves from his essential radicalism and from the radical demands with which his legacy still confronts us.

But it is not simply the radical King who makes us uncomfortable and about whom we are ill prepared and even unwilling to face the truth. King the deep and creative thinker, the man of ideas and letters, also presents the kind of challenge that makes many uncomfortable and afraid to honestly engage him.[32] King was never afraid to think, and he felt that "the great moments of history have been those moments when individuals have been free to think."[33] Lee E. Dirks trivialized King's significance as a thinker when he erroneously reported that King was "not an originator of ideas but a messenger of them"—that his ideas were merely "a synthesis of thoughts culled from other men's minds."[34] As chapter after chapter in this book shows, what King said about truth and untruth alone establishes him as one of the world's most gifted, creative, powerful, and provocative thinkers. Convinced that untruth enslaves the mind and spirit of whomever it victimizes and that truth frees the mind and spirit of the enslaved, King challenged humans everywhere to think in more creative and even unorthodox ways—in ways that many were not apt to even consider, let alone honor.[35] In this post-truth society, in which all too many are afraid to think and are afraid of thinkers, King and his legacy are likely to be subjected even more to embellished mythmaking. In a real sense, the very tools King deemed essential to a culture that lends itself to objective truth-telling are increasingly being eroded in our society and world; namely, an open and receptive mind, a belief in "the natural power of human reason," the capacity for objective appraisal and critical-analytical thinking, and an unwavering devotion to the search for truth.[36] Such qualities of mind and spirit cannot be sustained in a society and world in which solidly established evidence, facts, and truths no longer mean much.

Truth-telling about who and what King was as a human being exposes yet another set of concerns and challenges for both his admirers and detractors in these times. Scholars and journalists who have spoken and written about King's moral failures, especially his plagiarism and womanizing, over the last half century have accomplished a lot in terms of reconnecting him to his basic humanity, thus demythologizing him as a heroic figure.[37] They have reminded us that King, as Michael Eric Dyson points out, "was a man who was deeply human, deeply flawed, and yet truly amazing."[38] However, such an acknowledgment probably will not please the many African Americans who revere King and view truth-telling concerning his plagiarism and sex life as destructive and traitorous acts,[39] and it is most certainly insufficient and even unacceptable to those in the larger society and culture who either despise King, oppose what he stood and fought for, or feel that he is undeserving of the national and world recognition he has gotten and continues to get.[40]

The enduring preoccupation with the most explosive allegations about King's sexual activities undoubtedly appeals to more than simply those with a soap-opera mentality. As Barbara Ransby perceptively notes, because the charges about King's sexual activities are based largely on reports from Federal Bureau of Investigation (FBI) sources, whose mission was to thwart King, "we have to wonder where fact ends and fiction begins."[41] Ransby, Clayborne Carson, Donna Murch, and other highly reputable scholars have raised serious and probing questions about the reliability of the FBI accounts used by the likes of David J. Garrow,[42] who, in an article in *Standpoint*, a conservative British magazine, alleges that King may have observed and encouraged a rape.[43] It is not difficult to imagine the potential impact of such an allegation, though suspicious and unsubstantiated, on the image and legacy of the nation's most celebrated hero, especially in this era of alternative facts and anti-truth-telling. Not surprisingly, some readers immediately accepted the allegations as true and wondered if King's "statues would be removed now like monuments to the Civil War South generals."[44] We can rest assured that as the outcry for the removal of Confederate monuments continues, white nationalists, white supremacists, and neo-Confederates—who casually ignored President Donald Trump's self-admitted sexual exploits—will repeatedly call attention to the rumors and innuendoes concerning King's sexual adventures from FBI files and will insist that this justifies the abolishment of the King National Holiday and the elimination of the many other monuments to his memory.

The accounts juxtaposing King's vulnerabilities as a human being with his amazing heroism as a freedom fighter must also be considered on another level. Major biographers of King have long acknowledged his unwavering commitment, his indomitable courage, and his untiring efforts to liberate and empower humanity, but some have seemingly been more emphatic in variously characterizing King as "tortured," "always worried," "torn on the inside," chronically "self-critical," plagued by mounting "inner tension" and "self-doubts," and haunted by "consuming guilt" and "the menacing threat of despair." They have also explained in graphic terms King's "underlying loneliness"; his "growing pessimism"; his "deep" and "nearly incapacitating depression"; his persistent "despondency, confusion, and doubt"; the difficulties he faced "persevering" and living "comfortably"; and how he supposedly "drank more" during the final days of his life.[45] But this is only a part of that more gripping and penetrating story that must be told if the man behind the myth is to be better understood. Conspicuously absent from such accounts are significant references to the inner resources of strength and resilience King got from a powerful Black southern culture that was rooted in church, religion, and the extended family—a culture that kept him from reaching the breaking point physically, emotionally, and spiritually despite the tremendous demands on his person, time, and resources. King found in that culture rich and tasty soul food; great music; sports and a vital ethic of play; the gifts of wit, humor, and laughter; and a fervent and reassuring faith, all of which made him strong, resilient, driven, and energetically focused.[46] Apparently, he had this culture and more in mind when he declared that "the American Negro" will "eventually win his struggle for freedom and justice" because "he has in his nature the spiritual and worldly fortitude"—"a moral fortitude that has been forged by centuries of oppression."[47]

There are still other concerns that arise as we seek to reconnect with and honor the heroic and radical dimensions of King's legacy. We need to develop a sense of his global significance, for there is no honest way to affirm and celebrate him without taking into serious account his meaning for a globalized rights culture. The ruling elites seem to have no problem sculpting King's image in stone and naming streets, highways, and buildings after him[48] as long as we are not reminded of his scathing critique of the evils of capitalism, his oft-repeated call for a radical redistribution of the world's resources in the interest of the poor, his persistent denunciation of America's tendency to use "massive doses of violence" while posing as the "self-appointed world policeman," and his sincere belief that he and other crusaders for freedom in the United States were part of an unfolding "human rights revolution" with global ramifications. The rich and powerful would prefer that we forget about King's attack on the United States and Britain for propping up apartheid South Africa; his challenge to the wealthy nations "to provide capital and technical assistance" for underdeveloped countries in Africa, Asia, Latin America, and the Caribbean; his excoriation of America and other wealthy nations for using foreign aid "as a surreptitious means to control poor nations"; his exposure of the truth about his country's misadventure in Vietnam; and his insistence that Americans have much to learn from the rest of the world.[49] To truly remember this global King, or the King who called himself "a citizen of the world,"[50] is to commit and recommit ourselves to his vision and his incomplete mission for the uplift and empowerment of all human beings. His life teaches us that living daily with diversity is never easy but that humans everywhere need to become more mindful of the positive ways in which diversity defines and shapes our world and develop strategies for dealing with our God-given and healthy pluralism. This is much of what King was thinking when he stressed the need to pursue truthful ends through truthful means.

The symbolic has become more important in our memorialization of King today than the human virtues he embodied, but there may be some hope in the fact that he was and remains what Richard Lentz calls "a mutable symbol,"[51] especially if this ultimately leads to positive and more realistic portraits of who and what King was and what he means for humanity. The massive figure of King still hovers over the global horizon, for there is a certain timeless quality about so much of what he said and did. His very life was in essence a progressive march toward truth, and this is why his words and actions echo across generations. With the assassination of King, the lies we had long told about ourselves and our history confronted us in the form of spilled blood. These lies will live with us as long as we celebrate King annually while embracing the values of the post-truth age, which are antithetical to his vision of the highest human and ethical ideals. The challenge is to confront and engage the depths of King's humanity while refusing to undervalue his contributions and achievements. As Vincent Harding suggests, we cannot build on King's legacy in this "new century" if we become too comfortable with the image of "a convenient" or "a smoothed-down, lowest-common-denominator American hero."[52]

Unshared Values: The King Legacy, Trumpism, and the War on Truth

In carefully worded remarks at the opening of the Mississippi Civil Rights Museum in the city of Jackson on December 9, 2017, President Donald J. Trump paid homage to Martin Luther King Jr. and other "Christian pastors who started the Civil Right Movement in their own churches preaching." Trump referred specifically to King as "a man we have studied and watched and admired my entire life."[53] Roughly a month later, Trump issued his very first presidential proclamation in observance of the King National Holiday. In his comments on that occasion, the president alluded to some of the distinctive attributes King brought to his role as an ethical leader, calling him "a great American hero" who, through "bravery and sacrifice," "opened the eyes and lifted the conscience of our nation," "stirred the hearts of our people to recognize the dignity within every human soul," and changed "the course of human history."[54] In yet another statement marking the occasion, Trump declared, "The Reverend Dr. Martin Luther King, Jr. dedicated his life to a vision—that all Americans would live free from injustice and enjoy equal opportunity as children of God. His strong, peaceful, and lifelong crusade against segregation and discrimination brought our nation closer to the founding ideals set forth in the Constitution and the Declaration of Independence. Today, as we come to honor Dr. King, we know that America is stronger, more just, and more free because of his life and work."[55]

Trump also, apparently without fanfare, signed a measure that rededicated and renamed the Martin Luther King Jr. National Historic Site in Atlanta the Martin Luther King Jr. National Historic Park.[56] On April 4, 2018, the fiftieth anniversary of the King assassination presented yet another opportunity for Trump to pay tribute to King, and the president signed a proclamation in honor of the civil and human rights leader. While recalling that tragic event in our history, Trump also highlighted King's "legacy of justice and peace," and he urged fellow Americans "to make Dr. King's dreams of peace, unity, and justice a reality."[57] Trump's words echoed across a nation that remained deeply divided over the meaning and enduring relevance of King's life, leadership, and legacy and that was increasingly reflecting the adverse impact of the post-truth era.

However, quite unlike his predecessors—Bill Clinton, George W. Bush, and Barack Obama—Trump did essentially nothing on a practical level during his presidency to highlight the significance of the King National Holiday as a day of service to humanity. On that day in January 2018—after insisting that King's birthday be celebrated "with appropriate civic, community, and service activities"—Trump spent the day instead playing a few rounds of golf at his International Golf Club in West Palm Beach,

Florida.[58] On King Day a year later, Trump and his vice president, Mike Pence, marked the occasion with an unannounced, two-minute visit to the King Memorial on the National Mall in Washington, DC. After placing a wreath at the memorial, they quickly left without saying anything at all.[59] On King Day in 2020, the last of the Trump presidency, Trump and Pence made yet another quick and unannounced trip to the King Memorial, but Trump's mindset at that time was reflected in his attacks on Democratic presidential candidates, by his boastful comments about his support for gun ownership, and by his false claim that African American unemployment was at its lowest in the country's history.[60] President Trump's ambiguous and self-serving approach to King's memory and legacy could only have been expected of one whose characteristic tendency was to speak to one set of values while practicing another.

As president, Trump described King as the preeminent ethical leader and suggested that he respected King and had been greatly inspired by him. At another point, Trump claimed, without hesitation, "I think I am a great moral leader."[61] Here he was implying that an image so often associated with King was characteristic of him as well, or that he was not so different from King in terms of leadership qualities. But it is clear that Trump's casual disregard for and even aversion to objective truth and courageous truth-telling constituted a major challenge to King's legacy of ethical leadership. King held that a reverence for truth and truth-telling was absolutely essential to leadership that is ethical, prophetic, and transformative in nature—or, to put it more specifically, leadership that is driven by a keen capacity for critical-analytical thinking, a deep moral and spiritual grounding, personal integrity, and a healthy sense of social responsibility.[62] Furthermore, King desperately sought to embody this in his own life and in what became one of the most important ethical protest movements in American history. Telling the truth for him was the most vital, appealing, and defining feature of who and what the ethical leader is—an extension of the self-proclaimed ethical leader's very personality, being, existence, and life itself. This is why King himself constantly engaged in a process of self-introspection or honest self-analysis.[63] His widow, Coretta Scott

King, reported that her husband hated even the slightest appearance of being dishonest, deceptive, or untruthful. To illustrate her point, Coretta noted that although her husband was at times falsely accused of misusing movement money and falsifying his tax returns, he "was ruthlessly honest with himself in such matters" and that of all the attacks on his person, the ones "on his personal honesty hurt him most." Coretta went on to explain that if ever King "did something a little wrong," his "conscience devoured him" and that "his conscience was a formidable thing that kept him on the path he thought was right."[64]

This deep consciousness of honesty and dishonesty, right and wrong, was what King expected of all leaders who claimed to be ethical, particularly in politics and religion, for both fields had to do with serving and being, as much as humanly possible, role models for the masses of people. King's dealings with Dwight D. Eisenhower, John F. Kennedy, and Lyndon B. Johnson showed that he viewed US presidents not only as "the embodiment of the democratic personality of the nation, both domestically and internationally," but as ethical leaders who represented and largely determined the character and spirit of the country. "His own personal conduct," King said of the nation's leader, "influences and educates."[65] This alone stands as an indictment of Trump, who never measured up to high standards of behavior during his presidency. From the time he entered the White House in January 2017, Trump undermined democracy, sought to assume the role of an authoritarian, and fed the American public a steady stream of misinformation, outright fabrications and lies, exaggerated and misleading claims, rumors and half-truths, propaganda briefings and misrepresentations, and baseless conspiracy theories, thus attesting to the validity of King's assertion that "high status" should never be confused "with high character."[66] In any case, Trump's obsessive habit of creating false narratives as president highlighted his tendency to view life through a kaleidoscope, and most certainly his need for some "alternative reality," "reality distortion field," or "fantasy world" that "does not exist."[67] Trump's fabricated versions of truth and attacks on scientific facts, which too often denied the obvious and defied rationality, and which were designed "to sow confusion, doubt, and maybe even fatigue in the public,"[68] also seemed to be essentially a product of what King termed "self-delusion" "born of" or "wrapped in superficiality."[69]

In 2018, James B. Peterson reminded us that "Trump is precisely who King was so earnestly warning us about a half century ago."[70] King did suggest, indirectly and at times directly, that if Americans failed to be "tough-minded" and diligent in pursuing and creating democracy at its best, an authoritarian or fascist-minded figure with no regard for truth or integrity in government could possibly rise to the highest office in the land.[71] King referenced the case of Adolf Hitler to call attention to instances in which unethical people in power used lies and reality distortion to confuse and control the public and to advance their authority and self-interests, thus abusing power while ignoring the will of the people. "Adolf Hitler realized that soft-mindedness was so prevalent among his followers," King wrote, "that he said, 'I use emotion for the many and reserve reason for the few.'" King further noted that the German dictator, in his *Mein Kampf*, declared, "By means of shrewd lies, unremittingly repeated, it is possible to make people believe that heaven is hell—and hell heaven. . . . The greater the lie, the more readily it will be believed." King felt that Hitler's routine of exploiting falsehoods to his advantage presented a special challenge for persons of faith genuinely committed to truth-telling, a point that could be made of Trump and Trumpism as well:

> Hitler used to say that even if you tell a lie, tell a big one, and if you tell it long enough and loud enough, you'll convince everybody that it is true, even yourself. And he took that method and convinced the German people that the Jews were the cause of all of their misfortunes and led that great nation with all of its great minds to the killing of six million Jews. Now, if a man could tell a *lie* and turn a nation upside-down toward an evil end, it seems that we could tell the truth about Jesus Christ and turn this world right side-up.[72]

What King said here about Hitler is meaningful not only for framing a critique of Trump and his approach as president to truth and truth-telling[73] but also for assessing how leaders with moral and prophetic zeal might respond to the continuing challenges of Trumpism as a whole in this post-truth age. When considered in the larger context, Trump's determination to govern by lies—and to use lies and deception to secure and maintain power, with no intention of apologizing or correcting the record—actually constituted an assault on what King regarded as fundamental moral and ethical norms.[74] Trump and Trumpism are also classic examples of what King meant when he spoke of the inevitable decline and fall of powerful elites who represent a perversion of ethical leadership. King repeatedly declared that leaders who turn to falsehoods as a core aspect of governing inevitably open themselves to corruption, failure, the harsh judgments of the court of public opinion, and ultimately a fall from power, as evidenced, he felt, by the declines of the likes of Hitler and Mussolini.[75] The wisdom of King's perspective is being increasingly confirmed daily in the unfolding drama surrounding the many investigations of and legal challenges to Trumpism, which has become in the minds of many a symbol of and indeed a metaphor for political corruption.[76] This only confirms King's conviction that voters should always be intentional about putting only politicians who have credibility in public office, especially in a democracy that rests on certain self-evident truths.[77] Even so, the legacies of both Trump and King as leaders have so much to teach us about what it means to live in an age when truth is in peril—when all too many seem to forget what truth really means.

King is an immensely important critical resource for assessing how Trump put religion to the service of leadership based on deception and falsehoods. Trump used religion not only as a source to explain and justify his values, his ideas and worldview, his practices, his erratic approach to public-policy issues, and the ways in which he related to and interacted with people of various backgrounds and affiliations but also as a tool to sanction his authoritarian leadership and governing philosophy and style. It has been suggested that Trump's obsessive need to paint rosy and false pictures of what was going on around him—even when it was tragic, sad, and troubling—could be traceable to the influence of the late celebrity pastor Norman Vincent Peale, whom Trump greatly admired and who often spoke and "wrote about the ability of the mind to create its own more-positive reality."[78] Interestingly, King spoke about Peale's *The Power of Positive Thinking* (1952) in connection with what he termed "a sort of escape religion" that distorts truth and draws people "away from the realities of life,"[79] and this observation is relevant to any critical-analytical approach to not only Trump's own sense of his reality-based world but also the mindset of those, especially QAnon believers, who have been completely drawn into both Trump's cult of personality and his reality-distortion orbit. The same might be said of King's thoughts on what the philosopher William James called "the stream of consciousness," which means that human nature is such that an individual "has the power to adjust his mind to believe anything that he wants to" and "to convince himself" that what is untrue is true and that "the wrong is the right."[80]

Even more disturbing is the fact that as president, Trump surrounded himself with religious leaders, Black and white, who also demonstrated a lack of commitment to truth, and who questioned science and scientific facts in ways reminiscent of the old-line fundamentalism and the John T. Scopes trial of the 1920s.[81] White evangelicals gave Trump high approval ratings throughout his presidency and became part of the cult of personality surrounding him, and a smattering of Black preachers, who claimed to value King's legacy and who routinely proclaimed the power of Jesus's words about truth setting the captives free, defied their own orthodoxy regarding fidelity to faith, honesty, and truth-telling by remaining silent while bowing at the altar of Trumpism.[82] King's idea of the prophetic religious leader and the prophetic church that unapologetically speak truth to power had long been in decline since his death,[83] and Trumpism may well have inflicted the final death knell. It may be impossible for the Christian church, and especially its evangelical wing, to recover from the seductive and tranquilizing effects of Trumpism, let alone reclaim what King labeled "its prophetic zeal," "the sacrificial spirit," and those "certain truths which are essential parts of the Christian view of things." For King, "prophetic zeal," "sacrificial spirit," and "the Christian view of things" had to do with a genuine respect for and a willingness to risk all for not only religious truths but truth as "the whole."[84]

Trump's war on truth targeted people from all backgrounds and stations in life, but particularly communities of color, whom King had described as the "disinherited people all over the world."[85] Such attacks became more widely known during presidential candidate Trump's campaign of racial birtherism against Barack H. Obama, the nation's first Black president.[86] Trump's blatant lies about Obama's citizenship, coupled with the increasing "browning of America"—or the fact that the nation is becoming less Caucasian and more Black and brown—helped make Trump's volatile mix of populism, white nationalism, and reality distortion most appealing to many whites, and especially the more race-conscious working-class white folks, who have been led to believe that living in a multiracial democracy dominated numerically by people of color would be antithetical to their best interests—culturally, socially, intellectually, spiritually, psychologically, and otherwise.[87] Trump was actually elected president in 2016 largely because of the nation's changing demographics and a heavy voter turnout among non-college-educated, working-class white citizens who—constantly exposed to heavy doses of falsehoods, propaganda, and disinformation around issues of race from the candidate himself, and from Fox News and other right-wing media sources—increasingly feel displaced, disaffected, and even oppressed.[88] So many of these whites have never been interested in the fulfillment of King's vision of a multiracial nation that ultimately translates into a beloved community, but they easily consumed Trump's bombastic, racially charged messaging about "making America great again," which for them meant "making America white again."[89] Trump's self-appointed mission to "make America great again" suggested a looking back to some imagined, idealized past in race relations instead of a looking ahead in a sustained effort to, as King put it, "make the American dream a reality" for all.[90] Walter E. Fluker is right in saying that Trumpism "represents the nostalgic wanderings of an American past that never existed."[91] Put another way, Trumpism is about reliving the past and appealing to misguided forces of retrogression, but King looked to the future while challenging and inspiring the enlightened forces of progression.

Trump and his closest associates, Black and white, declared that he was not a white supremacist,[92] that his policies actually benefited African Americans,[93] and that King would be proud of what he achieved in the areas of Black employment and financial support for historically Black colleges and universities.[94] Most Blacks and many liberal whites strongly argue that such claims do not square with the facts, and they mock Trump's assertions that he did "more for the black community than any president since Abraham Lincoln" and that "nobody had ever heard of Juneteenth before he made it 'very famous.'"[95] Clearly, Trump took actions, pursued policies, and promoted falsehoods around race that put the country's majority European-descended population at ease and that convinced most Blacks that the civil rights gains made during the age of King were being slowly but surely eroded. Aside from "attacking voting rights" and "promoting white nationalism," Trump occasionally used racist rhetoric; verbally attacked Blacks in politics and the media who called him to accountability; refused to sincerely condemn the Ku Klux Klan (KKK), neo-Nazis, and other hate groups; slashed civil rights enforcement; encouraged police misconduct and abuses; "scaled back Obama-era efforts to hold police departments accountable"; and publicly defended Confederate heroes and monuments.[96] When Trump departed the White House in January 2021, Black-white relations had been wounded and fragmented in ways that will take generations to repair, if they ever can be, thus placing in bold relief King's stern prophecy, made in his very last speech, concerning the difficult times ahead.[97] To be sure, Trumpism, the lingering effects of which still cut into the soul of this nation, put the lie to the notion, held widely from the time of the election of Obama, that America had finally become the kind of postracial society King envisioned.[98] Trump's presidency actually emboldened the forces of white supremacy at every level of this nation's life, and also elevated the race debate to new levels of intensity.

Trump's America encouraged an absence of concern for the weak, the destitute, and the vulnerable that we have not seen since the King years—a spirit of sheer heartlessness and lack of empathy that is seemingly limitless, inexcusable in modern times, and really unfathomable. This became painfully real in policies aimed at immigrants, refugees, and asylum seekers, and especially the children among them. The United States, as King occasionally noted, has long been a safe haven for the persecuted of other countries, especially Europeans,[99] and it has been defined over time by the spirit and values of immigrants, but Trump and Trumpism ushered in a new wave of nativism, xenophobia, and anti-immigration fear-mongering that is reminiscent, in some ways at least, of the Know Nothing Party movement of the mid-nineteenth century and the anti-immigrant fervor of the 1920s.[100] During his presidential campaign, Trump, despite his denials, described immigrants from Mexico as "criminals" and accused them of taking "jobs that should go to people here legally,"[101] and he "was carried into the White House by an angry tribe" that felt "sidelined by history, that feared their country was slipping away," and that found hope in his promise "to give their country back to them and to win a future for their children."[102] The words "go back to your country" had long been associated with the poisonous race-baiting tendencies of the most radical and reactionary white supremacists, and they were being echoed at this time by the president of the United States. Immigrants, refugees, and asylum seekers of color, unlike newcomers of European and Canadian descent, were characterized as "the others," portrayed in terms of "an us versus them" scenario, and perceived as a menace and a public safety threat, and "diversity," "pluralism," "multiculturalism," "invasion," "infestation," "demographic replacement," and "the great replacement" were used as code words to stoke fear and to fan the flames of bigotry and intolerance, thus creating deep wounds in the domestic life of this nation. The resulting tension festered into occasional violent backlashes against immigrants, refugees, and asylum seekers by vigilantes and sometimes ordinary Americans who were inspired and motivated by the inciteful, hateful, untruthful rhetoric of Trump, hate groups, and their sympathizers.[103]

Trump's suggestion that he shared King's vision of a pluralistic and inclusive multiracial democracy, fueled by the rich presence and creative energies of people of different backgrounds, was disproven time and time again as he launched his campaign of fear, misinformation, and outright untruths and also his politics of distraction and division. Having no real, thoughtful, coordinated policy options to deal with the influx of newcomers to America, Trump targeted these Black and brown-skinned people with his authoritarianism by forcing them to linger in crowded detention centers, by putting their children in cages, by rounding up and deporting even "Dreamers," or those impacted by the Deferred Action on Childhood Arrivals program, and by building a wall that was not only technologically obsolete but totally impractical and immoral. Such actions were clearly designed to discourage the "outsiders"—and more specifically, people from Mexico, Central America, Haiti, and Africa—from coming to this country.[104] The overly crowded detention centers, cages for children, anti-immigrant raids, and walls became the most powerful symbols for how the Trump administration treated what King called "the least of these."[105] So much of what King said about the disturbing disparities in the treatment of white immigrants and immigrants of color in American history is useful for understanding and critiquing what happened under the banner of Trumpism, especially since King himself was often labeled an "outsider" and treated like a "resident alien."[106] King held that no child of God is an "outsider" or "resident alien" anywhere on this earth. Quoting Psalms 24:1—"the earth is the Lord's, and the fulness thereof; the world, and they that dwell therein"—he insisted that humans are caretakers and not owners of God's properties, and he denounced the notion that America belonged to whites and that all peoples of color were "outsiders." The terms "outsiders," "the others," "illegal immigrants," and "resident aliens" were never used by him to describe any segment of humanity, for they conflicted with his understanding of truth and his communitarian ideal.[107] King advocated building bridges, not walls, between people, and his wise use of Jesus's parable of the Good Samaritan to explain "ones duty to a wounded stranger" is helpful in reimagining how immigrants, refugees, and asylum seekers might be viewed and treated in any society in which people are judged by the color of their skin instead of "those inner qualities" that make them one with all humanity.[108] If there is no serious reckoning with truth concerning race in the years ahead, and if Americans of all shades do not prove equal to the challenge of building a new multiracial United States, the likely scenario is that the country will go the way of the old apartheid South Africa—that it's political culture will be defined by an authoritarian government in which a white minority desperately seeks to uphold white supremacy by whitewashing its past, through a carefully designed system of patriotic education, via voter suppression and intimidation, by widespread gerrymandering and election subversion, through continuing patterns of economic exploitation, by divide-and-conquer tactics aimed at communities of color, and through other means.

Because the Good Samaritan's "spiritual eyes" were not blinded by what King called "the cataracts of provincialism"—which made it possible for him to look "beyond the external accidents" and discern "those inner qualities that make all men human and, therefore, brothers"[109]—his story, as interpreted by King, is equally meaningful for addressing Trump's and Trumpism's role in the mainstreaming of religious bigotry and intolerance, which also targets immigrants, and especially Muslims. Before and during his presidency, Trump drank from the wellsprings of "a culture of demonization, fear, and incitement" aimed at practitioners of Islam—a culture that had, in an atmosphere of post–September 11 attacks hysteria, conditioned all too many Americans "to think of all Muslims as terrorists."[110] As early as December 2015, presidential candidate Trump called for "a total and complete shutdown of Muslims entering the United States until our country's representatives can figure out what the hell is going on."[111] He began his presidency with a ban that impacted citizens from several Muslim-majority countries—Iraq, Iran, Libya, Somalia, Sudan, and Yemen—and he surrounded himself with cabinet officials, advisers, representatives from conservative media, and evangelical Christian leaders who believed in his falsehoods about Muslims and shared his anti-Islamic sentiments, thus contributing to a national climate in which Islamophobia was defended and even normalized.[112] Anti-Muslim hate groups grew significantly, mosques were vandalized and burned in parts of this nation, and Muslims were increasingly and needlessly profiled and scapegoated, subjected to Islamophobic tropes and name-calling, and at times physically attacked and murdered.[113] The shooter who killed six Muslim men in Quebec City in January 2017 was referred to as a supporter of "Trump's immigration policies," and the Australian-born suspect who brazenly murdered forty-nine and seriously wounded twenty in two mosques in Christchurch, New Zealand, in March 2019 praised Trump in his manifesto. In both cases, Trump's images of immigrants, including Muslims, as "invaders" and "terrorists" had a noticeable and unfortunate impact, despite his assertions to the contrary.[114] King was horrified by the mere thought of people being persecuted and killed for their faith, and what he said about violence provoked by and committed in the name of religion is of timeless value, especially since he was a powerful advocate of interfaith dialogue and cooperation in the interest of world peace and community. King's thought and activism stand as a necessary corrective to Trumpism's tendency to distort and use religion as yet another tool to divide and subjugate people.[115]

Like King before him, President Trump consistently stressed the need for religious freedom, but for reasons that were quite different and certainly questionable. Unlike King, he never did so out of a genuine respect for religious diversity or pluralism, despite his claims to the contrary. Trump implemented policies that banned Muslims from some countries but not from those with which he had business interests—Egypt, Saudi Arabia, Turkey, and the United Arab Emirates[116]—which means that his advocacy of religious freedom, much like his silence in the face of hate groups that targeted Jews, was about being self-serving and playing politics and not necessarily about upholding the right of individuals and groups to believe in and practice their faiths without government interference. The only faith tradition that fits into the category marked "religious freedom" in "Trump's world," says Tisa Werger, "is a particular brand of Christianity that is politically conservative and overwhelmingly white."[117] In contrast, King represented a perspective that valued religious pluralism and rejected religious bigotry and intolerance in all forms, and this was more consistent with religious freedom in the best tradition of the United States. King actually saw the other great world religions—Hinduism, Buddhism, Judaism, and Islam—not as "rivals" but as "possible alternatives" to Christianity and also as different but nonetheless complementary paths to truth.[118] King's own search for truth was actually enhanced substantially through deep and genuine encounters with other religions than his own, as evidenced by his intense study of the Hindu leader Mohandas K. Gandhi and by his associations with the Jewish rabbi Abraham J. Heschel and the Buddhist monk Thich Nhat Hanh in the interest of social justice and peace.[119] King vehemently denied ever being "a victim of religious bigotry" and ever having "condemned" other religions, and he described Islam as "one of the great religions of the world."[120] He had so much to say about "the moral degeneracy of religious bigotry and the corroding effects of narrow sectarianism."[121] His open-mindedness in the face of ever-increasing religious diversity—and most certainly his vision of a new model of panreligious dialogue and cooperation grounded in Hindu-Buddhist-Jewish-Christian-Islamic solidarity against structures of oppression and exclusion[122]—should serve as a much-needed example, guide, and inspiration in this post-truth age of bigoted and tribalized religious thinking.

The poor and their living conditions proved to be yet another issue that exposed how Trump and Trumpism differed from King, theoretically and practically, when it came to addressing problems of institutional and structural evil and injustice in society. For King, ethical leadership was most important when taking on this issue because it, like those previously mentioned, required truth-telling and the willingness to transcend "arrogant individualism" and "compassionless detachment" to engage "the needs of the underprivileged" or "the least of these."[123] Throughout his public life, and especially during those last three years, King habitually approached the plight of the poor in a prophetic mode, which means that he was brutally honest and forthright about how the evils of capitalism bred economic injustice and particularly the conditions that kept large segments of the nation's population in menial jobs with low wages, no health care, and insufficient quantities of food and other basic necessities. It bothered King that so few Americans actually connected various forms of bigotry with economic exploitation. In his thinking, these two evils had to be viewed in terms of their "malignant kinship."[124] He was deeply troubled by a system in which the rich got richer and the poor poorer on a daily basis. "God never intended for one group of people to live in superfluous inordinate wealth while others live in abject deadening poverty," King declared.[125] President Trump brought a completely different perspective to the problem, even as he praised King for uplifting and empowering people at all levels of society.

Even before he was elected president, Trump brought his own set of facts to what he considered to be the cause of the conditions faced by poor people of all races. He commonly blamed the enormous cost of "illegal immigration" and the policies of past presidents— and especially Obama's—for contributing to a grim economic picture that, in his opinion, produced tremendous anxiety, and he occasionally mentioned "those 45 million people stuck in poverty," the declining middle class, and the absence of vital and affordable health care. On the campaign trail, Trump promised to put forth a plan for "full employment" and to repeal and replace Obamacare "with a much better option."[126] He "used populist appeals to gain power," but while in office, "his economic policies," including the massive tax cut, favored "society's most privileged sectors." The "billionaire populist," as Trump was called in some circles, also packed "his cabinet with billionaires, bankers, and lobbyists"[127]—the very people King had always said were the least prepared to understand the problems of poor people. Always looking to the stock market for ammunition to paint a rosy picture of the nation's economic health, Trump used falsehoods and deception in his messaging to the poor, seeking to convince them that their situation had improved enormously under his leadership. He constantly bragged about what he had done to improve the employment situation for communities of color, always inflating the numbers, but virtually every social tabulation showed that Black and brown people continued to rank below whites, from educational levels to employment and wages to health care to life expectancy.[128]

Although the plight of non-college-trained, working-class whites never really improved significantly, they consistently gave Trump high approval ratings. Apparently, this had more to do with Trump's appeal to their prejudices and anti-immigrant sentiments than with any policy initiatives or programmatic thrust for their economic uplift. Trump had long attributed the declining conditions of the poor and middle class to inadequate leadership, which he blamed for a "crippled America,"[129] but his presidency did more to benefit himself, his family, and his friends, from a material standpoint, than it did the country. Trump and many of his family members, friends, and associates reportedly made millions of dollars. Trump became the very embodiment of the kind of leader King dreaded the most—the kind who used the system to take "necessities from the masses to give luxuries to the classes." King taught us that any real advancement on the part of the poor requires a complete restructuring of such an edifice. He demanded major structural changes in society, which could only be achieved with militant and perhaps even defiant disruptions of the machinery of government through massive nonviolent civil disobedience.[130] Having seen democratic socialism at work during his visit to the Scandinavian countries in 1964, King stressed the need for "the nationalization of basic industries" to insure compliance with antisegregation rulings, universal education and health care, "massive expenditures to revive center cities and to provide jobs for ghetto residents," and "a guaranteed income for every adult citizen of the U.S."[131] This speaks volumes about the sheer radicality of the leadership model he advocated and represented during his time.

The type of ethical, prophetic, or transformational leadership King embodied and called for in the struggle to uplift and empower the poor is extremely rare today. Although more is being said and written about the need for such a model of leadership than ever before, which is not surprising in these post-truth times, it is too often discussed in ways that suggest that it has little if anything to do with the homeless, destitute, and helpless. King's leadership model is superbly represented today by Bishop William Barber—pastor of Greenleaf Christian Church in Goldsboro, North Carolina—who speaks truth to power about the conditions of the poor and is also involved in a movement that is referred to as a "renewed version" of King's Poor People's Campaign.[132] Barber, whom Cornel West calls "the closest person to Martin Luther King, Jr. in our midst," has consistently criticized Trumpism while mobilizing support, marching, and advocating for a fifteen-dollar minimum wage, universal health care, and women's and LGBTQ rights.[133] Barber has also joined with other Christians, Jews, and Muslims to protest white supremacy, police brutality, and the treatment of immigrants, refugees, and asylum seekers at the southern border.[134] Barber's work with people from different races, ethnic groups, and religions mirrors the coalition of conscience King and others formed during the struggles for voting rights and the planning for the Poor People's Campaign in the late 1960s. The goal involves strengthening multiracial democracy in the context of a changing economy, thus undermining the lingering effects of Trumpism.

King's stress on the need for America to live out the self-evident truths she put on paper with respect to her obligation to different segments of the society had much to do with how he viewed her image and role on the world stage. When he spoke in terms of "the final triumph" of the democratic and beloved community ideals, he had in mind an America that valued freedom for all her inhabitants while also being a force for freedom abroad. Thus, he urged his country to get on the right side of the global human rights revolution—to lead in "a revolution of values" that is supportive of "the freedom revolutions engulfing the earth."[135] This global outlook has not been sustained as a cherished aspect of King's leadership and legacy, and Trump and Trumpism have done more to undermine it than any other cultural and political force in the United States up to this point. On paper and in speeches, Trump proudly referred to America's leadership role in "the free world," and he insisted that "we've earned the right to boast and make it clear that we are ready and willing to do whatever is necessary to defend this country as well as liberty anywhere else in the world,"[136] but his actions as president belied this statement.

Trump's dealings with the world reflected levels of misunderstanding, insensitivity, hostility, and incompetence that King never witnessed in the three presidents with whom he frequently discussed domestic and world affairs. Trump attacked globalization for making "the financial elite wealthy" and for leaving "millions of our workers with nothing but poverty and headache,"[137] adopted an "America First" approach to foreign policy,[138] often conducted foreign policy by threatening tweets, pulled out of strategic partnerships with allies around the world,[139] dismissed NATO as obsolete,[140] cozied up to and lavishly praised dictators,[141] and solicited foreign influence on US presidential elections.[142] Equally disturbing is the fact that Trump, who claimed to share King's unifying vision of humanity, also reportedly made "racist remarks" about African countries, Haiti, and El Salvador;[143] senselessly exacerbated trade tensions with China;[144] repeatedly blamed the terrible death toll caused by the coronavirus pandemic on "the China Virus";[145] severed ties with the World Health Organization (WHO);[146] inspired white supremacists around the world;[147] and failed to make any meaningful and lasting contributions to world peace and community.[148] Trump's actions along these lines did not advance America's interests on the world stage and have actually weakened her leadership and influence globally. His "America First" approach, which essentially meant "America only" or "America alone," represented a stark contrast to King's vision of the "world house," which called for "a world-wide fellowship that lifts neighborly concern" beyond nation, and it forced the United States down a path of isolationism. King considered any "America First" doctrine to be a threat to not only world peace but human survival.[149] He mapped out "a literal path of global reconciliation, community, and spiritual love as radical as any in history,"[150] and it must be taken more seriously if we are to become a new humanity.

Although King and Trump, as self-proclaimed ethical leaders, brought a different set of ideas, principles, values, and strategies to their service to America and the world, both are critical resources for redefining what ethical leadership at its best should be in this post-truth age. Trump is no longer president, but Trumpism in one form or another will continue to exist while inspiring many with political aspirations. King has been gone for more than a half century, but he is still admired as one of the most effective models of ethical, prophetic, and transformational leadership in the history of Christianity. We can rest assured that the biographies of King and Trump will continue to function in American and world history as more than stories of individual lives. Many will continue to appeal to them to justify positions held on a range of concerns relative to race, religion, and politics.

Can Truth Prevail? The Looming Question

George Orwell—the English journalist, novelist, and fierce opponent of tyranny—once declared that "in a time of universal deceit, telling the truth is a revolutionary act."[151] Martin Luther King Jr. lived in such a time, and he acknowledged as much and more when he equated the habit and spirit of relentless truth-telling with cross-bearing and with the Calvary experience as epitomized in the suffering of Jesus of Nazareth. As a civil and human rights leader, and as a proclaimer of truth in the face of raw power and ruling elites, King lived his life on the cross,[152] and his crucifixion was a testimony to the revolutionary act of truth-telling. This explains in part why his legacy of ideas and struggle should take on new shades and applicability in these post-truth times. Although King spoke, engaged, acted on, and suffered for truth in his own world, he essentially anticipated certain concerns and challenges that confront Americans in these early decades of the twenty-first century, for there is still an absence of deep wellsprings of credibility at virtually every level of institutional life, and especially within the ranks of politics and religion.

Falsehoods have become mainstreamed and normalized in our culture, and all too many seem unconcerned about the conflicts or the blurred lines between truth and untruth.[153] Too many insist on choosing and defining their own realities. The old rules and standards regarding truth and truth-telling have been broken, and repairing them may take generations, if they can ever be repaired. Again, this is to some extent the legacy of Trumpism. Because King was a transformational figure—and because his life and legacy remain a monument to the meaning, indispensability, and power of truth and truth-telling—he is uniquely instructive to the contemporary situation. Put another way, there are lessons that we can apply from him as we respond to a culture that is increasingly becoming addicted to lies and lying. We might begin with King's conviction that the best life is the life devoted to an avid, untiring, and enduring search for truth, which he associated with "the highest good," or the summum bonum of life.[154] The determination to know, experience, and act on truth was for him the goal of human life, which transcends all dogmatic and doctrinal prescriptions, and he dedicated his mind, heart, and soul to this endless quest. This is also how King understood the lives of great sages like the Hebrew prophets, the Greek philosophers, Jesus, and Mohandas K. Gandhi, all of whom demonstrated, in word and deed, that the chief goal of life should be directed toward the noblest of moral and/or ethical and spiritual ends. King believed that the lifelong quest for truth is always liberating and empowering and that it is essential for wholeness or the integration of the personality. Once truth becomes irrelevant and meaningless in any life, he held, that life becomes inauthentic, disintegrated, and enslaved to untruth.[155] We need to echo and even amplify this same message today, for the failure to value and pursue truth as a lifelong quest is reducing too many lives in our society and world to what King called "moral" and "spiritual slavery."[156]

A serious reading of King also challenges us around the need to come to some shared understandings of what actually constitutes objective truths and facts, or those truths and facts that are knowable, established by proof, and universally accepted. All too many are ill prepared for a debate around what truth really means. King believed that truth and facts are equally important in coming to terms with objective reality. He occasionally illustrated the point by referencing the absolute truths of religion and the known and verifiable facts of science, which he viewed as not only complementary but also not dependent on human opinions or questionable on the grounds of common sense and rationality.[157] King understood and generally accepted the kind of cultural relativism that allowed for different opinions on many subjects but categorically rejected it in the case of objective truths and facts.[158] He felt that a society in which large segments of the population could not agree on fundamental truths and facts is invariably a society without a shared sense of what is real and unreal, rational and irrational, right and wrong.[159] Perhaps the greatest danger of this age of post-truth is the growing absence of shared standards of truth. Truth and untruth too often masquerade as one and the same, some speak of different or alternative truths, and any kind of verified knowledge is rendered questionable and even debatable.[160] In these post-truth times, the possibility of a discussion based on shared conceptions of truth and a common set of facts is very difficult and increasingly becoming impossible, for too many are deriving their accepted truths and facts from the dark corners of social media and from political and religious leaders who are more concerned about power, privilege, and maintaining a certain image than about common sense, rationality, honesty, and integrity.

The absence of general agreement on basic truths and facts mushroomed and spilled over into the 2020 US presidential election, placing America in the grip of extreme right-wing terrorist threats, violence, and insurrection. It also explains the outrageous claim, echoed and reechoed by powerful post-truth voices, of an equivalency between the lone Black state representative who was arrested for knocking on the governor of Georgia's door in protest against voter suppression and the hundreds of insurrectionists who stormed the US Capitol to prevent the peaceful transfer of power on January 6, 2021.[161] King was deeply concerned about both "the content of our character" and our survival and welfare as a nation, and a more concerted, intense, and protracted struggle for the full realization of his ideal of a society that functions in accordance with shared understandings of self-evident truths and verifiable facts is no longer a choice but an absolute necessity.[162] A unified struggle in pursuit of this goal, on the part of Americans of goodwill, is our best defense against antitruth advocates, who are engaged in an ongoing war with the facts of science, and whose "looseness with truth" is gradually degrading culture and turning this nation into what King dubbed "a soulless society."[163]

A cultural reawakening around the necessity for creating a new and more vital ethic of truth-telling exposes another level on which King's legacy still challenges and provokes us as a nation. King declared that truth-telling is always essential in modeling a civilized state of human existence, and he consistently raised the need for America to develop the type of "moral climate" and "mode of thinking" that result in a better ethic and culture of truth-telling and truth-sharing. In King's mind, this is what the civil rights movement in the United States was all about.[164] He opined that the kingdom of God exists wherever people love truth, and that truth-telling and lying cannot coexist equally in a culture supposedly designed to promote sanity, responsibility, and trust. Moreover, King believed that an ethic and culture of truth-telling was necessary for America to thrive and move forward socially, economically, politically, and otherwise. The collective responsibility for shaping and maintaining such a culture, in his judgment, fell on the shoulders of citizens from all walks of life—politicians, religious leaders, academics, poets and producers of other forms of popular literature, artists, entrepreneurs, and indeed ordinary citizens. There is a special challenge here for Americans who have apparently forgotten what truth looks, sounds, and feels like or what it means to live in a society where truth is constantly spoken, shared, listened to, and heard.[165]

This new ethic and culture would compel Americans to engage in a serious and renewed reckoning with truth regarding the ugly, uncomfortable, and shameful side of the country's past or its history and heritage, for this, too, reveals exactly who and what we are. King said over and over that engaging in soul-searching honesty about ourselves and our nation, especially with regard to the oppression of communities of color over time, is part of that grace that can set us free. He highlighted the critical need for all Americans to study and learn from "the truth of the situation," from "the facts of history"—or from "historical truths" or "the lessons of history"—which means being exposed to both one's own verifiable truths and the verifiable truths of others.[166] For King, such an engagement with truth on these various levels was central, and indeed of indispensable value, in transcending our age-old image of an "ambivalent nation"[167] and in achieving meaningful healing, reconciliation, and community between the different races. Stated more specifically, he knew that the communitarian ideal he envisioned, and for which he struggled so gallantly, could not find true meaning, fulfillment, and survival on a shaky foundation of false history or on what W. E. B. Du Bois called "the propaganda of history."[168]

Post-truth extremists on the right side of the political spectrum have revealed as much as any other force in our history the refusal of all too many Americans to come to terms with the troubling and painful truths and facts about this country's history. The fierce opposition to the 1619 Project and the banning of critical race theory are emblematic of their determination to distort and/or whitewash the nation's past, thus posing yet another challenge to both objective truth and a functioning democracy. Such actions are not only antihistory and antitruth but a clear violation of the First Amendment.[169] They constitute an assault on teachers, teaching, and truth. Ironically enough, the Texas state representative who authored the bill against critical race theory in his state argued that King would support his efforts—that the ban "echoes Dr. King's wish that we should judge people on the content of their character, not their skin."[170] This is a strange case of using King's language to undermine a theory that is obviously consistent with King's own views about race and how it should be a central category in the teaching of American history.[171] Critical race theory is usually taught in the nation's law schools, and not in public school systems, but there is still a loud and growing outcry against it on the part of uninformed white parents who mistakenly think their children are being exposed to it. Many whites who vehemently oppose and denounce critical race theory would likely have no problem with Eurocentric curricula and teaching content in public schools that affirm and reinforce white supremacy while suppressing the truth about the kidnapping and enslavement of Africans; genocidal efforts against Native Americans; Jim Crow; the countless violent attacks on communities of color by the likes of the KKK, skinheads, and the Nazi Party; and other social evils that are so much a part of this country's legacy.[172] They fail to see that America remains caught in the grip of racial polarization and tribalism largely because there is no shared knowledge and understanding across racial boundaries of what has long been true and untrue and right and wrong about its history and culture. King and the civil rights movement sought to bring Americans to such a shared realization and understanding by encouraging the kind of education that promotes critical-analytical thinking skills, for King knew that this remained essential in starting the healing process and moving the nation forward.[173] He also understood that speaking truth about America's failings and being patriotic are not mutually exclusive—that patriotism at its best demands nothing less.

We would do well to recall King's oft-repeated reminder that only truth can reconcile us with our history and heritage. He argued that we can never achieve "a just society" by "untruthful means."[174] Fortunately, King's efforts to force America to face the truth about herself are being echoed in the actions of many freedom-loving people who honor him today. National Football League players who kneel at pro football games are not disrespecting the national anthem and the flag; they are challenging the nation to be what it says it is on paper, or to live up to its self-evident truths.[175] The removal of Confederate monuments is not about dishonoring anyone's heritage; it is about peeling away the layers of untruth and getting at unadulterated truths that have been denied and covered up for much too long. The message conveyed through Black Lives Matter protests is not that only Black lives matter; it is about a larger truth concerning the intrinsic dignity and worth of all human personality, which means that all lives cannot matter until Black lives matter. As King so often pointed out, knowing truth is always a precondition for embracing and living the truth. The murder of George Floyd by policemen in Minnesota, in the full view of millions around the world, will likely do more than anything since the era of King and the civil rights movement to bring us face-to-face with certain raw and hard truths about what being American has been, is, is not, and should be.

King's challenge concerning the need for a new and more vital ethic and culture of truth-telling is also relevant at the level of the nation's politics. Lying has always been a modus operandi for all too many politicians, as highlighted during the Watergate crisis, but it was mainstreamed and normalized in unprecedented ways under Trump and Trumpism, thus heightening the need to reclaim and restore truth as a valued and positive force in American political life. This need became far more evident and critical with the concerted effort to overturn a legitimate, constitutionally mandated, and fair 2020 presidential election based on "the big lie," or the outrageous and false claim that massive fraud robbed the legitimate winner and put the loser in the White House. Compulsive lying is now a way of life for many who seek and hold public office. The practice of injecting lies, half-truths, propaganda, disinformation, and conspiracy theories into political discourse has become routine, thus contributing greatly to the deep and mindless tribalism that already prevails at virtually every level of American society. Having witnessed lying on the part of so many in government in his time, King warned about politicians who have a reckless disregard for truth and who resort to falsehoods in their bids for power, and his thoughts on the subject still resonate in powerful ways. He declared that outright lying does not square with democratic theory, and he agreed that much of the answer to this problem inhered in electing men and women with character and integrity to public office.[176]

What we are witnessing in these post-truth times is actually a ferocious attack on democracy by the forces of untruth. King wondered, particularly toward the end of his life, if America could actually become the embodiment of a participatory and representative democracy in the truest sense. Today the question is "Can America remain and expand as such a democracy?" Ironically, King and the civil rights movement successfully showed, albeit in a different fashion, what Trumpism and the forces of antitruth reveal today— namely, that the infrastructure of American democracy remains flawed, deficient, fragile, and vulnerable. The fact that former president Trump and his associates have so far escaped accountability for abysmal abuses of power and attacks on the nation's systems of laws, institutions, justice, and democratic governance makes this claim all the more valid. Trump and Trumpism have more than demonstrated what can happen to participatory and representative democracy when it is challenged and subverted by the power-thirsty forces of incivility, irrationality, and untruth. As president, Trump emerged as perhaps the most glaring and painful product and exemplar of what King called "the still ambivalent nation"—of America's historical tendency to proudly profess "the principles of democracy" while practicing "the very antithesis of those principles."[177] Because King himself was born in and lived through some of the most difficult and challenging times for democracy in America, his own struggles and insights into the supremacy of the moral law, truth as a regulating ideal, the wise and unselfish use of power, and service in the interest of the common good offer clues to how we might reclaim the very best qualities in the American democratic character and spirit in this post-truth era.[178] King was deeply interested in how truth and facts get manipulated within the realm of politics, and he taught us how we might appreciate, cherish, and sustain American democracy while also developing an informed sense of how the nation had fallen short of its democratic claims historically.

Confronted by "demagogues" like George Wallace, Ross Barnett, and Lester Maddox and by McCarthyism's "legacy of social paralysis," King recognized and actually spoke to frightening trends toward authoritarianism and fascism in this country in his times.[179] He saw how his own people had "been subject to the authoritarian and sometimes whimsical decisions of the white power structure,"[180] and he feared the crusading hordes of fascism.

310

King's experiences at home and abroad led him to conclude that the conflicts he and others were witnessing in the world between democracy and forms of authoritarianism, totalitarianism, and fascism were at bottom conflicts over not only the question "What is man?" but also "What is truth?"[181] As far as King was concerned, the "wisdom of democracy" over these more extreme and oppressive forms of government, which devalue truth, was never really in question.[182] He understood that blind loyalty to any single individual, as we have observed with Trumpism, is antithetical to the letter, spirit, and practice of democracy. When King thought in terms of strong, wise, and effective political leadership, or leadership that reflected what he termed "a positive democratic dynamism," he obviously had in mind not Machiavelli's image of "the prince," Nietzsche's idea of "the superman" or Übermensch, the German führer, Plato's "philosopher king," or even Donald Trump but one who embodied the values and spirit of Jesus "the practical realist" or "the prince of *satyagrahis*," who gave "himself to certain eternal truths and eternal principles that nobody could crucify and escape."[183] In King's opinion, Jesus delighted in and projected the profile of the strong leader who was driven by moral and/or ethical considerations rather than a lust for power and political expediency.

Many politicians who feast on vestiges of Trumpism are determined to take the nation back to Wallace, Barnett, and Maddox–era thinking, even McCarthy-era thinking, about truth and democracy. This is more than demonstrated in right-wing Republican opposition to both the John Lewis Voting Rights Act and the For the People Act, both of which are designed to protect voting rights for all Americans, and especially minorities of color, women, and young people.[184] This Republican-led attack is also evident in efforts to squash voices of dissent and protest. Words like "dissent," "protest," "resistance," and "revolution" are being smeared and distorted by the very forces largely responsible for the "crisis in truth" or "age of lies,"[185] thus striking at the very basics of democratic rights. These tactics are not new, for King's enemies at the highest levels of politics and government sought to restrict voting rights and to criminalize dissent and protest in a similar fashion. They, too, like those seduced by Trumpism in these times, were driven by "a nihilistic will to power."[186] If today's antidemocracy forces win, elections in the future will not be contests over who is most truthful, or who offers the most attractive policy options, but a struggle between those who represent democracy and those who do not. King often reminded us that antidemocratic forces never act in conformity with the highest values and traditions of America and that they triumph when the will of the people is not strong enough to resist them—that what "we the people" allow we in effect enable and empower. The people would ultimately determine, King held, "the potential for democracy's fulfillment or fascism's triumph."[187] "If American democracy should gradually disintegrate," he asserted, "it would be due as much to a lack of insight as a lack of commitment to right."[188] "Only when the people themselves begin to act are rights on paper given life blood," he noted. King often urged Americans who valued the principles of democracy not to allow "their consciences to sleep." Put another way, the challenge is never to be a Rip Van Winkle, to remain awake, to not sleep through a revolution, and certainly not the wrong revolution.[189] King knew that democracy survives only when its true saviors fight for it, and he admonished all Americans to exude something of the inner spirit of the founding fathers, who "broke with all traditions of imperial domination and established a unique and unprecedented form of government—the democratic republic."[190] King was fully convinced that "if democracy is to win its rightful place throughout the world, millions of people, Negro and white, must stand before the world as examples of democracy in action, not as voteless victims of the denial and corruption of our heritage."[191]

King viewed truth as the essential foundation, and indeed the life blood, of participatory and representative democracy at its best. It follows, then, that truth-telling is the healthiest and most essential ingredient of the democratic process—that it allows for the effective and productive workings of democracy. Post-truthism is a stern and much-needed wake-up call for Americans to take more seriously King's challenge concerning the need for a renewed and deeper consciousness of America's foundational democratic values, which affirm certain self-evident truths. Perhaps more forcefully than any other public figure in American history, King spoke to the need to go back to the revolutionary spirit and the loftiest mandates of this nation's democratic ethic as set forth in its founding documents.[192] He told us that democracy works best when its most cherished values are safeguarded and when the ethos of truth and truth-telling becomes an imperative for individual self-growth, activism, and social transformation. He felt that every generation has some responsibility to hold American democracy to this higher purpose and mission. This is always about an honest accounting of where America is and where it needs to go to fulfill the promises and possibilities of democracy. Otherwise, democracy becomes something other than a system guided by an of, for, and by the people ethic—it becomes a failed experiment.

What King said about the necessity for a new and more vital ethic and culture of truth-telling could not be more suggestive in terms of the prophetic duty to speak truth to power and to the conventions of authority wherever they might be. As Lawrence Edward Carter Sr. points out, in King, we "heard a man speak an eloquent and mighty truth to power and to speak from ultimate power the truth."[193] Whenever King mentioned leadership that is ethical, prophetic, or transformational, or the virtues that are so essential to public life and service, he included the moral obligation to speak truth to power in love but also with righteous indignation and a warning that God's judgment and wrath would not be withheld from those who refused to wield power with integrity, humility, compassion, and empathy. A serious student of Scripture and of the Hebraic-Christian tradition, King delighted in "the prophet's message of truth and decency,"[194] and he criticized corrupt rulers and evil in high places, always speaking and acting in the service of truth. In other words, King exemplified what he himself called "a transformed nonconformist" or "a maladjusted personality,"[195] and he demonstrated that prophetic rhetoric is always the rhetoric of discontent, critique, and truth. Also, King placed the primary burden of speaking truth to powerful and ruling elites squarely on religious leadership and the Christian church, which he called "the conscience of the state" and "the chief moral guardian of society."[196]

The courage and freedom to speak truth to power was threatened and significantly diminished during the Trump years. Many die-hard Bible-believing Christians and even some megachurch pastors, who had a platform to speak to the whole world, seemed incapable of outrage in the face of the barrage of lies told to Americans daily, and they chose silence over bold proclamations and moral cowardice over moral courage. Many African American preachers either remained silent and noncommittal or became outright enablers and supporters of, or apologists for, Trumpism, thus betraying a proud Black Christian prophetic tradition and the legacy of King. King only became important in their world when they needed his image, name, and legacy to support causes that were self-serving and that suited Trumpism and the conservative right-wing political agenda.[197] King himself was determined never to allow those who wielded great power in evil and selfish ways to become too comfortable with their deception, trickery, and falsehoods, and he was willing to pay for his moral boldness with his life. The prophetic King felt that the kingdom of God, or "the acceptable year of the Lord," would come only after the forces of truth are triumphant over untruth, and his message about the critical need for the type of righteous anger and discontent that disrupts and transforms the status quo stands as an enduring challenge to faith leaders who refuse to take seriously the prophetic dimension of ethical leadership.[198]

King majored in this prophetic side of ethical leadership not only by courageously speaking truth but also by struggling to undermine and to ultimately defeat untruth through words, actions, and the freedom campaigns he led. The pulpit, the streets, and jail cells all became important vehicles in this effort. As a preacher and pastor, King used the pulpit and the proclamation of God's word based in Scripture (kerygma) not only to create a healthy tension in the minds of his hearers—thus preparing them to rise above propaganda, disinformation, and half-truths "to the unfettered realm of creative analysis and objective appraisal"—but also to attack the myths of white superiority and Black inferiority and the many untruths advanced by segregationists about race, the human condition, and the meaning of the struggle for justice, human dignity, equal opportunity, and peace.[199] In his capacity as civil and human rights leader, King took that same gospel and repackaged and expanded on it as he set out to explain what he believed to be essentially a spiritual movement to the unchurched, Catholics, Jews, and other people of various backgrounds who marched with him in the streets and spent time with him in jail cells. The larger society was not to be excluded from this gospel, which always mixed scriptural passages with words and phrases from the Constitution and the Declaration of Independence. King's core message was always about the enslaving tendencies and routines of untruth and the power of truth to set the captives free. The civil rights campaigns he led were visible, living testimonies to the spirit and durability of truth in the face of untruth. In such instances, King actually mapped out and acted on a prophetic model of truth-telling that was as unique and radical as any since the times of the ancient Hebrew prophets and Jesus of Nazareth.

As we engage in conversation across this nation and the world about how to overcome the morally, spiritually, psychologically, and physically debilitating effects of post-truthism, and reclaim a culture of truth and truth-telling, we would be wise to recall what King said about the significance and indispensability of truthful means and truthful ends. Political philosophy from Machiavelli to Lenin and beyond, he noted, had separated the means and the ends, arguing that the ends actually justify the means if the ends are good.[200] Trumpism and other forms of post-truthism are among the most recent manifestations of this point of view. But King thought differently as he envisioned a new humanity and a higher global ideal:

> If we are to have peace in the world, men and nations must embrace the nonviolent affirmation that ends and means must cohere. One of the great philosophical debates of history has been over the whole question of means and ends. And there have always been those who argued that the end

justifies the means, that the means really aren't important. The important thing is to get to the end, you see. So if you're seeking to develop a just society, they say, the important thing is to get there, and the means are really unimportant; any means will do so long as they get you there—they may be violent, they may be untruthful means; they may even be unjust means to a just end. There have been those who have argued this throughout history. But we will never have peace in the world until men everywhere recognize that ends are not cut off from means, because the means represent the ideal in the making, and the end in process, and ultimately you can't reach good ends through evil means, because the means represent the seed and the end represents the tree.[201]

King's idea that only moral means can lead to moral ends and vice versa, which he viewed as the spiritual essence of the teachings of both the Hebrew prophets and Jesus, could not be more enlightening and meaningful in this twenty-first-century world, considering the dearth of vigorous ethical leadership and the climate in which unethical conduct at the highest levels of this nation's political and religious life is overlooked, excused, normalized, and at times rewarded. All too many among the powerful elites no longer consider truth a virtue, if they ever did, and they survive and prosper because the masses are unwilling or unable to demand accountability. Government mendacity and hard-core biblical conservatism are too often hardened by a growing culture of political violence, which can only lead to immoral and unethical ends. This failure to pursue truthful ends via truthful means is not simply a problem with politics and religion but one that extends across institutions worldwide—from the boardrooms of major corporations to newsrooms to the halls of academia to entertainment to the ranks of professional and Olympic sports.[202]

If there ever was a time for ethical leaders who speak, stand, and act as if truth is a respectable and commendable quality, it is now. King was no perfect ethical leader, but his ideas, wisdom, moral-spiritual vision and practice, prophetic-social activism, and eventual martyrdom in defense of truth explain why he is still viewed in so many circles as the quintessential model of ethical leadership. As America's one true spiritual genius and national hero, King's meaning and message are still amazingly fresh, and he still challenges us to reclaim a values-infused or values-laden culture that cherishes and elevates truth as the moral means that leads to moral ends.

The arc of truth is long, and its march and ultimate triumph in the universe was the gist of King's last prophecy as he stood before a cheering crowd on a drizzly night in Memphis. The message echoing through his entire speech, "I See the Promised Land," was that truth always marches on—even in strange, awkward, and unanticipated ways—to victory.[203] Truth marches on because nothing can stop or defeat it. It marches on because it is imbued with the power and spirit of no surrender. It marches on because it has a date with destiny. It marches on in this post-truth era with the people of all races who raise the banner of Black Lives Matter, with women who comprise the Me Too crusade, with youngsters involved in the March for Our Lives against gun violence, with those who struggle against voter suppression and intimidation, and with those who refuse to bow to Trumpism, post-truthism, or any other form of spiritual and moral perversion and antidemocracy. It marches on with those who honor and celebrate King's legacy not simply with words but also with deeds that change lives, structures, and institutions for the better. Truth marches on because only truth can have the last word in history.

Notes

Foreword

1 See chapter 6 in this volume.
2 Susannah Heschel, "Two Friends, Two Prophets: Abraham Joshua Heschel and Martin Luther King Jr.," *Plough Quarterly* 16, *America's Prophet* (Spring 2018), https://www.plough.com/en/topics/community/leadership/two-friends-two-prophets.
3 Martin Luther King Jr., "A Challenge to the Churches and Synagogues," speech, 1963 conference on "Religion and Race," National Conference of Christians and Jews (January 17, 1963). Quoted in Heschel, "Two Friends, Two Prophets."
4 See chapter 6 in this volume.
5 Quoted in Clayborne Carson and Peter Holloran, eds., *A Knock at Midnight: Inspiration from the Great Sermons of the Reverend Martin Luther King, Jr.* (New York: Warner, 1998), 111.

Introduction

1 David J. Garrow, *The FBI and Martin Luther King, Jr.: From "Solo" to Memphis* (New York: W. W. Norton, 1981), 122; Martin Luther King Jr., *Why We Can't Wait* (New York: New American Library, 1963), 88–89; Clayborne Carson, ed., *The Papers of Martin Luther King, Jr.*, vol. 7, *To Save the Soul of America, January 1961–August 1962*, ed. Tenisha Armstrong (Berkeley: University of California Press, 2014), 202, 404n18, 524–26, 527n1, 569.
2 In this regard, King was very much like Mohandas K. Gandhi, who called himself "a votary of truth from my childhood" and noted that "it was the most natural thing for me." See Thomas Merton, ed., *Gandhi on Non-violence: Selected Texts from Mohandas K. Gandhi's "Non-violence in Peace and War"* (New York: New Directions, 1965), 28.
3 Clayborne Carson, ed., *The Autobiography of Martin Luther King, Jr.* (New York: Warner, 1998), 16; Clayborne Carson, ed., *The Papers of Martin Luther King, Jr.*, vol. 1, *Called to Serve, January 1929–June 1951*, ed. Ralph E. Luker and Penny A. Russell (Berkeley: University of California Press, 1992), 363; Clayborne Carson, ed., *The Papers of Martin Luther King, Jr.*, vol. 6, *Advocate of the Social Gospel, September 1948–March*

1963, ed. Susan Carson et al. (Berkeley: University of California Press, 2007), 57.

4   Carson, *King Papers*, 7:209. King's statement here was taken from the title of Gandhi's autobiography. See Mohandas K. Gandhi, *An Autobiography: The Story of My Experiments with Truth* (Ahmadabad, India: Navajivan, 1927).

5   Walter Fluker stresses King's lifelong search for community, which he concludes began in the context of his family, church culture, and the larger Black community of Atlanta, Georgia. "The search for community," Fluker writes, "was the defining motif of Martin Luther King Jr.'s life and thought" (81). I submit that there is no essential conflict between Fluker's conclusions and my own, because King's search for community was a part of his larger search for truth. See Walter E. Fluker, *They Looked for a City: A Comparative Analysis of the Ideal of Community in the Thought of Howard Thurman and Martin Luther King, Jr.* (Lanham, MD: University Press of America, 1989), 81, 82–86.

6   Carson, *King Papers*, 1:361–63; Carson, *King Autobiography*, 6, 15–17.

7   Carson, *King Papers*, 1:122–24, 363; Carson, *King Autobiography*, 13–15; Clayborne Carson, *The Georgia Roots of Martin Luther King, Jr.: 1989 Georgia Week Lecture* (Atlanta: Georgia Humanities Council, 1989), 13–16.

8   Martin Luther King Jr., *Stride toward Freedom: The Montgomery Story* (New York: Harper & Row, 1958), 91–101; Martin Luther King Jr., *Strength to Love* (Philadelphia: Fortress, 1981; originally published in 1963), 147.

9   Carson, *King Papers*, 6:78, 110, 218, 397; Carson, *King Papers*, 7:408; Clayborne Carson, ed., *The Papers of Martin Luther King, Jr.*, vol. 5, *Threshold of a New Decade, January 1959–December 1960*, ed. Tenisha Armstrong et al. (Berkeley: University of California Press, 2005), 572; King, *Strength to Love*, 10; Martin Luther King Jr., *The Measure of a Man* (Philadelphia: Fortress, 1988; originally published in 1959), 36.

10   Carson, *King Papers*, 6:108.

11   Clayborne Carson, ed., *The Papers of Martin Luther King, Jr.*, vol. 2, *Rediscovering Precious Values, July 1951–November 1955*, ed. Stewart Burns et al. (Berkeley: University of California Press, 1994), 77, 89–90; Carson, *King Papers*, 6:172, 373–74, 461, 548, 600; Carson, *King Papers*, 7:408; King, *Strength to Love*, 10–11.

12   These different categories of truth are based on my own careful reading of King's writings, sermons, speeches, and interviews. See King, *Measure of a Man*, 36; Carson, *King*

Autobiography, 16; Carson, *King Papers*, 1:362; Carson, *King Papers*, 5:572; Carson, *King Papers*, 6:78, 108, 118, 171–73, 193–94, 218, 397; Carson, *King Papers*, 7:408–9, 491, 593; James M. Washington, ed., *A Testament of Hope: The Essential Writings and Speeches of Martin Luther King, Jr.* (New York: HarperCollins, 1991), 279; and King, *Strength to Love*, 10.

13   King, *Stride toward Freedom*, 101.

14   Both King and some of his associates used the word "Kingian" at times to describe the very personal and unique angle or element he brought to his thought. See Clayborne Carson and Peter Holloran, eds., *A Knock at Midnight: Inspiration from the Great Sermons of Reverend Martin Luther King, Jr.* (New York: Warner, 1998), 2, 25.

15   Carson and Holloran, *Knock at Midnight*, 195–96; Carson, *King Autobiography*, 357–58; King, *Stride toward Freedom*, 190–91; Carson, *King Papers*, 6:115, 383, 423–24; Carson, *King Papers*, 7:198, 212.

16   Carson, *King Papers*, 1:108–11; Carson and Holloran, *Knock at Midnight*, 86, 91–93; Fluker, *Looked for a City*, 87; Lewis V. Baldwin, *Behind the Public Veil: The Humanness of Martin Luther King, Jr.* (Minneapolis: Fortress, 2016), 32.

17   Lewis V. Baldwin, *There Is a Balm in Gilead: The Cultural Roots of Martin Luther King, Jr.* (Minneapolis: Fortress, 1991), 24–25; Carson, *King Autobiography*, 13.

18   Baldwin, *Behind the Public Veil*, 43–51.

19   John J. Ansbro, *Martin Luther King, Jr.: The Making of a Mind* (Maryknoll, NY: Orbis, 1982), 120–28, 151–60.

20   King described himself as "a dialectical thinker," meaning that he generally took "a both-and" rather than "an either-or" approach to reasoning. See Carson, *King Papers*, 7:180; and Alex Ayres, ed., *The Wisdom of Martin Luther King, Jr.: An A-to-Z Guide to the Ideas and Ideals of the Great Civil Rights Leader* (New York: Penguin, 1993), 58–59. King borrowed the phrase "the American dilemma" from the Swedish sociologist Gunnar Myrdal, who published *The American Dilemma* (1944), a study of Black-white relations in the United States. See Washington, *Testament*, 208–9, 477–78; Clayborne Carson, ed., *The Papers of Martin Luther King, Jr.*, vol. 4, *Symbol of the Movement, January 1957–December 1958*, ed. Susan Carson et al. (Berkeley: University of California Press, 2000), 363; King, *Stride toward Freedom*, 205; and Martin Luther King Jr., *Where Do We Go from Here: Chaos*

or Community? (Boston: Beacon, 1968; originally published in 1967), 84–85.

21 King, *Where Do We Go*, 35, 68, 80, 82, 88, 183; King, *Stride toward Freedom*, 190–91; King, *Strength to Love*, 49; Carson, *King Papers*, 7:113–14; Carson, *King Papers*, 6:305; King, *Why We Can't Wait*, 121; Washington, *Testament*, 282; Carson and Holloran, *Knock at Midnight*, 87.

22 King, *Where Do We Go*, 35, 68; King, *Stride toward Freedom*, 190–91.

23 I am indebted to Rufus Burrow Jr. for this understanding of King as an "ethical prophet." See Rufus Burrow Jr., *Ethical Prophets along the Way: Those Hall of Famers* (Eugene, OR: Cascade, 2020), 159–85. Also see J. Deotis Roberts, *Bonhoeffer and King: Speaking Truth to Power* (Louisville: Westminster John Knox, 2005), 111–23; and Baldwin, *Balm in Gilead*, 322–30. These important works suggest that King drew no distinction between prophetic leadership and moral or ethical leadership, especially when it came to speaking truth to power.

24 King, *Stride toward Freedom*, 19–20; Baldwin, *Balm in Gilead*, 322–30; Burrow, *Ethical Prophets*, 159–85.

25 Carson, *King Papers*, 6:527, 534; King, *Stride toward Freedom*, 134–35; Carson and Holloran, *Knock at Midnight*, 160–64.

26 Carson, *King Papers*, 7:471, 525; Washington, *Testament*, 103, 149; Carson, *King Papers*, 4:326; Carson, *King Papers*, 6:88, 453–54, 494; Clayborne Carson and Kris Shepard, eds., *A Call to Conscience: The Landmark Speeches of Dr. Martin Luther King, Jr.* (New York: Warner, 2001), 140; King, *Strength to Love*, 45–46; Carson, *King Autobiography*, 343.

27 Carson, *King Autobiography*, 146; Martin Luther King Jr., "A Challenge to the Churches and Synagogues," in *Race: A Challenge to Religion—Original Essays and an Appeal to the Conscience from the National Conference on Religion and Race*, ed. Mathew Ahmann (Chicago: Henry Regnery, 1963), 168–69; Carson, *King Papers*, 5:200; Carson, *King Papers*, 6:146–48, 451; Carson, *King Papers*, 4:125, 340; Carson, *King*

Papers, 7:477, 602–4; King, *Stride toward Freedom*, 208, 210; King, *Why We Can't Wait*, 90; Washington, *Testament*, 481.

28 King, *Where Do We Go*, 13; Carson, *King Papers*, 4:407.

29 Washington, *Testament*, 230; Carson, *King Papers*, 5:250, 289, 343, 375.

30 Carson, *King Papers*, 5:286, 370; Carson and Shepard, *Call to Conscience*, 144, 205; King, *Stride toward Freedom*, 105; Martin Luther King Jr., "Bold Design for a New South," *Nation* 196 (March 30, 1963): 259–62; Carson, *King Papers*, 4:273–74; Carson, *King Papers*, 7:340, 484; Carson and Holloran, *Knock at Midnight*, 147.

31 Washington, *Testament*, 331.

32 Washington, *Testament*, 101, 108, 137, 359; Martin Luther King Jr., "The 'New Negro' of the South: Behind the Montgomery Story," *Socialist Call*, June 1956, 16–19; King, *Where Do We Go*, 16, 18, 61–66; Carson, *King Papers*, 7:167; Carson, *King Papers*, 6:467–69, 475; King, *Stride toward Freedom*, 224; Baldwin, *Balm in Gilead*, 229–43.

33 Carson and Holloran, *Knock at Midnight*, 121–22, 186; Martin Luther King Jr., *The Trumpet of Conscience* (San Francisco: Harper & Row, 1968; originally published in 1967), 50; Carson, *King Papers*, 6:112, 182–83; Carson, *King Papers*, 4:178, 331–32, 334, 342.

34 Comments by Nicolle Wallace on *Deadline: White House*, "A Crisis of Credibility," aired March 12, 2020, on MSNBC; Christina Pazzanese, "National & World Affairs: Politics in the 'Post Truth' Age," *Harvard Gazette*, July 14, 2016, https://news.harvard.edu/gazette/story/2016/07/politics-in-a-post-truth-age/; Sophia Rosenfeld, *Democracy and Truth: A Short History* (Philadelphia: University of Pennsylvania Press, 2019), 2, 15, 20, 39, 136–37; Ralph Keyes, *The Post-truth Era: Dishonesty and Deception in Contemporary Life* (New York: St. Martin's, 2004), 10–30; Hillary McQuilkin and Meghna Chakrabarti, "In Search of Truth, Part IV: Are We Living in a Post-truth World?," *On Point*, February 27, 2020, https://www.wbur.org/onpoint/2020/02/27/part-iv-post-truth.

Chapter 1

1 Martin Luther King Sr. with Clayton Riley, *Daddy King: An Autobiography* (New York: William Morrow, 1980), 130; Martin Luther King Jr., *Stride toward Freedom: The Montgomery Story* (New York: Harper & Row, 1958), 18–19; Clayborne Carson, ed., *The Papers of*

Martin Luther King, Jr., vol. 1, *Called to Serve, January 1929–June 1951*, ed. Ralph E. Luker and Penny A. Russell (Berkeley: University of California Press, 1992), 359, 361–63.

2 Martin Luther King Jr., *Strength to Love* (Philadelphia: Fortress, 1981; originally

published in 1963), 147; King, *Stride toward Freedom*, 101.

3 Clayborne Carson, ed., *The Autobiography of Martin Luther King, Jr.* (New York: Warner, 1998), 6, 15–16; King, *Strength to Love*, 147; Carson, *King Papers*, 1:361–63.

4 King, *Strength to Love*, 147.

5 David Cortright, *Truth Seekers: Voices of Peace and Nonviolence from Gandhi to Pope Francis* (Maryknoll, NY: Orbis, 2020).

6 King, *Stride toward Freedom*, 18.

7 Carson, *King Autobiography*, 7; Clayborne Carson, ed., *The Papers of Martin Luther King, Jr.*, vol. 7, *To Save the Soul of America, January 1961–August 1962*, ed. Tenisha Armstrong (Berkeley: University of California Press, 2014), 164; King, *Stride toward Freedom*, 18–19.

8 King, *Stride toward Freedom*, 18–19; Carson, *King Autobiography*, 3–4.

9 King, *Stride toward Freedom*, 19; Carson, *King Autobiography*, 4–5; Coretta Scott King, *My Life with Martin Luther King, Jr.*, rev. ed. (New York: Henry Holt, 1993), 79–80.

10 King with Riley, *Daddy King*, 107–8, 123–25, 132–34; King, *Stride toward Freedom*, 19–20; Carson, *King Autobiography*, 4–5; Lewis V. Baldwin, *There Is a Balm in Gilead: The Cultural Roots of Martin Luther King, Jr.* (Minneapolis: Fortress, 1991), 120–22.

11 Clayborne Carson, ed., *The Papers of Martin Luther King, Jr.*, vol. 6, *Advocate of the Social Gospel, September 1948–March 1963*, ed. Susan Carson et al. (Berkeley: University of California Press, 2007), 98.

12 Carson, *King Papers*, 1:408.

13 Carson, *King Papers*, 6:301.

14 Carson, *King Papers*, 6:295.

15 Carson, *King Autobiography*, 6; Carson, *King Papers*, 1:361.

16 Lee E. Dirks, "'The Essence Is Love': The Theology of Martin Luther King, Jr.," *National Observer*, December 30, 1963, 1, 12; Carson, *King Papers*, 1:228–29; Carson, *King Papers*, 6:235, 382, 411.

17 Carson, *King Papers*, 1:362–63; Carson, *King Autobiography*, 16.

18 Morehouse College has never gotten the attention it deserves as a source for the intellectual development of Martin Luther King Jr. Rufus Burrow Jr. and Clayborne Carson have done more than any other scholars to correct this serious pattern of omission, and their work serves, on some levels, as a corrective to those intellectual biographies written by scholars such as Kenneth L. Smith, Ira G. Zepp Jr., and John J. Ansbro. See Kenneth L. Smith and Ira G. Zepp Jr., *Search for the Beloved Community: The Thinking of Martin Luther King, Jr.* (Valley Forge, PA: Judson, 1998; originally published in 1974), 3–4, 6, 11, 42, 123; John J. Ansbro, *Martin Luther King, Jr.: Nonviolent Strategies and Tactics for Social Change* (Lanham, MD: Madison, 2000; originally published in 1982), 15, 76, 106, 110, 166, 180, 283; Rufus Burrow Jr., *God and Human Dignity: The Personalism, Theology, and Ethics of Martin Luther King, Jr.* (Notre Dame, IN: University of Notre Dame Press, 2006), 6, 8, 17–18, 20, 27, 58, 157, 160, 184, 204; Clayborne Carson, "Martin Luther King, Jr.: The Morehouse Years," *Journal of Blacks in Higher Education*, no. 15 (Spring 1997): 121–25; and Carson, *King Papers*, 1:7n20, 14, 25–26, 37–46.

19 Carson, *King Papers*, 1:361–62; Carson, *King Autobiography*, 16.

20 Carson, *King Papers*, 1:40, 42–43.

21 Carson, *King Papers*, 1:362–63; King, *Strength to Love*, 147.

22 Carson, *King Autobiography*, 15.

23 King, *Strength to Love*, 147; Clayborne Carson, ed., *The Papers of Martin Luther King, Jr.*, vol. 5, *Threshold of a New Decade, January 1959–December 1960*, ed. Tenisha Armstrong et al. (Berkeley: University of California Press, 2005), 419–20.

24 Carson, *King Papers*, 1:363.

25 Martin Luther King Jr., "The Purpose of Education," *Maroon Tiger*, January–February 1947, 10; Carson, *King Papers*, 1:122.

26 King, "Purpose of Education," 10; Carson, *King Papers*, 1:122, 124.

27 Carson, *King Papers*, 5:412; King, *Strength to Love*, 45.

28 King, *Strength to Love*, 45; Carson, *King Papers*, 5:412; Carson, *King Papers*, 6:493–94.

29 Carson, *King Papers*, 1:151–55; Burrow, *God and Human Dignity*, 18.

30 Carson, *King Papers*, 1:152; Ervin Smith, *The Ethics of Martin Luther King, Jr.* (New York: Edwin Mellen, 1981), 3.

31 Martin Luther King Jr., *Where Do We Go from Here: Chaos or Community?* (Boston: Beacon, 1968; originally published in 1967), 67; Alex Ayres, ed., *The Wisdom of Martin Luther King, Jr.: An A-to-Z Guide to the Ideas and Ideals of the Great Civil Rights Leader* (New York: Penguin, 1993), 221.

32 Carson, *King Autobiography*, 13.

33 Burrow, *God and Human Dignity*, 17–18; Ansbro, *Martin Luther King*, 76, 166.

34 Ansbro, *Martin Luther King*, 165–66; Carson, *King Papers*, 1:43.

35 These institutes were often held in Sales Chapel at Morehouse while King was still a student there. See "Baptist Ministers' Institute

in Session," *Atlanta Daily World*, July 3, 1946, 2; and Carson, *King Papers*, 1:42.

36 Carson, *King Papers*, 6:563; Carson, *King Papers*, 7:116; Carson, *King Papers*, 5:170, 172, 285; James M. Washington, ed., *A Testament of Hope: The Essential Writings and Speeches of Martin Luther King, Jr.* (New York: HarperCollins, 1991), 251; Lewis V. Baldwin, ed., *"In a Single Garment of Destiny": A Global Vision of Justice—Martin Luther King, Jr.* (Boston: Beacon, 2012), 206–7; King, *Where Do We Go*, 92.

37 Carson, *King Papers*, 1:182, 188–89, 204–5; Carson, *King Autobiography*, 15–16; Carson, *King Papers*, 5:170, 172, 285; Carson, *King Papers*, 6:98, 102, 563; Carson, *King Papers*, 7:116, 408.

38 Carson, *King Papers*, 5:420.

39 Carson, *King Papers*, 1:40, 45; Ansbro, *Martin Luther King*, 15, 283n128; Burrow, *God and Human Dignity*, 6; Carson, *King Autobiography*, 359; Washington, *Testament*, 279; Clayborne Carson and Kris Shepard, eds., *A Call to Conscience: The Landmark Speeches of Dr. Martin Luther King, Jr.* (New York: Warner, 2001), 208.

40 Washington, *Testament*, 50, 291, 294–95; Carson, *King Papers*, 7:185, 201, 210, 290, 508, 537, 595; Carson, *King Papers*, 5:170; Carson, *King Papers*, 6:473; Carson, *King Autobiography*, 191, 194, 196, 305–6; Martin Luther King Jr., *Why We Can't Wait* (New York: New American Library, 1963), 85.

41 Carson, *King Papers*, 7:290–91.

42 Carson, *King Autobiography*, 17; Ansbro, *Martin Luther King*, 15.

43 Carson, *King Papers*, 1:234, 411, 423.

44 Washington, *Testament*, 46, 372.

45 Smith and Zepp, *Beloved Community*, 123.

46 Carson, *King Papers*, 1:154.

47 Smith and Zepp, *Beloved Community*, 3; Burrow, *God and Human Dignity*, 58; Carson, *King Papers*, 1:42–43. At Morehouse's Institute for Baptist Ministers in July 1946, Kelsey and others focused on themes such as "Studies in the Prophecies of Jeremiah," "The Message of Jesus and Jeremiah for Our Age," and "The Social Principles of Jesus"—all of which were in line with the Social Gospel. See "Institute in Session," 2.

48 Burrow, *God and Human Dignity*, 156–57, 184, and 204.

49 Burrow, *God and Human Dignity*, 183–84; Benjamin E. Mays, *Seeking to Be Christian in Race Relations* (New York: Friendship, 1946), 8.

50 "Moral Laws Objective, Universal as Laws of Science, Mays Says," *Atlanta Daily World*, October 6, 1948, 6.

51 See, for example, "Moral Laws," 6. For references to a speech in which Mays spoke of the need to believe in "the moral law" and in "the permanency in ethics and moral law," see "Mays Deplores Disregard for God in S.C. Sermon," *Atlanta Daily World*, April 26, 1946, 4. These lectures were occurring years before King enrolled at Morehouse. See "57 M'house Grads Hear Dr. Mays: Sound Principles for Rich Living Cited by Speakers," *Atlanta Daily World*, June 7, 1939, 1.

52 See "Wins Yale Doctorate," *Atlanta Daily World*, July 23, 1946, 1.

53 Clayborne Carson, *The Papers of Martin Luther King, Jr.*, vol. 2, *Rediscovering Precious Values, July 1951–November 1955*, ed. Stewart Burns et al. (Berkeley: University of California Press, 1994), 314. During the 1961–62 academic year at Morehouse College, King and Williams, his former professor, taught a social philosophy course in which they focused, among other matters, on "natural and divine law." See Carson, *King Papers*, 7:59, 258n1.

54 Carson, *King Autobiography*, 14; King, *Stride toward Freedom*, 91; Ansbro, *Martin Luther King*, 110–14.

55 Carson, *King Autobiography*, 14; King, *Stride toward Freedom*, 91.

56 Carson, *King Papers*, 1:39–41; Burrow, *God and Human Dignity*, 20.

57 Burrow, *God and Human Dignity*, 20; Baldwin, *Balm in Gilead*, 27.

58 Carson, *King Autobiography*, 16; Carson, *King Papers*, 1:43–45, 363; Burrow, *God and Human Dignity*, 19; Ansbro, *Martin Luther King*, 180.

59 Carson, *King Autobiography*, 33.

60 Keith D. Miller, *Voice of Deliverance: The Language of Martin Luther King, Jr. and Its Sources* (New York: Free Press, 1992), 40.

61 King, *Strength to Love*, 148–49; Carson, *King Autobiography*, 25–27.

62 Smith and Zepp, *Beloved Community*, 4.

63 King raised the issue of biblical truths in a paper he wrote for George Davis at Crozer, entitled "A View of the Cross Possessing Biblical and Spiritual Justification" (1949–50). In another paper for Davis's class, King showed a willingness "to abandon scriptural literalism" (226). See Carson, *King Papers*, 1:226–30, 236, 239–41, 263–67.

64 Carson, *King Papers*, 1:238.

65 Carson, *King Papers*, 1:162; James B. Pritchard to Coretta Scott King, unpublished and typed version (February 22, 1987), Martin Luther King Jr. Papers, Library and Archives of the Martin Luther King Jr. Center for Nonviolent Social Change (KCLA), Atlanta, GA, 1.

66 King made numerous references to the Hebrew prophets in his papers at Crozer. See Carson, *King Papers*, 1:47, 49, 176, 178, 181–95.

67 Dirks, "'Essence Is Love,'" 1; Smith and Zepp, *Beloved Community*, 8–10, 31.

68 Smith and Zepp, *Beloved Community*, 3, 8–11, 13–25; Carson, *King Papers*, 1:195–96, 211, 272–73, 382.

69 King, *Stride toward Freedom*, 91; Carson, *King Papers*, 1:49–51; Clayborne Carson, ed., *The Papers of Martin Luther King, Jr.*, vol. 4, *Symbol of the Movement, January 1957–December 1958*, ed. Susan Carson et al. (Berkeley: University of California Press, 2000), 474.

70 King, *Stride toward Freedom*, 91; Washington, *Testament*, 37–38; Carson, *King Papers*, 4:474.

71 Carson, *King Papers*, 1:49.

72 King, *Stride toward Freedom*, 92; Washington, *Testament*, 38; King, *Strength to Love*, 150; Carson, *King Papers*, 4:474.

73 See Carson, *King Papers*, 1:359–63.

74 King, *Stride toward Freedom*, 90–107; Washington, *Testament*, 35–40; Carson, *King Papers*, 4:473–81; King, *Strength to Love*, 147–55.

75 Carson, *King Papers*, 1:234, 294, 411, 422–23; Washington, *Testament*, 496; Carson, *King Papers*, 6:268, 410, 465; Washington, *Testament*, 279.

76 Carson, *King Papers*, 4:474; King, *Stride toward Freedom*, 97.

77 King, *Stride toward Freedom*, 97; Carson, *King Papers*, 4:474–75.

78 King, *Stride toward Freedom*, 92, 97; Washington, *Testament*, 45; Carson, *King Papers*, 6:99, 125–27, 146–50.

79 King, *Stride toward Freedom*, 92–95; King, *Strength to Love*, 96–102; Carson, *King Papers*, 6:146–50; Washington, *Testament*, 109; Carson, *King Papers*, 1:37, 249, 435–36; Carson, *King Autobiography*, 20–22.

80 Carson, *King Autobiography*, 23; Ansbro, *Martin Luther King*, 1–2.

81 This understanding differs from Ansbro's, who writes about the "intellectual and emotional crisis" King experienced as he read Nietzsche. See Ansbro, *Martin Luther King*, 1.

82 Carson, *King Autobiography*, 22–23; Carson, *King Papers*, 4:477.

83 Ansbro, *Martin Luther King*, 1–2; Carson, *King Autobiography*, 23–24.

84 Carson, *King Autobiography*, 23. The *Atlanta Daily World*, to which the King family subscribed throughout King's childhood, featured countless articles on Gandhi and the Indian independence struggle in the 1930s and '40s. This newspaper was started by W. A. Scott, a close friend of the Kings, in Atlanta, Georgia, in 1928, and its headquarters was located a few blocks from the King home on Auburn Avenue. See Vicki L. Crawford and Lewis V. Baldwin, eds., *Reclaiming the Great World House: The Global Vision of Martin Luther King, Jr.* (Athens: University of Georgia Press, 2019), 40, 54n24, 122n5–6; and Carson, *King Papers*, 1:37, 249.

85 Carson, *King Autobiography*, 23; King, *Stride toward Freedom*, 96; Carson, *King Papers*, 1:89; Carson, *King Papers*, 2:16–17; Carson, *King Papers*, 4:296–97.

86 King, *Stride toward Freedom*, 91; King, *Strength to Love*, 150; Carson, *King Papers*, 4:474.

87 This analysis relies heavily on Ansbro, *Martin Luther King*, 3. Also see King, *Stride toward Freedom*, 96–97; King, *Strength to Love*, 151; and Carson, *King Papers*, 4:478.

88 Carson, *King Papers*, 7:209.

89 Washington, *Testament*, 103, 149; Carson, *King Papers*, 5:505, 510–11; Carson, *King Papers*, 7:209.

90 This point is brilliantly made about Gandhi in Sophia Rosenfeld, *Democracy and Truth: A Short History* (Philadelphia: University of Pennsylvania Press, 2019), 170–71.

91 See Carson, *King Papers*, 4:322; Carson, *King Papers*, 7:198; Carson, *King Autobiography*, 23–24; and Walter Rauschenbusch, *Christianity and the Social Crisis* (New York: Harper & Row, 1964; originally published in 1907), 44–142. King's associate Wyatt Tee Walker declared that "the writings that influenced King most were the Gospels of Matthew, Mark, Luke, and John, which teach us about the crucified carpenter of Galilee and the sacrificial life that gave birth to the church." See Wyatt Tee Walker, foreword to *The Voice of Conscience: The Church in the Mind of Martin Luther King, Jr.*, by Lewis V. Baldwin (New York: Oxford University Press, 2010), ix–x. King frequently referred to love and the early church in his papers at Crozer. See Carson, *King Papers*, 1:205–6, 208, 211, 213, 218–19, 245.

92 Washington, *Testament*, 35; King, *Strength to Love*, 147.

93 King, *Strength to Love*, 147; Washington, *Testament*, 35.

94 King, *Strength to Love*, 147–48; Carson, *King Papers*, 1:204; Washington, *Testament*, 35–36.

95 King, *Stride toward Freedom*, 97; Carson, *King Papers*, 4:478.

96 Smith and Zepp, *Beloved Community*, 71.

97 King, *Strength to Love*, 148–49. In a paper written for George Davis at Crozer, entitled "The Place of Reason and Experience in Finding God" (1949), King contrasted the neoorthodox theology of Karl Barth

with the theological liberalism of Edwin E. Aubrey. See Carson, *King Papers*, 1:230–36.

98 King, *Stride toward Freedom*, 97–99; Carson, *King Papers*, 4:478–80.

99 King, *Stride toward Freedom*, 98; Carson, *King Papers*, 4:479.

100 King, *Stride toward Freedom*, 100.

101 Carson, *King Papers*, 4:480; King, *Stride toward Freedom*, 100.

102 At some points, King noted that he was working toward a PhD in systematic theology, and at others, he identified the area as philosophical theology. It is clear that his PhD studies covered both areas. See Carson, *King Papers*, 1:57, 390–91; King, *Strength to Love*, 149; Washington, *Testament*, 333; and Carson, *King Papers*, 2:221–22.

103 King, *Stride toward Freedom*, 100; Carson, *King Papers*, 4:480.

104 King, *Stride toward Freedom*, 99; Carson, *King Papers*, 4:479–80. The charge that there is insufficient documentary evidence to support King's claim, made in his *Stride toward Freedom*, that he had extensive "intellectual engagement with Niebuhr's ideas" at Crozer is open to question. An academic journey is always too complex to be measured merely on the basis of a documentary record, especially since so much of what happens is usually undocumented. See Carson, *King Papers*, 1:55. King wrote several papers at Boston University that are important for understanding how he, as an evangelical liberal, drew the contrast between Niebuhr and Karl Barth. See Carson, *King Papers*, 2:95–107, 139–51.

105 Rufus Burrow Jr., *Personalism: A Critical Introduction* (St. Louis, MO: Chalice, 1999), x, 77; Burrow, *God and Human Dignity*, 6; Smith and Zepp, *Beloved Community*, 104.

106 Burrow, *God and Human Dignity*, 90; Burrow, *Personalism*, 11–18.

107 See King's paper, "The Personalism of J. M. E. McTaggart under Criticism," written for DeWolf's class on personalism and the comparison he drew between McTaggart, William E. Hocking, and Brightman in a philosophy of religion course he had with Brightman. See Carson, *King Papers*, 2:61–92.

108 King, *Stride toward Freedom*, 100; Carson, *King Papers*, 4:480.

109 This "homespun personalism" speaks to the significance of King's family and Atlanta's Ebenezer Baptist Church in the origins and development of King's ideas about God and humanity. See Burrow, *God and Human Dignity*, 77–79.

110 Burrow, *Personalism*, 1.

111 Burrow, *Personalism*, 5.

112 Carson, *King Papers*, 2:76–77, 89–90.

113 King must have had this and more in mind when he stressed the need for "moral and spiritual development." See Burrow, *God and Human Dignity*, 269; and Carson, *King Papers*, 5:224.

114 Carson, *King Papers*, 2:77–78, 89–90.

115 Smith and Zepp, *Beloved Community*, 123–24; James H. Cone, "The Theology of Martin Luther King, Jr.," *Union Seminary Quarterly Review* 40, no. 4 (January 1986): 23; King, *Stride toward Freedom*, 100; Carson, *King Papers*, 4:480.

116 King, *Stride toward Freedom*, 100–101; Carson, *King Papers*, 4:480; Carson, *King Papers*, 2:63, 111, 121, 123, 153–55, 196–201, 216, 359–60, 436, 447, 532.

117 King, *Stride toward Freedom*, 100–101, 213; Carson, *King Papers*, 4:480. Numerous references to Hegel's dialectical method and to the broader dimensions of his logic appear in King's published works. See Carson and Shepard, *Call to Conscience*, 194; Martin Luther King Jr., *The Measure of a Man* (Philadelphia: Fortress, 1988; originally published in 1959), 10; King, *Strength to Love*, 9, 103, 148–49; King, *Where Do We Go*, 129, 187; Carson, *King Autobiography*, 21–22; Washington, *Testament*, 36, 123; Carson, *King Papers*, 4:477, 480; Carson, *King Papers*, 5:421; Carson, *King Papers*, 6:460; and Carson, *King Papers*, 7:180–81.

118 Walter Fluker rightly contends that "King's search for community was characterized by an insatiable thirst for truth and a deep-seated religious faith that began in his early years in the intimate contexts of his family, the black church, and the larger black community of Atlanta, Georgia." Fluker goes on to say that "the dialectical method" also gave King "a keen analytical tool with which he could exegete the inner tensions of the human psyche and life," a point that has profound implications for how King ultimately came to view the African American experience through the lens of that method. See Walter E. Fluker, *They Looked for a City: A Comparative Analysis of the Ideal of Community in the Thought of Howard Thurman and Martin Luther King, Jr.* (Lanham, MD: University Press of America, 1989), 81–82, 106. On this subject, also see Baldwin, *Balm in Gilead*, 24–25; and Burrow, *God and Human Dignity*, 25.

119 King, *Stride toward Freedom*, 101; Carson, *King Papers*, 4:480. It is possible that King's

understanding of the Hegelian idea of "truth as the whole" benefited from his reading of Alfred North Whitehead, a prominent figure in process philosophy, whom he studied in a course with Professor Nathaniel Lawrence at Harvard during those Boston years. Whitehead had raised "the philosophical paradox of 'the one and the many'—that is, the question of whether reality is composed of a unified whole or of numerous parts." See Carson, *King Papers*, 2:17, 19.

120 Cone, "Theology of King," 23.

121 Ansbro, *Martin Luther King*, 119–22; Washington, *Testament*, 135.

122 Ansbro, *Martin Luther King*, 47. Aristotelian philosophy was most certainly the topic of lengthy discussions in classes King had with DeWolf, and King covered certain dimensions of Aristotle's thought in his PhD qualifying examinations, but the extant papers King wrote at Boston reveal surprisingly little about this ancient Greek philosopher's thoughts on God and other topics. See Carson, *King Papers*, 2:243–44.

123 Ansbro, *Martin Luther King*, 71–76; Carson, *King Papers*, 6:103; Carson, *King Papers*, 2:121, 152–55, 197–98, 216–17, 246, 400.

124 Ansbro, *Martin Luther King*, 71–72; Clayborne Carson, ed., *The Papers of Martin Luther King, Jr.*, vol. 3, *Birth of a New Age, December 1955–December 1956*, ed. Stewart Burns et al. (Berkeley: University of California Press, 1997), 3:460; King, *Where Do We Go*, 97; Carson, *King Autobiography*, 193.

125 Carson, *King Papers*, 6:212; Crawford and Baldwin, *Great World House*, 219, 221.

126 Ansbro rightly argues that in portraying Kant in these terms, King was simply reinforcing an interpretation already current in philosophical circles. See Ansbro, *Martin Luther King*, 73.

127 Ansbro, *Martin Luther King*, 73–74.

128 Ansbro, *Martin Luther King*, 75.

129 Delores S. Williams, "Between Haggar and Jezebel: A Womanist Assessment of Martin Luther King, Jr.'s Beloved Community," January 13, 1997, All Faith Chapel, Vanderbilt University Divinity School, videotaped lecture, housed at the Jean and Alexander Heard Library, Nashville, TN.

130 King, *Strength to Love*, 149; Ansbro, *Martin Luther King*, 92.

131 King, *Strength to Love*, 149; Ansbro, *Martin Luther King*, 92–106.

132 Carson, *King Papers*, 2:398. King also mentioned an important "common denominator between atheistic and theistic existentialists" in his essay "Pilgrimage to Nonviolence." See King, *Strength to Love*, 149.

133 Carson, *King Papers*, 2:133, 349, 385, 396, 398–99, 402, 417; Carson, *King Papers*, 6:196, 263.

134 King, *Strength to Love*, 149.

135 King, *Strength to Love*, 149; Ansbro, *Martin Luther King*, 92.

136 Baldwin, *Balm in Gilead*, 170; Carson, *King Papers*, 6:325.

137 Ansbro, *Martin Luther King*, 60; Carson, *King Papers*, 2:446–47.

138 Fluker, *Looked for a City*, 141; Ansbro, *Martin Luther King*, 7–8; King, *Where Do We Go*, 37.

139 Ansbro, *Martin Luther King*, 15, 283n128; Burrow, *God and Human Dignity*, 30; Smith and Zepp, *Beloved Community*, 123; J. Deotis Roberts, *Bonhoeffer and King: Speaking Truth to Power* (Louisville: Westminster John Knox, 2005), 36.

140 Carson, *King Papers*, 2:109, 524–27; Carson, *King Papers*, 6:82; King, *Strength to Love*, 145. Mohandas K. Gandhi declared that "the quest for truth is the *summum bonum* of life," and King shared this idea. See Mohandas K. Gandhi, *An Autobiography: The Story of My Experiments with Truth* (Boston: Beacon, 1993; originally published in 1927), 251.

141 Carson, *King Papers*, 2:9–10; Carson, *King Autobiography*, 38; Roberts, *Bonhoeffer and King*, 36; Baldwin, *Balm in Gilead*, 40; Lawrence D. Reddick, *Crusader without Violence: A Biography of Martin Luther King, Jr.* (New York: Harper & Brothers, 1959), 88; King, *Stride toward Freedom*, 100.

142 Sam Lamerson, "Great Book," review of *Never to Leave Us Alone: The Prayer Life of Martin Luther King Jr.*, by Lewis V. Baldwin, Amazon, October 10, 2011, http://www.amazon.com/Never-Leave-Us-Alone-Prayer/dp/0800697448.

143 Traci West brilliantly critiques this tendency on the part of ministers who knew and marched with King—this tendency to believe that such association with the civil rights leader makes them authorities on what King actually believed or what he would say about certain matters today. See Traci C. West, "Gay Rights and the Misuse of Martin," in *The Domestication of Martin Luther King, Jr.: Clarence B. Jones, Right-Wing Conservatism, and the Manipulation of the King Legacy*, ed. Lewis V. Baldwin and Rufus Burrow Jr. (Eugene, OR: Cascade, 2013), 142–43.

144 Ansbro, *Martin Luther King*, 104.

145 See Carson, *King Papers*, 1:127–42, 162–80, 195–209, 211–42, 251–56, 294–326; and Carson, *King Papers*, 2:61–75, 196–201.

146 King, *Where Do We Go*, 124; Carson, *King Papers*, 3:417; Carson, *King Papers*, 4:375; Carson, *King Papers*, 7:491. While a student in Boston, King said that "the way of Christ is the only ultimate way to man's salvation," but he was speaking here of the Jesus ethic and not Western Christianity. He associated the ethic of Jesus with ultimate truth and, even at that time, could distinguish between the religion of Jesus and Western Christianity. See Carson, *King Papers*, 6:125.

147 Smith and Zepp, *Beloved Community*, 10–11.

148 Carson, *King Papers*, 2:95, 97, 99, 105–6, 131, 133, 137–38, 164–70, 204–10, 249–50.

149 Carson, *King Papers*, 2:137–38.

150 There are several different versions of King's "Pilgrimage to Nonviolence," published at various times, beginning in 1958. See King, *Stride toward Freedom*, 90–107; King, *Strength to Love*, 147–55; Carson, *King Autobiography*, 121–34; Washington, *Strength*, 35–40; and Carson, *King Papers*, 4:473–81.

151 Smith and Zepp, *Beloved Community*, xviii, 6.

152 Carson, *King Papers*, 1:122, 124; King, *Strength to Love*, 45; Carson, *King Papers*, 6:493–94.

153 Martin Luther King Jr., "The Meaning of Hope," sermon, unpublished and typed version, Dexter Avenue Baptist Church, Montgomery, AL (December 10, 1967), King Papers, KCLA, 17–18; "Hugh Downs Interview with Martin Luther King, Jr.," unpublished and typed version, *Today Show*, NBC (April 18, 1966), King Papers, KCLA, 5–6; Carson, *King Papers*, 6:417. King was distinguishing between "theoretical atheism" and "practical atheism" in the mid- to late 1950s and early '60s, when the works of "Death of God" theologians like Paul Van Buren, Thomas J. J. Altizer, and William Hamilton were emerging to prominence in philosophical-theological circles. See Carson, *King Papers*, 6:136, 171, 260, 294.

154 Carson, *King Papers*, 7:288–304.

155 King, *Why We Can't Wait*, 79; Carson, *King Papers*, 5:472; Carson, *King Papers*, 6:473.

156 Kenneth L. Smith, foreword to *Toward the Beloved Community: Martin Luther King, Jr. and South Africa*, by Lewis V. Baldwin (Cleveland: Pilgrim, 1995), x.

157 King, *Where Do We Go*, 67.

158 Alex Ayres, ed., *The Wisdom of Martin Luther King, Jr.: An A-to-Z Guide to the Ideas and Ideals of the Great Civil Rights Leader* (New York: Penguin, 1993), 221; King, *Where Do We Go*, 67; Carson, *King Papers*, 5:269.

159 King, *Strength to Love*, 151–52; King, *Stride toward Freedom*, 101; Carson, *King Papers*, 4:481.

160 King made wide use of the language of the spiritual when discussing the bus protest in Montgomery, as well as subsequent civil rights campaigns. See King, *Stride toward Freedom*, 44, 69, 89, 99, 138, 161, 172, 196, 199, 210, 216, 219, 224; Washington, *Testament*, 52, 84, 162, 170; Glenn Smiley, "Interview with Martin Luther King, Jr. regarding the Montgomery Bus Boycott," unpublished and typed version (February–March 1956), King Papers, KCLA, 1–2; and Lewis V. Baldwin and Victor Anderson, eds., *Revives My Soul Again: The Spirituality of Martin Luther King, Jr.* (Minneapolis: Fortress, 2018), 76–83. King was speaking of the importance of "the spiritual life" and of getting "the heart right" even before the protest began in Montgomery. See Carson, *King Papers*, 2:165, 249, 294.

161 King, *Stride toward Freedom*, 134–35; Carson and Holloran, *Knock at Midnight*, 160–62; Carson, *King Autobiography*, 77–78; King, *Strength to Love*, 112–13; Carson, *King Papers*, 6:533–34; Baldwin and Anderson, *Revives My Soul Again*, 156–59. David Garrow was among the first scholars to really highlight the significance of King's kitchen experience and vision. See David J. Garrow, *Bearing the Cross: Martin Luther King, Jr., and the Southern Christian Leadership Conference* (New York: William Morrow, 1986), 57–58.

162 Smith and Zepp, *Beloved Community*, 111.

163 Carson and Shepard, *Call to Conscience*, 140; Carson, *King Papers*, 6:527, 534.

164 Washington, *Testament*, 372; Carson, *King Papers*, 5:152–53; Carson, *King Papers*, 4:348, 356, 418, 472, 540; Carson, *King Papers*, 6:96.

165 William D. Watley, *Roots of Resistance: The Nonviolent Ethic of Martin Luther King, Jr.* (Valley Forge, PA: Judson, 1985), 15.

166 Watley, *Roots of Resistance*, 15.

167 Carson, *King Papers*, 7:198, 406, 409, 555, 598; Martin Luther King Jr., "Nonviolence: The Christian Way in Human Relations," *Presbyterian Life* 11 (February 8, 1958): 11–13; King, *Strength to Love*, 146; King, *Stride toward Freedom*, 102; Carson, *King Autobiography*, 125.

168 Carson, *King Papers*, 7:209, 532; Carson, *King Papers*, 5:505, 510–11; Washington, *Testament*, 38, 103, 149.

169 Carson, *King Papers*, 7:209.

170 King and Gandhi also agreed that it is possible to engage in a quest for truth without being nonviolent. See Gandhi, *Autobiography*, 412, 416, 503–4; Arvind Sharma,

"Truth and Nonviolence," *Gandhi Marg*, accessed August 13, 2020, https://www.mkgandhi.org/articles/truth_nonvio.htm; Carson, *King Papers*, 7:209, 532; and Carson, *King Papers*, 5:505, 510–11.

171 Carson, *King Papers*, 7:275, 288, 458, 532; Washington, *Testament*, 103, 164, 429.

172 Washington, *Testament*, 294; Carson, *King Papers*, 7:536–37, 595.

173 Carson, *King Papers*, 7:185, 201, 536–37, 595; Washington, *Testament*, 50, 294, 349; King, *Strength to Love*, 21–22. King noted that the early church, when "still a numerical minority," championed truth, but "then it began to grow in numbers until it finally captured the Roman Empire." King added, "Gradually, it became so entrenched in wealth and worldly prestige that it began to dilute the strong demands of the gospel and to conform to the status quo of the world. Ever since that time the church has been like a weak and ineffectual trumpet making uncertain sounds, rather than a strong trumpet sounding a clarion call for truth and righteousness." See Carson, *King Papers*, 6:473. Noel Smith, a white southern Baptist pastor, insisted that "King was guilty of a palpable falsehood when he implies that the New Testament and the practices of the early Christians authenticate his objectives and methods." "The first Christians violated only those laws that forbade them to preach Christ," this preacher believed. "Otherwise, they were model citizens, recognizing the divinely ordered authority." Other white southern fundamentalist pastors agreed, claiming that "the New Testament records no antics, no mob demonstrations, involving recalcitrant believers." See Bill J. Leonard, "A Theology for Racism: Southern Fundamentalists and the Civil Rights Movement," *Baptist History and Heritage* 34, no. 1 (Winter 1999): 57, 61.

174 King, *Why We Can't Wait*, 85; Carson, *King Papers*, 5:170; Carson, *King Papers*, 7:185, 201, 290, 537; Carson, *King Papers*, 5:170; Carson, *King Papers*, 6:473.

175 Washington, *Testament*, 50, 294–95; Carson, *King Papers*, 7:186, 201, 458, 537.

176 Carson, *King Papers*, 7:186, 201, 458, 537; Washington, *Testament*, 50.

177 Carson, *King Papers*, 6:473.

178 Carson, *King Papers*, 7:122; Carson, *King Papers*, 5:164, 168–75.

179 In an Easter sermon entitled "A Walk through the Holy Land," delivered at Dexter Avenue Baptist Church in March 1959, King spoke of Jesus's willingness to "act on truth." See Carson, *King Papers*, 5:168, 170–74; King, *Strength to Love*, 37–39, 49; and King, *Stride toward Freedom*, 105–6, 156–57, 169, 172.

180 Baldwin, *Balm in Gilead*, 320.

181 Carson, *King Autobiography*, 146; Carson, *King Papers*, 6:476; Carson, *King Papers*, 5:167–75; Washington, *Testament*, 345.

182 Carson, *King Papers*, 5:164, 172–74; Carson, *King Papers*, 7:443, 445, 448; Ayres, *Wisdom of King*, 132.

183 King, *Stride toward Freedom*, 169, 172.

184 Baldwin, *Voice of Conscience*, 207–16; Crawford and Baldwin, *Great World House*, 318–23; King, *Where Do We Go*, 167–91.

185 King, *Where Do We Go*, 167–91; King, *Stride toward Freedom*, 62, 100, 105, 107.

186 John J. Ansbro erroneously suggests that King, unlike Gandhi, actually found "the Truth he sought"—that "fixed and final theological and philosophical system" he needed to function in the context of the civil rights struggle. Ansbro argues that because Gandhi had no such "theological and philosophical system apart from his commitment to the principles of nonviolence," he was thus able "to choose insights from several creeds and philosophical systems." Ansbro goes on to claim that this caused Gandhi "in the course of his campaigns to be open to revising not only his tactics but also his strategies so that he could respond to the actions of his opponent." Strangely, this very same argument applies as well to King, who never claimed a "fixed" or "final" truth. See Ansbro, *Martin Luther King*, 140.

187 Washington, *Testament*, 35.

188 King, *Where Do We Go*, 124. Also see King, *Strength to Love*, 141.

189 Carson, *King Papers*, 3:417; Carson and Holloran, *Knock at Midnight*, 30.

190 Carson, *King Papers*, 4:471–72; Baldwin, *"Single Garment of Destiny,"* 196.

191 Martin Luther King Jr. to Mr. M. Bernard Resnikoff, unpublished and typed version (September 17, 1961), King Papers, KCLA, 1–2; Martin Luther King Jr. to Dr. Harold E. Fey, unpublished and typed version (June 23, 1962), King Papers, KCLA, 1–5; Baldwin, *"Single Garment of Destiny,"* 197–205; Carson, *King Papers*, 6:681; Carson, *King Papers*, 7:491.

192 Carson, *King Papers*, 7:408.

193 Carson, *King Papers*, 7:491.

194 As early as his student days at Crozer, King included Gandhi among those towering figures who greatly revealed "the working of the Spirit of God." The others were David

Livingstone, Albert Schweitzer, and Jesus of Nazareth. When King was assassinated in April 1968, an Alabama white Baptist pastor halfheartedly lamented his murder while simultaneously attacking the civil rights leader for rejecting "the cardinal tenets of

Biblical Christianity for the heathen philosophy of Mahatma Gandhi." See Carson, *King Papers*, 1:249; and Leonard, "Theology for Racism," 63.

195 Carson, *King Papers*, 1:154; Ansbro, *Martin Luther King*, 104.

Chapter 2

1 Martin Luther King Jr., *Stride toward Freedom: The Montgomery Story* (New York: Harper & Row, 1958), 101; Clayborne Carson, ed., *The Autobiography of Martin Luther King, Jr.* (New York: Warner, 1998), 32; Clayborne Carson, ed., *The Papers of Martin Luther King, Jr.*, vol. 4, *Symbol of the Movement, January 1957–December 1958*, ed. Susan Carson et al. (Berkeley: University of California Press, 2000), 480.

2 I am largely indebted to Dan Hayden for this idea. As I considered titles for chapter 2 of this book, Hayden's idea of "the Bible as a great symphony" of truth came together in my mind with King's occasional use of the word "symphony" to define aspects of his sense of reality and truth. King routinely used phrases like "a beautiful symphony of brotherhood," "meaningful symphonies of spiritual harmony," and "the beautiful symphony of life." See Dan Hayden, "Symphony of Truth," *Zion's Fire* 30, no. 5 (September–October 2019):16–17; Clayborne Carson, ed., *The Papers of Martin Luther King, Jr.*, vol. 7, *To Save the Soul of America, January 1961–August 1962*, ed. Tenisha Armstrong (Berkeley: University of California Press, 2014), 509; Clayborne Carson, ed., *The Papers of Martin Luther King, Jr.*, vol. 6, *Advocate of the Social Gospel, September 1948–March 1963*, ed. Susan Carson et al. (Berkeley: University of California Press, 2007), 360, 382; Clayborne Carson, ed., *The Papers of Martin Luther King, Jr.*, vol. 3, *Birth of a New Age, December 1955–December 1956*, ed. Stewart Burns et al. (Berkeley: University of California Press, 1997), 426; Clayborne Carson, ed., *The Papers of Martin Luther King, Jr.*, vol. 5, *Threshold of a New Decade, January 1959–December 1960*, ed. Tenisha Armstrong et al. (Berkeley: University of California Press, 2005), 571, 575; and James M. Washington, ed., *A Testament of Hope: The Essential Writings and Speeches of Martin Luther King, Jr.* (New York: HarperCollins, 1991), 219.

3 Carson, *King Papers*, 7:509; Washington, *Testament*, 219; King, *Stride toward Freedom*,

107; Martin Luther King Jr., "Some Things We Must Do," speech, unpublished and typed version, Montgomery, AL (December 5, 1957), Martin Luther King Jr. Papers, Library and Archives of the Martin Luther King Jr. Center for Nonviolent Social Change (KCLA), Atlanta, GA, 3.

4 Martin Luther King Jr., *The Measure of a Man* (Philadelphia: Fortress, 1988; originally published in 1959), 36; Carson, *King Autobiography*, 16; Clayborne Carson, ed., *The Papers of Martin Luther King, Jr.*, vol. 1, *Called to Serve, January 1929–June 1951*, ed. Ralph E. Luker and Penny A. Russell (Berkeley: University of California Press, 1992), 362; Carson, *King Papers*, 5:572; Carson, *King Papers*, 6:78, 108–9, 118, 171–73, 193–94, 218, 397; Carson, *King Papers*, 7:408, 491, 593; Washington, *Testament*, 279; King, *Strength to Love*, 10.

5 Carson, *King Papers*, 6:289, 351, 460, 506; Carson, *King Autobiography*, 286; Washington, *Testament*, 9, 18, 52–53, 88, 230, 243; Carson, *King Papers*, 7:445, 485; Carson, *King Papers*, 1:201–2; King, *Strength to Love*, 10, 110–11.

6 Carson, *King Papers*, 6:303, 345, 529; Carson, *King Papers*, 7:288, 290, 292–93, 296, 301; Washington, *Testament*, 279.

7 Carson, *King Papers*, 7:288.

8 This model or theory of truth dates at least as far back as the Greek philosopher Aristotle. See "Truth, Reality, and Knowledge: The Correspondence Theory of Truth," Media Lane, accessed September 1, 2020, https://media.lanecc.edu/users/borrowdalej/phl203_w19/phl203_w19_handout_0107_truth_reality_knowledge_1.html; and Marian David, "The Correspondence Theory of Truth," Stanford Encyclopedia of Philosophy, May 28, 2015, https://plato.stanford.edu/entries/truth-correspondence/.

9 Carson, *King Papers*, 6:88, 155, 372–74; Carson, *King Papers*, 7:213–14, 351, 500; Carson, *King Papers*, 5:280; Martin Luther King Jr., *Where Do We Go from Here: Chaos or Community?* (Boston: Beacon, 1968; originally published in 1967), 56.

10 Carson, *King Papers*, 6:108.

11 Carson, *King Papers*, 7:247; King, *Strength to Love*, 12.

12 See Rufus Burrow Jr., *God and Human Dignity: The Personalism, Theology, and Ethics of Martin Luther King, Jr.* (Notre Dame, IN: University of Notre Dame Press, 2006), 20; Carson, *King Papers*, 1:162–63; Carson, *King Papers*, 7:247–48, 351, 500; Carson, *King Autobiography*, 277; Clayborne Carson and Peter Holloran, eds., *A Knock at Midnight: Inspiration from the Great Sermons of Reverend Martin Luther King, Jr.* (New York: Warner, 1998), 5, 179; King, *Where Do We Go*, 56, 136; and Clayborne Carson and Kris Shepard, eds., *A Call to Conscience: The Landmark Speeches of Dr. Martin Luther King, Jr.* (New York: Warner, 2001), 178.

13 Martin Luther King Jr., "Speech Regarding Freedom Summer Project," unpublished and typed version, Jackson, MS (July 23, 1964), King Papers, KCLA, 1; Carson, *King Papers*, 5:280; Carson, *King Papers*, 7:407, 500.

14 Carson, *King Autobiography*, 15; Carson, *King Papers*, 1:251–56.

15 Clayborne Carson, ed., *The Papers of Martin Luther King, Jr.*, vol. 2, *Rediscovering Precious Values, July 1951–November 1955*, ed. Stewart Burns et al. (Berkeley: University of California Press, 1994), 326; King, *Where Do We Go*, 172; Carson, *King Papers*, 6:131.

16 Carson, *King Papers*, 6:495–96, 548.

17 Carson, *King Papers*, 5:578; Carson, *King Papers*, 1:162, 239; Carson, *King Papers*, 6:108, 131, 191, 203, 374; King, *Strength to Love*, 11.

18 King, *Strength to Love*, 11–12; Carson, *King Papers*, 6:374.

19 Carson, *King Papers*, 1:239; Carson, *King Papers*, 6:108.

20 Carson, *King Papers*, 6:110.

21 King, *Strength to Love*, 11; Carson, *King Papers*, 6:374, 548.

22 Carson, *King Papers*, 6:131, 203.

23 Carson, *King Papers*, 6:495–96; King, *Where Do We Go*, 172.

24 Carson, *King Papers*, 6:372–73.

25 Carson, *King Papers*, 6:366.

26 Carson, *King Papers*, 1:411; Carson, *King Papers*, 2:104; Carson, *King Papers*, 7:290–91.

27 Carson, *King Autobiography*, 254–64; Washington, *Testament*, 225.

28 Carson, *King Papers*, 1:282–83; Carson, *King Papers*, 6:415–17, 538; Martin Luther King Jr., *The Trumpet of Conscience* (San Francisco: Harper & Row, 1968; originally published in 1967), 69–70; Carson, *King Papers*, 2:104.

29 King, *Stride toward Freedom*, 92; King, *Strength to Love*, 97.

30 Carson, *King Papers*, 6:138.

31 Carson, *King Papers*, 6:97; Carson, *King Papers*, 1:239, 411; Carson, *King Papers*, 2:104.

32 Burrow, *God and Human Dignity*, 185.

33 Carson, *King Papers*, 6:88, 97, 135, 192, 204; Carson, *King Papers*, 4:475; Carson, *King Papers*, 2:104, 294; Carson, *King Papers*, 1:243–44, 408, 423.

34 King, *Where Do We Go*, 190–91.

35 Carson, *King Papers*, 6:78, 96, 108, 118, 365–67; Carson, *King Papers*, 4:513–14; Carson, *King Papers*, 5:510, 578–79; Carson, *King Papers*, 7:530, 592–93.

36 Carson, *King Autobiography*, 359; Carson, *King Autobiography*, 6:365–66.

37 Carson, *King Papers*, 6:417; King, *Stride toward Freedom*, 101.

38 King, *Stride toward Freedom*, 92; King, *Strength to Love*, 97–98. For other references King made to ethical relativism, see Carson, *King Papers*, 2:252; Carson, *King Papers*, 5:412; Carson, *King Papers*, 7:197; and Carson, *King Papers*, 6:160–61, 341, 402, 406, 448.

39 Carson, *King Papers*, 6:160–61, 181–84; Carson, *King Papers*, 2:251–52; Lewis V. Baldwin and Paul R. Dekar, eds., *"In an Inescapable Network of Mutuality": Martin Luther King, Jr. and the Globalization of an Ethical Ideal* (Eugene, OR: Cascade, 2013), 3–5.

40 Carson, *King Papers*, 2:252.

41 Carson, *King Papers*, 2:274; John J. Ansbro, *Martin Luther King, Jr.: Nonviolent Strategies and Tactics for Social Change* (Lanham, MD: Madison, 2000; originally published in 1982), 122.

42 Ansbro, *Martin Luther King*, 122–24; King, *Stride toward Freedom*, 101.

43 Carson, *King Papers*, 2:251–52; Carson, *King Papers*, 6:160–61; King, *Stride toward Freedom*, 92.

44 Carson, *King Papers*, 6:97, 135, 204; Carson, *King Papers*, 1:243–44. Mohandas K. Gandhi, one of King's major intellectual and spiritual sources, concluded that truth "is but another name for God." Describing himself as "a votary of truth," Gandhi declared, "My prayerful search gave me the revealing maxim 'truth is God' instead of the usual one, 'God is truth.' That maxim enables me to see God face to face as it were. I feel Him pervade every fiber of my being." See Thomas Merton, ed., *Gandhi on Nonviolence: Selected Texts from Mohandas K. Gandhi's "Non-violence in Peace and War"* (New York: New Directions, 1965), 27–28; and Carson, *King Papers*, 7:406n22.

45 Carson, *King Papers*, 6:78; Carson, *King Papers*, 1:239, 249, 429; Carson, *King Papers*, 2:90, 252; Carson, *King Papers*, 4:375; Carson, *King Papers*, 7:408; Carson, *King Papers*, 5:547; Martin Luther King Jr., "Moving to Another Mountain," *Wesleyan University Alumnus* 52, no. 4 (May 1968): 3.

46 King, *Where Do We Go*, 64, 182, 190–91; Washington, *Testament*, 102–3; Carson, *King Papers*, 6:293, 447–48; Carson, *King Papers*, 2:251–52.

47 Carson, *King Papers*, 1:124; Carson, *King Papers*, 6:218, 293, 447, 449, 578; King, *Strength to Love*, 10, 12.

48 Carson, *King Papers*, 1:124, 201, 207; King, *Strength to Love*, 10.

49 Carson, *King Papers*, 5:136.

50 King, *Stride toward Freedom*, 101.

51 King, *Strength to Love*, 44; Carson, *King Papers*, 6:374, 492.

52 Carson and Holloran, *Knock at Midnight*, 72–73; King, *Strength to Love*, 21; Lewis V. Baldwin, *The Voice of Conscience: The Church in the Mind of Martin Luther King, Jr.* (New York: Oxford University Press, 2010), 76–77, 79.

53 King, *Strength to Love*, 44; Carson, *King Papers*, 6:374, 492, 548.

54 Carson, *King Papers*, 6:374, 548, 576; Carson and Holloran, *Knock at Midnight*, 30; Carson, *King Papers*, 7:491.

55 Carson, *King Papers*, 6:492, 583–84.

56 Sophia Rosenfeld, *Democracy and Truth: A Short History* (Philadelphia: University of Pennsylvania Press, 2019), 15.

57 The pragmatic theory of truth has been traced back to thinkers such as C. S. Peirce, William James, and John Dewey. See John Capps et al., "The Pragmatic Theory of Truth," Stanford Encyclopedia of Philosophy, March 21, 2019, https://plato.stanford.edu/entries/truth-pragmatic/.

58 Carson, *King Papers*, 4:169.

59 King used the Greek word *Phi* to refer to the kind of truths that relate to the whole of human experience. See Carson, *King Papers*, 6:194, 228, 360; Carson, *King Papers*, 4:513; and Carson, *King Papers*, 7:288. Apparently, King agreed with the British philosopher John Locke's view that experience—along with reason, sensation, and reflection—is key in any serious quest for knowledge and truth. See Carson, *King Papers*, 2:245.

60 This idea of "experiential truth" courses through much of what King said and wrote about the Black experience in America and worldwide, though he, as far as this author knows, did not make specific use of the term.

"Experiential truth" is really about the factual ways in which the experiences of humans impact their self-concepts, daily lives, and thought processes. King often spoke of those truths derived from human experience. Much of what is said here about experiential truth was framed on the basis of my reading of Francois Tremblay, "The Experiential Theory of Truth," *The Prime Directive* (blog), January 27, 2015, https://francoistremblay.wordpress.com/2015/01/27/the-experiential-theory-of-truth/; and Tom Das, "Experiential vs Scientific Truth," *Liberation and Nonduality* (blog), September 25, 2017, https://tomdas.com/2017/09/25/experiential-vs-scientific-truth/. For an extensive treatment of the "experiential approach to truth," see Daniel Erway (a.k.a. Nirmala), *Living from the Heart* (Scotts Valley, CA: CreateSpace, 2008).

61 King, *Stride toward Freedom*, 18.

62 Lawrence Reddick, a close friend of King and King's very first major biographer, reports that King "was about eleven years old" when this incident occurred. The important point is that it did in fact take place. See John Freeman, "Interview with Martin Luther King, Jr." unpublished and typed version, *Face to Face*, BBC Television, London, England (October 29, 1961), King Papers, KCLA, 4–5; Lewis V. Baldwin, *There Is a Balm in Gilead: The Cultural Roots of Martin Luther King, Jr.* (Minneapolis: Fortress, 1991), 21–22; and Lawrence D. Reddick, *Crusader without Violence: A Biography of Martin Luther King, Jr.* (New York: Harper & Brothers, 1959), 59–60.

63 Carson, *King Papers*, 5:198; King, *Stride toward Freedom*, 90; Carson, *King Papers*, 4:473; Carson and Holloran, *Knock at Midnight*, 208.

64 Carson, *King Papers*, 4:473–74; Carson, *King Papers*, 1:359–60, 362.

65 Carson, *King Papers*, 6:228.

66 King, *Measure of a Man*, 21–23; Martin Luther King Jr., "The Meaning of Hope," sermon, unpublished and typed version, Dexter Avenue Baptist Church, Montgomery, AL (December 10, 1967), King Papers, KCLA, 1–2; King, *Where Do We Go*, 102–3.

67 Carson and Shepard, *Call to Conscience*, viii.

68 The development of the notion of "historical truth" is attributed to Sigmund Freud, the father of psychoanalysis. King read and had some familiarity with Freud and his work, and King himself used the terms "historical truth" and "historical truths" and wrote about the tendency to equate these with "legendary truth" as early as his

Crozer Seminary years. This discussion of King in relation to historical truths benefited from a reading of James M. Banner Jr., "Historical Truth and Personal Truths," Origins: Current Events in Historical Perspective, June 27, 2001, https://origins.osu.edu/history-news/historical-truth-and-personal-truths; Paul Ricoeur, *History and Truth*, Studies in Phenomenology and Existential Philosophy (Evanston, IL: Northwestern University Press, 2007), 3–368; Alan B. Spitzer, *Historical Truth and Lies about the Past* (Chapel Hill: University of North Carolina Press, 1996), 3–176; Sophie de Mijolla-Mellor, "Historical Truth," Encyclopedia.com, accessed September 19, 2020, https://www.encyclopedia.com/psychology/dictionaries-thesauruses-pictures-and-press-releases/historical-truth; Carson, *King Papers*, 1:162–63.

69 Carson, *King Papers*, 1:162–63; Carson, *King Papers*, 4:230, 407; Carson, *King Papers*, 6:193, 219; Carson, *King Papers*, 7:378, 405, 477.

70 Carson, *King Papers*, 1:162–63; Carson, *King Papers*, 6:216–19, 511; Carson, *King Papers*, 3:265; Washington, *Testament*, 401–2; Carson, *King Papers*, 4:407; Carson, *King Papers*, 7:221, 335, 592–93. For one of King's most important statements on "the lessons of history," see Martin Luther King Jr., "Discerning the Signs of History," sermon, unpublished and typed version, Ebenezer Baptist Church, Atlanta, GA (November 15, 1964), King Papers, KCLA, 1–7.

71 Carson, *King Papers*, 1:359; Christine King Farris, *Through It All: Reflections on My Life, My Family, and My Faith* (New York: Atria, 2009), 12.

72 King, *Stride toward Freedom*, 18–19; Carson, *King Autobiography*, 3–4; Farris, *Through It All*, 16–17.

73 Carson, *King Papers*, 3:265; Farris, *Through It All*, 12; Martin Luther King Jr., "What a Mother Should Tell Her Child," sermon, unpublished and transcribed version, Ebenezer Baptist Church, Atlanta, GA (May 12, 1963), King Papers, KCLA, 1–14; Martin Luther King Jr., "Training Your Child in Love," sermon, unpublished and typed version, Ebenezer Baptist Church, Atlanta, GA (May 8, 1966), King Papers, KCLA, 1–11.

74 Sydney Ahlstrom made this point about the Black religious experience and American history back in 1972, as the world grappled with the legacy of King and the civil rights movement, and I am indebted

to him for much of this insight. He writes, "The basic paradigm for a renovation of American church history is the black religious experience, which has been virtually closed out of all synoptic histories written so far—closed out despite the obvious fact that any history of America that ignores the full consequences of slavery and non-emancipation is a fairy tale." Undoubtedly, King would have agreed with this point, but his focus was always on the Black experience as a whole and what it meant in terms of our understanding of certain truths about both American and world history. See Sydney E. Ahlstrom, *A Religious History of the American People* (New Haven, CT: Yale University Press, 1972), 12–13.

75 King, *Where Do We Go*, 103.

76 See Richard W. Wills, *Martin Luther King, Jr. and the Image of God* (New York: Oxford University Press, 2009), 33; King, *Stride toward Freedom*, 18–19.

77 Carson, *King Papers*, 6:219; Carson, *King Papers*, 3:74; Carson, *King Papers*, 7:378, 405; King, *Where Do We Go*, 178; Martin Luther King Jr., "A Cry of Hate or a Cry for Help?," statement, unpublished and typed version (August 1965), King Papers, KCLA, 4; Baldwin, *Voice of Conscience*, 92–93, 294n211.

78 Carson, *King Autobiography*, 6; Carson, *King Papers*, 1:360–63; Farris, *Through It All*, 16–18. The term "Hebrew Bible," not "Old Testament," is more commonly used in the circles of biblical scholarship today, but "Old Testament" is employed here as a way of being true to the age in which King himself lived. There is reason to believe that King would have been open to the use of the term "Hebrew Bible" as well. See Carson, *King Papers*, 1:163, 179–80, 286–87; and Martin Luther King Jr., "An Address," unpublished and typed version, Synagogue Council of America, Waldorf Astoria Hotel, New York, NY (December 5, 1965), King Papers, KCLA, 8–11.

79 Carson, *King Autobiography*, 6; Carson, *King Papers*, 1:360–63; King, *Strength to Love*, 147; Baldwin, *Balm in Gilead*, 163. The five essential truths of the old-line biblical fundamentalism, also known as "the five points of Christian belief" and "the five basic doctrines of fundamentalism," reportedly sprung from the Niagara Bible Conference of 1895 and were reaffirmed by the Presbyterian General Assembly and with the publication of *The Fundamentals* in 1910. See Jerald C. Brauer et al., *The Westminster Dictionary of Church*

History (Louisville: Westminster John Knox, 1971), 348–49; and J. D. Douglas et al., eds., *The New International Dictionary of the Christian Church* (Grand Rapids, MI: Zondervan, 1979), 396.

80 Carson, *King Autobiography*, 6, 16; Carson, *King Papers*, 1:195, 226–29, 236–42, 251–56, 361–63.

81 Carson, *King Papers*, 2:229.

82 At the same time, King criticized liberal theology for "too often" losing "itself in 'higher criticism.'" See Carson, *King Papers*, 1:43, 180, 241–42, 251–53; Carson, *King Papers*, 2:137–38, 213; Carson, *King Papers*, 6:78, 80.

83 King had put forth this argument in some form at least as far back as his Morehouse College days. See Keith D. Miller, *Voice of Deliverance: The Language of Martin Luther King, Jr. and Its Sources* (New York: Free Press, 1992), 39–40, 223n68, 248; Lee E. Dirks, "'The Essence Is Love': The Theology of Martin Luther King, Jr.," *National Observer*, December 30, 1963, 1, 12; Carson, *King Papers*, 1:225–26, 228–29; and Carson, *King Papers*, 6:71, 80, 128–29.

84 Dirks, "'Essence Is Love,'" 1.

85 Carson, *King Papers*, 6:83, 235–37, 411; Carson, *King Papers*, 1:271; Carson, *King Papers*, 7:446. Lee E. Dirks noted in 1963 that King's "sermons contain no 'hard' preaching on Heaven and Hell, no preoccupation with sin and salvation." Constantly looking for an angle from which to attack and insult King, prominent southern white clergy turned to his views on the five fundamentals. John R. Rice argued that while King called himself a Christian, he did "not believe the Bible." Rice further noted of King, "He is not a Christian in the historic sense of holding to the great essentials of the Christian faith; he is a 'minster' who doesn't preach the gospel, doesn't save souls . . . , and does not believe in the Christian faith nor trust in the virgin-born Savior." Noel Smith contended that "Dr. King's Christ has nothing in common with the Christ of the Bible." Smith went on to conclude that "anybody who knows the Bible's definition of a Christian . . . has little if any evidence that King was a Christian. He denied the virgin birth of Christ." Archer Weniger called King "pro-communist" and "a modernist" because "he denied that hell is 'a place of literal burning fire.'" By "definition," Weniger concluded, "Dr. Martin Luther King is an apostate." See Dirks, "'Essence Is Love,'" 1; and Bill J. Leonard,

"A Theology for Racism: Southern Fundamentalists and the Civil Rights Movement," *Baptist History and Heritage* 34, no. 1 (Winter 1999): 61, 63.

86 Carson, *King Autobiography*, 16; Miller, *Voice of Deliverance*, 39; Carson, *King Papers*, 2:228–29; Carson, *King Papers*, 1:180, 226, 228–29, 234–35, 241, 287.

87 Carson, *King Papers*, 1:286–87.

88 Carson, *King Papers*, 1:287.

89 This is part of what King had in mind when he, quoting from the American religious historian William Warren Sweet, spoke of becoming "Christians in deed, and in truth." Carson, *King Papers*, 6:499–501; Carson and Holloran, *Knock at Midnight*, 71–74; Carson, *King Papers*, 1:340.

90 Carson, *King Papers*, 1:204–7; Carson, *King Papers*, 2:205–10.

91 Carson, *King Papers*, 4:408–9.

92 "If we accept the Old Testament as being 'true,'" King declared during his seminary years, "we will find it full of errors, contradictions, and obvious impossibilities—as that the Pentateuch was written by Moses." "But if we accept it as 'truth,'" King continued, "we will find it to be one of the most logical vehicles of mankind's deepest devotional thoughts and aspirations, couched in language which still retains its original vigor and its moral intensity." See Carson, *King Papers*, 1:180.

93 To highlight this nexus of truth and justice in the Bible, King occasionally mentioned the *imago Dei* principle in Genesis in connection with other biblical passages, such as Acts 17:26, which states, "[God] hath made of one blood all nations of men for to dwell on all the face of the earth, and hath determined the times before appointed, and the bounds of their habitation." Strangely enough, southern white fundamentalist clergy in the 1950s and '60s used this very same verse in Acts to defend segregation. See Wills, *Image of God*, 61–62, 66–68, 70, 78, 94–95, 100, 113–14, 124–27; Carson, *King Papers*, 4:124, 274, 334; Carson, *King Papers*, 7:594; Carson, *King Papers*, 3:378–79, 417; Carson, *King Papers*, 6:343, 441, 481; and Andrew M. Manis, "'Dying from the Neck Up': Southern Baptist Resistance to the Civil Rights Movement," *Baptist History and Heritage*, 34, no. 1 (Winter 1999): 39.

94 Carson, *King Papers*, 4:87, 155, 157, 161, 163; Carson, *King Papers*, 5:288, 410; Martin Luther King Jr., "A Christian Movement in a Revolutionary Age," speech, unpublished and typed version (Fall 1966), King

Papers, KCLA, 1; King, *Strength to Love*, 77–82; Carson, *King Autobiography*, 113; Carson, *King Papers*, 6:511; Martin Luther King Jr., "Nobel Lecture," unpublished and typed version, Aula of the University, Oslo, Norway (December 11, 1964), King Papers, KCLA, 6.

95 King, "Christian Movement," 2; King, "Nobel Lecture," 6.

96 Carson, *King Papers*, 7:116.

97 Carson, *King Papers*, 2:165, 169; Carson, *King Papers*, 3:286, 418; Carson, *King Papers*, 4:125, 191, 276, 342, 397; Carson, *King Papers*, 7:594; Carson, *King Autobiography*, 198.

98 King, "Address," Synagogue Council of America, 7–8; Carson, *King Papers*, 1:181–82, 187–89; Carson, *King Papers*, 7:116, 408; King, *Strength to Love*, 129.

99 King held that God "is found in Christ and the Prophets." See Carson, *King Papers*, 6:563. King acknowledged that "the New Testament was a great influence in my life in the philosophical, from a moral, from a spiritual point of view." See Martin Luther King Jr., "Doubts and Certainties Link," interview, unpublished, transcribed, and typed version, London, England (Winter 1968), King Papers, KCLA.

100 Dirks, "'Essence Is Love,'" 1; Carson, *King Papers*, 5:172; Carson, *King Papers*, 6:115.

101 King called this "the manifesto of Jesus." See Carson, *King Papers*, 4:476; King, *Strength to Love*, 100; Carson and Holloran, *Knock at Midnight*, 105–6.

102 King, *Stride toward Freedom*, 210–11; Carson, *King Papers*, 7:594; Washington, *Testament*, 16, 447; Carson, *King Papers*, 3:326; King, *Stride toward Freedom*, 101.

103 Dirks, "'Essence Is Love,'" 1; Carson, *King Papers*, 2:138; King, *Strength to Love*, 26–35, 56–75; Carson, *King Papers*, 6:125, 184–85, 238, 406; Carson, *King Papers*, 5:147; Carson, *King Papers*, 4:472; Carson, *King Papers*, 7:491; Martin Luther King Jr., "A Knock at Midnight," sermon, unpublished and typed version, All Saints Community Church, Los Angeles, CA (June 25, 1967), King Papers, KCLA, 1.

104 Kenneth Smith and Ira Zepp contend that "the Kingdom of God and the Beloved Community were synonymous in King's thought." See Kenneth L. Smith and Ira G. Zepp Jr., *Search for the Beloved Community: The Thinking of Martin Luther King, Jr.* (Valley Forge, PA: Judson, 1998; originally published in 1974), 141; and King, "Meaning of Hope," 11.

105 King held that it was Jesus Christ's "Love for God and Truth" that "precipitated the evil act of his execution." See Carson, *King Autobiography*, 306, 351; Martin Luther King Jr., *Why We Can't Wait* (New York: New American Library, 1963), 89; and Washington, *Testament*, 298.

106 King, "Christian Movement," 3; King, *Strength to Love*, 41–42; Washington, *Testament*, 493–94; Baldwin, *Voice of Conscience*, 151–71.

107 Carson, *King Papers*, 6:118, 343; Carson, *King Papers*, 7:408, 491; Carson, *King Papers*, 3:259; Carson, *King Papers*, 4:375; King, *Where Do We Go*, 190. King's openness to truths in other religions and sacred texts goes at least as far back as his Crozer Seminary years (1948–51), when he wrote papers on topics such as Mithraism, a sect of Zoroastrianism, referring to the god of Mithra as "the defender of truth," "the spirit of light and truth," "the protector of truth," and one destined "to attain purity and truth." See Carson, *King Papers*, 1:211, 213, 218–19.

108 Carson, *King Papers*, 6:78, 118.

109 The term "Bible Belt" was coined by the nationally known writer H. L. Mencken (1880–1956) in reference to those parts of America, especially the rural South and Midwest, which were dominated by a belief in the inerrancy or literal authenticity of the Bible. Mencken used "Bible Belt" as a term of derision, but many over time have attached a positive connotation to the term. See Charles Reagan Wilson and William Ferris, eds., *Encyclopedia of Southern Culture* (Chapel Hill: University of North Carolina Press, 1989), 890, 1312–13.

110 Carson, *King Papers*, 6:97, 135, 204; Burrow, *God and Human Dignity*, 185. King did not quote the Scriptures in making this point, but clearly, there are some verses in the Bible that affirm that God is truth, such as Deuteronomy 32:4, Psalms 31:5, and Isaiah 65:16. It is well established in the scholarship on King, particularly by authorities in theology, that King was indeed a theologian, but not a systematic theologian. See Martin Luther King Jr., "A Comparison of the Conceptions of God in the Thinking of Paul Tillich and Henry Nelson Wieman" (PhD diss., Boston University, June 1955); Herbert W. Richardson, "Martin Luther King—Unsung Theologian," in *New Theology No. 6: On Revolution and Non-revolution, Violence and Non-violence, Peace and Power*, ed. Martin E. Marty and

Dean G. Peerman (New York: Macmillan, 1969), 178–84; Paul R. Garber, "Martin Luther King, Jr.: Theologian and Precursor of Black Theology" (PhD diss., Florida State University, December 1973); John C. Harris, "The Theology of Martin Luther King, Jr." (PhD diss., Duke University, April 1974); James H. Cone, "The Theology of Martin Luther King, Jr.," *Union Seminary Quarterly Review* 40, no. 4 (January 1986): 21–39; Noel Leo Erskine, *King among the Theologians* (Cleveland: Pilgrim, 1994); Luther D. Ivory, *Toward a Theology of Radical Involvement: The Theological Legacy of Martin Luther King, Jr.* (Nashville: Abingdon, 1997); and Rufus Burrow Jr., *Martin Luther King, Jr., and the Theology of Resistance* (Jefferson, NC: McFarland, 2015). Paul Garber refers to King as "literally a theologian on the run, spending more time in airports and aboard planes than in office or study," which holds some significance for assessing King's approach to theological truth. See Paul R. Garber, "Too Much Taming of Martin Luther King?," *Christian Century* 9, no. 22 (June 5, 1974): 616.

111 These ideas find expression to some extent in King's PhD dissertation. See Carson, *King Papers*, 2:70–71, 91–92, 108, 167–68, 188, 406, 408–10, 424–32, 490–92, 503–7, 510–17, 524–27, 534, 546–47; Carson, *King Papers*, 6:512; Ansbro, *Martin Luther King*, 40, 48, 52–53, 58–59, 60–70; and King, *Strength to Love*, 106–14.

112 King had essentially the same thing in mind when he asserted that "history is ultimately guided by spirit, not matter." Here he was attacking the Marxists' materialistic view of history. See Carson, *King Papers*, 6:218, 230; Carson, *King Papers*, 1:290, 294; King, *Strength to Love*, 109–10, 131, 135–36; Washington, *Testament*, 506–7; Burrow, *God and Human Responsibility*, 95; Carson, *King Papers*, 4:475; and Ansbro, *Martin Luther King*, 37–38.

113 Alex Ayres, ed., *The Wisdom of Martin Luther King, Jr.: An A-to-Z Guide to the Ideas and Ideals of the Great Civil Rights Leader* (New York: Penguin, 1993), 74–75.

114 Carson, *King Papers*, 1:226–27, 246, 257–62; Carson, *King Papers*, 7:163; Dirks, "'Essence Is Love,'" 1.

115 Carson, *King Papers*, 7:442, 491; Carson, *King Papers*, 1:227, 257; Carson, *King Papers*, 2:138; Carson, *King Papers*, 4:472.

116 King declared that "Jesus' ability to match words with actions"—to "match his sublime teachings with matchless living"—clearly separated him from most of humanity. He consistently made this point when addressing human hypocrisy. See Carson, *King Papers*, 6:406, 487; and Carson, *King Papers*, 5:168.

117 King's emphasis here is not on Christ the person as the only savior, which was typical of biblical fundamentalists, but on "the way of Christ," which is love, or that "supreme unifying principle of life" as expressed in all the great religions of the world. "The way of Christ" is the way of truth, and this way is not confined to any one faith tradition. King also delighted in quoting the great theologian Karl Barth, who stated that "Jesus desires to speak truth to us." See Carson, *King Papers*, 6:102, 115, 125, 185; Carson, *King Papers*, 7:205, 491; Carson, *King Papers*, 3:208; Dirks, "'Essence Is Love,'" 1, 12; and King, *Where Do We Go*, 190–91.

118 King insisted as early as his Crozer Seminary years that "the church," being "one of the chief exponents of racial bigotry," is "far from Christ"—that "the great tragedy of the church" is that "it has confused the vices of the church with the virtues of Christ." King reminded Christians that Jesus challenged his disciples to become "true propagandizers" of his word in a global context, which, in King's mind, contrasted with Western Christianity and the sense of missionary compassion and urgency associated with it. See Carson, *King Papers*, 6:105–6, 184–85; Carson, *King Papers*, 5:170.

119 Carson and Holloran, *Knock at Midnight*, 186.

120 Carson, *King Papers*, 6:51, 78, 402, 478; Carson, *King Papers*, 2:229; Carson, *King Papers*, 1:226, 268, 301–2.

121 Carson, *King Papers*, 6:78–79.

122 Richard Wills observes that King found this *imago Dei* principle affirmed not only in the Bible, theology, and anthropology but also in "the language of the Declaration of Independence." See Wills, *Image of God*, 25.

123 King, *Measure of a Man*, 9–55; Carson, *King Papers*, 5:399–400, 507; Carson, *King Papers*, 7:228; Carson, *King Papers*, 4:243.

124 Carson, *King Papers*, 6:95, 328–37, 481; Carson, *King Papers*, 4:318, 334; King, *Strength to Love*, 149; Ansbro, *Martin Luther King*, 92–106.

125 King, *Measure of a Man*, 9–55; King, *Strength to Love*, 67–75; Carson and Holloran, *Knock at Midnight*, 121–64. King attributed both "masculinity" and "femininity" to God, noting that the "tough

mindedness of God is expressed in an austere masculinity" and God's "tender heartedness" "in a gentle femininity." He went on to say that "God possesses the firmness of a father and the softness of a mother." But in his use of the *imago Dei* language and other language about God, he almost never used gender-inclusive language. In a sermon entitled "The Christian Doctrine of Man," preached in March 1958, he declared, "And when I am speaking of man at this point I must make it clear that I'm not talking about the male sex; this is generic in its setting including men and women." King also said at another point that "when I say men, I'm speaking in a generic sense, I mean women also." Although he seemed aware of some of the potential problems involved in the use of gender-exclusive language, even at that time, he never addressed them specifically. See Carson, *King Papers*, 6:330, 377; and Carson, *King Papers*, 4:337.

126 Wills focuses on what he calls King's "theological anthropology," placing King in the African American Christian tradition and that larger Christian tradition as well. See Wills, *Image of God*, 23, 25. For another source that embodies some significance for analyzing King's *imago Dei* concept, see Garth Baker-Fletcher, *Somebodyness: Martin Luther King, Jr., and the Theory of Dignity* (Minneapolis: Fortress, 1993), 107–35.

127 Carson, *King Papers*, 6:268, 328–37, 424; Carson, *King Papers*, 7:199; Carson, *King Papers*, 4:318, 341; Lewis V. Baldwin and Victor Anderson, eds., *Revives My Soul Again: The Spirituality of Martin Luther King, Jr.* (Minneapolis: Fortress, 2018), 66.

128 King, *Measure of a Man*, 9–22; Carson, *King Papers*, 6:176–78, 268, 328, 334, 424; Carson, *King Papers*, 7:199, 442; Carson, *King Papers*, 1:412; Baldwin and Anderson, *Revives My Soul Again*, 66.

129 King, *Measure of a Man*, 18, 21; Carson, *King Papers*, 6:178, 334; Carson, *King Papers*, 7:198–99; Ayres, *Wisdom of King*, 111; Washington, *Testament*, 47; Baldwin and Anderson, *Revives My Soul Again*, 66. For King, the image of God in humanity afforded one of his strongest arguments in favor of the agape love ethic. "And when you come to the point that you look into the face of every man and see deep down within him what religion calls 'the image of God,' you begin to love him in spite of. No matter what he does, you see God's image there." Of the white segregationist in the South, King's point was even more powerful and moving: "We must

somehow stand up before our white brothers in this Southland and see within them the image of God. No matter how bad they are as we think, no matter what they do to us, no matter what they said about us, we must still believe that in the most recalcitrant segregationist there is the image of God. If we keep on loving him, we must believe that he can be transformed. This is the hope that we must live by." See Carson, *King Papers*, 4:318, 341.

130 King, *Measure of a Man*, 9, 12–14; Carson, *King Papers*, 6:176–78; King, *Stride toward Freedom*, 100; Burrow, *God and Human Dignity*, 126.

131 Carson, *King Papers*, 4:187, 335; Washington, *Testament*, 211; Carson, *King Papers*, 3:300, 323.

132 Carson, *King Papers*, 6:551; Washington, *Testament*, 211.

133 Baldwin and Dekar, *"Inescapable Network,"* 4; Washington, *Testament*, 121–22.

134 King, *Where Do We Go*, 180–81; King, *Strength to Love*, 70.

135 King, *Why We Can't Wait*, 77.

136 King, *Measure of a Man*, 12–14; Carson, *King Papers*, 6:176–79, 416–17, 530–31; King, *Where Do We Go*, 97, 187.

137 Carson, *King Papers*, 4:280; King, *Where Do We Go*, 181. For a longer version of this statement, see King, *Trumpet of Conscience*, 69–70; and Carson and Holloran, *Knock at Midnight*, 132–33, 151–52.

138 King seems to have been referring here to humanity's "self-transcending qualities," and perhaps its "readjusting qualities." See King, *Measure of a Man*, 9, 17, 21; Carson, *King Papers*, 6:176–78; Baldwin and Anderson, *Revives My Soul Again*, 67; and King, "Doubts and Certainties Link," 1–2.

139 Carson, *King Papers*, 6:177–78; Carson, *King Papers*, 1:244; King, *Measure of a Man*, 11–21; Baldwin and Anderson, *Revives My Soul Again*, 67.

140 King, "Moving to Another Mountain," 3; Martin Luther King Jr., "See You in Washington," speech, unpublished and typed version, SCLC Staff Retreat, Ebenezer Baptist Church, Atlanta, GA (January 17, 1968), King Papers, KCLA, 11; King, *Where Do We Go*, 171; King, "Doubts and Certainties Link," 2–3; Baldwin and Anderson, *Revives My Soul Again*, 67; Ansbro, *Martin Luther King*, 92, 101, 289n82.

141 Carson, *King Papers*, 6:177–78; Baldwin and Anderson, *Revives My Soul Again*, 68.

142 Carson, *King Papers*, 6:178, 386; Baldwin and Anderson, *Revives My Soul Again*, 68.

143 King held that "one of the great problems of mankind is that we suffer from a poverty of the spirit which stands in glaring contrast to our scientific and technological abundance." He felt that an obsession with materialism was gradually eroding humanity's moral and spiritual fiber. See Carson, *King Papers*, 6:176, 190, 335, 424; Carson, *King Papers*, 5:579; King, *Where Do We Go*, 171; Carson, *King Papers*, 7:293; Baldwin and Anderson, *Revives My Soul Again*, 68.

144 King, *Strength to Love*, 4, 154–55; Carson, *King Papers*, 7:576; Carson, *King Papers*, 2:294; Carson, *King Papers*, 5:123; Carson, *King Papers*, 6:84, 194, 197; King, *Trumpet of Conscience*, 45; Carson, *King Papers*, 4:444; Carson and Holloran, *Knock at Midnight*, 122; Carson and Shepard, *Call to Conscience*, 140; Baldwin and Anderson, *Revives My Soul Again*, 69, 72–73.

145 King was trained in systematic theology but also tended to see himself as a philosophical theologian, and he would have included himself among those whom he described as "religious" with "a philosophical bent." Robert Birt views King as "a philosophical man of action" or "an insurgent philosopher-activist," which is also important for understanding King's approach to philosophical truth. Birt does not include King among "academic" or "systematic philosophers." King himself said that "I don't consider myself a philosopher, although I did most of my studying in philosophy, but I'm not a systematic philosopher." "I do try to follow many of the insights I've gained from philosophy, and many of these insights have guided my life," he added, "but I wouldn't say I was a philosopher in the sense of a professor of philosophy." King went on to report that "as a philosophical thinker, I was greatly influenced by Plato and Aristotle and Hegel and Immanuel Kant. Some of the philosophical theologians that have greatly influenced me have been Augustine and Aquinas, those great Catholic theologians, and more contemporary theologians have been Reinhold Niebuhr and Paul Tillich." See King, "Doubts and Certainties Link," 3–4; Robert E. Birt, ed., *The Liberatory Thought of Martin Luther King, Jr.: Critical Essays on the Philosopher King* (Lanham, MD: Lexington, 2012), 1–6; Carson, *King Papers*, 2:221–22; and Carson, *King Papers*, 7:158.

146 King has not gotten the attention he deserves as a philosopher. One might agree with Charles R. Johnson's claim that King was "our most prominent moral philosopher of the second half of the Twentieth Century." See Birt, *Liberatory Thought*, 1–6; and Charles R. Johnson, "The King We Need: Teachings for a Nation in Search of Itself," *Shambhala Sun*, January 2005, 42.

147 Carson, *King Papers*, 6:248, 303, 345; Carson, *King Papers*, 1:423; Carson, *King Papers*, 7:296.

148 Carson, *King Papers*, 7:442; Carson, *King Papers*, 1:124.

149 King, *Strength to Love*, 45; Carson, *King Papers*, 1:243; King, *Stride toward Freedom*, 212; Carson, *King Papers*, 7:120, 197.

150 Carson, *King Papers*, 7:279; Carson, *King Papers*, 6:303, 345; Ansbro, *Martin Luther King*, 3.

151 Carson, *King Papers*, 6:303, 345; King, *Strength to Love*, 55; Carson, *King Papers*, 2:251–53; Carson, *King Papers*, 7:506, 531; King, *Where Do We Go*, 167–91; Birt, *Liberatory Thought*, 6; Carson, *King Papers*, 4:75; Washington, *Testament*, 135, 286, 335; Ayres, *Wisdom of King*, 56, 140, 212.

152 Carson, *King Papers*, 1:230–36, 394, 411, 422–23; Carson, *King Papers*, 2:229; Carson, *King Papers*, 5:420.

153 Carson, *King Papers*, 6:165, 167, 303, 335; Birt, *Liberatory Thought*, 1–12.

154 King argued that "the Christian ethic is never a bundle of do-nots but it's a bushel of dos." He typically made no sharp distinction between "ethical truths" and "moral truths." See Carson, *King Papers*, 2:165, 167, 251–52; Carson, *King Papers*, 6:384, 386; King, *Strength to Love*, 47; Carson, *King Papers*, 5:521; and Carson, *King Papers*, 7:443.

155 Carson, *King Papers*, 2:252; Carson and Holloran, *Knock at Midnight*, 13; Carson, *King Papers*, 6:496; Carson, *King Papers*, 5:411–12; Carson, *King Papers*, 1:122; Carson, *King Papers*, 4:278; Carson, *King Papers*, 7:192–93.

156 King, *Stride toward Freedom*, 104; Carson, *King Papers*, 3:308; King, *Trumpet of Conscience*, 45.

157 Carson, *King Autobiography*, 23–24, 351; Smith and Zepp, *Beloved Community*, 22; Carson, *King Papers*, 6:578, 584.

158 Carson, *King Papers*, 6:218.

159 King, "Signs of History," 2.

160 Carson, *King Papers*, 6:110, 218, 224, 242, 245, 247, 330, 364, 488, 513, 519, 563, 593–95; Carson, *King Papers*, 2:80, 356; Carson, *King Papers*, 7:297, 299, 302–3, 334; Carson, *King Papers*, 1:282–83, 290–91, 318, 355, 411; Carson, *King Papers*, 5:173; Ansbro, *Martin Luther King*, 117–19.

161 King, *Stride toward Freedom*, 101; Carson, *King Papers*, 4:480.

162 Carson, *King Papers*, 1:16, 122, 124, 361, 363.

163 King, *Strength to Love*, 12–13; Carson, *King Papers*, 6:460–61.

164 King, *Strength to Love*, 12–13; Carson, *King Papers*, 6:460.

165 King, "Freedom Summer Project," 1; Carson, *King Papers*, 6:578; Carson, *King Autobiography*, 277.

166 King, *Strength to Love*, 15, 39, 45, 135; Carson, *King Papers*, 1:248–49; Carson, *King Papers*, 6:115, 185, 200, 335, 348, 460–62, 494, 578, 598; Carson, *King Papers*, 7:166, 286; King, *Trumpet of Conscience*, 45; Washington, *Testament*, 10, 88, 357–58; King, *Stride toward Freedom*, 179, 202, 210; King, "Doubts and Certainties Link," 3.

167 Carson, *King Papers*, 4:427, 447, 491; Carson, *King Papers*, 6:132, 147, 427, 447, 453, 491; Carson, *King Papers*, 5:502, 505; Carson, *King Papers*, 7:240, 531.

168 Carson, *King Papers*, 6:599; King, *Trumpet of Conscience*, 70–71; Carson, *King Papers*, 5:521, 547; King, *Why We Can't Wait*, 27–46.

169 Carson, *King Papers*, 6:599; Carson, *King Papers*, 5:521, 547; Washington, *Testament*, 349–50.

170 Carson, *King Autobiography*, 178.

171 Carson, *King Papers*, 4:189; Carson, *King Autobiography*, 257; Carson, *King Papers*, 6:185; Carson and Holloran, *Knock at Midnight*, 6–7; Carson, *King Papers*, 2:249.

172 Burrow, *God and Human Dignity*, 185.

173 Carson, *King Autobiography*, 357; King, *Strength to Love*, 79; Carson and Shepard, *Call to Conscience*, 163; Washington, *Testament*, 243; Carson, *King Papers*, 6:418, 506, 508; Carson, *King Papers*, 7:485.

174 Carson, *King Papers*, 6:216, 218–19; Carson, *King Papers*, 7:443; King, "Doubts and Certainties Link," 3.

175 Washington, *Testament*, 199; Carson, *King Papers*, 4:189; Carson, *King Papers*, 6:138, 465.

176 At Easter, King was apt to speak of truth in terms of "the ultimate triumph of good." At other times, he considered truth in relationship to justice, noting that "*justice* will triumph in the universe over all of the forces on injustice." See Washington, *Testament*, 52–53, 230; Carson, *King Papers*, 6:532; Carson, *King Papers*, 7:443; and Carson, *King Papers*, 3:327.

177 Carson, *King Papers*, 6:289.

178 Carson, *King Papers*, 6:532; King, *Strength to Love*, 110–11.

179 King, *Strength to Love*, 76–85; Carson, *King Papers*, 4:155.

180 Carson, *King Papers*, 5:422, 505, 510–11; Washington, *Testament*, 103, 149.

181 Carson, *King Papers*, 3:447; King, *Stride toward Freedom*, 171. Also see Carson, *King Papers*, 5:173; and Carson, *King Papers*, 7:485.

182 King, "Doubts and Certainties Link," 3.

183 Washington, *Testament*, 141; Carson, *King Papers*, 5:413.

184 Washington, *Testament*, 141; King, *Stride toward Freedom*, 90.

185 For a discussion that is quite enlightening around this claim as it relates to King, see James H. Cone, *The Cross and the Lynching Tree* (Maryknoll, NY: Orbis, 2011), 65–92.

186 Washington, *Testament*, 9, 257; King, *Trumpet of Conscience*, 75. For the many references King made to Easter as symbolic of the triumph of truth, see Carson, *King Papers*, 5:170, 172; Carson, *King Papers*, 3:344, 459; Carson, *King Papers*, 6:494; King, *Stride toward Freedom*, 171; and Carson, *King Papers*, 7:444–45.

187 Carson, *King Papers*, 7:444–45; Carson, *King Papers*, 6:360, 494.

Chapter 3

1 King referred to these words of Thomas Jefferson as a "ringing truth." See Clayborne Carson, ed., *The Papers of Martin Luther King, Jr.*, vol. 7, *To Save the Soul of America, January 1961–August 1962*, ed. Tenisha Armstrong (Berkeley: University of California Press, 2014), 417; Martin Luther King Jr., *Why We Can't Wait* (New York: New American Library, 1963), 93; James M. Washington, ed., *A Testament of Hope: The Essential Writings and Speeches of Martin Luther King, Jr.* (New York: HarperCollins, 1991), 89–90; Clayborne Carson, ed., *The Papers of Martin Luther King, Jr.*, vol. 6, *Advocate of the Social Gospel, September 1948–March 1963*, ed. Susan Carson et al. (Berkeley: University of California Press, 2007), 327; and Clayborne Carson, ed., *The Autobiography of Martin Luther King, Jr.* (New York: Warner, 1998), 242.

2 Clayborne Carson and Peter Holloran, eds., *A Knock at Midnight: Inspiration from the*

Great Sermons of Reverend Martin Luther King, Jr. (New York: Warner, 1998), 1995–96; Carson, *King Autobiography*, 357–58; Carson, *King Papers*, 7:198–99; Carson, *King Papers*, 6:115, 137–38, 190–92, 225, 335–36, 383, 423–24.

3   Clayborne Carson, ed., *The Papers of Martin Luther King, Jr.*, vol. 1, *Called to Serve, January 1929–June 1951*, ed. Ralph E. Luker and Penny A. Russell (Berkeley: University of California Press, 1992), 109–11; Clayborne Carson and Kris Shepard, eds., *A Call to Conscience: The Landmark Speeches of Dr. Martin Luther King, Jr.* (New York: Warner, 2001), 85; Carson and Holloran, *Knock at Midnight*, 217; Washington, *Testament*, 208; Carson, *King Papers*, 6:475.

4   Martin Luther King Jr., *Where Do We Go from Here: Chaos or Community?* (Boston: Beacon, 1968; originally published in 1967), 68, 79–81, 83–85; Washington, *Testament*, 208, 282; Martin Luther King Jr., *Stride toward Freedom: The Montgomery Story* (New York: Harper & Row, 1958), 190; Carson and Holloran, *Knock at Midnight*, 87; Martin Luther King Jr., *Strength to Love* (Philadelphia: Fortress, 1981; originally published in 1963), 49.

5   William E. B. Du Bois, *The Souls of Black Folk*, unabridged ed. (New York: Dover, 2016; originally published in 1903), 2–3.

6   John Freeman, "Interview with Martin Luther King, Jr.," unpublished and typed version, *Face to Face*, BBC Television, London, England (October 29, 1961), Martin Luther King Jr. Papers, Library and Archives of the Martin Luther King Jr. Center for Nonviolent Social Change (KCLA), Atlanta, GA, 3; Lewis V. Baldwin, *There Is a Balm in Gilead: The Cultural Roots of Martin Luther King, Jr.* (Minneapolis: Fortress, 1991), 22–23.

7   Freeman, "Interview with King," 2–5; King, *Stride toward Freedom*, 18–21, 90; Carson, *King Papers*, 1:110, 362.

8   Baldwin, *Balm in Gilead*, 24–25; King, *Stride toward Freedom*, 90; Carson, *King Papers*, 1:362; Carson, *King Papers*, 7:164.

9   Freeman, "Interview with King," 1–3; King, *Stride toward Freedom*, 19–20; Carson, *King Papers*, 1:362; Carson, *King Autobiography*, 4–5; Christine King Farris, *Through It All: Reflections on My Life, My Family, and My Faith* (New York: Atria, 2009), 16–18; Martin Luther King Sr. with Clayton Riley, *Daddy King: An Autobiography* (New York: William Morrow, 1980), 82, 108–9.

10 From the time he entered the first grade at Yonge Street Elementary School in Atlanta, King was surrounded by teachers and principals who were deeply interested in Black history and culture. A case in point was Marie Hill, King's elementary school principal, who studied African influences on Black life and culture. At David T. Howard Elementary and Junior High School in Atlanta, which King also attended, there was for years a "Negro History Study Club." King was exposed to much of the same during his years at Atlanta University Laboratory High School and Booker T. Washington High School in that city, where Negro History Week programs were commonly held. See "Miss Marie Hill Writes Original Play, Is Featured at English Ave. PTA Meet," *Atlanta Daily World*, May 23, 1954, 5; "News of David T. Howard Elementary-Junior High School," *Atlanta Daily World*, December 6, 1936, 7; "World Editor Lauds DuBois in Message," *Atlanta Daily World*, February 11, 1938, 1; "Jr. NAACP to Meet at Lab High," *Atlanta Daily World*, February 28, 1941, 1; and S. Grace Bradley, "Negro History Week Holds Interest," *Atlanta Daily World*, February 14, 1943, 6.

11 King with Riley, *Daddy King*, 82; Carson, *King Autobiography*, 15–16; King, *Stride toward Freedom*, 35–36; Lewis V. Baldwin, *The Voice of Conscience: The Church in the Mind of Martin Luther King, Jr.* (New York: Oxford University Press, 2010), 132–34.

12 Carson, *King Papers*, 1:109–11; Baldwin, *Balm in Gilead*, 25.

13 Carson, *King Autobiography*, 13; Carson, *King Papers*, 1:109–11; Lewis V. Baldwin, *Behind the Public Veil: The Humanness of Martin Luther King, Jr.* (Minneapolis: Fortress, 2016), 98–99.

14 Carson, *King Papers*, 6:94–95; Carson, *King Autobiography*, 358; Washington, *Testament*, 47.

15 Carson, *King Papers*, 6:305, 383; Clayborne Carson, ed., *The Papers of Martin Luther King, Jr.*, vol. 4, *Symbol of the Movement, January 1957–December 1958*, ed. Susan Carson et al. (Berkeley: University of California Press, 2000), 4:318; Carson and Holloran, *Knock at Midnight*, 45.

16 King, *Strength to Love*, 29; Carson, *King Papers*, 6:330–32, 551.

17 Carson, *King Papers*, 6:95.

18 Clayborne Carson, ed., *The Papers of Martin Luther King, Jr.*, vol. 2, *Rediscovering Precious Values, July 1951–November 1955*, ed. Stewart Burns et al. (Berkeley: University of

California Press, 1994): 2:180, 190; King, *Strength to Love*, 147–49; Carson, *King Papers*, 6:175, 549; Carson, *King Papers*, 7:198; Martin Luther King Jr., *The Measure of a Man* (Philadelphia: Fortress, 1988; originally published in 1959), 9–31; John J. Ansbro, *Martin Luther King, Jr.: Nonviolent Strategies and Tactics for Social Change* (Lanham, MD: Madison, 2000; originally published in 1982), 69.

19 King, *Strength to Love*, 9.

20 Carson and Holloran, *Knock at Midnight*, 45–46; Carson, *King Papers*, 4:318; Carson, *King Papers*, 6:95–96, 115, 335, 383–84, 423, 487.

21 Carson, *King Papers*, 6:384; Carson, *King Autobiography*, 358; King, *Where Do We Go*, 78; Carson and Holloran, *Knock at Midnight*, 196; Carson, *King Papers*, 4:318.

22 Carson, *King Papers*, 7:198; Carson, *King Papers*, 6:115, 335, 384, 386; Carson, *King Autobiography*, 357.

23 King, *Strength to Love*, 149; Ansbro, *Martin Luther King*, 92, 102.

24 Carson, *King Papers*, 7:198–99; Carson, *King Papers*, 6:190, 372, 383; King, *Measure of a Man*, 10; Carson, *King Papers*, 4:342; Baldwin, *Behind the Public Veil*, 98–99. Interestingly, King spoke to this dualism in the self in sermons and prayers. In one sermon, he declared that the Prodigal Son was not "his real self" or "whole self" when he abandoned the love and security of his own home environment and ventured into some foreign, unknown country. See Martin Luther King Jr., "The Prodigal Son," sermon, unpublished and typed version, Ebenezer Baptist Church, Atlanta, GA (September 4, 1966), King Papers, KCLA, 4; Carson, *King Papers*, 6:190; and Baldwin, *Behind the Public Veil*, 98–99n132.

25 Carson, *King Papers*, 6:266, 329, 494.

26 Carson, *King Papers*, 6:190.

27 Carson, *King Papers*, 6:320, 329.

28 Clayborne Carson, ed., *The Papers of Martin Luther King, Jr.*, vol. 5, *Threshold of a New Decade, January 1959–December 1960*, ed. Tenisha Armstrong et al. (Berkeley: University of California Press, 2005), 420; Carson, *King Papers*, 6:190, 253; King, *Strength to Love*, 148; Carson, *King Papers*, 7:453.

29 Clayborne Carson, ed., *The Papers of Martin Luther King, Jr.*, vol. 3, *Birth of a New Age, December 1955–December 1956*, ed. Stewart Burns et al. (Berkeley: University of California Press, 1997), 325; King, *Strength to Love*, 38; Carson, *King Papers*, 6:272; Carson, *King Papers*, 7:453.

30 Carson, *King Papers*, 6:382.

31 King, *Strength to Love*, 148; Carson, *King Papers*, 7:453; Carson, *King Papers*, 6:138, 335, 384.

32 King, *Strength to Love*, 22, 42, 51, 58; Carson, *King Papers*, 6:88, 200, 384; Carson, *King Papers*, 5:412; Carson and Holloran, *Knock at Midnight*, 13, 68.

33 Carson and Holloran, *Knock at Midnight*, 175; Carson, *King Papers*, 5:388; King, *Stride toward Freedom*, 116–17, 120, 122, 124–26.

34 Carson, *King Papers*, 6:578.

35 Washington, *Testament*, 251; Carson, *King Papers*, 6:465.

36 King, *Strength to Love*, 76.

37 Carson and Holloran, *Knock at Midnight*, 13; Carson, *King Papers*, 2:252.

38 King, *Where Do We Go*, 96.

39 Carson, *King Papers*, 6:171, 487; King, *Strength to Love*, 37.

40 Carson, *King Papers*, 4:407; Carson, *King Papers*, 5:502; Carson, *King Papers*, 6:132, 145; Washington, *Testament*, 102, 109, 132, 145, 356, 493; King, *Where Do We Go*, 63, 70.

41 Carson, *King Papers*, 4:407; Carson, *King Papers*, 5:264, 283, 325–26; King, *Where Do We Go*, 152–53; Carson, *King Papers*, 6:450; Washington, *Testament*, 128, 299, 310, 321, 373, 608.

42 King said in an interview in 1962, "But in all seriousness I don't think I have a split personality." At other times, he admitted that "we all observe within ourselves something of what psychiatrists and psychologists call schizophrenia or split personality." See Carson, *King Papers*, 7:540; Carson, *King Papers*, 6:190–91; Rufus Burrow Jr., *God and Human Dignity: The Personalism, Theology, and Ethics of Martin Luther King, Jr.* (Notre Dame, IN: University of Notre Dame Press, 2006), 8–10; David Levering Lewis, "Failing to Know Martin Luther King, Jr.," *Journal of American History* 78, no. 1 (June 1991): 81–85; Theodore Pappas, *Plagiarism and the Culture War: The Writings of Martin Luther King, Jr., and Other Prominent Americans* (Tampa, FL: Hallberg, 1998), 65–83, 149–86; Clayborne Carson, "Documenting Martin Luther King, Jr.'s Importance—and His Flaws," *Chronicle of Higher Education*, February 24, 1993, B4; and Peter Waldman, "To Their Dismay, Scholars of Martin Luther King Find Troubling Citation Pattern in Academic Papers," *Wall Street Journal*, November 9, 1990, 1.

43 Burrow, *God and Human Dignity*, 10–12; Cheryl A. Kirk-Duggan, "Drum Major for Justice or Dilettante of Dishonesty: Martin Luther King, Jr., Moral Capital, and Hypocrisy of Embodied Messianic Myths," in *The Domestication of Martin Luther King, Jr.: Clarence B. Jones, Right-Wing Conservatism, and the Manipulation of the King Legacy*, ed. Lewis V. Baldwin and Rufus Burrow Jr. (Eugene, OR: Cascade, 2013), 100–119; Lewis V. Baldwin and Amiri YaSin Al-Hadid, *Between Cross and Crescent: Christian and Muslim Perspectives on Malcolm and Martin* (Gainesville: University Press of Florida, 2002), 178.

44 Washington, *Testament*, 105, 160, 206; King, *Strength to Love*, 75, 117; Carson, *King Autobiography*, 358; Carson, *King Papers*, 4:336, 348, 392–94, 401–2, 417–18, 472; King, *Stride toward Freedom*, 133–34; Carson, *King Papers*, 6:571; Baldwin and Al-Hadid, *Between Cross and Crescent*, 178.

45 Tavis Smiley, *Death of a King: The Real Story of Dr. Martin Luther King, Jr.'s Final Year* (New York: Little, Brown, 2014), 155–56.

46 Rufus Burrow Jr. is right in saying that in King's case, the keen observer has "to see a whole life rather than a single moment of either brilliance or defect. Faithfulness to God is a long-term project! I see King as a faithful person." Here Burrow is quoting David Bundy, "a white theological librarian and early church historian" who taught at Christian Theological Seminary in Indianapolis, IN. See Burrow, *God and Human Dignity*, 9–10.

47 Carson, *King Papers*, 7:166; Carson, *King Autobiography*, 46.

48 Carson and Holloran, *Knock at Midnight*, 198–99; Carson, *King Autobiography*, 358–59; Carson, *King Papers*, 7:163.

49 Frye Gaillard, foreword to *Behind the Public Veil*, by Baldwin, xi, xiii.

50 Carson, *King Papers*, 6:225, 255, 307; Carson and Holloran, *Knock at Midnight*, 123–24.

51 Carson and Holloran, *Knock at Midnight*, 123; Carson, *King Papers*, 6:315; King, *Where Do We Go*, 123.

52 Martin Luther King Jr., "The Sword That Heals," *Critic*, June–July 1964, 14; Baldwin, *Balm in Gilead*, 236–37; Carson, *King Papers*, 6:334; Carson, *King Papers*, 7:186–87.

53 Carson, *King Papers*, 7:187.

54 Ansbro, *Martin Luther King*, 155.

55 Carson, *King Papers*, 6:484–85.

56 Ansbro, *Martin Luther King*, 113.

57 Ansbro, *Martin Luther King*, 113, 155–56. King also reminded his readers that "Niebuhr makes it clear that a perfect democracy is just as impossible to reach as either a perfect society or a perfect individual." See Carson, *King Papers*, 2:148.

58 Carson, *King Papers*, 6:210.

59 King, *Where Do We Go*, 83.

60 Carson, *King Papers*, 6:591.

61 Here King was speaking of us as humans standing outside of ourselves while passing judgment on ourselves. As far as King was concerned, this constitutes the height of maturity. Anything short of this was for him escapist mysticism. See Carson, *King Papers*, 6:96, 98; Carson, *King Papers*, 7:164, 166; Carson, *King Papers*, 4:317–18; King, *Where Do We Go*, 83; and Carson, *King Papers*, 5:152–53.

62 Mohandas K. Gandhi, *An Autobiography: The Story of My Experiments with Truth*, trans. Mahadev Desai (Boston: Beacon, 1993; originally published in 1927), 350; Carson, *King Papers*, 5:152–53.

63 Carson, *King Papers*, 6:96–97.

64 Carson and Holloran, *Knock at Midnight*, 6; Carson, *King Papers*, 2:165, 249; King, *Strength to Love*, 45; Carson, *King Papers*, 6:493.

65 Carson, *King Papers*, 2:165, 249, 252; Carson, *King Papers*, 6:493; Carson and Holloran, *Knock at Midnight*, 6–7.

66 King, *Stride toward Freedom*, 33–34. While stressing the significance of education, King also made it clear that this is not "to say that one must be a philosopher or a possessor of extensive academic training before he can achieve the good life." At another point, he conceded that "knowledge and discipline are as indispensable as courage and self-sacrifice." See Carson, *King Papers*, 6:493; and Carson, *King Papers*, 7:214.

67 King, *Strength to Love*, 44–45; Carson, *King Papers*, 6:406.

68 Carson, *King Papers*, 2:249; King, *Strength to Love*, 68–69; Carson and Holloran, *Knock at Midnight*, 6–7.

69 Martin Luther King Jr., "Nobel Lecture," unpublished and typed version, Aula of the University, Oslo, Norway (December 11, 1964), King Papers, KCLA, 1; Carson, *King Papers*, 6:207, 209, 232, 246, 260, 266, 474, 484; King, *Strength to Love*, 111; Carson, *King Papers*, 5:170. Beverly Lanzetta provides rich and hard insights into the ways in which head and heart came together in Gandhi's experiments with and understanding of truth. My reading of Lanzetta

impacted my discussion at this point. See Beverly Lanzetta, *The Monk Within: Embracing a Sacred Way of Life* (Sebastopol, CA: Blue Sapphire, 2018), 154, 255–56, 258–59, 273–74, 310–12.

70 Carson, *King Papers*, 6:191. Also see Lewis V. Baldwin and Victor Anderson, eds., *Revives My Soul Again: The Spirituality of Martin Luther King, Jr.* (Minneapolis: Fortress, 2018), 19–295.

71 King, "Prodigal Son," 4; Baldwin, *Behind the Public Veil*, 98–99; Carson, *King Papers*, 6:190, 337–38; Carson, *King Papers*, 4:521.

72 Carson, *King Papers*, 6:189–90; Washington, *Testament*, 314.

73 King criticized the Protestant Reformation, which "so concentrated on the wickedness of man that it overlooked the capacity for goodness." See Carson, *King Papers*, 6:178–79, 190, 336, 549; and Carson, *King Papers*, 4:306.

74 This is how former president Barack Obama views King's challenge to humanity. Obama is quoted in Vicki L. Crawford and Lewis V. Baldwin, eds., *Reclaiming the Great World House: The Global Vision of Martin Luther King, Jr.* (Athens: University of Georgia Press, 2019), 305. Also see Carson, *King Papers*, 6:192.

75 Nietzsche's exact words were "I walk amongst men as the fragments of the future; that future which I contemplate." Of course, the future he contemplated was radically different from that envisioned by King. And yet, King had no problem quoting Nietzsche to make his point. See Carson, *King Papers*, 6:115n11, 192, 255.

76 King, *Measure of a Man*, 33–56; Carson, *King Papers*, 6:150–56; Carson and Holloran, *Knock at Midnight*, 65–78; Carson, *King Papers*, 7:212.

77 King, *Measure of a Man*, 36–38, 41; Carson, *King Papers*, 6:152–53, 192, 281; Carson, *King Papers*, 4:375.

78 King asserted that man "must realize that the most meaningful life is a life whose center is a fixed point outside of his own being." See Carson, *King Papers*, 7:452.

79 King brought the philosopher Immanuel Kant into his analysis of character and the highest good. He wrote, "Kant believes that if a rational being is honest, he will admit as a self-evident proposition that the only absolutely good thing conceivable in the world is 'a good will,' or as we should say, 'good character.' Even such virtues as courage and perseverance can be used for evil purposes, so they cannot be regarded as intrinsically good. But a good will is good in itself, in that it acts solely on the basis of duty regardless of consequences." See Carson, *King Papers*, 7:214, 303; and Carson, *King Papers*, 6:87.

80 Carson, *King Papers*, 7:452.

81 Carson, *King Papers*, 6:484–85; Carson, *King Papers*, 7:170–71.

82 King referred to Jesus's willingness "to die on Calvary" as "history's most magnificent expression of obedience to the unenforceable." See Carson, *King Papers*, 5:170–71; King, *Strength to Love*, 35, 45; Carson, *King Papers*, 7:303; and Carson, *King Papers*, 6:484, 493.

83 King, *Measure of a Man*, 41–42.

84 King, *Measure of a Man*, 42–44; King, *Strength to Love*, 26–35; King, *Where Do We Go*, 180; Carson, *King Papers*, 6:239–40.

85 King, *Where Do We Go*, 180.

86 Here again, King made it clear that "an inner spiritual transformation" was absolutely necessary in overcoming the evil self but also in fighting "vigorously the evils of the world in a humble and loving spirit." See King, *Measure of a Man*, 50–51, 54–56; Carson, *King Papers*, 6:255, 474; and King, *Strength to Love*, 23.

87 Referring in part to good and evil, King argued that "this element of conflict presents itself to all areas of life." He noted on another occasion that "in a sense, the whole of life is the history of a struggle between good and evil. There seems to be a tension at the very core of the universe." See Carson, *King Papers*, 6:95, 506; and Carson, *King Papers*, 3:259.

88 Carson and Holloran, *Knock at Midnight*, 46.

89 Carson, *King Papers*, 7:198.

90 Carson, *King Papers*, 6:320.

91 Ansbro, *Martin Luther King*, 161.

92 Apparently, Douglass's views on the Constitution changed over time. He ultimately concluded that this document, if "'construed in the light of well-established rules of legal interpretation, might be made consistent in its details with the noble purposes in its preamble,' and that in the future he would insist that the Constitution 'be wielded in behalf of emancipation.'" See Philip S. Foner, ed., *The Life and Writings of Frederick Douglass*, vol. 2, *Pre–Civil War Decade: 1850–1860* (New York: International Publishers, 1975), 50–54.

93 Foner, *Frederick Douglass*, 2:52.

94 Walter E. Fluker, *They Looked for a City: A Comparative Analysis of the Ideal of Community*

in the *Thought of Howard Thurman and Martin Luther King, Jr.* (Lanham, MD: University Press of America, 1989), 87; Baldwin, *Behind the Public Veil*, 31–32; Carson, *King Papers*, 1:109–11; Carson, *King Autobiography*, 9–10. Jonathan Eig is currently writing a biography of King in which he challenges many of the claims regarding "The Negro and the Constitution." He informed me that King plagiarized much of the speech and that, despite reports to the contrary, he was not the winner of the oratorical contest. More specifics surrounding Eig's findings will appear in his forthcoming King biography. Be that as it may, Eig's findings should not obscure the fact that young King used the content of the speech because it was consistent with his own emerging perspective on the Black experience and America's founding documents. It has been argued also that the speech "reflected King's early political views." See Lewis V. Baldwin, notes from a telephone conversation with Jonathan Eig, handwritten version, November 17, 2020; Lewis V. Baldwin et al., *The Legacy of Martin Luther King, Jr.: The Boundaries of Law, Politics, and Religion* (Notre Dame, IN: University of Notre Dame Press, 2002), 127; "Contest Winner, M. L. King, Jr," *Atlanta Daily World*, April 16, 1944, 2; Martin Luther King Jr., "Segregation Is Not Just a Southern Problem," interview, unpublished and typed version, Chicago, IL (July 28, 1965), King Papers, KCLA, 2; Washington, *Testament*, 342–43; Baldwin, *Balm in Gilead*, 22; and Coleman B. Brown, "Grounds for American Loyalty in a Prophetic Christian Ethic—with Special Attention to Martin Luther King, Jr." (PhD diss., Union Theological Seminary, April 1979), 188, 248, 253–54.

95 Carson, *King Papers*, 1:109–10.

96 Carson, *King Papers*, 1:110.

97 Washington, *Testament*, 342–43; Carson, *King Autobiography*, 9–10; Baldwin, *Balm in Gilead*, 22.

98 Carson, *King Papers*, 1:121–24.

99 In another draft of the Declaration of Independence, Jefferson wrote, "We hold these truths to be sacred and undeniable, that all men are created equal and independent, that from that equal creation they derive rights inherent and inalienable, among which are the preservation of life, and liberty, and the pursuit of happiness." See Jill Lepore, *These Truths: A History of the United States* (New York: W. W. Norton, 2018), xiv. Although Lepore makes numerous references to King in her otherwise brilliant history of the United States, she could have done much more with King's perspective on Thomas Jefferson's idea of "self-evident" truths as stated in the Declaration of Independence. This is not too much to ask, since King was such a pivotal figure in twentieth-century American history. For King's repeated references to Jefferson's words, see Carson and Shepard, *Call to Conscience*, 85; Carson, *King Autobiography*, 226; King, *Strength to Love*, 24; Carson and Holloran, *Knock at Midnight*, 86, 91–93, 100, 217; Washington, *Testament*, 208, 377; Carson, *King Papers*, 6:475; and Carson, *King Papers*, 5:508.

100 Carson, *King Autobiography*, 17, 24; King, *Stride toward Freedom*, 92; Carson, *King Papers*, 7:299–300, 302; Baldwin et al., *Legacy of King*, 126.

101 Reinhold Niebuhr, *Moral Man and Immoral Society: A Study in Ethics and Politics* (New York: Charles Scribner's Sons, 1960; originally published in 1932), 95. Also see Carson, *King Papers*, 6:335.

102 Niebuhr, *Moral Man*, xi–xii; Ansbro, *Martin Luther King*, 152; Carson, *King Papers*, 2:271.

103 King, *Stride toward Freedom*, 190–91; King, *Strength to Love*, 49; King, *Where Do We Go*, 68, 80; Carson and Holloran, *Knock at Midnight*, 45–46; Carson, *King Papers*, 4:318; Carson, *King Papers*, 5:508; Carson, *King Papers*, 6:305, 335, 383–84, 423; Carson, *King Papers*, 7:113–14; Washington, *Testament*, 208–9.

104 King, *Where Do We Go*, 75–78; Baldwin et al., *Legacy of King*, 128.

105 King, *Why We Can't Wait*, 121; King, *Where Do We Go*, 79–80, 84–85, 102; Martin Luther King Jr., "The Negro Speaks—the Negro Is the Most Glaring Evidence of White America's Hypocrisy," *St. Louis Post Dispatch*, August 25, 1963, 1, 3.

106 King, *Where Do We Go*, 78–79.

107 Much of this idea comes from Cornel West, *Prophesy Deliverance! An Afro-American Revolutionary Christianity* (Philadelphia: Westminster, 1982), 30.

108 King, *Where Do We Go*, 79–80; Baldwin, *Balm in Gilead*, 42. For another side of King's perspective on America as a nation of immigrants, see Washington, *Testament*, 181.

109 King, *Where Do We Go*, 75; Carson, *King Papers*, 6:491; Carson, *King Papers*, 7:114, 185, 482, 497; King, *Why We Can't Wait*, 25, 47; King, *Stride toward Freedom*, 199; Carson, *King Autobiography*, 60.

110 King, *Where Do We Go*, 80, 88; King, *Why We Can't Wait*, 120.

111 Washington, *Testament*, 477; King, *Where Do We Go*, 84–85; Carson, *King Papers*, 7:228.

112 Carson, *King Papers*, 7:228, 474–86; Martin Luther King Jr., "America's Chief Moral Dilemma," address, unpublished and typed version, United Church of Christ—General Synod, Palmer House, Chicago, IL (July 6, 1965), King Papers, KCLA, 1–20.

113 King, *Where Do We Go*, 84–85; Washington, *Testament*, 161, 209, 477; Carson, *King Papers*, 6:130–33; King, "America's Chief Moral Dilemma," 2–5, 9–11, 13–14, 16–20.

114 Carson, *King Papers*, 7:271; Washington, *Testament*, 161.

115 King, *Strength to Love*, 80; Carson, *King Papers*, 6:509; Washington, *Testament*, 217, 219; Carson, *King Autobiography*, 223–24, 226.

116 King, *Where Do We Go*, 80–81.

117 Washington, *Testament*, 320; Baldwin et al., *Legacy of King*, 148.

118 Martin Luther King Jr. to Mr. Earl Kennedy, unpublished and typed version (October 30, 1956), King Papers, KCLA, 1; Carson, *King Papers*, 3:384, 409, 460, 476; Carson, *King Papers*, 4:235.

119 King, *Where Do We Go*, 10–11.

120 King, *Where Do We Go*, 26.

121 Carson and Holloran, *Knock at Midnight*, 217.

122 King, *Where Do We Go*, 183; Martin Luther King Jr., "Doubts and Certainties Link," interview, unpublished, transcribed, and typed version, London, England (Winter 1968), King Papers, KCLA, 8.

123 Martin Luther King Jr., "Untitled Column on European Tour," article, unpublished and typed version (September 17, 1964), King Papers, KCLA, 1. This piece was apparently written for the *New York Amsterdam News*, but there is some uncertainty about whether it appeared in that newspaper in its original or any other form. We do know that King gave a speech on his European tour almost two years later and that a piece on the topic also appeared in the *SCLC Newsletter*. See Martin Luther King Jr., "European Tour," speech, unpublished and typed version (March 1966), King Papers, KCLA, 1–10; and "King's Europe Tour Gigantic Success," *SCLC Newsletter* 3, no. 2 (March–April 1966): 1, 6.

124 Carson, *King Papers*, 6:487; Carson and Holloran, *Knock at Midnight*, 217.

125 Carson, *King Papers*, 1:124; King, *Where Do We Go*, 68, 75–79; King, *Stride toward Freedom*, 190–91; King, *Why We Can't Wait*, 126, 132.

126 This was analogous to King's determination to define the civil rights struggle not in terms of Black versus white, which is what it was at least on some levels, but from the standpoint of justice versus injustice. As early as the Montgomery struggle in the mid-1950s, King declared, "The tension in this city is not between white people and Negro people. The tension is at bottom between justice and injustice, between the forces of light and the forces of darkness." King repeatedly made this point throughout his public life. See Washington, *Testament*, 8; and Carson, *King Papers*, 7:121, 212.

127 King, *Where Do We Go*, 173–76; King, "Doubts and Certainties Link," 1–2. King was saying here not that whites are innately unique in this regard but rather that they tended to think and act out of a sense of their stranglehold on world power. After all, he, as noted earlier, saw truth and untruth as part of the tension at the very center of the universe. See Carson, *King Autobiography*, 357–58.

128 Carson, *King Papers*, 5:145, 224–25, 248, 268–69, 288; Carson, *King Papers*, 6:162; King, *Where Do We Go*, 186; Baldwin and Anderson, *Revives My Soul Again*, 6–7.

129 Washington, *Testament*, 251, 358; Carson and Holloran, *Knock at Midnight*, 146–47; Carson and Shepard, *Call to Conscience*, 130, 144, 214; Baldwin and Anderson, *Revives My Soul Again*, 74–75; Carson, *King Papers*, 6:332; Carson, *King Papers*, 7:237, 529; Carson, *King Papers*, 5:370, 546.

130 Martin Luther King Jr., *The Trumpet of Conscience* (San Francisco: Harper & Row, 1968; originally published in 1967), 44; Baldwin and Anderson, *Revives My Soul Again*, 74–75; King, *Strength to Love*, 75.

131 Carson, *King Papers*, 3:305; Carson, *King Papers*, 6:416; Carson, *King Papers*, 7:114, 122.

132 Washington, *Testament*, 219; King, *Where Do We Go*, 5–10, 75; Carson, *King Papers*, 7:229–30, 484, 496, 500.

133 King, *Stride toward Freedom*, 31–32; King, *Where Do We Go*, 75, 80, 103, 105; Carson, *King Papers*, 5:190–91, 335; Carson, *King Papers*, 7:482.

134 King laid bare the facts of southern life, at times in gruesome detail, in his writings, speeches, and sermons. See Martin Luther King Jr., "The Truth about Atlanta: The Danger of a Little Progress," *SCLC Newsletter*, February 1964, 7–8; Martin Luther King Jr., "Who Speaks for the South," *Liberation* 2

(March 1958): 13–14; and Martin Luther King Jr., "The Burning Truth in the South," *Progressive* 24 (May 1960): 8–10.

135 King, *Stride toward Freedom*, 200; Carson and Shepard, *Call to Conscience*, 50; Carson, *King Papers*, 7:521, 524.

136 King, *Strength to Love*, 43.

137 King, *Strength to Love*, 29; Washington, *Testament*, 211; Martin Luther King Jr., "The Mission to the Social Frontiers," speech, unpublished and typed version (n.d.), King Papers, KCLA, 2; Carson, *King Papers*, 3:300, 323; Carson, *King Papers*, 6:96.

138 King, *Where Do We Go*, 67.

139 King, *Where Do We Go*, 67, 70–71, 75–77, 152–53; King, *Why We Can't Wait*, 91; King, *Strength to Love*, 42–43; Washington, *Testament*, 140, 211, 228; Carson, *King Papers*, 5:273; Carson, *King Papers*, 6:323, 491.

140 King was most concerned about how the system "segregated southern minds from honest thinking." See Carson, *King Papers*, 7:461; Washington, *Testament*, 228.

141 King, *Where Do We Go*, 11, 75; King, *Strength to Love*, 29, 42.

142 Carson, *King Papers*, 3:73; Carson, *King Papers*, 7:472.

143 King, *Strength to Love*, 42; King, *Where Do We Go*, 75.

144 King, *Why We Can't Wait*, 144.

145 African American slaves quoted in Lawrence W. Levine, *Black Culture and Black Consciousness: Afro-American Folk Thought from Slavery to Freedom* (New York: Oxford University Press, 1977), 123.

146 Carson, *King Papers*, 1:359; Farris, *Through It All*, 16–18; King, *Stride toward Freedom*, 79, 82; Baldwin, *Behind the Public Veil*, 297–98; Martin Luther King Jr., "True Dignity," essay, unpublished and typed version (n.d.), King Papers, KCLA, 1–10; King, *Why We Can't Wait*, 28–29; King, *Where Do We Go*, 16.

147 See Levine, *Black Consciousness*, 102–32; William J. Faulkner, *The Days When the Animals Talked: Black American Folktales and How They Came to Be* (Chicago: Follett, 1977), 75–177; and Sterling Stuckey, *Slave Culture: Nationalist Theory and the Foundations of Black America* (New York: Oxford University Press, 1987), 17–19, 169, 256. There is every reason to believe that King read the Black philosopher of religion Howard Thurman's chapter on "Deception" in Howard Thurman, *Jesus and the Disinherited* (Nashville: Abingdon, 1949), 58–73. Also see Fluker, *Looked for a City*, 111–12, 197–99n2, 238n19.

148 King heard Faulkner "speak on several occasions." Also, Faulkner knew King's paternal grandfather, the Reverend Adam D. Williams, pastor of Atlanta's Ebenezer Baptist Church (1894–1931) and social activist. In any case, Brer Rabbit emerges as a master of deception in Faulkner's collection of tales. See Carson, *King Papers*, 3:167–68, 292; and Faulkner, *When the Animals Talked*, 75–177.

149 Levine, *Black Consciousness*, 300; Baldwin, *Behind the Public Veil*, 12, 261, 298, 305.

150 King, "True Dignity," 1.

151 King, "True Dignity," 1–2.

152 Lawrence Levine brilliantly makes a similar point in relation to the conduct of slaves, who desperately sought not only to survive but to maintain some semblance of human dignity and worth under the power of the plantation system. He holds that slaves rationalized "their need to lie, cheat, and steal without holding these actions up as models to be followed in all instances, without creating, that is, a counter-morality." See Levine, *Black Consciousness*, 123; Carson, *King Papers*, 7:144; and Carson, *King Papers*, 4:126, 542.

153 King, *Trumpet of Conscience*, 5; Carson, *King Papers*, 7:404; Washington, *Testament*, 327; King, *Why We Can't Wait*, 28–29.

154 Martin Luther King Jr., "The Dilemma of the Negro," *New York Amsterdam News*, January 29, 1966, 14.

155 Carson, *King Papers*, 6:221–22; King, *Stride toward Freedom*, 36.

156 Carson, *King Papers*, 6:212.

157 Washington, *Testament*, 91; Carson, *King Papers*, 4:368.

158 King, *Where Do We Go*, 80–81.

159 Baldwin et al., *Legacy of King*, 126, 128; King, *Where Do We Go*, 6.

160 A similar argument might be made concerning the founding fathers and their use of these documents of freedom, but they clearly were not thinking along the same lines as King. They had a different understanding of what constituted freedom, justice, and human community. It is also important to note that the founding fathers lived in a different age and cultural context. See Baldwin et al., *Legacy of King*, 126.

161 Baldwin et al., *Legacy of King*, 126; Washington, *Testament*, 119, 217, 315, 377; King, *Why We Can't Wait*, 94, 128, 131; King, *Where Do We Go*, 70–71; Carson, *King Papers*, 7:113.

162 Sylvester Johnson, review of *The Legacy of Martin Luther King, Jr.: The Boundaries of Law, Politics, and Religion*, by Lewis V. Baldwin

et al., *Journal of Southern Religion*, accessed February 14, 2019, http://jsr.fsu.edu/2003/Reviews/johnson.htm.

163 Baldwin et al., *Legacy of King*, 126.

164 King used both "Judeo-Christian tradition" (or "Judeo-Christian heritage") and "Hebraic-Christian tradition" at times, but "Hebraic-Christian tradition" is the more proper term employed today. See Baldwin et al., *Legacy of King*, 127; Martin Luther King Jr., "The Negro and the American Dream," speech, unpublished and typed version, Meeting of the Charlotte Branch of the NAACP, Charlotte, NC (September 25, 1960), Martin Luther King Jr. Papers, Special Collections, Mugar Memorial Library, Boston University, Boston, MA, 2; Carson, *King Papers*, 7:472, 602; and Carson, *King Papers*, 3:259.

165 Quoted in Michael Eric Dyson, *I May Not Get There with You: The True Martin Luther King, Jr.* (New York: Free Press, 2000), 38–39; and Baldwin et al., *Legacy of King*, 126.

166 Washington, *Testament*, 217; Carson and Shepard, *Call to Conscience*, 82; Baldwin et al., *Legacy of King*, 128–29.

167 King, *Stride toward Freedom*, 190; King, *Strength to Love*, 24; King, *Why We Can't Wait*, 47, 88, 93; King, *Where Do We Go*, 70–71, 76–77; Carson, *King Papers*, 1:109–10; Carson, *King Papers*, 3:286; Carson, *King Papers*, 4:191, 276; Carson, *King Papers*, 5:563; Carson, *King Papers*, 6:327, 472, 475, 509–10; Carson, *King Papers*, 7:163, 417.

168 King, *Where Do We Go*, 70; Baldwin et al., *Legacy of King*, 127.

169 King, "Negro and American Dream," 1; Martin Luther King Jr., "Moral and Religious Imperatives for Brotherhood," speech, unpublished and typed version, Congregation B'nai Jeshurun, New York, NY (September 9, 1963), King Papers, KCLA, 1–3; Baldwin et al., *Legacy of King*, 127; Muriel Knight, "Martin Luther King, Jr. and the American Dream," *Roxbury (Massachusetts) City News*, January 21, 1965, 1.

170 Knight, "King and American Dream," 1; Baldwin et al., *Legacy of King*, 127; Brown, "Grounds for American Loyalty," 248; Martin Luther King Jr., "Racism Is Not Just a Southern Problem," interview, unpublished and typed version, Chicago, IL (July 28,

1965), King Papers, KCLA, 2; Carson, *King Papers*, 7:113.

171 Carson, *King Papers*, 4:407; Martin Luther King Jr., "Statement on the Declaration of Independence, the Constitution, and the Emancipation Proclamation," unpublished and typed version (December 1962), King Papers, KCLA, 1–3; Martin Luther King Jr., "An Address," unpublished and typed version, New York Civil War Centennial Commission, Park Sheraton Hotel, New York, NY (September 12, 1962), King Papers, KCLA, 1, 3, 5–10, 12; Martin Luther King Jr., "Emancipation Proclamation," *New York Amsterdam News*, November 10, 1962, 13; Martin Luther King Jr., "The Luminous Promise," essay, unpublished and typed version (December 1962), King Papers, KCLA, 1–3.

172 Brown, "Grounds for American Loyalty," 289.

173 King, *Where Do We Go*, 77–78, 80–85; Brown, "Grounds for American Loyalty," 109–10; Carson, *King Autobiography*, 359; Washington, *Testament*, 279–80; King, *Strength to Love*, 80–81; Carson, *King Papers*, 1:111; Baldwin et al., *Legacy of King*, 130–31, 161n26–27.

174 King, *Where Do We Go*, 78.

175 Baldwin et al., *Legacy of King*, 131; Martin Luther King Jr., "The South—a Hostile Nation," *New York Amsterdam News*, May 11, 1963, 10, 12.

176 King, *Why We Can't Wait*, 23; Carson, *King Autobiography*, 223–24.

177 King, *Strength to Love*, 81.

178 King, *Strength to Love*, 81; Baldwin et al., *Legacy of King*, 131–32.

179 Carson, *King Autobiography*, 219.

180 Washington, *Testament*, 282; Carson and Shepard, *Call to Conscience*, 213.

181 Carson and Holloran, *Knock at Midnight*, 98; Carson, *King Papers*, 7:111, 122.

182 King, *Why We Can't Wait*, 25; Washington, *Testament*, 377; Baldwin et al., *Legacy of King*, 129.

183 Washington, *Testament*, 217, 219, 377; Carson, *King Papers*, 5:387.

184 Carson, *King Papers*, 7:122; Carson, *King Papers*, 6:197; Carson, *King Papers*, 1:111; King, *Why We Can't Wait*, 93; Washington, *Testament*, 219.

Chapter 4

1 King became quite familiar with the deep sense of loneliness often endured by the leader who proclaims and acts on truth. See Martin Luther King Jr., *Why We Can't Wait* (New York: New American Library, 1963), 72–73.

2 See Rufus Burrow Jr., *Ethical Prophets along the Way: Those Hall of Famers* (Eugene, OR: Cascade, 2020), 159–85; Clayborne Carson and Peter Holloran, eds., *A Knock at Midnight: Inspiration from the Great Sermons of Reverend Martin Luther King, Jr.* (New York: Warner, 1998), 110–11; Lewis V. Baldwin, *There Is a Balm in Gilead: The Cultural Roots of Martin Luther King, Jr.* (Minneapolis: Fortress, 1991), 322–30; Lewis V. Baldwin, *To Make the Wounded Whole: The Cultural Legacy of Martin Luther King, Jr.* (Minneapolis: Fortress, 1992), 52–55; and Peter J. Paris, "The Bible and the Black Churches," in *The Bible and Social Reform*, ed. Ernest R. Sandeen (Philadelphia: Fortress, 1982), 140–44.

3 Martin Luther King Jr., "My Jewish Brother," *New York Amsterdam News*, February 26, 1966, 1, 12; Burrow, *Ethical Prophets*, 159–85; Lewis V. Baldwin, ed., *"In a Single Garment of Destiny": A Global Vision of Justice—Martin Luther King, Jr.* (Boston: Beacon, 2012), 206–8; Martin Luther King Jr., "An Address," unpublished and typed version, Synagogue Council of America, Waldorf Astoria Hotel, New York, NY (December 5, 1965), Martin Luther King Jr. Papers, Library and Archives of the Martin Luther King Jr. Center for Nonviolent Social Change (KCLA), Atlanta, GA, 8–9.

4 Rufus Burrow takes a slightly different position here, noting that "King insisted that the ethical prophet always asks the moral question: Is it right?" According to Burrow, this is the question that King "persistently asked." See Burrow, *Ethical Prophets*, 162–63.

5 Martin Luther King Jr., *Stride toward Freedom: The Montgomery Story* (New York: Harper & Row, 1958), 134–35; Martin Luther King Jr., *Strength to Love* (Philadelphia: Fortress, 1981; originally published in 1963), 113; Clayborne Carson, ed., *The Papers of Martin Luther King, Jr.*, vol. 6, *Advocate of the Social Gospel, September 1948–March 1963*, ed. Susan Carson et al. (Berkeley: University of California Press, 2007), 533–34; Carson and Holloran, *Knock at Midnight*, 160–62.

6 Carson, *King Papers*, 6:88; King, *Strength to Love*, 25; Clayborne Carson, ed., *The Papers of Martin Luther King, Jr.*, vol. 7, *To Save the Soul of America, January 1961–August 1962*, ed. Tenisha Armstrong (Berkeley: University of California Press, 2014), 602–3; Clayborne Carson, ed., *The Papers of Martin Luther King, Jr.*, vol. 5, *Threshold of a New Decade, January 1959–December 1960*, ed. Tenisha Armstrong et al. (Berkeley: University of California Press, 2005), 167, 285; James M. Washington, ed., *A Testament of Hope: The Essential Writings and Speeches of Martin Luther King, Jr.* (New York: HarperCollins, 1991), 481.

7 King, *Stride toward Freedom*, 210; Washington, *Testament*, 481; King, *Strength to Love*, 106; Carson, *King Papers*, 7:602–3; King, *Why We Can't Wait*, 92.

8 Paris, "Bible and Black Churches," 140–44.

9 Martin Luther King Sr., *Daddy King: An Autobiography*, with Clayton Riley (New York: William Morrow, 1980), 82–85, 90; "Noted Atlanta Divine Dies Suddenly: Sudden Death of Reverend A. D. Williams Shocks Entire Nation," *Georgia Baptist*, April 10, 1931, 1; Lizzie Hunnicut, "In Memoriam," *Georgia Baptist*, August 25, 1931, 1–3; *Program for Rev. Adam Daniel Williams' Funeral Service*, March 24, 1931, Christine King Farris Personal Collection, Atlanta, Georgia; Clayborne Carson ed., *The Papers of Martin Luther King, Jr.*, vol. 1, *Called to Serve, January 1929–June 1951*, ed. Ralph E. Luker and Penny A. Russell (Berkeley: University of California Press, 1992), 10–26; *Atlanta Constitution*, March 22, 1931, 16A; Baldwin, *Balm in Gilead*, 95; Lewis V. Baldwin, *The Voice of Conscience: The Church in the Mind of Martin Luther King, Jr.* (New York: Oxford University Press, 2010), 20–21.

10 King Jr. reported that Jennie C. Parks Williams, Adam D. Williams's widow and his maternal grandmother, "spent many evenings telling [them] interesting stories," some of which most certainly included Pastor Williams. See Carson, *King Papers*, 1:102, 359. For beautiful but short poems the King family published in Williams's memory on the first and eighth anniversaries of his death, see "In Memoriam," *Atlanta Daily World*, March 21, 1932, 3; and Carson, *King Papers*, 1:102.

11 Clayborne Carson, ed., *The Autobiography of Martin Luther King, Jr.* (New York: Warner, 1998), 5.

12 John Freeman, "Interview with Martin Luther King, Jr.," unpublished and typed version,

for *Face to Face*, BBC Television, London, England (October 29, 1961), King Papers, KCLA, 1; Carson, *King Autobiography*, 5; King, *Stride toward Freedom*, 20.

13 King, *Stride toward Freedom*, 20.

14 Carson, *King Autobiography*, 4; King, *Stride toward Freedom*, 20.

15 Strangely, even leading King scholars have failed to seriously discuss Adam D. Williams and Martin Luther King Sr. in relation to that prophetic tradition that produced King Jr. It is not excessive to conclude that the prophetic stream of the Black Christian tradition was passed down from Williams to King Sr. and ultimately King Jr. See Paris, "Bible and Black Churches," 140–44; Burrow, *Ethical Prophets*, 159–85; and Baldwin, *Make the Wounded Whole*, 52–55.

16 Carson, *King Papers*, 1:162, 181–95; Burrow, *Ethical Prophets*, 166.

17 Carson, *King Papers*, 1:181–95.

18 Clayborne Carson, ed., *The Papers of Martin Luther King, Jr.*, vol. 2, *Rediscovering Precious Values, July 1951–November 1955*, ed. Stewart Burns et al. (Berkeley: University of California Press, 1994), 165, 167–70.

19 Clayborne Carson and Kris Shepard, eds., *A Call to Conscience: The Landmark Speeches of Dr. Martin Luther King, Jr.* (New York: Warner, 2001), 196; Carson, *King Papers*, 6:182.

20 King, "Address," Synagogue Council of America, 7; Burrow, *Ethical Prophets*, 164; Carson, *King Papers*, 1:182–95; Carson, *King Papers*, 2:169; Carson, *King Papers*, 7:116; Carson, *King Papers*, 5:285.

21 Carson, *King Papers*, 1:182–95; Carson, *King Papers*, 2:165–70; Carson, *King Papers*, 7:116; Carson, *King Papers*, 5:285.

22 Martin Luther King Jr., "Transformed Nonconformist," sermon, unpublished and typed version, Ebenezer Baptist Church, Atlanta, GA (January 16, 1966), King Papers, KCLA, 7, 13; Carson, *King Papers*, 6:327, 475; Clayborne Carson, ed., *The Papers of Martin Luther King, Jr.*, vol. 3, *Birth of a New Age, December 1955–December 1956*, ed. Stewart Burns et al. (Berkeley: University of California Press, 1997), 130; Clayborne Carson, ed., *The Papers of Martin Luther King, Jr.*, vol. 4, *Symbol of the Movement, January 1957–December 1958*, ed. Susan Carson et al. (Berkeley: University of California Press, 2000), 191, 276; King, *Why We Can't Wait*, 88–89.

23 King, *Why We Can't Wait*, 77.

24 Martin Luther King Jr., "A Lecture," unpublished and typed version, Federation

Protestante de France Mutualite, Paris, France (October 24, 1965), King Papers, KCLA, 2; Carson, *King Papers*, 5:167.

25 King, *Where Do We Go from Here: Chaos or Community?* (Boston: Beacon, 1968; originally published in 1967), 92; King, "Address," Synagogue Council of America, 8–9; Burrow, *Ethical Prophets*, 165.

26 See Kenneth L. Smith and Ira G. Zepp Jr., *Search for the Beloved Community: The Thinking of Martin Luther King, Jr.* (Valley Forge, PA: Judson, 1998; originally published in 1974), 34.

27 Smith and Zepp, *Beloved Community*, 31–32.

28 King, "Transformed Nonconformist," 2, 5, 7, 10; Carson, *King Papers*, 6:327, 473, 475; Carson, *King Papers*, 4:191, 276; Washington, *Testament*, 297–98, 300; King, *Why We Can't Wait*, 88–89.

29 Carson, *King Papers*, 1:249; Carson, *King Papers*, 5:146–48; Carson, *King Papers*, 7:156.

30 King's respect for prophets from various religious traditions extended at least as far back as his Crozer years, when he wrote papers on both the Hebrew prophets and other prophetic traditions. He knew then that prophecy and prophetic utterances figured prominently in the cultures of the ancient Near East. In 1966, King called the Buddhist Zen master Thich Nhat Hanh "a holy man," suggesting that he too was in some sense a prophet. Evidently, this expansive understanding of and appreciation for different prophetic traditions was consistent with King's religious and theological liberalism. See Carson, *King Papers*, 1:162–209, 211–25, 249; and Carson, *King Papers*, 7:408, 491. Also see King's statement of endorsement on the back cover of Thich Nhat Hanh, *Fragment Palm Leaves: Journals 1962–1966* (New York: Riverhead, 1999; originally published in 1966).

31 Many of King's closest friends and associates— among them Benjamin E. Mays, John Lewis, and Wyatt Tee Walker—viewed him as a prophet in the tradition of the Hebrew prophets and Jesus but unique to his own times and circumstances. They all described King as a twentieth-century prophet who spoke primarily to human problems in the 1950s and '60s. See Carson and Shepard, *Call to Conscience*, 111, 115; Carson and Holloran, *Knock at Midnight*, 1; *Martin Luther King, Jr., 1929–1968: An Ebony Picture Biography* (Chicago: Johnson, 1968), 4; and Burrow, *Ethical Prophets*, 162.

32 In response to a question raised to him in a Christian ethics class at Southern Baptist

Theological Seminary in Louisville, Kentucky, in April 1961, King declared, "Well I'm an extremist. I believe in the extreme of love, not the extreme of hate. I believe in the extreme of goodwill and not the extreme of ill will. I'm never worried about being an extremist. I think the world is in great need of extremists, and I say that very seriously." King's answer was immediately greeted with laughter before he, apparently in an effort to end that in-the-moment reaction, quickly explained what he meant. The extremist label was often attached to him by white bigots who desired to discredit him and his activities. But King's idea of extremism obviously had a philosophical depth that extended beyond the most common definitions of the word and most certainly the definitions used by his enemies and detractors. See Carson, *King Papers*, 7:202, 527n1.

33 Carson and Holloran, *Knock at Midnight*, 110–11.

34 King, *Stride toward Freedom*, 134–35; King, *Strength to Love*, 113; Carson, *King Papers*, 6:303, 345, 533–34; Carson and Holloran, *Knock at Midnight*, 160–62; Carson, *King Papers*, 7:471, 473, 525.

35 King would have fully agreed with the British novelist George Orwell, who declared that "if liberty means anything at all it means the right to tell people what they do not want to hear." Orwell "insisted on the truth even when the truth was most inconvenient." See George Orwell, "The Freedom of the Press: Orwell's Proposed Preface to *Animal Farm*, 1945," *Times Literary Supplement*, September 15, 1972, 9, https://www.marxists.org/archive/orwell/1945/preface.htm; George Orwell, *Animal Farm: A Fairy Story* (New York: New American Library, 1996), ix.

36 Carson, *King Papers*, 7:156, 163.

37 Carson and Holloran, *Knock at Midnight*, 208.

38 King, *Where Do We Go*, 173.

39 King, *Where Do We Go*, 173; Carson, *King Autobiography*, 331.

40 Martin Luther King Jr., "America's Chief Moral Dilemma," speech, unpublished and typed version, United Church of Christ—General Synod, Palmer House, Chicago, IL (July 6, 1965), King Papers, KCLA, 16–17.

41 King, *Where Do We Go*, 176.

42 King, *Where Do We Go*, 177–79; Martin Luther King Jr., "The Octopus of Poverty," *The Mennonite*, January 5, 1965, 4; Martin Luther King Jr., "Nobel Lecture," unpublished and

typed version, Aula of the University, Oslo, Norway (December 11, 1964), King Papers, KCLA, 16.

43 King, *Strength to Love*, 19, 102–3; King, *Where Do We Go*, 177–79, 181; King, "Octopus of Poverty," 4; Martin Luther King Jr., "En Granslos Kval Pa Operan: Remarks," unpublished and typed version, Stockholm, Sweden (March 31, 1966), King Papers, KCLA, 3; Baldwin, *"Single Garment of Destiny,"* 118, 121.

44 King, *Where Do We Go*, 64, 183; Washington, *Testament*, 233; Martin Luther King Jr., "The Meaning of Hope," sermon, unpublished and typed version, Dexter Avenue Baptist Church, Montgomery, AL (December 10, 1967), King Papers, KCLA, 6; Washington, *Testament*, 232–33.

45 Carson, *King Autobiography*, 337; Carson and Shepard, *Call to Conscience*, 141.

46 Martin Luther King Jr., "Transcript of an Interview with Local Newscasters," unpublished and typed version, KNXT TV, Los Angeles, CA (July 10, 1965), King Papers, KCLA, 2; Martin Luther King Jr., "Transcript of an Interview on *Face the Nation*," unpublished and typed version, CBS Television Network, New York, NY (August 29, 1965), King Papers, KCLA, 3; Lewis V. Baldwin, "The Minister as Preacher, Pastor, and Prophet: The Thinking of Martin Luther King, Jr.," *American Baptist Quarterly* 7, no. 2 (June 1988): 85; Baldwin, *Balm in Gilead*, 322.

47 Carson and Shepard, *Call to Conscience*, 142; King, "Interview with Local Newscasters," 2; King, "*Face the Nation* Interview," 3; Martin Luther King Jr., *The Trumpet of Conscience* (San Francisco: Harper & Row, 1968; originally published in 1967), 22.

48 For a discussion of King's many other reasons for opposing and speaking out against US involvement in the Vietnam War, see Baldwin, *Make the Wounded Whole*, 273–81; John J. Ansbro, *Martin Luther King, Jr.: Nonviolent Strategies and Tactics for Social Change* (Lanham, MD: Madison, 2000; originally published in 1982), 256–62; and Carson and Shepard, *Call to Conscience*, 141–46.

49 Washington, *Testament*, 233, 235–36; Carson and Shepard, *Call to Conscience*, 146–49.

50 King, *Where Do We Go*, 182–83.

51 Washington, *Testament*, 233; Carson and Shepard, *Call to Conscience*, 143.

52 *Dr. Martin Luther King, Jr.: An Amazing Grace* (New York: McGraw Hill Films, 1978), VHS, part 2; Carson, *King Autobiography*,

345; Baldwin, *"Single Garment of Destiny,"* 156.

53   Carson, *King Papers*, 7:340, 569; King, *Why We Can't Wait*, 77.

54   According to family members, King "hated being alone," especially when he was in jail, but he needed time to be with and by himself. Apparently, the problem for King was not so much being alone but loneliness, which he occasionally felt "even in the presence of family, friends, and his closest and most trusted aides." See Freeman, "Interview with King," 9; King, *Daddy King*, 174–75; Coretta Scott King, *My Life with Martin Luther King, Jr.* (New York: Henry Holt, 1993; originally published in 1969), 179; Lewis V. Baldwin, *Behind the Public Veil: The Humanness of Martin Luther King, Jr.* (Minneapolis: Fortress, 2016), 74; and King, *Why We Can't Wait*, 72–73.

55   Carson, *King Autobiography*, 334, 342.

56   Kenneth Smith argues that during this time frame, "King broadened both his vision of the kind of society required to eliminate racism and achieve justice for everyone and his view of the tactics necessary to actualize such a society." More specifically, writes Smith, "it is necessary to understand his broadened social vision in terms of 'democratic socialism' and the tactic of 'mass civil disobedience' he thought would be required to achieve it." See Kenneth L. Smith, "The Radicalization of Martin Luther King, Jr.: The Last Three Years," *Journal of Ecumenical Studies* 26, no. 2 (Spring 1989): 270.

57   *An Amazing Grace*, part 2; Ralph W. McGill to Martin Luther King Jr., unpublished and typed version (May 1, 1967), King Papers, KCLA, 1; Lewis V. Baldwin et al., *The Legacy of Martin Luther King, Jr.: The Boundaries of Law, Politics, and Religion* (Notre Dame, IN: University of Notre Dame Press, 2002), 35–36.

58   Carson, *King Autobiography*, 334; Baldwin, *Make the Wounded Whole*, 278; Ralph McGill, "Says NAACP Follows Best Course in Rejecting Dr. King's Proposal," *Akron Beacon Journal*, April 20, 1967, A6; Ansbro, *Martin Luther King*, 255–56, 264; Richard Lentz, *Symbols, the News Magazines, and Martin Luther King, Jr.* (Baton Rouge: Louisiana State University Press, 1990), 175–82, 197, 202, 207, 225.

59   King called Wilkins's claim "a myth about [his] views," insisting that he had no plans to fuse these two movements. "I challenged the NAACP and other critics of my position to take a forthright stand on the rightness or wrongness of this war," King remarked, "rather than going off creating a nonexistent issue." See Carson, *King Autobiography*, 343.

60   King quoted in James H. Cone, "The Theology of Martin Luther King, Jr.," *Union Seminary Quarterly Review* 40, no. 4 (1986): 34–35.

61   Carson and Shepard, *Call to Conscience*, 145; Carson, *King Papers*, 6:473.

62   King, *Strength to Love*, 9–16, 18, 21, 24–25; Carson, *King Papers*, 6:327–28, 466, 473; Carson, *King Papers*, 4:276; Carson, *King Autobiography*, 331.

63   Carson, *King Autobiography*, 342.

64   King said at another point, "I draw not from Marxism or any other secular philosophy but from the prophets of Israel; from their passion for justice and cry for righteousness. The ethic of Judaism is central to my faith." See Martin Luther King Jr. to Mr. Sam Wyler, unpublished and typed version (July 20, 1967), King Papers, KCLA; Samuel Newman, "Martin Luther King, Jr.," *The Jewish Spectator* 33, no. 6 (1962): 16–17; and Rabbi Marc Schneier, *Shared Dreams: Martin Luther King, Jr. and the Jewish Community* (Woodstock, VT: Jewish Lights, 1999), 32. For similar statements that appear in King's sermons and speeches, see Carson, *King Autobiography*, 342–43; Martin Luther King Jr., "An Address to the Ministers' Leadership Training Program," unpublished and typed version, Miami, FL (February 23, 1968), King Papers, KCLA, 2–5; and King, "Meaning of Hope," 6.

65   On that occasion, King also referred to Rabbi Heschel as "a truly great prophet"— "one of the persons who is relevant for all times, always standing with prophetic insights to guide us through these difficult days." Interestingly enough, Heschel's questions about King on that occasion were also raised at times by Black preachers like Kelly Miller Smith Sr., who reminded King that "the mantle of the prophets rests well upon [his] shoulders." Smith worked closely with King in the SCLC. See Washington, *Testament*, 658–59; Burrow, *Ethical Prophets*, 160–61; Schneier, *Shared Dreams*, 138–41; Carson, *King Papers*, 3:143; and Susannah Heschel, "Theological Affinities of Abraham Joshua Heschel and Martin Luther King, Jr.," *Conservative Judaism* 50, no. 2–3 (1998): 140.

66   Earl E. Shelp and Ronald H. Sunderland, eds., *The Pastor as Prophet* (New York: Pilgrim, 1985), 15, 33; Thomas Hoyt Jr., "The

Biblical Tradition of the Poor and Martin Luther King, Jr.," *Journal of the Interdenominational Theological Center* 4, no. 2 (Spring 1977): 12–32; Joseph M. Thompson, "Martin Luther King, Jr. and Christian Witness" (PhD diss., Fordham University, 1981), 3; Baldwin, *Balm in Gilead*, 327.

67 Walter Harrelson, "Martin Luther King, Jr. and the Hebrew Prophets" (notes from a lecture delivered in a religious studies class, Vanderbilt University, February 6, 1986), 1–5.

68 Harrelson, "Hebrew Prophets," 1–8; Baldwin, "Preacher, Pastor, and Prophet," 86–87; Carson, *King Papers*, 5:285; Carson, *King Papers*, 4:397; Baldwin, *Balm in Gilead*, 328.

69 Baldwin, *Balm in Gilead*, 328; Harrelson, "Hebrew Prophets," 1–8; Carson, *King Papers*, 7:163–64; Shelp and Sunderland, *Pastor as Prophet*, 17.

70 Harrelson, "Hebrew Prophets," 1–10; Shelp and Sunderland, *Pastor as Prophet*, 17; King, *Stride toward Freedom*, 224; Martin Luther King Jr., "People to People," essay, unpublished version, prepared for *New York Amsterdam News* (September 17, 1964), King Papers, KCLA, 2–3; Baldwin, *Balm in Gilead*, 230–43, 328; Baldwin, *Voice of Conscience*, 188–89.

71 This idea of Black Americans having a special spiritual and ethical link to the biblical Israelites and the ancient Hebrew prophets is deeply rooted in African American history, religion, and culture, stretching back to the earliest days of slavery. See Albert J. Raboteau, "African Americans, Exodus, and the American Israel," in *African American Christianity: Essays in History*, ed. Paul E. Johnson (Berkeley: University of California Press, 1994), 1–17; and Baldwin, *Voice of Conscience*, 105.

72 Harrelson, "Hebrew Prophets," 1–10; Baldwin, *Balm in Gilead*, 329; King, *Trumpet of Conscience*, 75; King, *Stride toward Freedom*, 106–7; Carson, *King Papers*, 2:251–53. When King sang these Negro spirituals with or in the presence of large numbers of Jews, as he did occasionally, his sense of a connection with the Hebrew prophets and the Jews' spiritual and cultural commitment to social justice must have been powerful indeed. See Schneier, *Shared Dreams*, 147; Washington, *Testament*, 220, 658; and Yvonne Chireau and Nathaniel Deutsch, eds., *Black Zion: African American Religious Encounters with Judaism* (New York: Oxford University Press, 2000), 156–57.

73 Harrelson, "Hebrew Prophets," 5–10; Baldwin, *Balm in Gilead*, 329.

74 Carson and Shepard, *Call to Conscience*, 222–23; Washington, *Testament*, 286.

75 Carson and Shepard, *Call to Conscience*, 140; Washington, *Testament*, 231; King, *Strength to Love*, 65.

76 J. Deotis Roberts seems to suggest that King's ability to "effectively witness against the powers of evil" was limited by his failure to lift up "the importance of the Christian belief in the resurrection and the guidance and power of the Holy Spirit" in his theological perspective. This claim is refuted to some degree by Aaron J. Howard. See J. Deotis Roberts, *Bonhoeffer and King: Speaking Truth to Power* (Louisville: Westminster John Knox, 2005), 128; and Aaron J. Howard, "The Manifestation of an Immanent God: The Holy Spirit in the Theology of Martin Luther King, Jr.," in *Revives My Soul Again: The Spirituality of Martin Luther King, Jr.*, ed. Lewis V. Baldwin and Victor Anderson (Minneapolis: Fortress, 2018), 91–111.

77 Lentz, *Symbols*, 8, 31, 33–34, 238–62.

78 Carson, *King Papers*, 6:373–74, 461.

79 Carson, *King Papers*, 5:371–72.

80 Carson, *King Papers*, 5:542–43.

81 Carson, *King Papers*, 7:311, 314.

82 King debunked six myths largely perpetrated by media outlets about the civil rights movement and its leadership in a speech at the 53rd Annual Convention of the NAACP in Atlanta, Georgia, in July 1962. See Carson, *King Papers*, 7:183–84, 496, 504.

83 Carson, *King Papers*, 7:194, 218–21.

84 Martin Luther King Jr. to Mr. Edward R. Ball, unpublished and typed version (December 14, 1961), King Papers, KCLA, 1–2.

85 Lentz, *Symbols*, 79, 82–83, 86–88; S. Jonathan Bass, *Blessed Are the Peacemakers: Martin Luther King, Jr., Eight White Religious Leaders, and the "Letter from Birmingham Jail"* (Baton Rouge: Louisiana State University Press, 2001), 2–4; King, *Why We Can't Wait*, 59, 65, 67, 77, 79, 82, 97.

86 Lentz, *Symbols*, 80, 82–83, 87–88; King, *Why We Can't Wait*, 59, 65, 67, 77, 79–84, 97.

87 King, *Why We Can't Wait*, 97.

88 Lentz, *Symbols*, 78–80.

89 Bass, *Blessed Are the Peacemakers*, 229; Lentz, *Symbols*, 152–53; William D. Watley, *Roots of Resistance: The Nonviolent Ethic of Martin Luther King, Jr.* (Valley Forge, PA: Judson, 1985), 83–86; Carson, *King Autobiography*, 281; Washington, *Testament*, 127, 130.

90 Washington, *Testament*, 54.

91 Quoted in Bass, *Blessed Are the Peacemakers*, 229; King, *Where Do We Go*, 32.

92 Carson, *King Autobiography*, 323.

93 S. Jonathan Bass's claim that King "always believed the national media was an important ally" is open to debate. See Bass, *Blessed Are the Peacemakers*, 229; Carson, *King Papers*, 7:340; Michael Friedly and David Gallen, *Martin Luther King, Jr.: The FBI File* (New York: Carroll & Graf, 1993), 38.

94 Carson, *King Papers*, 7:36, 464–65.

95 Carson, *King Papers*, 1:137.

96 Carson, *King Papers*, 6:132–33.

97 Carson, *King Papers*, 4:230; Martin Luther King Jr., "A Knock at Midnight," sermon, unpublished and typed version, All Saints Community Church, Los Angeles, CA (June 25, 1967), King Papers, KCLA, 3; Carson, *King Papers*, 7:444.

98 Carson, *King Papers*, 3:73.

99 Carson, *King Papers*, 3:431.

100 King, *My Life with King*, 108; Carson, *King Papers*, 5:266, 284, 340.

101 Carson, *King Papers*, 3:322n2, 357–58, 448, 475; Washington, *Testament*, 469–70; Carson, *King Papers*, 7:487; Carson, *King Papers*, 4:118, 172, 272.

102 Martin Luther King Jr., "The Drum Major Instinct," sermon, unpublished and typed version, Ebenezer Baptist Church, Atlanta, GA (February 4, 1968), King Papers, KCLA, 5; Carson and Holloran, *Knock at Midnight*, 178.

103 Carson, *King Autobiography*, 53; King, *Stride toward Freedom*, 49–51; Carson, *King Papers*, 7:202–3; Carson, *King Papers*, 5:509.

104 Carson, *King Papers*, 7:336; Carson, *King Papers*, 6:472.

105 Washington, *Testament*, 362.

106 Carson, *King Papers*, 5:206.

107 King, *Stride toward Freedom*, 110–26, 192.

108 Carson, *King Papers*, 5:456–58.

109 King routinely referred to these men as "demagogues" who all too often made "utterly ridiculous and erroneous" charges regarding himself and the movement. They constituted for him part of an "unholy" alliance who called "for open defiance of law and constituted authority," thus inflaming and inciting "those who committed" atrocities. See Washington, *Testament*, 373; King, *Where Do We Go*, 152–53; Carson, *King Papers*, 5:206, 258; and Martin Luther King Jr., "Complete Text of a Statement," unpublished and typed version, released to *Atlanta Journal and Constitution* (July 13, 1963), King Papers, KCLA, 1.

110 Washington, *Testament*, 373; King, *Where Do We Go*, 152–53; Carson, *King Autobiography*, 200; Carson, *King Papers*, 4:295–96, 364, 407; Carson, *King Papers*, 6:169.

111 King, *Stride toward Freedom*, 116, 192.

112 Carson, *King Papers*, 7:365.

113 Carson, *King Autobiography*, 315–16, 319.

114 Carson, *King Autobiography*, 295, 311.

115 King, *Where Do We Go*, 128.

116 King, *Where Do We Go*, 2.

117 King, *Strength to Love*, 77.

118 Carson and Shepard, *Call to Conscience*, 211.

119 Carson, *King Papers*, 5:336; King, *Where Do We Go*, 148–49; Carson, *King Papers*, 7:462.

120 Carson, *King Papers*, 4:99–101, 132–34, 414–15; King, *Why We Can't Wait*, 143–46; Washington, *Testament*, 114, 171–72; Carson, *King Autobiography*, 345; Baldwin et al., *Legacy of King*, 133–48; Carson, *King Papers*, 7:145–48, 161–62, 561; Southern Christian Leadership Conference (SCLC), "King Urges JFK to Support Dynamic South in Civil Rights," press release (March 24, 1963), King Papers, KCLA, 1–2.

121 Carson, *King Autobiography*, 345.

122 Washington, *Testament*, 320. An article appeared in "several prominent newspapers" on "several groups and individuals" who urged King to "become a candidate for the presidency of the United States in the 1968 elections," but King, "quite surprised by these sentiments," declined because, as an ethical prophet, he had come to see his "role as one which operates outside the realm of partisan politics." See Martin Luther King Jr., "A Statement," unpublished and typed version, Atlanta, GA (April 25, 1967), King Papers, KCLA, 1.

123 Carson, *King Papers*, 7:122.

124 Martin Luther King Jr. to Mr. Earl Kennedy (October 30, 1956), King Papers, KCLA, 1; Carson, *King Papers*, 3:429; Carson, *King Papers*, 5:264, 484; Carson, *King Autobiography*, 246–48, 252, 254; Carson, *King Papers*, 6:441; Carson, *King Papers*, 4:81, 176, 370; Washington, *Testament*, 93, 320, 372–73; Carson, *King Papers*, 7:171–72, 199–200; Martin Luther King Jr., "A Christian Movement in a Revolutionary Age," speech, unpublished and typed version (Fall 1966), King Papers, KCLA, 4; Martin Luther King Jr., "The Republican Presidential Nomination," statement, unpublished and typed version (April 1, 1964), King Papers, KCLA, 2; King, *Where Do We Go*, 146–47.

125 "Statement Issued by Dr. King on Statement of J. Edgar Hoover regarding FBI Agents," unpublished and typed version (February 1961), King Papers, KCLA, 1; Martin Luther King Jr., "Equality Now," *Nation*, February 4, 1961, 91–95; "Martin

Luther King's Reaction—A Statement and a Disagreement," *U.S. News & World Report*, November 30, 1964, 58.

126 Quoted in Alex Ayres, ed., *The Wisdom of Martin Luther King, Jr.: An A-to-Z Guide to the Ideas and Ideals of the Great Civil Rights Leader* (New York: Penguin, 1993), 79–80.

127 David J. Garrow, *The FBI and Martin Luther King, Jr.: From "Solo" to Memphis* (New York: W. W. Norton, 1981), 55, 246n78; "Dr. King Says F.B.I. in Albany, Ga., Favors Segregationists," *New York Times*, November 19, 1962, 21; *Atlanta Constitution*, November 19, 1962, 18.

128 Ayres, *Wisdom of King*, 80; "The FBI and Civil Rights—J. Edgar Hoover Speaks Out," *U.S. News & World Report*, November 30, 1964, 56; Lentz, *Symbols*, 136; Garrow, *FBI and King*, 121–22.

129 "FBI and Civil Rights," 58.

130 Martin Luther King Jr., "When a Negro Faces Southern Justice," *New York Amsterdam News*, April 16, 1966, 3; Martin Luther King Jr., "The Verdict," *New York Amsterdam News*, November 20, 1965, 16; King, *Stride toward Freedom*, 32; Martin Luther King Jr., "Negro Faces Dixie Justice," *Chicago Defender*, April 23, 1966, 10.

131 King, "Negro Faces Southern Justice," 3; Freeman, "Interview with King," 5; Martin Luther King Jr., "Something Happening in Mississippi," *New York Amsterdam News*, October 17, 1964, 20.

132 Carson, *King Autobiography*, 91, 237; King, *Stride toward Freedom*, 160–62, 164, 171, 186, 191–93, 199; Watley, *Roots of Resistance*, 72–73.

133 King, *Where Do We Go*, 10–11, 80–81; King, *Why We Can't Wait*, 18–19.

134 Carson, *King Papers*, 5:168.

135 Watley, *Roots of Resistance*, 71–72.

136 Carson and Holloran, *Knock at Midnight*, 71; King, "Lecture," Federation Protestante de France Mutualite, 1.

137 King, "Knock at Midnight," 7–9; Baldwin, *"Single Garment of Destiny,"* 190–97, 201, 204–5; Baldwin, *Voice of Conscience*, 182–216.

138 King, *Where Do We Go*, 145; King, *Strength to Love*, 10; Carson, *King Papers*, 6:564.

139 King, *Strength to Love*, 19–21; King, "Transformed Nonconformist," 4–5.

140 King, "Knock at Midnight," 9.

141 Washington, *Testament*, 143; Carson, *King Papers*, 5:287; Carson, *King Papers*, 3:461; Carson, *King Papers*, 4:190.

142 Malinda Snow, "Martin Luther King's 'Letter from Birmingham Jail' as Pauline Epistle," in *Martin Luther King, Jr.: Civil Rights Leader, Theologian, Orator*, vol. 3, ed. David J. Garrow (Brooklyn, NY: Carlson, 1989), 857–73; King, *Why We Can't Wait*, 89–92.

143 Bill J. Leonard, "A Theology for Racism: Southern Fundamentalists and the Civil Rights Movement," *Baptist History and Heritage* 34 no. 1 (Winter 1999): 61, 63; Carson, *King Papers*, 7:278–79, 281, 488–92; Carson, *King Papers*, 5:480–81.

144 Lee E. Dirks, "'The Essence Is Love': The Theology of Martin Luther King, Jr.," *National Observer*, December 30, 1963, 1; Leonard, "Theology for Racism," 61, 63.

145 Carson, *King Papers*, 7:488–92.

146 Carson, *King Papers*, 7:278–79, 488–92; Carson, *King Papers*, 5:480–81. King never devoted time to responding to the many charges southern white ministers made against him. He knew that these ministers were always die-hard segregationists and that there was no point in dignifying the many nasty and untrue accusations they volleyed at him.

147 King strongly attacked the Catholic Church's claim that it possessed "the only truth," and its dogma of papal infallibility as well. See Carson and Holloran, *Knock at Midnight*, 30; and Carson, *King Papers*, 3:417.

148 Cone, "Theology of King," 35.

149 Martin Luther King Jr., "An Address," closing session of the Second Mobilization of Clergy and Laymen Concerned about the War in Vietnam, New York Avenue Presbyterian Church, Washington, DC (February 5–6, 1968), King Papers, KCLA, 1. This address was included in a pamphlet entitled "In Whose Name?"

150 Carson and Shepard, *Call to Conscience*, 140; Washington, *Testament*, 231.

151 King also added other layers of meaning to the word "witness." He said that it meant "verbal affirmation," or "talking about the life and the death and the resurrection of Jesus Christ." It also meant "living a triumphant life," which involves service to God and humanity. See Carson, *King Papers*, 6:453.

152 Martin Luther King Jr., "Excerpts from an Address," unpublished and typed version, Public Meeting of the Charlotte Branch of the NAACP, Charlotte, North Carolina (September 25, 1960), King Papers, KCLA, 4; Carson, *King Papers*, 6:344, 476; Carson, *King Papers*, 5:338. As early as his college years, King had spoken of loving and sacrificing for truth. See Carson, *King Papers*, 1:122.

153 Carson, *King Papers*, 6:453.

154 Washington, *Testament*, 103, 149; Carson, *King Papers*, 5:336; Carson, *King Papers*, 7:471, 525.

155 Martin Luther King Jr., "First Day of Selma March," statement, unpublished and typed version (March 9, 1965), King Papers, KCLA, 1–2.

156 Carson, *King Papers*, 5:170.

157 *An Amazing Grace*, part 2; Carson, *King Papers*, 6:251–52, 266; Carson, *King Autobiography*, 343; Carson, *King Papers*, 7:285–86. David Garrow appropriately uses the "bearing the cross" theme in the title of his Pulitzer Prize–winning biography of King. See David J. Garrow, *Bearing the Cross: Martin Luther King, Jr., and the Southern Christian Leadership Conference* (New York: William Morrow, 1986).

158 Carson, *King Autobiography*, 181; Washington, *Testament*, 347; Carson, *King Papers*, 6:219, 252, 275, 279, 282–84, 287–89, 348, 418–19, 427, 429; Carson, *King Papers*, 7:340, 394, 509.

159 Carson, *King Papers*, 6:474.

160 Martin Luther King Jr., "To Chart Our Course for the Future," speech, unpublished and typed version, SCLC Retreat, Penn Center, Frogmore, SC (May 29–31, 1967), King Papers, KCLA, 31–32; *An Amazing Grace*, part 2; Carson, *King Papers*, 6:266.

161 Carson, *King Autobiography*, 181, 183; King, *Why We Can't Wait*, 71.

162 Carson, *King Autobiography*, 182–83; King, *Why We Can't Wait*, 71–73.

163 Carson, *King Papers*, 5:167; King, "Lecture," Federation Protestante de France Mutualite, 2; King, *Stride toward Freedom*, 210.

164 Carson, *King Papers*, 5:170.

165 Washington, *Testament*, 347; Carson, *King Papers*, 6:348.

166 Carson, *King Papers*, 6:452–53, 476; Washington, *Testament*, 62.

167 Carson, *King Papers*, 6:251–52; Washington, *Testament*, 356. King offered a somewhat different perspective on this question of being like Jesus in Carson, *King Papers*, 7:156, 163; and Dirks, "'Essence Is Love,'" 1.

168 King, "Transformed Nonconformist," 9–10; King, *Why We Can't Wait*, 91.

169 Carson, *King Papers*, 5:546; James H. Cone, *The Cross and the Lynching Tree* (Maryknoll, NY: Orbis, 2011), 81–82; "Martin Luther King, Jr.: A Personal Portrait," videotaped interview, distributed by Carroll's Marketing and Management Service, Goldsboro, NC, (1966–67); Washington, *Testament*, 41–42; Carson, *King Autobiography*, 344.

170 Carson, *King Autobiography*, 219; Martin Luther King Jr., "On the Murder of Medgar Evers," statement, unpublished and typed version (June 12, 1963), King Papers, KCLA, 1; Carson, *King Papers*, 4:369; Washington, *Testament*, 221.

171 Carson, *King Papers*, 6:251, 482.

172 Carson, *King Papers*, 7:598.

173 Carson, *King Autobiography*, 344; Carson, *King Papers*, 5:269, 505; King, "Meaning of Hope," 14; Carson, *King Papers*, 5:269, 505.

174 Carson, *King Papers*, 6:377; Carson, *King Autobiography*, 344.

175 At the same time, King admitted, "I can never turn my eyes from that Cross without realizing that it symbolizes a strange mixture of greatness and smallness, of good and evil." He went on to proclaim, "As I behold that uplifted Cross I am not only reminded of the unlimited power of God, but also of the sordid weakness of man. I not only think of the glory of the divine, but of the tang of the human. I am reminded not only of Christ at his best, but also of man at his worst." See Carson, *King Papers*, 6:494.

176 Coretta Scott King, *My Life, My Love, My Legacy*, as told to the Rev. Dr. Barbara Reynolds (New York: Henry Holt, 2017), 154.

177 Ayres, *Wisdom of King*, 56.

178 Miss D. McDonald to Rev. Robert W. Towner, unpublished and typed version (May 11, 1964), King Papers, KCLA, 1; Robert W. Towner to Dr. Martin Luther King Jr., unpublished and typed version (May 4, 1964), King Papers, KCLA, 1; Carson, *King Papers*, 5:145, 175; Cone, *Cross and Lynching Tree*, 73.

179 Cone, *Cross and Lynching Tree*, 73. This was equally true for those who, like Pope Paul VI and the Reverend Joseph Barndt, associated the events surrounding King's assassination with the images of Holy Week and "the sufferings" or "the tragic story of the passion of Christ." See Gerald Miller, "Pope's Palm Mass Deplores Slaying," *Atlanta Constitution*, April 8, 1968, 11; and Baldwin, *Voice of Conscience*, 218, 345–46n2–3. King himself associated these images with the many "courageous people who have been caught up in the gallant spirit of the entire freedom movement, even to offering their bodies as personal sacrifices to achieve the human dignity we all seek." See Martin Luther King Jr. to Mr. Henry R. Luce, unpublished and typed version (January 16, 1964), King Papers, KCLA, 1.

180 King, *My Life with King*, 280, 291–92; King, *My Life*, 154; Garrow, *Bearing the Cross*, 307,

354

311; Ralph David Abernathy, *And the Walls Came Tumbling Down: An Autobiography* (New York: Harper & Row, 1989), 176, 309, 437, 476–78, 488–92.

181 This is the conclusion set forth in Baldwin, *Voice of Conscience*, 248–49. Also see King, *Stride toward Freedom*, 210; and King, "America's Chief Moral Dilemma," 16–17.

182 King, *Why We Can't Wait*, 89–92.

183 King, "Transformed Nonconformist," 5–6; King, "America's Chief Moral Dilemma," 16–17; King, *Stride toward Freedom*, 210.

184 Carson, *King Papers*, 7:602–3; Carson and Shepard, *Call to Conscience*, 213–14; Carson, *King Papers*, 4:125n11. King appreciated "the moral insights of a religious prophet." See Carson, *King Papers*, 3:398.

185 King, *Stride toward Freedom*, 210; Washington, *Testament*, 481.

186 King, "America's Chief Moral Dilemma," 17.

187 Carson, *King Papers*, 6:185.

188 Carson, *King Papers*, 6:185.

189 King, *Strength to Love*, 25.

190 King, "Christian Movement," 8.

191 Carson, *King Papers*, 6:549; King, "Transformed Nonconformist," 8.

192 Undoubtedly, the cross was central to King's interpretation of the Christian faith. See Ansbro, *Martin Luther King*, 93–95; Carson and Shepard, *Call to Conscience*, 202; King, *Strength to Love*, 25; Carson, *King Papers*, 7:122; and Carson and Holloran, *Knock at Midnight*, 108.

193 Washington, *Testament*, 10, 149.

194 King, "Transformed Nonconformist," 9–10; Carson, *King Papers*, 6:473.

195 King, *Why We Can't Wait*, 92.

196 King, *Strength to Love*, 77–78, 82–83; King, "Meaning of Hope," 10.

Chapter 5

1 James M. Washington, ed., *A Testament of Hope: The Essential Writings and Speeches of Martin Luther King, Jr.* (New York: HarperCollins, 1991), 84, 162, 170; Glenn Smiley, "Interview with Martin Luther King, Jr. regarding the Montgomery Bus Boycott," unpublished and typed version (February–March 1956), Martin Luther King Jr. Papers, Library and Archives of the Martin Luther King Jr. Center for Nonviolent Social Change (KCLA), Atlanta, GA, 1–2; Clayborne Carson, ed., *The Papers of Martin Luther King, Jr.*, vol. 3, *Birth of a New Age, December 1955–December 1956*, ed. Stewart Burns et al. (Berkeley: University of California Press, 1997), 92, 200, 280; Clayborne Carson, ed., *The Papers of Martin Luther King, Jr.*, vol. 7, *To Save the Soul of America, January 1961–August 1962*, ed. Tenisha Armstrong (Berkeley: University of California Press, 2014), 197, 212; Clayborne Carson, ed., *The Papers of Martin Luther King, Jr.*, vol. 5, *Threshold of a New Decade, January 1959–December 1960*, ed. Tenisha Armstrong et al. (Berkeley: University of California Press, 2005), 289, 328; Lewis V. Baldwin and Victor Anderson, eds., *Revives My Soul Again: The Spirituality of Martin Luther King, Jr.* (Minneapolis: Fortress, 2018), 76.

2 Alex Ayres, ed., *The Wisdom of Martin Luther King, Jr.: An A-to-Z Guide to the Ideas and Ideals of the Great Civil Rights Leader* (New York: Penguin, 1993), 43.

3 King, *Where Do We Go from Here: Chaos or Community?* (Boston: Beacon, 1968; originally published in 1967), 13; Clayborne Carson, ed., *The Papers of Martin Luther King, Jr.*, vol. 4, *Symbol of the Movement, January 1957–December 1958*, ed. Susan Carson et al. (Berkeley: University of California Press, 2000), 407.

4 Washington, *Testament*, 230; Carson, *King Papers*, 5:250, 289, 343, 375.

5 Washington, *Testament*, 112–16; Carson, *King Papers*, 4:230; Carson, *King Papers*, 7:340; Clayborne Carson and Peter Holloran, eds., *A Knock at Midnight: Inspiration from the Great Sermons of Reverend Martin Luther King, Jr.* (New York: Warner, 1998), 121–22, 147; Martin Luther King Jr., *Trumpet of Conscience* (San Francisco: Harper & Row, 1968; originally published in 1967), 50.

6 Washington, *Testament*, 331.

7 Washington, *Testament*, 359; Martin Luther King Jr., "The 'New Negro' of the South: Behind the Montgomery Story," *The Socialist Call*, June 1956, 16–19; King, *Where Do We Go*, 16, 18, 61–66; Carson, *King Papers*, 7:167; Clayborne Carson, ed., *The Papers of Martin Luther King, Jr.*, vol. 6, *Advocate of the Social Gospel, September 1948–March 1963*, ed. Susan Carson et al. (Berkeley: University of California Press, 2007), 467–69, 475; Martin Luther King Jr., *Stride toward Freedom: The Montgomery Story* (New York: Harper & Row, 1958), 224; Lewis V. Baldwin, *There Is a Balm in Gilead: The Cultural*

Roots of Martin Luther King, Jr. (Minneapolis: Fortress, 1991), 229–43; Carson, *King Papers*, 3:181, 266; Carson, *King Papers*, 7:114, 156, 163, 167, 275; Carson, *King Papers*, 4:80, 125; Carson, *King Papers*, 5:129, 410.

8   Clayborne Carson and Kris Shepard, eds., *A Call to Conscience: The Landmark Speeches of Dr. Martin Luther King, Jr.* (New York: Warner, 2001), 15, 115, 130, 214; Carson and Holloran, *Knock at Midnight*, 147; Carson, *King Papers*, 7:164, 340, 484, 557; Carson, *King Papers*, 6:96, 209, 332; King, *Where Do We Go*, 19–20, 50, 66, 165; Washington, *Testament*, 282, 358.

9   Carson, *King Papers*, 3:336–37; Carson, *King Papers*, 7:229–30, 500.

10   See Charles Reagan Wilson, *Baptized in Blood: The Religion of the Lost Cause, 1865–1920* (Athens: University of Georgia Press, 1980), 1–2; Martin Luther King Jr., "The South—a Hostile Nation," *New York Amsterdam News*, May 11, 1963, 10.

11   Washington, *Testament*, 521; King, *Where Do We Go*, 82; Martin Luther King Jr., "A Christian Movement in a Revolutionary Age" (speech, Fall 1966), unpublished and typed version, King Papers, KCLA, 4.

12   Washington, *Testament*, 521; Carson, *King Papers*, 4:103, 105; Carson, *King Papers*, 3:210.

13   Washington, *Testament*, 228; Clayborne Carson, ed., *The Autobiography of Martin Luther King, Jr.* (New York: Warner, 1998), 284; Carson, *King Papers*, 6:406; Martin Luther King Jr., *Strength to Love* (Philadelphia: Fortress, 1981; originally published in 1963), 42–43.

14   Lillian Smith, "A Strange Kind of Love," *Saturday Review*, October 20, 1962, 18; King, *Where Do We Go*, 75; Martin Luther King Jr., *Why We Can't Wait* (New York: New American Library, 1963), 120.

15   King, *Where Do We Go*, 13–14, 72–73; Martin Luther King Jr., "Civil Rights at the Crossroads," speech, unpublished and typed version, Shop Stewards of Local 815, Teamsters and Allied Trades Council, New York, NY (May 2, 1967), King Papers, KCLA, 4.

16   Martin Luther King Jr., "A Speech at a Dinner Honoring Him as a Nobel Prize Recipient," unpublished and typed version, Dinkler Plaza Hotel, Atlanta, GA (January 27, 1965), King Papers, KCLA, 6–7; Baldwin, *Balm in Gilead*, 84.

17   Carson, *King Papers*, 4:104; King, "Speech," Dinkler Plaza Hotel, 6–7; Baldwin, *Balm in Gilead*, 84.

18   Carson, *King Papers*, 7:398.

19   Martin Luther King Jr., "Segregation Is Not Just a Southern Problem," speech, unpublished and typed version, Chicago, IL (July 28, 1965), King Papers, KCLA, 1–6; Martin Luther King Jr., "A Realistic Look at Race Relations," speech, unpublished and typed version, second anniversary of the NAACP Legal Defense and Educational Fund, Waldorf Astoria Hotel, New York, NY (May 17, 1956), King Papers, KCLA, 5; Carson, *King Papers*, 3:284; Carson, *King Papers*, 7:500.

20   King, "The South—a Hostile Nation," 10; Martin Luther King Jr., "America's Chief Moral Dilemma," speech, unpublished and typed version, United Church of Christ—General Synod, Palmer House, Chicago, IL (July 6, 1965), King Papers, KCLA, 1; King, "Realistic Look," 5; Martin Luther King Jr., "A Second Emancipation Proclamation," questions and answers exercise, unpublished and typed version, San Francisco, CA (October 16, 1961), King Papers, KCLA, 1.

21   Washington, *Testament*, 358; Carson, *King Papers*, 4:444.

22   Martin Luther King Jr., "En Granslos Kval Pa Operan: Remarks," unpublished and typed version, Stockholm, Sweden (March 31, 1966), King Papers, KCLA, 1–3; Martin Luther King Jr., "A Speech," unpublished and typed version, European Tour (March 1966), King Papers, KCLA, 7.

23   King, "En Granslos Kval Pa Operan: Remarks," 1–3.

24   King, *Where Do We Go*, 117.

25   William D. Watley, *Roots of Resistance: The Nonviolent Ethic of Martin Luther King, Jr.* (Valley Forge, PA: Judson, 1985), 97; Carson, *King Autobiography*, 308.

26   Martin Luther King Jr., "An Address," unpublished and typed version, mass meeting, Marks, MS (March 19, 1968), King Papers, KCLA, 5–6; Washington, *Testament*, 358–59; Baldwin, *Balm in Gilead*, 78–79.

27   Carson, *King Papers*, 5:462, 472–73.

28   Washington, *Testament*, 358.

29   Carson, *King Papers*, 3:429.

30   Martin Luther King Jr. to H. E. Tate, unpublished and typed version (February 20, 1958), King Papers, KCLA.

31   Frederick L. Downing, "A Review of David J. Garrow's *Bearing the Cross: Martin Luther King, Jr., and the Southern Christian Leadership Conference*," *Theology Today* 44, no. 3 (October 1987): 391; F. Gavin Davenport,

The Myth of Southern History: Historical Consciousness in Twentieth-Century Southern Literature (Nashville: Vanderbilt University Press, 1970), 196–97; Baldwin, *Balm in Gilead*, 79.

32 Pat Watters, "The Spring Offensive," *Nation*, February 3, 1964, 119–20; Baldwin, *Balm in Gilead*, 79–80.

33 Carson, *King Papers*, 3:429.

34 Washington, *Testament*, 404.

35 Southern Christian Leadership Conference (SCLC), "King Urges JFK to Support Dynamic South in Civil Rights," press release (March 24, 1963), King Papers, KCLA, 1; Washington, *Testament*, 475; King, *Stride toward Freedom*, 201; Carson, *King Papers*, 4:440.

36 In 1963, five years after offering this breakdown of white southern attitudes, King argued that the white South was "split" or "fissured into two parts; one ready for extensive change, and the other opposed to any but most trivial alterations." Here he was making a distinction between "the dynamic South" and "the reactionary South." See SCLC, "King Urges JFK," 1–2; Washington, *Testament*, 475; King, *Stride toward Freedom*, 201; and Carson, *King Papers*, 4:331.

37 Carson, *King Papers*, 7:225; Martin Luther King Jr., "A Suggested Preamble for the SCLC," statement, unpublished and typed version, Atlanta, GA (n.d.), King Papers, KCLA, 1–2; Martin Luther King Jr., "When Peace Becomes Obnoxious," *The Louisville Defender*, March 29, 1956, 1; Martin Luther King Jr., "An Address," unpublished and typed version, First Annual Institute on Nonviolence and Social Change under the Auspices of the Montgomery Improvement Association, Holt Street Baptist Church, Montgomery, AL (December 3, 1956), King Papers, KCLA, 1; Martin Luther King Jr., "A Statement regarding the Mississippi Freedom Democratic Party at the COFO Rally," unpublished and typed version, Jackson, MS (July 22, 1964), King Papers, KCLA, 1; Baldwin, *Balm in Gilead*, 68–69, 84.

38 Martin Luther King Jr., "The Meaning of Hope," sermon, unpublished and typed version, Dexter Avenue Baptist Church, Montgomery, AL (December 10, 1967), King Papers, KCLA, 3; Baldwin, *Balm in Gilead*, 64; Martin Luther King Jr., "An Address," unpublished and typed version, 47th NAACP Annual Convention, San Francisco, CA (June 27, 1956), King Papers, KCLA, 8–9; King, "Address," First Annual Institute on Nonviolence, 1–2; Lewis V. Baldwin et al., *The Legacy of Martin Luther King, Jr.: The Boundaries of Law, Politics, and Religion* (Notre Dame, IN: University of Notre Dame Press, 2002), 46; Carson, *King Papers*, 3:151.

39 Carson, *King Papers*, 4:104.

40 Martin Luther King Jr., "Bold Design for a New South," *Nation*, March 30, 1963, 260.

41 Small wonder that King could speak in terms of "a Declaration of Independence of a New South" by 1963, though his optimism at this point seemed, in hindsight, to have been premature. See Washington, *Testament*, 115; and King, "Bold Design," 260–61.

42 Washington, *Testament*, 357–58.

43 Carson, *King Papers*, 4:298.

44 Washington, *Testament*, 147.

45 Washington, *Testament*, 315.

46 Carson and Shepard, *Call to Conscience*, 120; Martin Luther King Jr., "Nobel Lecture," unpublished and typed version, Aula of the University, Oslo, Norway (December 11, 1964), King Papers, KCLA, 9.

47 Carson and Shepard, *Call to Conscience*, 191; Washington, *Testament*, 249; King, *Where Do We Go*, 62.

48 King, *Where Do We Go*, 63; Carson, *King Papers*, 4:189.

49 King also referred to the movement as a "dramatic social revolution." He was highly impressed with Gandhi's "Salt March to the Sea," and he undoubtedly related this event to Gandhi's understanding of "Truth-force" or "holding on to Truth" (*satyagraha*). See "King's Europe Tour Gigantic Success," *Southern Christian Leadership Conference Newsletter* 3, no. 2 (March–April 1966): 3; Martin Luther King Jr., "Pathos and Hope," *New York Amsterdam News*, March 3, 1962, 9–10; Martin Luther King Jr., "Annual Report," unpublished and typed version, Eighth Annual Convention of the Southern Christian Leadership Conference, Savannah, GA (September 28–October 2, 1964), KCLA, 1, 20–21; Carson, *King Papers*, 7:112, 542; Washington, *Testament*, 227, 229–30, 517; Carson, *King Papers*, 3:151, 427, 447; King, *Strength to Love*, 125; King, *Where Do We Go*, 17; Carson, *King Papers*, 4:478; King, *Why We Can't Wait*, 38; Carson and Shepard, *Call to Conscience*, 112, 114, 116, 119–20; Carson, *King Papers*, 5:150, 250, 289, 343; and Ayres, *Wisdom of King*, 147.

50 Carson and Shepard, *Call to Conscience*, 114.

51   King, "Annual Report," 20; Washington, *Testament*, 229; Carson, *King Papers*, 4:163, 166; Ayres, *Wisdom of King*, 188.

52   King, "Annual Report," 20–21; Carson, *King Papers*, 5:166.

53   King, *Strength to Love*, 81; Carson, *King Papers*, 3:259–61, 433; King, "Nobel Lecture," 6, 8–9; Carson, *King Papers*, 4:155, 163; King, "Christian Movement," 1–3.

54   King, "Annual Report," 20–21; King, *Strength to Love*, 80–82; King, "Nobel Lecture," 8–9; Carson, *King Papers*, 3:259–61, 433; Carson, *King Papers*, 4:155, 163; King, *Strength to Love*, 81; Harold Courlander, *Negro Folk Music, U.S.A* (New York: Columbia University Press, 1963), 42–43; King, "Christian Movement," 1; Bill J. Leonard, "A Theology for Racism: Southern Fundamentalists and the Civil Rights Movement," *Baptist History and Heritage* 34, no. 1 (Winter 1999): 56–64.

55   King, *Why We Can't Wait*, 132; Carson, *King Papers*, 4:255; Carson, *King Papers*, 3:113–14; Carson, *King Papers*, 5:333, 360; Carson, *King Autobiography*, 105.

56   Even William Faulkner, the Nobel Prize–winning author from Mississippi and the greatest white southern writer of his time, was "trapped by the myth" that "the Negro is happy." See Carson, *King Autobiography*, 197; King, *Stride toward Freedom*, 44; King, *Why We Can't Wait*, 28–29, 67–68, 77, 79–80, 84–87; Washington, *Testament*, 80; Harry Golden, *Mr. Kennedy and the Negroes* (Cleveland: World, 1963), 22; Franklin H. Littell, *From State Church to Pluralism: A Protestant Interpretation of Religion in American History* (New York: Macmillan, 1971), 161–62; Carson, *King Papers*, 7:496, 502; and Baldwin et al., *Legacy of King*, 70n160, 83.

57   King, *Why We Can't Wait*, 28–29; Martin Luther King Jr., "True Dignity," essay, unpublished and typed version (n.d.), King Papers, KCLA, 7; Carson, *King Papers*, 7:496, 502.

58   King argued that "only in death is there an absence of tension." He also declared, "Our nonviolent direct-action program has as its objective not the creation of tensions, but the *surfacing* of tensions already present." See King, *Why We Can't Wait*, 84–86; Ayres, *Wisdom of King*, 217; Carson, *King Papers*, 7:496, 502; and Washington, *Testament*, 135, 350. For an interesting and insightful discussion of how King's studies of Heraclitus and Hegel heightened "his awareness" of the tension or "the dialectic at work" in

civil rights campaigns, see John J. Ansbro, *Martin Luther King, Jr.: Nonviolent Strategies and Tactics for Social Change* (Lanham, MD: Madison, 2000; originally published in 1982), 125–26.

59   King, "Realistic Look," 4.

60   King, *Why We Can't Wait*, 84–86; Ayres, *Wisdom of King*, 217; Washington, *Testament*, 350.

61   King declared that "we must get rid of the false notion that there is some miraculous quality in the flow of time that inevitably heals all evils." See King, *Why We Can't Wait*, 86; King, *Where Do We Go*, 128; Washington, *Testament*, 295–96, 355; Carson, *King Autobiography*, 195–96; Carson, *King Papers*, 5:266–67, 283; Carson, *King Papers*, 7:496, 501; and Carson and Holloran, *Knock at Midnight*, 209–10.

62   King further illustrated his point by noting that the comings of Jesus, Martin Luther, and Abraham Lincoln were examples of times when history was ready to accept a new idea and/or event. See Carson, *King Papers*, 6:193–94; Carson, *King Papers*, 7:270, 418, 528; Washington, *Testament*, 59, 99, 106, 160, 618–19; King, *Where Do We Go*, 169; and Carson, *King Papers*, 5:360, 368, 415.

63   King, *Why We Can't Wait*, 80.

64   King, *Stride toward Freedom*, 50–51; Carson, *King Papers*, 3:486.

65   Ayres, *Wisdom of King*, 135–36; King, *Why We Can't Wait*, 82, 90.

66   King, *Why We Can't Wait*, 70–71.

67   Carson, *King Papers*, 5:561–64; Ayres, *Wisdom of King*, 41; King, *Why We Can't Wait*, 83–84.

68   Adam Fairclough, *To Redeem the Soul of America: The Southern Christian Leadership Conference and Martin Luther King, Jr.* (Athens: University of Georgia Press, 1987), 2–4; Carson, *King Papers*, 7:504.

69   King's speech at the 53rd NAACP Annual Convention debunked a range of myths about the movement advanced by various sectors of white society. See Carson, *King Papers*, 7:496–509.

70   Fairclough, *Soul of America*, 1–4; Adam Fairclough, "The Southern Christian Leadership Conference and the Second Reconstruction, 1957–1973," *Southern Atlantic Quarterly* 8, no. 2 (Spring 1981): 178; Baldwin, *Balm in Gilead*, 192.

71   Fairclough, *Soul of America*, 4.

72   Carson, *King Papers*, 7:504–5.

73   Carson, *King Papers*, 7:505.

74   King, *Why We Can't Wait*, 78.

75 Both the "four basic steps" and the "six principles" were influenced by Gandhi. See King, *Why We Can't Wait*, 78; King, *Stride toward Freedom*, 102–6; Carson, *King Papers*, 5:123–25; Carson, *King Papers*, 4:232–33.

76 King, *Stride toward Freedom*, 102–6; Carson, *King Papers*, 7:496, 506–7.

77 Carson, *King Papers*, 5:438; Carson, *King Papers*, 3:92, 200, 202, 308. Albert Raboteau rightly points out that King drew upon and appropriated "the spiritual tradition of black suffering Christianity." In another source, he skillfully argues that King, "better than any other leader," explained "the religious meaning of civil rights for the nation." See Albert J. Raboteau, *A Sorrowful Joy: The Spiritual Journey of an African-American Man in Late Twentieth-Century America* (Mahwah, NJ: Paulist, 2002), 29, 50; and Albert J. Raboteau, "Martin Luther King, Jr. and the Tradition of Black Religious Protest," in *Religion and the Life of the Nation: American Recoveries*, ed. Rowland A. Sherrill (Urbana: University of Illinois Press, 1990), 47.

78 Carson, *King Papers*, 5:438; Carson, *King Papers*, 3:200, 202, 308, 428, 430; Carson, *King Papers*, 7:505.

79 See W. E. B. Du Bois, *The Gifts of Black Folk: The Negroes in the Making of America* (Garden City Park, NY: Square One, 2009; originally published in 1924), 151–62; King, *Stride toward Freedom*, 224; Carson, *King Papers*, 6:365; Martin Luther King Jr., "Pre-Washington Campaign," speech, unpublished and typed version, Mississippi Leaders on the Washington Campaign Meeting, St. Thomas AME Church, Birmingham, AL (February 15, 1968), King Papers, KCLA, 12; and Lewis V. Baldwin, *Behind the Public Veil: The Humanness of Martin Luther King, Jr.* (Minneapolis: Fortress, 2016), 186.

80 Carson, *King Papers*, 7:505.

81 King, "Christian Movement," 1–2, 8; King, *Strength to Love*, 109, 111, 114; Washington, *Testament*, 506–7, 509; Carson, *King Papers*, 6:530–34.

82 King also used the term "spiritual reevaluation." See King, *Where Do We Go*, 173; and King, "Nobel Lecture," 22.

83 King, "Nobel Lecture," 3–4.

84 Carson, *King Papers*, 5:269.

85 King, *Where Do We Go*, 173.

86 Referring to the climate in which he lived, King talked about "the conflict of soul," or, as he put it, "the moral choices that confront our people, both Negro and white, in these fateful times." "We are seeking to free the soul of America," he declared repeatedly. See King, "Nobel Lecture," 3; Carson, *King Papers*, 5:281, 583; and Carson, *King Papers*, 4:497.

87 Carson, *King Papers*, 3:181, 208; King, *Stride toward Freedom*, 218; King, *Trumpet of Conscience*, 75; Carson, *King Papers*, 7:409. King said that "the philosophy of nonviolence is concerned mainly with spiritual strategy." See Carson, *King Papers*, 4:184.

88 Washington, *Testament*, 87; Carson, *King Papers*, 6:324; Carson, *King Papers*, 3:325; Carson, *King Papers*, 5:521.

89 King, *Strength to Love*, 54; Carson, *King Papers*, 5:505, 521; King, "Nobel Lecture," 2–3.

90 Carson, *King Autobiography*, 305–6.

91 Carson, *King Papers*, 7:557.

92 Carson, *King Papers*, 5:369; Carson, *King Papers*, 3:447; King, *Stride toward Freedom*, 171.

93 Carson, *King Papers*, 3:71–73, 79; Carson, *King Papers*, 7:552.

94 No reply from the former president has been found. See Carson, *King Papers*, 5:437–38.

95 King, "Pathos and Hope," 9–10; Carson, *King Papers*, 7:201, 340, 416, 536–37, 595; Carson and Holloran, *Knock at Midnight*, 183; Washington, *Testament*, 349; Carson, *King Papers*, 5:340–41.

96 Carson, *King Papers*, 7:114, 138; Carson, *King Papers*, 4:295.

97 Martin Luther King Jr. to Mr. Edward D. Ball, unpublished and typed version (December 14, 1961), King Papers, KCLA, 2; Martin Luther King Jr., "Complete Text of a Statement," unpublished and typed version, released to *Atlanta Journal and Constitution* (July 13, 1963), King Papers, KCLA, 1; John Freeman, "Interview with Martin Luther King, Jr.," unpublished and typed version, *Face to Face*, BBC Television, London, England (October 29, 1961), King Papers, KCLA, 12; Paul Niven and Benjamin Bradlee, "Transcript of an Interview with Martin Luther King, Jr.," unpublished and typed version, CBS Television Network, New York, NY (May 10, 1964), King Papers, KCLA, 18–19.

98 Carson, *King Papers*, 4:307; Carson, *King Papers*, 5:502.

99 King, "Nobel Lecture," 4.

100 Carson, *King Papers*, 7:186, 201, 462, 508; Washington, *Testament*, 50, 91–92.

101 Washington, *Testament*, 91–92; Carson, *King Papers*, 4:368.

102 Martin Luther King Jr., "Excerpts from an Address," unpublished and typed version,

Public Meeting of the Charlotte, NC, Branch of the NAACP (September 25, 1960), King Papers, KCLA, 2; Martin Luther King Jr., "A Statement," unpublished and typed version, Credentials Committee of the Democratic National Committee (August 22, 1964), King Papers, KCLA, 1; Martin Luther King Jr., "People to People," article, unpublished and typed version, prepared for *New York Amsterdam News* (October 17, 1964), King Papers, KCLA, 1–2; Martin Luther King Jr., "Ready in Mississippi," *New York Amsterdam News*, August 29, 1964, 18; Martin Luther King Jr., "Something Happening in Mississippi," *New York Amsterdam News*, October 17, 1964, 20.

103 Martin Luther King Jr., "On the Murder of Medgar Evers," statement, unpublished and typed version (June 12, 1963), King Papers, KCLA, 1; Washington, *Testament*, 221–23; Carson, *King Autobiography*, 282–83; Carson, *King Papers*, 4:408; Carson, *King Papers*, 5:206; King, *Where Do We Go*, 2.

104 Carson, *King Papers*, 4:408, 488; Carson, *King Papers*, 5:206.

105 Carson, *King Papers*, 4:513.

106 In 1961, King actually agreed to participate in a film documentary concerning HUAC, but he changed his mind and opted out after hearing that Bert Edises, one of the producers, had been involved with the Communist Party. Undoubtedly, King also knew of the Black activist and artist Robeson and his appearance before hostile members of the HUAC around his embrace of Russia and Communism in the 1950s. When asked about his "personal view of Robeson" on one occasion, King simply said "no comment," but it is not difficult to surmise that he would have seen the glaring contradiction between the HUAC's treatment of Blacks like Robeson and its seeming lack of interest in white terrorist groups. See Carson, *King Papers*, 7:328–29; and Carson, *King Papers*, 5:128. For some indication of how King felt about the HUAC's charge of Communism against certain of SCLC's supporters, see his "Statement on House Committee on Un-American Activities Hearings on the United Packinghouse Workers of America" in Carson, *King Papers*, 5:226–27.

107 Carson, *King Papers*, 7:594; Carson, *King Papers*, 3:418; Carson, *King Papers*, 4:106, 125, 397.

108 Carson, *King Papers*, 7:357.

109 King made this statement in the typed manuscript version of what would eventually become one of his last books, entitled *Where Do We Go from Here: Chaos or Community?* See Baldwin, *Balm in Gilead*, 342n37.

110 Carson, *King Papers*, 5:188.

111 Carson, *King Papers*, 5:283–84; Carson, *King Papers*, 4:369.

112 Martin Luther King Jr., "Doubts and Certainties Link," interview, unpublished, transcribed, and typed version, London, England (Winter 1968), King Papers, KCLA, 1; King, "Nobel Lecture," 4; Carson, *King Papers*, 5:333, 368, 394; Carson, *King Papers*, 3:144, 254, 324–25.

113 Martin Luther King Jr., "Statement regarding the Legitimacy of the Struggle in Montgomery, Alabama," unpublished and typed version (May 4, 1956), Martin Luther King Jr. Papers, Special Collections, Mugar Memorial Library, Boston University, Boston, MA, 1; Lewis V. Baldwin, *To Make the Wounded Whole: The Cultural Legacy of Martin Luther King, Jr.* (Minneapolis: Fortress, 1992), 247.

114 Martin Luther King Jr., "Dreams of Brighter Tomorrows," *Ebony*, 20 (March 1965):34–35; King, *Where Do We Go*, 169–70; Baldwin, *Make the Wounded Whole*, 250; Carson, *King Papers*, 4:542.

115 King, "Christian Movement," 8.

116 King, *Why We Can't Wait*, 77; Carson, *King Autobiography*, 343–44; King, *Trumpet of Conscience*, 69–70; King, *Where Do We Go*, 181, 190.

117 Carson, *King Papers*, 4:103; King, *Where Do We Go*, 167.

118 King, *Where Do We Go*, 190.

119 Carson, *King Papers*, 5:368.

120 Carson, *King Papers*, 6:182–83; Carson, *King Papers*, 4:76, 438.

121 Washington, *Testament*, 280–81; King, *Trumpet of Conscience*, 49–50, 62–64, 68; Martin Luther King Jr., "An Address," unpublished and typed version, Fiftieth Anniversary of the Women's International League for Peace and Freedom, Philadelphia, PA (October 15, 1965), King Papers, KCLA, 1; Martin Luther King Jr., "What a Mother Should Tell Her Child," sermon, unpublished and typed version, Ebenezer Baptist Church, Atlanta, GA (May 12, 1963), King Papers, KCLA, 4–5; Baldwin, *Make the Wounded Whole*, 252–54; King, *Where Do We Go*, 167–91; Ayres, *Wisdom of King*, 234.

122 Carson, *King Papers*, 4:317, 369.

123 King, "Statement," Credentials Committee, 2.

124 Carson, *King Papers*, 7:114; King, *Stride toward Freedom*, 196; Ayres, *Wisdom of King*, 57; King, "Excerpts from an Address," 1.

125 King, "Speech," European Tour, 2.

126 Carson, *King Papers*, 7:468.

127 Carson, *King Papers*, 3:308.

128 Washington, *Testament*, 228–29.

129 Washington, *Testament*, 230. King agreed with his wife Coretta's observation that "walking for freedom has been an integral part of man's struggle for freedom and dignity" and that "the future belongs to those who march toward freedom." See Carson, *King Papers*, 4:514–15.

130 Carson, *King Papers*, 4:407; King, *Where Do We Go*, 13; Carson, *King Papers*, 5:521; Washington, *Testament*, 118.

131 Washington, *Testament*, 118; Carson, *King Papers*, 5:191–92; King, "America's Chief Moral Dilemma," 15; King, "Doubts and Certainties Link," 7–8.

132 Washington, *Testament*, 118.

133 Lewis V. Baldwin, *Toward the Beloved Community: Martin Luther King, Jr. and South Africa* (Cleveland: Pilgrim, 1995), 2.

134 King, "Bold Design," 259–62; Carson, *King Papers*, 4:230.

135 Carson and Holloran, *Knock at Midnight*, 147; Carson, *King Papers*, 7:340.

136 Carson, *King Papers*, 4:331; Carson and Holloran, *Knock at Midnight*, 186; King, *Trumpet of Conscience*, 50.

137 Baldwin, *Make the Wounded Whole*, 247–48; Baldwin, *Toward the Beloved Community*, 6.

138 Charles R. Wilson and William Ferris, eds., *Encyclopedia of Southern Culture* (Chapel Hill: University of North Carolina Press, 1989), 146, 931–32, 1113–14; Samuel S. Hill, ed., *Encyclopedia of Religion in the South* (Macon, GA: Mercer University Press, 1984), 471; Wilson, *Baptized in Blood*, 84–84; Baldwin et al., *Legacy of King*, 2–3.

139 Wilson and Ferris, *Encyclopedia of Southern Culture*, 146, 931–32, 1113–14; Hill, *Encyclopedia of Religion*, 471; Wilson, *Baptized in Blood*, 84–85, 92–93; Baldwin et al., *Legacy of King*, 2–3. Some studies claim that the Southern Methodist Bishop Atticus G. Haygood first used the term "New South." Others report that the term was used as early as January 1874 by *Harper's New Monthly Magazine* and as early as March of that same year by Henry W. Grady in an editorial in the *Atlanta Daily Herald*. See Raymond B. Nixon, *Henry W. Grady: Spokesman of the New South* (New York: Alfred A. Knopf, 1943), 240n6; Nancy Keever Andersen, "Cooperation for Social Betterment: Missions and Progressives in the Methodist

Episcopal Church, South, 1894–1921" (PhD diss., Vanderbilt University, 1999), 14; and Baldwin et al., *Legacy of King*, 2–4, 52n8.

140 Wilson and Ferris, *Encyclopedia of Southern Culture*, 146, 176, 206–7, 229–30, 929; Baldwin et al., *Legacy of King*, 2, 68n139.

141 For the first and most extensive treatment of this subject to date, see Baldwin et al., *Legacy of King*, 2–42.

142 Martin Luther King Jr., "An Address," unpublished and typed version, National Press Club, Washington, DC (July 9, 1962), King Papers, KCLA, 4; Baldwin et al., *Legacy of King*, 30; Baldwin, *Balm in Gilead*, 84–85; Washington, *Testament*, 100; Carson, *King Papers*, 4:129, 273–74.

143 Baldwin et al., *Legacy of King*, 5.

144 Carson, *King Papers*, 7:147–48.

145 King, *Where Do We Go*, 155, 193, 195; Carson, *King Papers*, 5:268, 284, 412; King, *Stride toward Freedom*, 33.

146 King, *Where Do We Go*, 67; Carson, *King Papers*, 5:284; Washington, *Testament*, 149–50.

147 Carson, *King Papers*, 4:408; Carson, *King Papers*, 6:492–93; King, *Where Do We Go*, 122–25, 194–95; Baldwin, *Balm in Gilead*, 57–61. King said at one point, "The white Southerner must be educated. We, the American Negro must educate him." At other points, he spoke of bringing "Negroes up to higher educational levels," of closing "the gap between their educational levels and those of whites." See Carson, *King Papers*, 7:233; and Ayres, *Wisdom of King*, 70–71.

148 Carson, *King Papers*, 7:214; King, "Nobel Lecture," 12–13.

149 Carson, *King Papers*, 7:213–14.

150 Atticus G. Haygood, *The New South: Gratitude, Amendment, Hope; A Thanksgiving Sermon for November 25, 1880* (Oxford, GA, 1880), 3–12; Atticus G. Haygood, *Our Brother in Black: His Freedom and His Future* (New York: Phillips & Hunt, 1881), 5–8, 17–23, 39–83, and 112–241; Atticus G. Haygood, *Pleas for Progress* (Nashville: Publishing House of the M. E. Church, South, 1889), 5–24, 137–46, and 212–49; Baldwin et al., *Legacy of King*, 4, 53–54n16.

151 Haygood, *Our Brother in Black*, 112–27; King, "Address," Marks, MS, 5–6; Washington, *Testament*, 189–94, 315–16, 563–66, 621–23; Paul M. Gaston, *The New South Creed: A Study in Southern Mythmaking* (New York: Alfred A. Knopf, 1970), 137–41, 224–25; Harold E. Davis, *Henry Grady's New South: Atlanta, a Brave and Beautiful*

City (Tuscaloosa: University of Alabama Press, 1990), 133–66; Baldwin et al., *Legacy of King*, 4–5.

152 Carson, *King Autobiography*, 90; Carson, *King Papers*, 4:76–77, 119, 171, 231, 271; Baldwin et al., *Legacy of King*, 5–6; Lee E. Dirks, "'The Essence Is Love': The Theology of Martin Luther King, Jr.," *National Observer*, December 30, 1963, 12. King occasionally used the term "racist ethos" in reference to institutions and structures that degraded, exploited, and segregated his people. See Carson, *King Papers*, 7:338.

153 Carson, *King Papers*, 5:273.

154 Carson, *King Papers*, 4:336.

155 Washington, *Testament*, 211; Carson, *King Papers*, 4:334–35.

156 King, *Where Do We Go*, 70; Carson, *King Papers*, 7:472.

157 Carson, *King Papers*, 5:360, 427; Washington, *Testament*, 118 and 317; King, "Doubts and Certainties Link," 7–8.

158 Carson, *King Papers*, 4:281.

159 James H. Cone, *Martin & Malcolm & America: A Dream or a Nightmare* (Maryknoll, NY: Orbis, 1991), 234; Washington, *Testament*, 317, 319, 665–66.

160 Washington, *Testament*, 91, 93; King, *Why We Can't Wait*, 89; Carson, *King Papers*, 3:273–74; Carson, *King Papers*, 4:371, 464–65, 510, 543; Carson, *King Papers*, 5:306–7, 508; Carson, *King Papers*, 6:357; Carson, *King Papers*, 7:473–74; Baldwin et al., *Legacy of King*, 11–36.

161 King, *Why We Can't Wait*, 89.

162 Michael K. Honey, *Southern Labor and Black Civil Rights: Organizing Memphis Workers* (Urbana: University of Illinois Press, 1993), 118; David L. Chappell, *Inside Agitators: White Southerners and the Civil Rights Movement* (Baltimore: John Hopkins University Press, 1994), 55; Baldwin, *Balm in Gilead*, 80; Baldwin et al., *Legacy of King*, 32.

163 Carson, *King Papers*, 7:137, 207; Carson, *King Papers*, 3:292–93; Baldwin et al., *Legacy of King*, 32.

164 Carson, *King Papers*, 3:347, 355; Carson, *King Papers*, 4:123; Baldwin et al., *Legacy of King*, 32.

165 Carson, *King Papers*, 4:508; Carson, *King Papers*, 5:115; Martin Luther King Jr., "A Statement," *News from the Southern Christian Leadership Conference*, unpublished and typed version (November 1, 1960), King Papers, KCLA, 1.

166 The paternalism of these and other white New South idealists, which may have been unconscious to some degree, was quite evident in their efforts to determine which Blacks were most suitable to lead a movement designed to eliminate white supremacist policies, institutions, and structures. See Carson, *King Papers*, 3:169–70; Ralph McGill, "Says NAACP Follows Best Course in Rejecting Dr. King's Proposal," *Akron Beacon Journal*, April 20, 1967, A6; Ralph McGill to Martin Luther King Jr., unpublished and typed version (May 1, 1967), King Papers, KCLA, 1; and Baldwin et al., *Legacy of King*, 34–35, 69–70n152–56.

167 Carson, *King Papers*, 3:169–70, 253, 478; Carson, *King Papers*, 4:273, 359, 408.

168 Carson, *King Papers*, 4:409.

169 King, "America's Chief Moral Dilemma," 19; Lewis V. Baldwin, *The Voice of Conscience: The Church in the Mind of Martin Luther King, Jr.* (New York: Oxford University Press, 2010), 176; Carson, *King Papers*, 4:211–13. King included southern white moderates and liberals, along with Negroes, in what he termed "the enlightened South." Also, he felt that even the "President of the United States" had to "be a genuine humanitarian." See SCLC, "King Urges JFK," 2; and Martin Luther King Jr., "The Republican Presidential Nomination," statement, unpublished and typed version (April 1, 1964), King Papers, KCLA, 2.

170 Martin Luther King Jr., "Introduction," in William Bradford Huie, *3 Lives for Mississippi* (New York: New American Library, 1968), 7–8; King, *Stride toward Freedom*, 202; Carson, *King Papers*, 4:129, 211–13, 331–32, 398, 409; Washington, *Testament*, 316; Carson, *King Papers*, 7:140, 145.

171 At times, King spoke of the socially active southern Negro minister as "a symbol of the new Negro." See King, "'New Negro' of the South," 16–19; Carson, *King Papers*, 3:264, 283, 285, 301, 305, 324, 456; Carson, *King Papers*, 4:126, 129, 170–71, 326, 364; Carson, *King Papers*, 7:378, 530; and Carson, *King Papers*, 5:127.

172 Carson, *King Papers*, 3:285; King, "Realistic Look," 7; Carson, *King Papers*, 4:126.

173 Carson, *King Papers*, 5:521; Carson, *King Papers*, 7:472. King also spoke of the use of nonviolent means to achieve the ends of the integrated society as being equivalent to putting on "the breastplate of righteousness" and "the armor of truth." See Martin Luther King Jr., "Moving to Another Mountain," *Wesleyan Alumnus* 52, no. 4 (May 1968), see quote from King's 1964 commencement address at Wesleyan University on magazine's front cover.

174 King, *Where Do We Go*, 16. King apparently believed that true integration is in essence "internal"—that it must occur from within before finding expression externally. See Carson, *King Papers*, 7:212.

175 Washington, *Testament*, 359; Carson, *King Papers*, 4:340; Carson, *King Papers*, 5:288. King offered one of the most brilliant accounts of the "reversal of truth" that produced "the Uncle Tom and the invincible Mr. Charlie" on record, focusing especially on how "the Negro" learned to blame himself "rather than his oppressor or his environment" for his condition and also "to honor his exploiter and dishonor himself." See King, "True Dignity," 2.

176 Carson, *King Papers*, 5:359; Carson, *King Papers*, 4:230; Martin Luther King Jr., "The Mission to the Social Frontiers," speech, unpublished and typed version (n.d.), King Papers, KCLA, 4; Carson, *King Papers*, 4:273; Carson, *King Papers*, 3:475.

177 Martin Luther King Jr., "Going to Chicago," *New York Amsterdam News*, January 15, 1966, 10.

178 King seemingly embraced this team or group leadership model in principle but not so much in practice, a point supported by his attitude toward female leaders in the civil rights movement. He criticized W. E. B. Du Bois's "talented tenth" leadership model, which "urged the 'talented tenth' to rise and pull behind it the mass of the race," noting that it left "no role for the whole people"—that "it was a tactic for an aristocratic elite who would themselves be benefited while leaving behind the 'untalented' 90 percent." See King, "America's Chief Moral Dilemma," 19; and King, *Why We Can't Wait*, 33.

179 Martin Luther King Jr. to Mrs. Katie E. Whickam, unpublished and typed version (July 7, 1958), King Papers, KCLA, 1; Carson, *King Papers*, 6:585.

180 King was in essence an ambivalent soul when it came to these matters. Evidently, he was quite familiar with the long history of sexism and female subordination, for he referred to the Greek philosopher Aristotle's "idea of the inferiority of women." He also occasionally quoted in his own way the apostle Paul's words: "In Christ there is neither male nor female" (Galatians 3:28). He made other statements praising the contributions of women to the freedom struggle, but he never became a fierce advocate of women's liberation. See Carson, *King Papers*, 7:292; King, *Trumpet of Conscience*, 72; Carson,

King Papers, 6:585; Carson, *King Papers*, 4:291; King, "People to People," 1–2; King, "Something Happening in Mississippi," 20; King, "Address," Fiftieth Anniversary of the Women's International League, 1; and Vicki L. Crawford and Lewis V. Baldwin, eds., *Reclaiming the Great World House: The Global Vision of Martin Luther King, Jr.* (Athens: University of Georgia Press, 2019), 219–45.

181 King, "En Granslos Kval Pa Operan: Remarks," 3. For King's use of the terms "new America" and "new nation" at other points, see Carson, *King Papers*, 7:340, 484; Carson and Holloran, *Knock at Midnight*, 147; Carson, *King Papers*, 6:332.

182 Dirks, "'Essence Is Love,'" 1; Carson, *King Papers*, 5:330; Washington, *Testament*, 250.

183 King, "Address," Public Meeting of the Charlotte, NC, Branch of the NAACP, 3; Carson, *King Papers*, 4:104, 190; Carson, *King Papers*, 3:137–38, 309; Carson, *King Papers*, 5:125; Carson, *King Papers*, 7:114; King, *Stride toward Freedom*, 224.

184 Ansbro, *Martin Luther King*, 111; King, *Stride toward Freedom*, 224; Carson, *King Papers*, 4:183, 474; Carson, *King Papers*, 5:129, 149, 410; Carson, *King Papers*, 7:167, 458, 484; Carson, *King Papers*, 6:467, 475.

185 Gandhi's point most certainly owed much to his exposure to the old Negro spirituals, which he loved very much, and which gave him insight into the mind, heart, and soul of Negro people. Gandhi also said, in words that seemingly anticipated a Martin Luther King Jr., that "one day the black races will rise like the avenging Attila against their white oppressors unless someone presents to them the weapon of *satyagraha*." Gandhi offered a strikingly different view of people of European descent, noting that "the people of Europe are sure to perish if they continue to be violent." See Homer A. Jack, ed., *The Gandhi Reader* (Bloomington: Indiana University Press, 1956), 312–16; Baldwin, *Balm in Gilead*, 232; and Thomas Merton, ed., *Gandhi on Non-violence: Selected Texts from Mohandas K. Gandhi's "Non-violence in Peace and War"* (New York: New Directions, 1965), 34, 56.

186 Reinhold Niebuhr, *Moral Man and Immoral Society: A Study in Ethics and Politics* (New York: Charles Scribner's Sons, 1960; originally published in 1932), 252–54.

187 The African American scholar St. Clair Drake mentioned this insight from Toynbee in a letter to King as early as March 1956, and interestingly enough, King subsequently

referenced it occasionally in his own writings and speeches. See Carson, *King Papers*, 3:181; Carson, *King Papers*, 4:80; King, *Stride toward Freedom*, 224; and Carson, *King Papers*, 5:125.

188 Carson, *King Papers*, 3:137–38; Carson, *King Papers*, 4:104, 190.

189 King, *Where Do We Go*, 50; Carson, *King Papers*, 5:503–4.

190 King, "Social Frontiers," 3; James R. Wood to Mr. L. F. Palmer Jr., unpublished and typed statement dictated by Martin Luther King Jr. (February 23, 1961), King Papers, KCLA, 1–2.

191 Washington, *Testament*, 368–69.

192 King denounced the "back-to-Africa" program and the Black separate nation ideal of Marcus Garvey. King knew that such a political philosophy and ideal ran like a thread through Black history, but he mostly blamed the white supremacist system that had for so long oppressed and segregated Black people. See King, *Why We Can't Wait*, 33, 35; Carson, *King Papers*, 7:203–4, 539; Carson, *King Papers*, 4:219–20; Martin Luther King Jr., "A Knock at Midnight," sermon, unpublished and typed version, All Saints Community Church, Los Angeles, CA (June 25, 1967), King Papers, KCLA, 6; and Washington, *Testament*, 665.

193 King, "Knock at Midnight," 6.

194 King, *Stride toward Freedom*, 169, 172; Carson, *King Papers*, 5:359–60.

195 Carson, *King Papers*, 7:139, 162–63, 208–10; King, "Social Frontiers," 10; Carson, *King Papers*, 5:188, 280, 283, 510; King, "Christian Movement," 6–7; King, "Bold Design," 259.

196 King, "Christian Movement," 5–7; Carson, *King Papers*, 7:375, 425; Carson, *King Papers*, 6:171; King, "Address," National Press Club, 6; King, "Social Frontiers," 16; Clayborne Carson, ed., *The Papers of Martin Luther King, Jr.*, vol. 1, *Called to Serve, January 1929–June 1951*, ed. Ralph E. Luker and Penny A. Russell (Berkeley: University of California Press, 1992), 268.

197 Carson, *King Papers*, 7:212.

198 Martin Luther King Jr., "A Lecture," unpublished and typed version, Federation Protestante de France Mutualite, Paris, France (October 24, 1965), King Papers, KCLA, 18; Carson, *King Papers*, 6:449, 469; Carson, *King Papers*, 3:73, 79; Carson, *King Papers*, 5:188; Baldwin, *Balm in Gilead*, 272; King, *Where Do We Go*, 20; *Trumpet of Conscience*, 40–41; Carson, *King Papers*, 4:208–10n4.

199 Carson, *King Papers*, 7:192.

200 Carson and Shepard, *Call to Conscience*, 115. Here John Lewis takes a position in stark contrast with that of Patrick Buchanan—a newspaper columnist, television personality, and former Republican presidential candidate—who scoffed at the idea of comparing King to the founding fathers. Buchanan argued that despite King's achievements, he "was not remotely so great a man or historic figure as George Washington, who led the army of independence, presided at our constitutional convention, and became our first president." "To raise Dr. King to a niche in the pantheon of American heroes alongside our founding father, as equally deserving of a holiday," Buchanan added, "is affirmative action at its most absurd." But the fact is that King freed America in ways that Washington and the other founding fathers did not. Put another way, King was instrumental in bringing freedom to people whom the original founding fathers, by both acts of commission and omission, helped enslave. See Patrick Buchanan, "A Rascal's Bedroom Escapades Diminish His Status as a Saint," *Tennessean*, October 22, 1989, 5G; and Baldwin, *Make the Wounded Whole*, 297.

201 Carson, *King Papers*, 5:258.

202 King, *Stride toward Freedom*, 103, 220; Washington, *Testament*, 41–42.

203 Washington, *Testament*, 225.

204 King, *Where Do We Go*, 3, 11, 67–101; King, "En Granslos Kval Pa Operan: Remarks," 3.

205 King, "En Granslos Kval Pa Operan: Remarks," 3.

206 King, "Speech," European Tour, 3.

207 King often used the phrases *new world* or *new world order*, and at times *new earth*. See King, "Address," Fiftieth Anniversary of the Women's International League, 9; Carson and Holloran, *Knock at Midnight*, 121–22, 186; King, *Trumpet of Conscience*, 50; Carson, *King Papers*, 6:112, 181–83; Carson, *King Papers*, 3:478; Carson, *King Papers*, 5:418; and Carson, *King Papers*, 4:178, 331–32, 334, 342.

208 Carson, *King Papers*, 5:221–24, 254, 275; King, "Lecture," Federation Protestante de France Mutualite, 3; Washington, *Testament*, 280; King, "Doubts and Certainties Link," 1; Carson, *King Papers*, 4:542.

209 King, "Lecture," Federation Protestante de France Mutualite, 2–6; King, *Where Do We Go*, 186–91; Carson, *King Papers*, 6:438–39.

210 Carson, *King Papers*, 6:169, 197–98, 327; Carson, *King Papers*, 5:170; King, *Trumpet*

of Conscience, 31; Martin Luther King Jr., "Speech," (unpublished speech, March 17, 1966), Methodist University, Dallas, Texas, King Papers, KCLA.

211 King, *Where Do We Go*, 57.

212 Lewis V. Baldwin and Paul R. Dekar, eds., *"In an Inescapable Network of Mutuality": Martin Luther King, Jr. and the Globalization of an Ethical Ideal* (Eugene, OR: Cascade, 2013), 49; Washington, *Testament*, 318–19.

213 Martin Luther King Jr., "A Statement to the Press regarding Nobel Trip," unpublished and typed version, Sheraton Atlantic Hotel, Atlantic City, NJ (December 4, 1964), King Papers, KCLA, 1; Carson, *King Papers*, 4:502; Baldwin, *Balm in Gilead*, 229, 235.

214 King, "Nobel Trip," 1; Baldwin, *Balm in Gilead*, 237; Martin Luther King Jr., "Untitled Column on European Tour," unpublished and typed version, prepared for *New York Amsterdam News* (September 17, 1984), King Papers, KCLA, 1–2; Baldwin and Dekar, *"Inescapable Network,"* 49.

215 King made this assertion while acknowledging that he was being criticized, during his speeches against US involvement in the Vietnam War, for his "role in international affairs." See King, "Christian Movement," 7–8. King realized that Blacks had already contributed enormously, and perhaps more than any other single group, to building bridges between the United States and other parts of the world through folklore, the arts, spiritual values, and most certainly the civil rights movement. See Baldwin et al., *Legacy of King*, 21, 263.

216 Martin Luther King Jr. to Mr. Sam Wyler, unpublished and typed version (July 20, 1967), King Papers, KCLA, 2.

217 Carson, *King Papers*, 5:125.

218 Carson, *King Papers*, 7:181; Carson, *King Papers*, 5:224, 231; Carson, *King Papers*, 4:103; King, "En Granslos Kval Pa Operan: Remarks," 1.

219 King, *Where Do We Go*, 167; King, "Social Frontiers," 5; Washington, *Testament*, 209.

220 King, *Where Do We Go*, 173–76.

221 Carson, *King Papers*, 4:175; Carson, *King Papers*, 6:344; King, "En Granslos Kval Pa Operan: Remarks," 3–4.

222 Carson, *King Papers*, 6:112, 138.

223 King, "Untitled Column on European Tour," 1; King, "Excerpts from an Address," 1–2.

224 King, "Doubts and Certainties Link," 1–2.

225 King, "Lecture," Federation Protestante de France Mutualite, 2.

226 King, "Christian Movement," 8; King, "Nobel Lecture," 17.

227 King, *Where Do We Go*, 49–50, 81–82, 132–33, 161–66, 176–81; King, "Nobel Lecture," 13–17; Carson, *King Papers*, 6:413–17; King, *Trumpet of Conscience*, 53–64.

228 King, "Knock at Midnight," 2.

229 Miss D. McDonald to M. G. Ramachandran, unpublished and typed statement dictated by Martin Luther King Jr. (December 20, 1961), King Papers, KCLA, 1.

230 Carson, *King Papers*, 5:122.

231 King, "Address," Fiftieth Anniversary of the Women's International League, 1.

232 King, "Knock at Midnight," 11; Martin Luther King Jr., "Transformed Nonconformist," sermon, unpublished and typed version, Ebenezer Baptist Church, Atlanta, GA (January 16, 1966), King Papers, KCLA, 6; Martin Luther King Jr., "The Drum Major Instinct," sermon, unpublished and typed version, Ebenezer Baptist Church, Atlanta, GA (February 4, 1968), King Papers, KCLA, 7.

233 Martin Luther King Jr., "An Address," unpublished and typed version, Synagogue Council of America, Waldorf Astoria Hotel, New York, NY (December 5, 1965), King Papers, KCLA, 10.

234 King, "Address," Fiftieth Anniversary of the Women's International League, 2, 5; King, "Nobel Lecture," 20; Carson, *King Papers*, 5:416.

235 King, "Address," Synagogue Council of America, 11; King, "Drum Major Instinct," 6; Carson, *King Papers*, 6:133; Carson, *King Papers*, 5:416.

236 King, "Speech," European Tour, 2.

237 Carson, *King Papers*, 5:122.

238 Carson, *King Papers*, 5:234; Carson and Shepard, *Call to Conscience*, 101, 191, 205; King, *Where Do We Go*, 62–63; Washington, *Testament*, 331; Carson, *King Papers*, 4:514; Carson, *King Papers*, 7:507, 531; King, *Trumpet of Conscience*, 72.

239 Martin Luther King Jr., "A Statement," unpublished and typed version, news from the Southern Christian Leadership Conference (November 1, 1960), King Papers, KCLA, 1.

240 King was convinced that all of the great religions expressed through their "ethical systems" the moral obligation to pursue the truthful ends of human community through truthful or peaceful means. To illustrate his point regarding the essential unity of world religions around these and other concerns, he noted that "the Gandhian concept of noninjury parallels the Hebraic-Christian teaching of the sacredness of every human being."

365

See King, *Where Do We Go*, 190–91; Washington, *Testament*, 124; and Lewis V. Baldwin, ed., *"In a Single Garment of Destiny": A Global Vision of Justice—Martin Luther King, Jr.* (Boston: Beacon, 2012), 204–5.

241   Wood to Palmer, 1–2.

242   Kenneth L. Smith and Ira G. Zepp Jr., *Search for the Beloved Community: The Thinking of Martin Luther King, Jr.* (Valley Forge, PA: Judson, 1998; originally published in 1974), 141.

243   Carson, *King Papers*, 6:182, 511–12, 567; Ayres, *Wisdom of King*, 132; King, "Social Frontiers," 16; King, "Meaning of Hope," 11; King, "Nobel Lecture," 27, and Carson, *King Papers*, 5:120.

Chapter 6

1   Gunnar Jahn, who headed the Nobel Committee when King received the Nobel Peace Prize in December 1964, essentially supported this view when he noted that King "was the first person in the Western world to have shown us that a struggle can be waged without violence." See "Dr. King Accepts Nobel Peace Prize as 'Trustee,'" *New York Times*, December 11, 1964, 1.

2   Ralph Keyes, *The Post-truth Era: Dishonesty and Deception in Contemporary Life* (New York: St. Martin's, 2004), 10–30; Comments by Nicolle Wallace on "A Crisis of Credibility," *Deadline: White House*, aired March 12, 2020, on MSNBC; Christina Pazzanese, "National & World Affairs: Politics in the Post-truth Age," *Harvard Gazette*, July 14, 2016, https://news.harvard.edu/gazette/story/2016/07/politics-in-a-post-truth-age/; Sophia A. Rosenfeld, *Democracy and Truth: A Short History* (Philadelphia: University of Pennsylvania Press, 2019), 2, 15, 20, 39, 136–37; Hillary McQuilkin and Meghna Chakrabarti, "In Search of Truth, Part IV: Are We Living in a Post-truth World?," *On Point*, February 27, 2020, https://www.wbur.org/onpoint/2020/02/27/part-iv-post-truth; Johan Farkas and Jannick Schou, *Post-truth, Fake News and Democracy: Mapping the Politics of Falsehood* (New York: Routledge, 2020), 43–158.

3   I am indebted to the world-renowned scholar Beverly J. Lanzetta for this description of King. See Beverly Lanzetta, email message to author, June 26, 2021, 1–2.

4   The term "post-truth politics" was first used as far back as 1992 by Steve Tesich, the Serbian-American playwright. Used interchangeably with *post-factual politics* and *post-reality politics*, it refers to "a political culture in which debate is framed largely by appeals to emotion disconnected from the details of policy, and by the repeated assertion of talking points to which factual rebuttals are ignored." See Wikipedia, s.v., "Post-truth politics," accessed July 1, 2021, https://en.wikipedia.org/wiki/Post-truth_politics; and Richard Kreitner, "Post-truth and Its Consequences: What a 25-Year-Old Essay Tells Us about the Current Moment," *Nation*, November 30, 2016, https://www.thenation.com/article/archive/post-truth-and-its-consequences-what-a-25-year-old-essay-tells-us-about-the-current-moment/.

5   Lee McIntyre, *Post-truth* (Cambridge, MA: MIT Press, 2018), 1–122, 151–72; Hamid Foroughi et al., "Leadership in a Post-truth Era: A New Narrative Disorder?," *Leadership* 15, no. 2 (March 2019): 1–25, accessed May 17, 2021, https://journals.sagepub.com/doi/full/10.1177/1742715019835369.

6   Michiko Kakutani, "The Death of Truth: How We Gave Up on Facts and Ended Up with Trump," *Guardian*, July 14, 2018, https://www.theguardian.com/books/2018/jul/14/the-death-of-truth-how-we-gave-up-on-facts-and-ended-up-with-trump; Sverre Spoelstra, "Donald Trump's War on Facts Is the Latest Play in a Long-Established Tradition to Create a Post-truth Reality," *Conversation*, October 24, 2019, https://theconversation.com/donald-trumps-war-on-facts-is-the-latest-play-in-a-long-established-tradition-to-create-a-post-truth-reality-125755. Sophia Rosenfeld rightly notes that former president Trump is "widely considered both a symptom and an accelerant of our move away from any shared standards of truth." See Rosenfeld, *Democracy and Truth*, 5–6.

7   Vincent Harding, *Martin Luther King: The Inconvenient Hero* (Maryknoll, NY: Orbis, 2008; originally published in 1996), ix; Kalamu ya Salaam, "Rest in Peace and Power: Dr. Vincent G. Harding, July 25, 1931–May 19, 2014," *Neo-griot* (blog), May 20, 2014, kalamu.com/neogriot/2014/05/21/obit-video-dr-vincent-g-harding/.

8   Harding, *Martin Luther King*, vi–xii.

9   Michael Dyson makes a bold and at times brilliant effort to reveal "the true" King by

dispelling the "romantic images" and treating the "deeply flawed and yet amazing" human being. He has taken a giant step in exposing the man behind the myth. See Michael Eric Dyson, *I May Not Get There with You: The True Martin Luther King, Jr.* (New York: Free Press, 2000), xv–xvii, 1–8. Also See Lewis V. Baldwin, *Behind the Public Veil: The Humanness of Martin Luther King, Jr.* (Minneapolis: Fortress, 2016), 1–319.

10 Clarence B. Jones, *What Would Martin Say?*, with Joel Engel (New York: HarperCollins, 2008), 33–67, 78–99, 110–24, 134–41, 164–78.

11 For the most extensive critique of Clarence Jones's mythmaking surrounding King, see Lewis V. Baldwin and Rufus Burrow Jr., eds., *The Domestication of Martin Luther King, Jr.: Clarence B. Jones, Right-Wing Conservatism, and the Manipulation of the King Legacy* (Eugene, OR: Cascade, 2013), xix–xxii (Introduction), 1–235.

12 King had a great relationship with Black civil rights leaders for the most part in his day, and he was never known to criticize them publicly. His statements about and communications with Ralph D. Abernathy, Thurgood Marshall, Adam Clayton Powell Jr., Bayard Rustin, and A. Philip Randolph are quite revealing in this regard. See Clayborne Carson, ed., *The Papers of Martin Luther King, Jr.*, vol. 3, *Birth of a New Age, December 1955–December 1956*, ed. Stewart Burns et al. (Berkeley: University of California Press, 1997), 253, 376–78; Clayborne Carson, ed., *The Papers of Martin Luther King, Jr.*, vol. 4, *Symbol of the Movement, January 1957–December 1958*, ed. Susan Carson et al. (Berkeley: University of California Press, 2000), 158, 175, 195–96, 229, 235, 260, 270–71, 360, 420–21, 527–28; Clayborne Carson, ed., *The Papers of Martin Luther King, Jr.*, vol. 5, *Threshold of a New Decade, January 1959–December 1960*, ed. Tenisha Armstrong et al. (Berkeley: University of California Press, 2005), 350, 354, 361, 390, 480–81; and Clayborne Carson, ed., *The Papers of Martin Luther King, Jr.*, vol. 7, *To Save the Soul of America, January 1961–August 1962*, ed. Tenisha Armstrong (Berkeley: University of California Press, 2014), 132, 153–54, 306–8, 337, 428–29, 496.

13 King called for "compensatory measures" as part of a larger "Economic Bill of Rights" or "Bill of Rights for the Disadvantaged." See Martin Luther King Jr., *Why We Can't Wait* (New York: New American Library, 1963), 134–41.

14 Clayborne Carson, ed., *The Papers of Martin Luther King, Jr.*, vol. 6, *Advocate of the Social Gospel, September 1948–March 1963*, ed. Susan Carson et al. (Berkeley: University of California Press, 2007), 484; Martin Luther King Jr., *Where Do We Go from Here: Chaos or Community?* (Boston: Beacon, 1968; originally published in 1967), 79–80, 103; Martin Luther King Jr., "A Knock at Midnight," sermon, unpublished and typed version, All Saints Community Church, Los Angeles, CA (June 25, 1967), Martin Luther King Jr. Papers, Library and Archives of the Martin Luther King Jr. Center for Nonviolent Social Change, Inc. (KCLA), 14–16; Martin Luther King Jr., *The Trumpet of Conscience* (San Francisco: Harper & Row, 1968; originally published in 1967), 12; James M. Washington, ed., *A Testament of Hope: The Essential Writings and Speeches of Martin Luther King, Jr.* (New York: HarperCollins, 1991), 317.

15 Carson, *King Papers*, 4:460; "Of Riots and Wrongs against Jews," *SCLC Newsletter*, July–August 1964, 11; Washington, *Testament*, 370, 668–70; King, *Where Do We Go*, 63, 91–93.

16 King, *Where Do We Go*, 14, 72–101, 118–19, 152, 173–76; Martin Luther King Jr., "Doubts and Certainties Link," interview, unpublished, transcribed, and typed version, London, England (Winter 1968), King Papers, KCLA, 1–2.

17 Martin Luther King Jr., *Stride toward Freedom: The Montgomery Story* (New York: Harper & Row, 1958), 213; King, *Where Do We Go*, 61, 181–86; King, *Trumpet of Conscience*, 63–64; Washington, *Testament*, 7–8, 19, 32–34, 55, 83, 87–88, 179, 224–25, 233, 360–61, 365–66, 374, 403–5, 482–83, 589–94.

18 Carolyn Garris, "Martin Luther King's Conservative Legacy," Heritage Foundation, January 12, 2006, https://www.heritage.org/conservatism/report/martin-luther-kings-conservative-legacy.

19 Alveda King is partially right in saying that her grandfather, Martin Luther King Sr., was a Republican for much of his life. That changed in 1960, however, after the Democratic presidential candidate John F. Kennedy intervened to have his son King Jr. released from Reidsville State Prison in Georgia. The Republican presidential candidate Richard M. Nixon knew King Sr. and King Jr., but he refused to advocate for the release of King Jr. At that point, King Sr., or Daddy King as he was affectionately called,

367

switched to the Democratic Party and was instrumental in the Black voter turnout that elected Kennedy the thirty-fifth US president. See Alveda C. King, "A Covenant with Life: Reclaiming MLK's Legacy," quoted in Fred Decker, "Letters to the Editor," *Carolina Coast—Online*, October 26, 2012, https://www.carolinacoastonline.com/news_times/opinions/letters_to_editor/article_03134e28-236c-11e2-a81e-0019bb2963f4.html; John Blake, "MLK was a Republican and Other Myths," updated version, CNN, January 18, 2016, https://www.cnn.com/2016/01/15/us/mlk-myths/index.html; and Clayborne Carson, ed., *The Autobiography of Martin Luther King, Jr.* (New York: Warner, 1998), 142–50.

20 Baldwin and Burrow, *Domestication of King*, 15; James D. Hunter, *Culture Wars: The Struggle to Define America* (New York: Basic, 1991), 17.

21 Baldwin and Burrow, *Domestication of King*, 15; Justin Watson, *The Christian Coalition: Dreams of Restoration, Demands for Recognition* (New York: St. Martin's, 1999), 45, 79, 136.

22 Watson, *Christian Coalition*, 136; Baldwin and Burrow, *Domestication of King*, 15–16; Daniel C. Maguire, *The New Subversives: Anti-Americanism of the Religious Right* (New York: Continuum, 1982), 39–40.

23 Maguire, *New Subversives*, 40.

24 Lewis V. Baldwin et al., *The Legacy of Martin Luther King, Jr.: The Boundaries of Law, Politics, and Religion* (Notre Dame, IN: University of Notre Dame Press, 2002), 104; Baldwin and Burrow, *Domestication of King*, 16; George E. Curry, ed., *The Affirmative Action Debate* (Reading, MA: Addison-Wesley, 1996), 60–63, 133, 212; Obery M. Hendricks, "The Domestication of Martin Luther King, Jr.," *A.M.E. Church Review*, April–June 1998, 53–54.

25 King, *Why We Can't Wait*, 19–20; Washington, *Testament*, 142, 198; Carson, *King Papers*, 5:467–68, 482–86.

26 Washington, *Testament*, 660; Carson, *King Autobiography*, 144, 149–50; Carson, *King Papers*, 7:133; Carson, *King Papers*, 5:518–19, 535–37, 542–43, 565.

27 Washington, *Testament*, 660; Carson, *King Papers*, 7:321–23.

28 Carson, *King Papers*, 7:182.

29 King, *Where Do We Go*, 146; Washington, *Testament*, 307.

30 Carson, *King Papers*, 5:287; Washington, *Testament*, 198.

31 Harding, *Martin Luther King*, vii–ix.

32 Rufus Burrow has done more than any other King scholar to highlight King's significance as a thinker. See Rufus Burrow Jr., *God and Human Dignity: The Personalism, Theology, and Ethics of Martin Luther King, Jr.* (Notre Dame, IN: University of Notre Dame Press, 2006), 1–269; Rufus Burrow Jr., *Extremist for Love: Martin Luther King, Jr., Man of Ideas and Nonviolent Social Action* (Minneapolis: Fortress, 2014), 1–364; and Rufus Burrow Jr., *Martin Luther King, Jr., and the Theology of Resistance* (Jefferson, NC: McFarland, 2015), 5–244.

33 "Interview with Martin Luther King, Jr.," unpublished, transcribed, and typed version, *Merv Griffin Show*, syndicated talk show for Westinghouse Broadcasting, New York, NY (July 6, 1967), King Papers, KCLA, 17.

34 Lee E. Dirks, "'The Essence Is Love': The Theology of Martin Luther King, Jr.," *National Observer*, December 30, 1963, 12.

35 King, *Where Do We Go*, 67.

36 Martin Luther King Jr., *Strength to Love* (Philadelphia: Fortress, 1981; originally published in 1963), 147.

37 Burrow, *God and Human Dignity*, 8–15; David J. Garrow, *Bearing the Cross: Martin Luther King, Jr., and the Southern Christian Leadership Conference* (New York: William Morrow, 1986), 374–76; Dyson, *May Not Get There*, 139–63, 280–81; Preston N. Williams, "The Public and Private Burdens of Martin Luther King, Jr.," *Christian Century* 104, no. 6 (February 25, 1987): 198.

38 Dyson, *May Not Get There*, xv.

39 Dyson, *May Not Get There*, ix.

40 See "The Beast as Saint: The Truth about Martin Luther King, Jr," A Historical Examination, accessed January 25, 2014, http://www.martinlutherking.org/the beast.html; and Patrick Buchanan, "A Rascal's Bedroom Escapades Diminish His Status as a Saint," *Tennessean*, October 22, 1989, 5G.

41 Barbara Ransby, "A Black Feminist's Response to Attacks on Martin Luther King Jr.'s Legacy," *New York Times*, June 3, 2019, https://www.nytimes.com/2019/06/03/opinion/martin-luther-king-fbi.html.

42 Ransby, "Black Feminist's Response," 1–4; Clayborne Carson, *Martin's Dream: My Journey and the Legacy of Martin Luther King, Jr.—A Memoir* (New York: Palgrave Macmillan, 2013), 117–18; Donna Murch, "A Historian's Claims about Martin Luther King Are Shocking—and Irresponsible," *Guardian*, June 8, 2019, https://www

.theguardian.com/commentisfree/2019/jun/
08/martin-luther-king-david-garrow-essay
-claims.

43 Daniel J. Flynn, "The MLK Story No One
Wanted to Read: New Revelations Undermined by Who Was Doing the Spying,"
American Spectator, May 31, 2019, https://
spectator.org/the-mlk-story-no-one
-wanted-to-read/.

44 "'Time for Some Statue Removals?': Twitter
Reacts to MLK Sex Life Claims, Rape Comments," *RT USA News*, May 26, 2019, https://
www.rt.com/usa/460321-martin-luther-king
-fbi-sex/; Flynn, "MLK Story," 6–13.

45 Stewart Burns, *To the Mountaintop: Mar-
tin Luther King, Jr.'s Sacred Mission to Save
America: 1955–1968* (San Francisco: Harp-
erCollins, 2004), 226, 260–61, 265, 280,
287, 345–47, 355, 377–78, 394, 403, 406–
7, 421–22, 427, 435–37; David J. Garrow,
*The FBI and Martin Luther King, Jr.: From
"Solo" to Memphis* (New York: W. W. Nor-
ton, 1981), 216–19; Baldwin and Burrow,
Domestication of King, 126–27, 131, 137;
Garrow, *Bearing the Cross*, 603–7; Richard
Lischer, *The Preacher King: Martin Luther
King, Jr. and the Word that Moved America*
(New York: Oxford University Press, 1995),
167–72; David L. Chappell, *Waking from
the Dream: The Struggle for Civil Rights
in the Shadow of Martin Luther King, Jr.*
(New York: Random House, 2014), 13,
186n7, 187n12, and 188n26–27; Taylor
Branch, *Parting the Waters: America in the
King Years, 1954–63* (New York: Simon &
Schuster, 1988), 702, 706; Taylor Branch,
*At Canaan's Edge: America in the King Years,
1965–68* (New York: Simon & Schuster,
2006), 194–95, 641; Adam Fairclough, *To
Redeem the Soul of America: The Southern
Christian Leadership Conference and Mar-
tin Luther King, Jr.* (Athens: University of
Georgia Press, 1987), 345, 354–55, 375–
81; Baldwin, *Behind the Public Veil*, 13–14.

46 Baldwin, *Behind the Public Veil*, 13–319;
Burrow, *Theology of Resistance*, 122.

47 Washington, *Testament*, 316.

48 Vicki L. Crawford and Lewis V. Baldwin,
eds., *Reclaiming the Great World House: The
Global Vision of Martin Luther King, Jr.*
(Athens: University of Georgia Press, 2019),
306–23.

49 King, *Strength to Love*, 102–3; King, *Where
Do We Go*, 173–81; King, *Trumpet of Conscience*, 69–70; Washington, *Testament*, 233,
238, 280; Carson, *King Autobiography*, 339–
40, 343.

50 King, *Trumpet of Conscience*, 31.

51 Richard Lentz, *Symbols, the News Magazines,
and Martin Luther King, Jr.* (Baton Rouge:
Louisiana State University Press, 1990),
237.

52 Harding, *Martin Luther King*, vi.

53 Earl Ofari Hutchinson, *50 Years Later: Why
the Murder of Dr. King Still Hurts* (Los Angeles, CA: Middle Passage, 2018), 104; Mythili
Sampathkumar, "Trump Says He 'Admired'
Martin Luther King at Civil Rights Museum
Opening amid Boycotts over His Atten-
dance," *Independent*, December 9, 2017,
https://www.independent.co.uk/news/
world/americas/us-politics/donald-trump
-civil-rights-museum-mississippi-martin
-luther-king-jr-a8101491.html.

54 "Remarks by President Trump at Signing of
Proclamation to Honor Dr. Martin Luther
King, Jr. Day," Roosevelt Room, White House,
Washington, DC (January 12, 2018), accessed
July 5, 2018, https://trumpwhitehouse.archives
.gov/briefings-statements/remarks-president
-trump-signing-proclamation-honor-dr
-martin-luther-king-jr-day/; Sally Persons,
"Donald Trump Remembers Martin Luther
King Jr. Holiday in Video," *Washington
Times*, January 15, 2018, https://www
.washingtontimes.com/news/2018/jan/15/
donald-trump-remembers-martin-luther
-king-jr-holid/; CNBC, "President Donald
Trump to Sign Martin Luther King, Jr. Day
Proclamation," January 12, 2018, YouTube
video, https://www.youtube.com/watch?v=
PWxY5RxoAt0.

55 Matthew Rozsa, "Awkward: Trump Praises
Martin Luther King, Jr. after His Racist Comments," *Salon*, January 12, 2018, https://www
.salon.com/2018/01/12/awkward-trump
-praises-martin-luther-king-jr-after-his-racist
-comments/.

56 "Remarks by President Trump," 1; Allie
Malloy, "Trump Signs MLK Jr. Proclamation Amid Cries of Racism," *CNN Politics*,
January 12, 2018, https://www.cnn.com/
2018/01/12/politics/donald-trump-martin
-luther-king-jr/index.html.

57 "President Donald Trump Proclaims 50th
Anniversary of the Assassination of Dr. Martin Luther King, Jr.," April 4, 2018, accessed
July 5, 2018, https://br.usembassy.gov/
president-donald-j-trump-proclaims-50th
-anniversary-assassination-dr-martin-luther
-king-jr/.

58 Jeremy Diamond, "Trump Spends MLK Jr.
Day Golfing," *CNN Politics*, January 15,
2018, https://www.cnn.com/2018/01/15/
politics/mlk-jr-day-donald-trump-schedule/
index.html.

59 Louis Nelson, "Trump Marks MLK Day with 2-Minute Memorial Visit," *Politico*, January 21, 2019, https://www.politico.com/story/2019/01/21/trump-mlk-day-memorial-visit-1116559; Kathryn Watson, "Trump and Pence Make Surprise Visit to MLK Memorial," *CBS News*, January 21, 2019, https://www.cbsnews.com/news/trump-and-pence-make-surprise-visit-to-mlk-memorial/.

60 On this occasion, strangely enough, the counselor to the president, Kellyanne Conway, assured reporters in the briefing room that Donald Trump "agrees with many of the things that Dr. Martin Luther King stood for and agreed with for many years, including unity and equality." Conway also opined that King would not have agreed with Trump's impeachment, insisting, "I don't think it was within Dr. King's vision to have Americans dragged through a process where the President is not going to be removed from office, is not being charged with bribery, extortion, high crimes or misdemeanors." See Betsy Klein, "Trump Commemorates Martin Luther King, Jr. Day with Memorial Visit," CNN Politics, January 20, 2020, https://edition.cnn.com/2020/01/20/politics/donald-trump-martin-luther-king-jr-day/index.html; Brian Niemietz, "Trump Criticized for Making Martin Luther King, Jr. Holiday about Himself, Sending Pro-gun Tweets," *New York Daily News*, January 20, 2020, https://www.nydailynews.com/news/politics/ny-trump-mlk-martin-luther-king-day-pro-guns-20200120-k2vjj6fhz5byvocowxaagbsvia-story.html.

61 Sampathkumar, "Trump Says," 1; Elise Viebeck, "Trump: 'I Think I Am a Great Moral Leader,'" *Washington Post*, November 7, 2018, https://www.washingtonpost.com/politics/2018/live-updates/midterms/midterm-election-updates/trump-i-think-i-am-a-great-moral-leader/; Donald J. Trump, *Crippled America: How to Make America Great Again* (New York: Threshold Editions, 2015), x, 130–31.

62 My definition of ethical leadership is based largely on a reading of Walter E. Fluker, *Ethical Leadership: The Quest for Character, Civility, and Community* (Minneapolis: Fortress, 2009), vii–xi, 11–56; and Rufus Burrow Jr., "Martin Luther King, Jr., and Ethical Leadership," *Telos* 182 (Spring 2018): 11–28. Also see Carson, *King Papers*, 5:287; Carson, *King Papers*, 4:190; and Carson, *King Papers*, 3:461.

63 Carson, *King Papers*, 4:348, 418, 472, 504, 540; Washington, *Testament*, 372; Carson, *King Papers*, 5:152–53; Lewis V. Baldwin, *The Prayer Life of Martin Luther King, Jr.* (Minneapolis: Fortress, 2010), 67–70, 123n5.

64 Coretta Scott King, *My Life with Martin Luther King, Jr.* (New York: Henry Holt, 1993; originally published in 1969), 59, 169.

65 Washington, *Testament*, 154–55, 391–92; Carson, *King Papers*, 7:140, 144, 230; Baldwin et al., *Legacy of King*, 133–48; Carson, *King Autobiography*, 101.

66 King, *Where Do We Go*, 159.

67 Calvin Woodward, "AP Fact Check: Trump Presidency Creates an Alternative Reality," *AP News*, January 18, 2018, https://www.apnews.com/795740757d724bcca5749fb61a784fb5/AP-FACT-CHECK:-Tru; Benjamin Hart, "Trump's Reality Distortion Field Could Be a Huge Asset for Democrats this Fall," *New York Magazine*, April 28, 2018, https://nymag.com/intelligencer/2018/04/trumps-reality-distortion-field-could-help-tank-republicans.html; Comments by Steve Schmidt, *Deadline: White House*, aired November 9, 2020, on MSNBC.

68 Rosenfeld, *Democracy and Truth*, 7.

69 Carson, *King Papers*, 6:548; Carson, *King Papers*, 7:500. King equated living in "a world of illusion" or in a false reality with taking the easy path in life—with substituting "the soothing lemonade of escape for the bitter cup of reality." Harking back to Jesus's parables in the New Testament, King argued that the Prodigal Son "was the tragic victim of a threefold illusion" in that he mistakenly thought that "pleasure is the end of life," that "he was independent," and that "he could live happily outside his father's house and his father's will." In other words, he not only lived with lies but tragically misunderstood reality, the essence of freedom. See Carson, *King Papers*, 6:251, 271–72, 305.

70 Peterson goes on to conclude that Trump and Trumpism have cast an "inimitable shadow" over King's "radical call for America to live up to its Constitutional principles"—that "Trumpism" has utterly displaced "King's utopian dreams." See James Braxton Peterson, "Commentary: Martin Luther King, Jr. Tried to Warn Us about Donald Trump," *Fortune*, January 15, 2018, https://fortune.com/2018/01/15/martin-luther-king-jr-day-federal-holiday-donald-trump/. For similar arguments, made with a broader focus on how Trump has related to Blacks over time, see Hutchinson, *50 Years Later*, 103–9.

71 Peterson, "Commentary: Martin Luther King, Jr.," 1–2; King, *Strength to Love*, 12; King, *Stride toward Freedom*, 196; Washington, *Testament*, 314.

72 Carson, *King Papers*, 6:185, 453; Carson, *King Papers*, 7:594–95.

73 Some of Trump's critics have concluded that it is not difficult to draw comparisons between Trump and Hitler when it comes to truth and truth-telling. Based on what has been reported by both close associates and critics of Trump, we might assume that Trump read at least some of Hitler's speeches and seemingly admired him greatly. See "Trump's Ex-Wife Says He Kept Hitler's Book of Speeches by Bedside," Quint, February 26, 2016, https://www.thequint.com/news/world/trumps-ex-wife-says-he-kept-hitlers-book-of-speeches-by-bedside; Jon Levine, "Tina Brown: Trump Dumped Wine on Reporter after She Wrote about Hitler's Speeches He Kept," Wrap, November 9, 2017, https://www.thewrap.com/trump-dumped-wine-on-reporter-after-she-wrote-about-hitler-speeches-he-kept/; Thomas Colson, "Trump 'Obviously Admired Hitler', Says Anne Frank's Step Sister, Referring to Claims He Studied His Speeches," Yahoo News, April 9, 2021, https://news.yahoo.com/trump-obviously-admired-hitler-says-123359718.html; Bill McCann, "Commentary: Trump Takes Tactics from Hitler's Playbook," *Austin American-Statesman*, August 13, 2020, https://www.statesman.com/story/special/2020/08/13/commentary-trump-takes-tactics-from-hitler rsquos-playbook/113764796/; Kyle Smith, "Trump vs. Hitler: Let's Run the Numbers—a Celebration of Charles Blow, the First Pundit to Compare the Two Figures," *National Review*, October 19, 2017, https://www.nationalreview.com/2017/10/charles-blows-novel-idea-trump-hitler/; Charles M. Blow, "Trump Isn't Hitler—But the Lying," *New York Times*, October 19, 2017, https://www.nytimes.com/2017/10/19/opinion/trump-isnt-hitler-but-the-lying.html; and Horace Bloom, *Trump and Hitler: A Responsible Consideration*, 2nd ed. (Scotts Valley, CA: CreateSpace, 2017), 1–5, 15–107.

74 King believed deeply in "the moral world" and in "certain absolute moral laws," and he focused with piercing clarity on those "principles out of harmony with the moral laws of the universe." All of this has to be seriously considered in any serious analysis of his concept of ethical leadership. See Carson, *King Papers*, 6:530–31.

75 Carson, *King Papers*, 6:217, 595, 600.

76 Any suggestion that Trump's behavior—especially his incitement of an insurrection to block the peaceful transfer of presidential power—would be viewed as politically and morally acceptable today by King is mind-boggling. See Matt Stieb, "Kellyanne Conway: Martin Luther King, Jr. Would Be against Trump Impeachment," *New York Magazine*, January 20, 2020, https://nymag.com/intelligencer/2020/01/kellyanne-conway-mlk-would-be-against-trump-impeachment.html.

77 Carson, *King Papers*, 5:287; Washington, *Testament*, 198.

78 Trump has written about his admiration of Peale as a person, indicating that he "especially loved his sermons." "He would instill a very positive feeling about God that also made me feel positive about myself," Trump added. "I would literally leave that church feeling like I could listen to another three sermons." Apparently, Trump read Peale's *The Power of Positive Thinking* (1952). See Tamara Keith, "Trump Crowd Size Estimate May Involve 'The Power of Positive Thinking,'" January 22, 2017, in *NPR Politics Podcast*, https://www.npr.org/2017/01/22/510655254/trump-crowd-size-estimate-may-involve-the-power-of-positive-thinking; Gwenda Blair, "How Norman Vincent Peale Taught Donald Trump to Worship Himself: The Magnate's Biographer Explains the Spiritual Guide behind His Relentless Self-confidence," *Politico Magazine*, October 6, 2015, https://www.politico.com/magazine/story/2015/10/donald-trump-2016-norman-vincent-peale-213220; and Trump, *Crippled America*, 130.

79 King held that, on the other hand, "high religion" or "genuine religion gives you the capacity to accept the realities of life, not only yourself but the external circumstances that beat up against you in life." See Carson, *King Papers*, 6:266, 299–300.

80 Carson, *King Papers*, 6:96; Carson, *King Papers*, 3:300, 323.

81 See George M. Marsden, *Fundamentalism and American Culture: The Shaping of Twentieth-Century Evangelicalism, 1870–1925* (New York: Oxford University Press, 1980), 6, 184–88, 222; and Jeff Tollefson, "How Trump Damaged Science—and Why It Could Take Decades to Recover," *Nature*, October 7, 2020, https://www.nature.com/articles/d41586-020-02800-9.

82 Jessica Taylor, "After 'Choosing Donald Trump,' Is the Evangelical Church in Crisis?,"

NPR Politics, October 29, 2017, https://www.npr.org/2017/10/29/560097406/after-choosing-donald-trump-is-the-evangelical-church; Alexander Hurst, "Escape from the Trump Cult: Millions of Americans Are Blindly Devoted to Their Dear Leader—What Will It Take for Them to Snap Out of It?," *New Republic*, December 14, 2018, https://newrepublic.com/article/152638/escape-trump-cult; Dante Scala, "Trump and Evangelicals: Cult of Personality or Marriage of Convenience?," *Medium*, March 11, 2021, https://medium.com/3streams/cult-of-personality-or-marriage-of-convenience-23d629b0b1da; Lulu Garcia-Navarro, "Black Pastors and Trump," NPR, August 5, 2018, https://www.npr.org/2018/08/05/635748598/black-pastors-and-trump.

83 King, *Why We Can't Wait*, 89–92; Clayborne Carson and Peter Holloran, eds., *A Knock at Midnight: Inspiration from the Great Sermons of Reverend Martin Luther King, Jr.* (New York: Warner, 1998), 108–15; Lewis V. Baldwin, *The Voice of Conscience: The Church in the Mind of Martin Luther King, Jr.* (New York: Oxford University Press, 2010), 79, 248.

84 Kin, *Where Do We Go*, 96; King, *Strength to Love*, 11–12, 62, 99; King, *Why We Can't Wait*, 92; Carson, *King Papers*, 6:448–49.

85 King, *Trumpet of Conscience*, 53; Baldwin, *Voice of Conscience*, 92–93; Martin Luther King Jr., "A Cry of Hate or a Cry for Help?," statement, unpublished and typed version (August 1965), King Papers, KCLA, 4; Martin Luther King Jr., "Revolution and Redemption," speech, unpublished and typed version, European Baptist Assembly, Amsterdam, Holland (August 16, 1964), King Papers, KCLA, 1.

86 John Nichols writes in graphic terms about "the politics of anti-Obama 'birtherism.'" See John Nichols, *Horsemen of the Trumpocalypse* (New York: Nation, 2017), 24; and Amanda Carpenter, *Gaslighting America: Why We Love It When Trump Lies to Us* (New York: Broadside, 2018), 9–15, 80, 187–88.

87 William H. Frey, *Diversity Explosion: How New Racial Demographics Are Remaking America* (Washington, DC: Brookings Institution Press, 2018), 1–20, 43–148, 131–48, 167–90, 213–44; Christopher Caldwell, "The Browning of America," review of *Diversity Explosion: How New Racial Demographics Are Remaking America*, by William H. Frey, *Claremont Review of Books* 15, no. 1 (Winter 2014–15): 1–9, accessed May 22, 2021, https://claremontreviewofbooks.com/the-browning-of-america/. Interestingly enough, King had some sense of how the future might unfold in terms of the nation's changing demographics. In an article on Black Power in 1967, he alluded to the "political significance" of "this changing composition of the cities," noting, "By 1970 ten of our larger cities will have Negro majorities if present trends continue." King added, "We can shrug off this opportunity or use it for a new vitality to deepen and enrich our family and community life." See Washington, *Testament*, 306, 312.

88 Brian Bennett and Justin Worland, "Beyond the Base: Donald Trump's Coalition Is Broader Than the Democrats' Caricature," *Time*, October 22, 2018, 32–35; Southern Poverty Law Center (SPLC), "Ten Ways Trump Promoted an 'Alt-right' Agenda in Year One," *America the Trumped: 10 Ways the Administration Attacked Civil Rights in Year One* (2018): 4–23; "SPLC Helps Nation Combat Hate after Charlottesville," *SPLC Report* 47, no. 3 (Fall 2017): 1, 3; Adam Serwer, "Conservatives Have a White-Nationalism Problem," *Atlantic*, August 6, 2019, https://www.theatlantic.com/ideas/archive/2019/08/trump-white-nationalism/595555/; Dean Obeidallah, "Trump Is Trying to Whip Up Fear about the Browning of America," CNN Opinion, November 4, 2018, https://cnn.com./2018/11/04/opinions/trump-whip-up-browing-of-america-obeidallah/index.html; Peter Grier, "Is America's Media Divide Destroying Democracy?," *Christian Science Monitor*, April 16, 2019, https://www.csmonitor.com/USA/Politics/2019/0416/Is-America-s-media-divide-destroying-democracy; Eugene Robinson, "Trump Might Go down in History as the Last President of the Confederacy," *Washington Post*, June 11, 2020, https://www.washingtonpost.com/opinions/trump-might-go-down-in-history-as-the-last-president-of-the-confederacy/2020/06/11/590194e2-ac13-11ea-94d2-d7bc43b26bf9_story.html.

89 David Waters, "'White Again' Billboard Candidate Needs American History Lesson," *Tennessean*, July 3, 2016, 2H; Jason Devaney, "Pelosi: Trump Trying to 'Make America White Again,'" Newsmax, July 10, 2019, https://www.newsmax.com/newsfront/nancy-pelosi-cansus-/2019/07/10/id/923911/?ns_mail_uid=062c44f1-1244-472d-8161-46c4dd79aa28&ns_mail_i. Michael Dyson is right in saying that "the election of President Trump was all about Whiteness." See Michael Eric Dyson, *Tears We*

Cannot Stop: A Sermon to White America (New York: St. Martin's, 2017), 219, 221–22.

90 Trump, *Crippled America*, 6, 10, 13, 59, 126, 141–42, 159–69; Martin Luther King Jr. to A. Philip Randolph, unpublished and typed version (November 2, 1964), King Papers, KCLA, 1; Justin Rose, "Martin Luther King, Jr. on Making America Great Again," *Black Perspectives: AAIHS*, January 21, 2019, https://www.aaihs.org/martin-luther-king-jr-on-making-america-great-again/.

91 Rich Barlow, "Walter Fluker, MLK Professor of Ethical Leadership, to Retire after Coming Academic Year," *BU Today*, June 5, 2019, https://www.bu.edu/articles/2019/walter-fluker-mlk-prof-retiring/.

92 Ian Haney Lopez, "Op-Ed: Why Do Trump Supporters Deny the Racism That Seems So Evident to Democrats?," *Los Angeles Times*, August 13, 2019, https://www.latimes.com/opinion/story/2019-08-13/trump-voters-racism-politics-white-supremacy; Jon Levine, "Martin Luther King, Jr.'s Niece Defends Trump: 'I Don't Believe He Is a Racist,'" Wrap, January 15, 2018, https://www.thewrap.com/martin-luther-king-jrs-niece-defends-trump-dont-believe-racist-vi; Robert Farley, "Trump Has Condemned White Supremacists," Factcheck Posts, February 11, 2020, https://www.factcheck.org/2020/02/trump-has-condemned-white-supremacists/; Mallory Simon and Sara Sidner, "Trump Says He's Not a Racist: That's Not How White Nationalists See It," CNN Politics, July 16, 2019, https://www.cnn.com/2018/11/12/politics/white-supremacists-cheer-midterms-trump/index.html.

93 Fred Lucas, "Economy News: Trump 'Most Pro-Black President', Pastor Says in White House Meeting," Daily Signal, August 2, 2018, https://www.dailysignal.com/2018/08/02/trump-most-pro-black-president-pastor-says-in-white-house-meeting/; Dave Boyer, "Black Pastor Calls Trump More 'Pro-Black' than Obama," *Washington Times*, August 2, 2018, https://www.washingtontimes.com/news/2018/aug/2/black-pastor-calls-donald-trump-more-pro-black-bar/; Eugene Scott, "Steve Bannon Says Martin Luther King, Jr. Would Be 'Proud' of Donald Trump: King's Daughter Says Otherwise," *Washington Post*, May 24, 2018, https://washingtonpost.com/news/the-fix/wp/2018/05/23/steve-bannon-thinks-martin-luther-king-jr-would-be-proud-of-donald-trump/.

94 Scott, "Steve Bannon Says"; Kate Brumback, "MLK Daughter: No, Bannon, My Dad Wouldn't Be Proud of Trump," *AP News*, May 24, 2018, https://apnews.com/article/0101ee28b7844391bbbf9ba5ef5b7180.

95 John Bellamy Foster, "Neofascism in the White House," *Monthly Review: An Independent Socialist Magazine*, April 1, 2017, https://monthlyreview.org/2017/04/01/neofascism-in-the-white-house/; Connor O'Brien, "'I Think He Is a Racist', John Lewis Says of Trump," *Politico*, January 14, 2018, https://www.politico.com/story/2018/01/14/john-lewis-trump-racist-mlk-340365; Cathy Burke, "George Wallace's Daughter Sees Parallels with Father, Trump," Newsmax, July 31, 2019, https://www.newsmax.com/newsfront/george-wallace-segregation-racism-alabama/2019/07/31/id/926705/; Sam McKenzie Jr., "Trump Is George Wallace, but George Wallace Was Less Evil," Medium, June 28, 2018, https://sammckenziejr.medium.com/trump-is-george-wallace-but-george-wallace-was-less-evil-6ab463a08735; Tim Reid, "Joe Biden Compares Trump to Segregationist George Wallace," AOL News, July 20, 2019, https://www.aol.com/article/news/2019/07/20/joe-biden-compares-trump-segregationist-george-wallace/23773688/; Dahleen Glanton, "Column: Trump's Claim That He Has Done More for Black People Than Any President since Abraham Lincoln Makes Me Sick," *Chicago Tribune*, October 28, 2020, https://www.chicagotribune.com/columns/dahleen-glanton/ct-donald-trump-black-community-20201028-h6muhdj5ufarzimwhdbzqcxxfi-story.html; Maegan Vazquez et al., "Trump Claims He Deserves Credit for Making Juneteenth 'Very Famous,'" CNN, June 18, 2020, https://www.cnn.com/2020/06/18/politics/donald-trump-juneteenth-credit/index.

96 SPLC, "Ten Ways Trump," 6–9, 16–17; "AME Church Responds to Trump's Racist Rhetoric," *Los Angeles Sentinel*, January 17, 2018, https://lasentinel.net/ame-church-responds-to-trumps-racist-rhetoric.html; Dara Lind, "Donald Trump's Attack on Civil Rights Leader John Lewis, Explained," *Vox*, January 15, 2017, https://www.vox.com/2017/1/15/14273532/john-lewis-donald-trump-history; Marlam Khan, "Trump Calls Waters 'Extraordinarily Low IQ Person' in Wake of Restaurant Controversy," ABC News, June 25, 2018, https://abcnews.go.com/politics/trump-calls-waters-extremely-low-iq-person-wake/story?id=56140886; Joe Tacopino, "Don Lemon Fires Back against 'Nasty, Hateful' Trump Attack," *New York Post*, August 7, 2018, https://nypost.com/2018/08/07/don-lemon-calls-trump

-attack-one-of-oldest-canards-of-racism/; Robinson, "Trump Might Go Down."

97 Washington, *Testament*, 286.

98 Baldwin and Burrow, *Domestication of King*, 42; Frederick Wine, "The Rev. King's Dream Has Finally Come True: Letters to the Editor," *Tennessean*, November 6, 2008, 15A; Tim Wise, *Between Barack and a Hard Place: Racism and White Denial in the Age of Obama*, Open Media (San Francisco: City Lights, 2009), 7–110; Dylan Lovan, "Church Revisits Interracial Ban after Uproar," *Tennessean*, December 3, 2011, 5A.

99 King, *Where Do We Go*, 79–80.

100 The Know Nothing Party originated and thrived for a time as an expression of anti-Catholicism in parts of the United States. In the 1920s, fear of foreigners, especially within the ranks of Christian fundamentalism, triggered a series of restrictive anti-immigration legislation. See Randall Miller and Jon Wakelyn, eds., *Catholics in the Old South: Essays on Church and Culture* (Macon, GA: Mercer University Press, 1999), 35, 95–97, 231; Linda Gordon, "The Last Time a Wall Went Up to Keep Out Immigrants," *New York Times*, May 20, 2019, https://www.nytimes.com/2019/05/20/books/review/guarded-gate-daniel-okrent.html; and David R. Morse, *An American Legacy: Racism, Nativism, and White Supremacy* (Hartford, CT: PYP Academy Press, 2020), 3–400.

101 Trump, *Crippled America*, x, 14.

102 Stephen Mansfield, *Choosing Donald Trump: God, Anger, Hope, and Why Christian Conservatives Supported Him* (Grand Rapids, MI: Baker, 2017), 99; Trump, *Crippled America*, 23; Donna Brazile, *Hacks: The inside Story of Break-Ins and Breakdowns That Put Donald Trump in the White House* (New York: Hachette, 2917), 177.

103 Clyde Hughes, "91-Year-Old Beaten, Told—'Go Back to Your Own Country,'" Newsmax, July 10, 2018, https://www.newsmax.com/thewire/91-year-old-man-beaten-brick/2018/07/10/id/870822/?; Masha Gessen, "How the Media Normalizes Trump's Anti-immigrant Rhetoric," *New Yorker*, October 25, 2018, https://www.newyorker.com/news/our-columnists/how-the-mainstream-media-normalizes-trumps-anti-immigrant-rhetoric; "SPLC Wages Legal Battles against Trump's Assault on Immigrants," *SPLC Report* 49, no. 2 (Summer 2019): 5, 8; Nichols, *Horsemen of the Trumpocalypse*, 24; Alexia Fernandez Campbell, "Trump Described an Imaginary 'Invasion' at the Border 2 Dozen Times in the Past Year," *Vox*, August 7, 2019, https://www.vox.com/identities/2019/8/7/20756775/el-paso-shooting-trump-hispanic-invasion.

104 "Amid Covid-19 Crisis, SPLC and Allies Fight to Free Immigrants from Deadly Detention Centers," *SPLC Report* 50, no. 2 (Summer 2020): 5; "'Papa! Papa!': Audio of Children Stokes Rage over Separation," *MPR News*, June 19, 2018, https://www.mprnews.org/story/2018/06/19/papa-papa-audio-of-children-stokes-rage-over-separation; Andrea Delgado, "SIFI Open Eyes to Reality Immigrants Face inside Today's Deportation Machine," *SPLC Report* 48, no. 3 (Fall 2018): 3; Alan Gomez, "1st Deported 'Dreamer' Drops Lawsuit against Trump Administration," *USA Today and Tennessean*, October 20, 2017, 2B; Diarese George, "Congress Can Honor the Legacy of King with Dream Act," *Tennessean*, January 14, 2018, 3H; "Mississippi Immigration Raids Target Longtime Latinx Residents," *SPLC Report* 49, no. 3 (Fall 2019): 5; "Trump Administration Says It Will Build 20 Miles of New 'Border Barrier,'" Newsmax, August 27, 2019, https://www.newsmax.com/politics/trumps-border-wall/2019/08/27/id/930251/?ns_mail_uid=062c44f1-1244-472d-8161-46c4dd79aa28&ns_mail_job=D.

105 King, *Strength to Love*, 19; Washington, *Testament*, 290, 349; King, *Why We Can't Wait*, 77.

106 Lewis V. Baldwin, *There Is a Balm in Gilead: The Cultural Roots of Martin Luther King, Jr.* (Minneapolis: Fortress, 1991), 42; King, *Where Do We Go*, 79–80; Washington, *Testament*, 317; King, *Trumpet of Conscience*, 12.

107 Baldwin and Burrow, *Domestication of King*, 174; Carson and Holloran, *Knock at Midnight*, 136.

108 "MLK Built Bridges Not Walls Because 'Love Not Hate Makes America Great,'" *Milwaukee Independent*, January 25, 2019, http://www.milwaukeeindependent.com/curated/mlk-built-bridges-not-walls-love-not-hate-makes-america-great/; Carson, *King Papers*, 6:483–84; King, *Strength to Love*, 29.

109 King, *Strength to Love*, 29; Carson, *King Papers*, 6:240, 479, 483–84.

110 The British political journalist Mehdi Raza Hasan said as much and more on *AM Joy*, hosted by Joy Reid, aired March 15, 2019, on MSNBC.

111 Jessica Taylor, "Trump Calls for 'Total and Complete Shutdown of Muslims Entering' US," NPR News, December 7, 2015, https://

www.npr.org/2015/12/07/458836388/trump-calls-for-total-and-complete-shutdown-of-muslims-entering-u-s.

112 Maha Hilal, "Trump's Year in Islamophobia: Five Ways the Administration Has Waged War on Muslims at Home and Abroad in Its First Year," Institute for Public Policy Studies, December 21, 2017, https://ips-dc.org/trumps-year-islamophobia/; Brian Klaas, "Opinion: A Short History of President Trump's Anti-Muslim Bigotry," *Washington Post*, March 15, 2019, https://washingtonpost.com/opinions/2019/03/15/short-history-president-trumps-anti-muslim-bigotry/; SPLC, "Anti-immigrant and Anti-Muslim Hostility Reigns," *The Year in Hate and Extremism: A Report from the Southern Poverty Law Center* (2019): 13–14; Brian Stelter, *Hoax: Donald Trump, Fox News, and the Dangerous Distortion of Truth* (New York: One Signal, 2020), 47, 171, 176, 229, 242, 267.

113 Heidi Beirich and Susy Buchannan, "The Year in Hate and Extremism," *Intelligence Report*, Southern Poverty Law Center, Spring 2018, 41; SPCL, "Hostility Reigns," 13–14; Heidi Beirich, "The Year in Hate and Extremism: Rage against Change," *Intelligence Report*, Southern Poverty Law Center, Spring 2019, 38; Mariah Timms, "Murfreesboro: Second Man Indicted in Mosque Vandalism," *Tennessean*, October 1, 2017, 10A; Jonathan Montpetit, "Quebec City Shooter Supported Trump's Immigration Policies, Newly Public Court Documents Show," CBC News, March 29, 2018, https://www.cbc.ca/news/canada/montreal/mosque-shooting-bissonette-1.4597998; "New Zealand Mosque Attacks Suspect Praised Trump in Manifesto: Suspected Gunman behind the Christchurch Rampage Dubbed the U.S. President 'a Symbol of Renewed White Identity,'" *Al-Jazeera*, March 16, 2019, https://www.aljazeera.com/news/2019/3/16/new-zealand-mosque-attacks-suspect-praised-trump-in-manifesto.

114 Montpetit, "Quebec City Shooter"; "New Zealand Mosque Attacks."

115 Baldwin, *Voice of Conscience*, 201–16; King, *Where Do We Go*, 190–91; Lewis V. Baldwin, ed., *"In a Single Garment of Destiny": A Global Vision of Justice—Martin Luther King, Jr.* (Boston: Beacon, 2012), 190–209.

116 Timothy L. O'Brien, "Look Who's Not in Trump's Travel Ban: Five Majority Muslim Countries Are Covered—Four Aren't—Guess Where the President Does Business,"

Bloomberg, June 26, 2018, https://www.bloomberg.com/opinion/articles/2018-06-26/trump-travel-ban-doesn-t-cover-saudi-arabia-or-the-u-a-e.

117 Tisa Werger, "Religious Freedom after Trump," Berkley Forum, Georgetown University, Washington, DC, December 7, 2020, https://berkleycenter.georgetown.edu/responses/religious-freedom-after-trump.

118 King, *Strength to Love*, 96; Carson, *King Papers*, 6:146–47; King, *Where Do We Go*, 190–91; Martin Luther King Jr. to Mr. M. Bernard Resnikoff, unpublished and typed version (September 17, 1961), King Papers, KCLA, 1.

119 King, *Stride toward Freedom*, 84–85, 96–98; Washington, *Testament*, 16–17, 658–59; Baldwin, *Voice of Conscience*, 212, 215–16; Carson, *King Autobiography*, 287–88.

120 King to Resnikoff (September 17, 1961), 1; Carson, *King Papers*, 7:476n4.

121 King, *Strength to Love*, 24; Carson, *King Papers*, 6:475; Carson, *King Papers*, 7:195, 204–5. King strongly disagreed with the anti-Catholic sentiment that existed on some levels before and during the presidency of John F. Kennedy, who was an adherent of this faith, and he also spoke out against religious persecution in Russia. See Carson, *King Papers*, 7:460; Berl I. Bernhard, "Interview with Martin Luther King, Jr.," unpublished and typed version, Oral History Project for the John F. Kennedy Library (March 9, 1964), King Papers, KCLA, 2–3; and Carson, *King Papers*, 4:534.

122 Baldwin, *Voice of Conscience*, 207–8; King, *Where Do We Go*, 167, 190–92; Martin Luther King Jr., "On Interfaith Conference on Civil Rights," statement, unpublished and typed version, Chicago, IL (January 15, 1963), King Papers, KCLA, 1.

123 Carson, *King Papers*, 6:469.

124 King, *Why We Can't Wait*, 24; Alex Ayres, ed., *The Wisdom of Martin Luther King, Jr.: An A-to-Z Guide to the Ideas and Ideals of the Great Civil Rights Leader* (New York: Penguin, 1993), 67.

125 Carson and Holloran, *Knock at Midnight*, 29.

126 Trump, *Crippled America*, x, xiii, 23, 169; Nichols, *Horsemen of the Trumpocalypse*, 14.

127 E. J. Dionne et al., *One Nation after Trump: A Guide for the Perplexed, the Disillusioned, the Desperate, and the Not-Yet Deported* (New York: St. Martin's, 2017), 9; Nichols, *Horsemen of the Trumpocalypse*, 1, 14.

128 Rashawn Ray and Keon L. Gilbert, "Has Trump Failed Black Americans?," *Brookings*, October 15, 2020, https://www.brookings.edu/blog/how-we-rise/2020/10/15/has

-trump-failed-black-americans/; Nolan D. McCaskill, "Fact Check: Trump's Policies for Black Americans," *Politico*, November 1, 2020, https://www.politico.com/news/2020/11/01/trump-black-americans-policies-433744.

129 This seems to be the thesis coursing through Trump, *Crippled America*, ix–176.

130 Carson, *King Papers*, 3:416, 479; Ayres, *Wisdom of King*, 67; Washington, *Testament*, 282–83, 315, 324, 326; Carson, *King Autobiography*, 346–55.

131 Martin Luther King Jr., "Statement Delivered at Stockholm Airport Arrival," unpublished and typed version, Stockholm, Sweden (December 1964), King Papers, KCLA, 1; Martin Luther King Jr., "Nobel Peace Prize," statement, unpublished and typed version, Oslo, Norway (December 1964), King Papers, KCLA, 1–3; Kenneth L. Smith, "Equality and Justice: A Dream or Vision of Reality," *Report from the Capitol* 39, no. 1 (January 1984): 5.

132 Martha Waggoner, "'Poor People's Campaign' Readies Its efforts for Nationwide Mobilization: Activists Say Government Ignoring Poverty in US," *Tennessean*, February 5, 2018, 14A.

133 Reverend William J. Barber, II et al., *Revive Us Again: Vision and Action in Moral Organizing* (Boston: Beacon, 2018), 143–48; Jeremy Ray Jewel, "Book Review: 'Revive Us Again'—Rev. Dr. William Barber II's Quest to Revive Compassion," *Arts Fuse*, December 24, 2018, https://artsfuse.org/177734/book-review-revive-us-again-rev-dr-william-barber-ii-s-quest-to-revive-compassion/.

134 Jack Jenkins, "Washington Bishop Joins Rev. William Barber and Other Clergy for Prayer Rally at St. John's Church," *Episcopal News Service*, June 18, 2020, https://www.episcopalnewsservice.org/2020/06/18/washington-bishop-joins-rev-william-barber-and-other-clergy-for-prayer-rally-at-st-johns-church/; Mallory Falk, "Religious Leaders Stand Up for Immigrants at Border," *Kera News*, August 1, 2019, https://www.keranews.org/news/2019-07-30/religious-leaders-stand-up-for-immigrants-at-border.

135 Carson, *King Papers*, 7:150; King, *Where Do We Go*, 186–89; Washington, *Testament*, 280; King, *Trumpet of Conscience*, 31–33, 43–44.

136 Trump, *Crippled America*, 136.

137 David Jackson, "Trump Targets Globalization and Trade: Assails Clinton, China and 'Failed Policies' for Job Losses," *USA Today* and *Tennessean*, June 29, 2016, 3B.

138 Oren Dorell, "Analysts: 'America First' Leaves America Alone—President's Actions

Cost Country Respect, They Say," *USA Today* and *Tennessean*, January 20, 2018, 2B.

139 Leah Mills, "US Pulls Out of Open Skies Treaty, Trump's Latest Treaty Withdrawal," *Reuters*, May 21, 2020, https://www.pri.org/stories/2020-05-21/us-pulls-out-open-skies-treaty-trumps-latest-treaty-withdrawal.

140 "Trump Worries NATO with 'Obsolete Comment,'" *BBC News*, January 15, 2017, https://www.bbc.com/news/world-us-canada-38635181.

141 Hillary Rodham Clinton, *What Happened* (New York: Simon & Schuster, 2017), 334.

142 Jane Mayer, "How Russia Helped Swing the Election for Trump," *New Yorker*, September 24, 2018, https://www.newyorker.com/magazine/2018/10/01/how-russia-helped-to-swing-the-election-for-trump.

143 Holly Meyer, "Trump's Language Called 'Offensive' by Those from Haiti and El Salvador," *Tennessean*, January 13, 2018, 3A.

144 David Jackson, "Promising Tariffs on Metals, Trump Says Trade Wars Are 'Easy to Win,'" *USA Today* and *Tennessean*, March 3, 2018, 2B.

145 Jerome Viala-Gaudefroy and Dana Lindaman, "Donald Trump's 'Chinese Virus': The Politics of Naming," *Conversation*, April 21, 2020, https://theconversation.com/donald-trumps-chinese-virus-the-politics-of-naming-136796.

146 "Coronavirus: Trump Moves to Pull US Out of World Health Organization," *BBC News*, July 7, 2020, https://www.bbc.com/news/world-us-canada-53327906.

147 Montpetit, "Quebec City Shooter," 1–3; "New Zealand Mosque Attacks," 1–6.

148 "President Trump Is a Threat to World Peace," World Peace Foundation, February 3, 2017, https://sites.tufts.edu/reinventingpeace/2017/02/03/president-donald-trump-is-a-threat-to-world-peace/.

149 Dorell, "'America First,'" 2B; "Trump Is a Threat," 1–2; King, *Where Do We Go*, 190; Carson, *King Papers*, 6:132.

150 I am indebted to Beverly Lanzetta for this insight. See Lanzetta to Baldwin, June 26, 2021, 1–2.

151 Quoted in Randy Patrick, "'In a Time of Universal Deceit,' Watch Those Quotes," *Kentucky Standard*, February 11, 2017, https://www.kystandard.com/content/%E2%80%98-time-universal-deceit%E2%80%99-watch-those-quotes.

152 Clayborne Carson and Kris Shepard, eds., *A Call to Conscience: The Landmark Speeches of Dr. Martin Luther King, Jr.* (New York: Warner, 2001), 202.

153 Former president Barack Obama referred to this as a period of "truth decay," which means that "not only do we not have to tell the truth, but truth doesn't even matter." We are in "a contest where facts no longer matter," he added. "It's all about beating the other guy." See Barack H. Obama interview, *60 Minutes*, aired November 15, 2020, on CBS.

154 King, *Strength to Love*, 45; Clayborne Carson, ed., *The Papers of Martin Luther King, Jr.*, vol. 1, *Called to Serve, January 1929–June 1951*, ed. Ralph E. Luker and Penny A. Russell (Berkeley: University of California Press, 1992), 154; Carson, *King Papers*, 7:290, 296; Carson, *King Papers*, 6:303.

155 Carson, *King Papers*, 6:88; King, *Where Do We Go*, 67.

156 King, *Where Do We Go*, 67.

157 King, *Strength to Love*, 11–12; Carson, *King Papers*, 6:108.

158 This is why King habitually listened to arguments on all sides of an issue, "finding some merit in each argument." See Carson, *King Papers*, 4:195.

159 Clayborne Carson, *The Papers of Martin Luther King, Jr.*, vol. 2, *Rediscovering Precious Values, July 1951–November 1955*, ed. Stewart Burns et al. (Berkeley: University of California Press, 1994), 251–52.

160 Rosenfeld, *Democracy and Truth*, 5, 7.

161 Ishena Robinson, "Really, Now?: Cop Who Arrested Georgia State Rep. Park Cannon for Knocking on Governor's Door Claims Events of Jan. 6 Were on His Mind," *Root*, March 30, 2021, https://www.theroot.com/really-now-cop-who-arrested-georgia-state-rep-park-c-1846585142. President Joseph R. Biden Jr. had this in mind when he, in his inaugural address, urged Americans to "reject the culture in which facts are manipulated and even manufactured." See Joseph R. Biden Jr., "Inaugural Address," aired January 20, 2021, on MSNBC.

162 Washington, *Testament*, 206, 219, 377; King, *Strength to Love*, 11; Carson, *King Papers*, 6:576; King, *Why We Can't Wait*, 119.

163 Rosenfeld, *Democracy and Truth*, 7; King, *Trumpet of Conscience*, 44.

164 Carson, *King Papers*, 4:278, 407; Carson, *King Papers*, 5:432; Carson, *King Papers*, 1:122; Carson and Holloran, *Knock at Midnight*, 112; King, *Where Do We Go*, 13, 165; King, *Stride toward Freedom*, 171.

165 Carson, *King Papers*, 6:192–93; Carson, *King Papers*, 7:287; Carson, *King Papers*, 4:402, 434; Washington, *Testament*, 296–302.

166 King, *Where Do We Go*, 67, 105, 109–10, 128, 154–55; Washington, *Testament*, 338, 401–2; Carson, *King Papers*, 1:162–63; Carson, *King Papers*, 4:407; Carson, *King Papers*, 3:265; Carson, *King Papers*, 6:216–19; Carson, *King Papers*, 7:221, 335, 592–93; Martin Luther King Jr., "Discerning the Signs of History," sermon, unpublished and typed version, Ebenezer Baptist Church, Atlanta, GA (November 15, 1964), King Papers, KCLA, 1–7.

167 King, *Where Do We Go*, 79–81, 83–85, 102.

168 We know that King read at least parts of Du Bois's reflections on the subject and most certainly would have agreed with what he said. See W. E. B. Du Bois, *Black Reconstruction in America: An Essay toward a History of the Part Which Black Folk Played in the Attempt to Reconstruct Democracy in America, 1860–1880* (New York: Atheneum, 1975; originally published in 1935), 711–28; Martin Luther King Jr., "Honoring Dr. DuBois," *Freedomways* 8 (1968): 104–11; "News: Dr. Martin Luther King on Reconstruction," Zinn Education Project, January 16, 2021, https://www.zinnedproject.org/news/dr-king-on-reconstruction.

169 These insights benefited from a conversation concerning the 1619 Project and critical race theory between Joy Reed and Nicole Hannah-Jones, the director of the 1619 Project, on *Reid Report*, aired June 14, 2021, on MSNBC.

170 Marquise Francis, "Author of Texas Bill to Ban Critical Race Theory Says Martin Luther King, Jr. Would Approve of It," Yahoo News, June 4, 2021, https://news.yahoo.com/author-of-texas-bill-to-ban-critical-race-theory-says-martin-luther-king-jr-would-approve-of-it-195058754.html.

171 King, *Where Do We Go*, 41–44.

172 King often outlined all of these social evils and more in his sermons, speeches, and writing. See, for example, King, *Where Do We Go*, 67–101.

173 King believed that those who define the past control history, at least in some sense. He clearly understood the wisdom of George Orwell's statement "He who controls the past controls the future. He who controls the present controls the past." See George Orwell, *1984: A Novel* (New York: New American Library, 1984), 32.

174 Washington, *Testament*, 255; King, *Trumpet of Conscience*, 70–71.

175 Kneel-ins were as much a part of the tactics of the civil rights movement as sit-ins, especially during King's involvement in the Albany Movement (1961–62). See King, *Why We Can't Wait*, 69; Carson, *King Autobiography*, 163; and Carson, *King Papers*, 7:565.

176 Washington, *Testament*, 143, 307; Carson, *King Papers*, 5:287; Carson, *King Papers*, 3:461.

177 King, *Where Do We Go*, 79–81, 83–85, 102; Washington, *Testament*, 208.

178 King often said in his time that American "democracy is on trial" and that "the outcome of our struggle" will determine not only America's destiny but, "in large measure," the "destiny of the world." See Martin Luther King Jr., "The Right to Vote, the Quest for Jobs: Civil Rights '65," essay, unpublished and typed version (March 1965), King Papers, KCLA, 9.

179 King, *Where Do We Go*, 152–53; Washington, *Testament*, 373, 644–45; Carson, *King Papers*, 7:240; Carson, *King Papers*, 6:132, 472; King, *Strength to Love*, 12, 21.

180 King, *Where Do We Go*, 36.

181 Martin Luther King Jr., *The Measure of a Man* (Philadelphia: Fortress, 1988; originally published in 1959), 9; King, *Where Do We Go*, 67; King, *Strength to Love*, 12; Carson, *King Papers*, 6:132–33, 453.

182 Washington, *Testament*, 152, 164, 208; Carson, *King Papers*, 7:139; King, *Strength to Love*, 12, 21; Carson, *King Papers*, 6:132–33, 453; King, *Stride toward Freedom*, 220–21; Carson, *King Papers*, 5:486.

183 Carson, *King Papers*, 7:291, 299, 506, 508, 531, 595; Carson, *King Papers*, 6:422, 453; Carson, *King Papers*, 5:172, 411; King, "Doubts and Certainties Link," 4. Donald Trump is the classic example of the kind of leader King associated with a "perverted definition of democracy" and with a Machiavellian and Nietzschean approach to power and governing. See Steven Ogden, "Opinion: The Problem of Strong Man Politics," ABC Religion and Ethics, March 16, 2020, https://www.abc.net.au/religion/strong-man-politics/12060722; and Washington, *Testament*, 307.

184 Peter W. Stevenson, "How Is the John Lewis Voting Rights Act Different from H.R. 1?," *Washington Post*, June 8, 2021, https://www.washingtonpost.com/politics/2021/06/08/how-is-john-lewis-voting-rights-act-different-hr-1; Ines Pohl, "Opinion: US Voting Rights Restrictions Are a Warning to All Democracies," *DW*, April 6, 2021, https://www.dw.com/en/opinion-us-voting-rights-restrictions-are-a-warning-to-all-democracies/a-57781184.

185 These terms are used in Rosenfeld, *Democracy and Truth*, 3, 137–76.

186 The term "nihilistic will to power" came from the presidential historian Jon Meacham, who used it in a conversation with Don Lemon on *Don Lemon Tonight*, aired May 4, 2021, on CNN.

187 King, *Stride toward Freedom*, 196; Washington, *Testament*, 314.

188 Carson, *King Papers*, 6:493; King, *Strength to Love*, 44.

189 Carson, *King Papers*, 7:506; Carson, *King Papers*, 5:504; King, *Where Do We Go*, 170; Washington, *Testament*, 268–69.

190 King, *Trumpet of Conscience*, 16.

191 Carson, *King Papers*, 4:370.

192 Carson, *King Papers*, 7:215. E. J. Dionne and his coauthors are making essentially the same point when they call for "a new patriotism" to counter the worst aspects of Trumpism. They contend that this "new patriotism" should involve a commitment "to an equality that Martin Luther King, Jr. insisted was 'a dream deeply rooted in the American dream.'" See Dionne et al., *One Nation after Trump*, 13.

193 Lawrence Edward Carter Sr., *A Baptist Preacher's Buddhist Teacher: How My Interfaith Journey with Daisaku Ikeda Made Me a Better Christian* (Santa Monica, CA: Middleway, 2018), 59.

194 Martin Luther King Jr., "My Jewish Brother," *New York Amsterdam News*, February 26, 1966, 1.

195 King, *Strength to Love*, 17–18; Washington, *Testament*, 14–15; Carson, *King Papers*, 6:197.

196 King, *Strength to Love*, 62; Martin Luther King Jr., "America's Chief Moral Dilemma," address, unpublished and typed version, United Church of Christ—General Synod, Palmer House, Chicago, IL (July 6, 1965), King Papers, KCLA, 2; Baldwin, *Voice of Conscience*, 76–77.

197 King, "Covenant with Life," 1; Garcia-Navarro, "Black Pastors and Trump," 1–3.

198 Carson and Holloran, *Knock at Midnight*, 112; Carson, *King Papers*, 4:398. King held that "no righteous" person "could fail to resist evil." See Carson, *King Papers*, 5:247.

199 King's "Letter from the Birmingham City Jail" (1963) suggests that his role—as preacher, pastor, and prophet—was to use the pulpit and other platforms to tell the truth about the movement and to create the kind of tension in the minds of movement foot soldiers (and indeed the society as a whole) that opened and made them more receptive of this truth. Here King's role was not far removed from that of Socrates. See King, *Why We Can't Wait*, 79–80.

200 Ayres, *Wisdom of King*, 73; King, *Trumpet of Conscience*, 70–71; Carson, *King Papers*, 7:299, 506, 531.

201 King, *Trumpet of Conscience*, 70–71; Carson, *King Papers*, 5:521.

202 James Comey, *A Higher Loyalty: Truth, Lies, and Leadership* (New York: Flatiron, 2018), ix–x.

203 Washington, *Testament*, 279–86; Carson and Shepard, *Call to Conscience*, 204.

Index